Short Guide to Theme Correction

Guide and Handbook
for Writing

IRWIN GRIGGS

DAVID H. WEBSTER

Temple University

AMERICAN BOOK COMPANY

New York

Acknowledgments

Grateful acknowledgment is made to the following publishers and individuals for permission to reprint material which is in copyright or of which they are the authorized publishers:

THE AMERICAN MERCURY: For "Hunting" by Alan Devoe, from the February, 1951, issue. By permission of Jason Matthews, *The American Mercury.*

THE AMERICAN SCHOLAR: For excerpt from William G. Carleton's "Are We Politically Adolescent?" reprinted from *The American Scholar,* Volume 16, Number 1, Winter, 1946–47. Copyright 1946 by the United Chapters of Phi Beta Kappa. By permission of the publishers.

THE ATLANTIC MONTHLY: For William Barrett's review of "The Fall of the Dynasties." Copyright © 1963, by The Atlantic Monthly Company, Boston 16, Mass.

THE BOBBS-MERRILL COMPANY: For excerpt from *Academic Procession,* copyright, 1953, by Ernest Earnest, reprinted by permission of the publishers, The Bobbs-Merrill Company, Inc.

HENRY STEELE COMMAGER: For excerpt from "Who Is Loyal to America," which appeared in the September, 1947, issue of *Harper's Magazine.* Reprinted by permission of the author.

E. P. DUTTON: For excerpt from the book *Far Away and Long Ago* by W. H. Hudson. Copyright, 1918, by E. P. Dutton & Co., Inc. Renewal, 1946, by Royal Society for the Protection of Birds. Reprinted by permission of the publishers, The Royal Society for the Protection of Birds, and The Society of Authors.

HARCOURT, BRACE & WORLD: For excerpt from "Dickens" in *Dickens, Dali and Others,* copyright, 1946, by George Orwell. For excerpt from *The Economic Consequences of the Peace* by John Maynard Keynes, copyright, 1920, by Harcourt, Brace & World, Inc.; renewed, 1948, by Lydia Lopokova Keynes. For excerpt from *Barren Ground* by Ellen Glasgow. For excerpt from *Noon Wine,* copyright, 1936, 1937, 1939, © 1964 by Katherine Anne Porter. All reprinted by permission of Harcourt, Brace & World, Inc.

Preface

This book combines materials for three parts of the usual freshman composition course: first, the study of the craft of writing; second, models and assignments of various kinds; and third, a handbook of usage. There is no necessary tie between the three main parts; any one of them may be used separately. We suppose that the first two divisions, or portions of them, will be assigned for study and as source material for student themes; we expect that the third division, the handbook, will often be used only as a reference book.

We owe a debt to many colleagues who have suggested changes and who have helped us in various ways. For earlier help we are obliged to Harper Brown, William Rossky, and Elkan Buchhalter. For recent help we are especially indebted to three colleagues who have aided in the chapter on the research paper: Marie Stone, Paul A. Brown, and Charles Burkhart.

I. G.

D. H. W.

Contents

I
The Craft of Writing

vii

CONTENTS

II
Types, Models, and Writing Assignments

CONTENTS

III
The Handbook

GRAMMAR

CONTENTS

x

CONTENTS

CONTENTS

EFFECTIVE SENTENCES

CONTENTS

PUNCTUATION AND MECHANICS

xiii

CONTENTS

CONTENTS

SPELLING

GLOSSARY

I

The Craft of Writing

1
Introduction to Writing

All your life you have been learning to use words, and if your mind does not become stagnant, you will continue to learn as long as you live. For no one, not even the greatest poet, ever "masters" the art of using words—masters it in the sense that he has nothing more to learn or in the sense that he succeeds automatically and without effort. For most of you, however, this class will be the last formal study of the subject. You should enter it with the belief that no matter how well or how poorly you write this September, by next May you can have learned to write much better. For, like throwing a baseball or playing a violin, writing is a skill and can be studied and learned; and though no one can achieve perfection in it, everyone, if he tries, can make progress.

First of all, you must wish to develop your skill—and not simply to get a grade and pass a course. You must wish to develop the skill because you understand its value to you. People seldom become expert at anything unless they wish to, even in the simpler skills like preparing a good dinner, and no one ever learned to write well without study and prolonged effort.

THINKING AND WRITING

Your most obvious and immediate motive for learning to use effective English lies in realizing that your success in other college courses depends in good part on your ability to express yourself in clear, forceful language. Even in mathematics you will use words as well as mathematical symbols; in chemistry you will get nowhere by merely memorizing formulas and manipulating test tubes; and subjects like his-

3

tory and economics are largely verbal. You will probably find —and this should not surprise you—that your history professor, for example, speaks and writes as well as your English professor and, just as much as your English professor, expects you to speak and write with clarity, fullness, and correctness. In none of the subjects you will take in college, including English composition, is the ability to speak and write well a substitute for knowledge; but in all of them, including mathematics, the *in*ability to speak and write well imposes the severest handicap.

When you leave college to enter business or one of the professions, you will continue to speak and write, and your success will depend in part, probably in large part, on whether you speak and write well or poorly. President J. C. Warner of the Carnegie Institute of Technology has said, "Without the ability to read accurately and to write clear, coherent prose, no engineer, scientist, architect or business executive can achieve distinction in his profession." President Warner does not mention the teacher, presumably because the teacher's dependence on words is so obvious, as is also the lawyer's, the politician's, the minister's, the journalist's. The business and professional world functions largely and often almost entirely through the medium of words.

To help you in college and afterwards is not, however, the only benefit you can expect from developing your skill with words. It might be if the only reason for using words were to communicate, to pass thought from one person to another: from the professor to the student in a lecture; from the student to the professor in an examination; from the doctor to the patient; from the executive to his assistant. But to communicate thought is only one of the two reasons for using language. The second is to *formulate* thought. It is possible to think without words, to be sure. The painter and the musician do so constantly, and we all do sometimes. For most of the activity of the mind, however, we must use words not only to tell the other person (to communicate) but to tell ourselves (to formulate). Most kinds of thinking we simply cannot do in a wordless vacuum. We may not speak the words or write

4

them or even be aware of them, but our minds are using them. Without them, large areas of our minds could not function. The most important reason for you to develop your skill with words is to develop your capacity to think.

WRITING THEMES: CHOOSING A SUBJECT

Your instructor may give you the subject on which you are to write, but even if he does, you will have to make some selection within the general area of the subject he assigns. If, for example, he asks you to write about some problem you have encountered in college, you still have to select the problem. If he is more specific in his assignment—if he specifies that it is to be an academic problem—you still have to select a specific academic problem. You always have to make some kind of selection.

Students often wonder what to select. Sometimes they expend more nervous energy in wondering what to write about than in the actual writing. Sometimes, indeed, they start out with the feeling that they have nothing to write about.

Whatever else may be true of you, this, at least, is not true—that you have nothing to write about. One of the better resolutions you might make now at the beginning of your college career is never to say it and never to think it. For if it were true it would mean—it would have to mean—that you had been not quite alive these last eighteen years.

So start looking around. Get into the habit of seeing everything as possible theme material. You will find before long that you have a great deal more to write about than you can ever use in the assignments in this course. All your memories, your feelings, and your opinions are raw material. They are likely, it is true, to be in a jumble; what you need to do is think about your experiences and ideas in such a way that you can put them to use. You need to examine them to find out what they are like and what part they have played in your life. You should not write on big, vague matters like your impressions of baseball or music, but you can sort out of these impressions your desire to be a shortstop or a violinist,

5

and you can write a theme on why you would rather play shortstop than third base or why you would rather play the violin than the viola. Neither you nor anyone else would be much interested in a collection of random impressions of your family, but if you show how you can't stand Aunt Edith because she is so opinionated and so self-righteous, you will have a good theme. Your scattered ideas about life at college won't make a good theme, but you can write about the advantages (or disadvantages) of belonging to a fraternity or of living in a dormitory instead of commuting between home and college.

For some assignments your material will be personal experiences—a party where you were happy or disappointed or embarrassed, your first falling in love, the games and sports you took part in, the intense friendships of adolescence. For other assignments personal opinion on familiar subjects will make good material. What do you think of a certain book or movie, of people you have met, of places you have visited? What do you think of the food in the cafeteria? Of the freshman orientation program? Of the first convocation?

Some assignments may call for less personal material. To see the wealth of possible subjects that do not arise directly from one's own experience, look at a daily newspaper. On the front page you may find a dozen subjects: why taxes will be raised, what the issues are in the coming election, what caused a strike, what is responsible for a series of accidents. The sports page can suggest subjects: why the once-respected sport of wrestling has fallen into disrepute; why some people think that college athletics will be ruined if schools keep trying to make money out of them. Even in the comics you can find subjects, for the comics are full of characters reflecting aspects of American life: the superman, the career girl, the rural boob, the city slicker, the domineering woman, the henpecked husband.

Last night, let us say, you looked at television and listened to a commercial after each act of a rather good play. They were well-bred commercials as commercials go, only the softest kind of soft sell. But just the same, you did not like

6

them. You have a subject right there. Or perhaps you were recalling the long debate last spring over whether you should go to the state university or the small college near home. Perhaps you were thinking about the girl back home and wondering whether it is true that absence makes the heart grow fonder. At breakfast you heard people talking about anti-American riots in a South American nation and you wondered why there should be this hostility to our country. Later in the morning you listened to your history professor lecture about ancient Greece and you were fascinated and for a few moments at least you wondered if you might rather be a historian than a doctor. Or perhaps you have just been pretty homesick this last week. Or perhaps, against your expectations, you have not been.

Of course, you do not know enough to write about some subjects, but don't be too modest. About one subject—yourself—you are the world's greatest authority, and no one who is interested in human nature will be uninterested in you. About a great many less personal subjects you can also write with confidence. You may know parts of the country that no one else in the class, including the instructor, has seen. You may have a skill for doing something no one else in the class can do as well, such as making an upside-down cake, repairing a transmission, transforming an old hat into a new one, or not keeping your mouth shut. Certainly you are an authority on Aunt Edith.

Of all the subjects mentioned above, the one you probably know least about is the rioting in the South American country. You did not see it—in fact, you have never been in South America. So how could you possibly write on this subject? But you did work at the desk in a resort hotel last summer. You had to deal with people who demanded rooms though they had made no reservations and every room in the hotel was booked. You had to try to quiet down more than one party at two o'clock in the morning. And the waitress you took canoeing one afternoon told you that being growled at because she could not serve breakfast to everyone at once was standard practice. You have seen so much rudeness at home that you wonder if the rudeness of some Americans may not be a factor in anti-American feeling abroad. Then, perhaps, you see that you have the subject for a theme—an excellent subject, in fact, and one about which, it turns out, you know a good deal.

LIMITING THE SUBJECT

After you find a subject that looks promising, you will probably have to cut it down to workable size. Your first idea is likely to be something much too big for a theme of, say, five hundred words. If it is, you should reflect that it is far better to treat a smaller subject thoroughly than a larger one superficially.

You can always cut down. You can always limit a subject in one way or another. Suppose you start out with the idea of writing about literature. Clearly this is not a subject at all but an area in which you might find a subject. An obvious way to begin is to cut it down to American literature, then perhaps to twentieth-century American fiction, and then perhaps to Hemingway. At this point and not before, you may have a subject. You might, even in so short a space as five hundred words, write a good theme on Hemingway—that is, on something like why you enjoy reading him. You would perhaps be wise, however, to continue to limit the subject, first, say, to *A Farewell to Arms* and finally, if this has interested you and you have some ideas about it, to the attitude toward war expressed in this novel. Here, at last, you would have a subject sufficiently limited to be treated with some fullness in so short a space as five hundred words. And it would not be a minor subject after all. It would tell the reader something about an important writer and something about the modern world. That would be plenty for a five-hundred-word theme.

No one can tell you how far you should limit your subject. In the research paper, to be discussed later, there is no question but that the subject should be limited severely. In other themes, you may not carry limitation so far as Hemingway's

8

treatment of war in *A Farewell to Arms*. Some instructors have received good themes on such subjects as "The Trouble with Women," surely a very big subject, and "What's Wrong with Men," an even bigger one. All that can be said is that limiting your subject will help you treat it with some thoroughness. It will help you cover a subject instead of skipping through it.

Perhaps we have said enough about finding and limiting a subject. Actually, whether your syllabus is made up of some of the great classics, like Sophocles' *Antigone* and Plato's *Apology,* or whether it is restricted to contemporary essays, many of your subjects will rise out of your reading this year. So let us move on from finding a subject to writing a theme.

SEVEN BASIC CHARACTERISTICS OF A GOOD
THEME: A CHECKLIST

Every theme should have at least the characteristics summarized below. A list of this sort is not complete, to be sure, but because it is brief and pointed, you can the more easily measure everything you write against it.

1. A theme should have a *thesis,* a clear central purpose that can be stated in a single sentence. This thesis or controlling idea should determine everything that goes into the theme.

If writing has no thesis, it has no reason for being. This is precisely what is wrong with some writing—it seems to have no reason for being. We wonder what the writer is driving at, and when we get to the end we feel much as we do when we have listened to a pointless joke. "So what?" we think.

A thesis is not an announcement that you are going to say something. In briefest form, it is what you are going to say. One of the following sentences, assuming that the theme carries it out, is a thesis; the other is not. (You should not need to be told which is which.)

A. I am going to write about why our state needs more junior colleges.

B. Our state needs more junior colleges to meet the needs

9

of students who can afford to go neither to the state university nor to a private college.

The thesis should be written out *before* you write your first draft. Though you write it out, however, you should not ordinarily include it in the theme itself.

2. A theme should have *substance*. It should express ideas and feelings, observation and experience, and express them as fully, with as much detail, as is needed.

Contrast these sentences describing the same event:

A. The weather was very disagreeable while we were at camp.

B. The last time we scouts in Monmouth Troop 1 saw the sun was the Thursday afternoon we set up tents and unpacked at Camp Tioga. That night the wind and rain came out of the northeast and we shivered under our thin cotton blankets. The wind stopped the next morning but the rain went on. Sunday afternoon we packed up and drove home in the rain.

The first example is a vague, general remark that tells us almost nothing about the experience. The second brings in enough detail to make the reader share it. The second passage, in contrast with the first, has substance.

When a student who does the first kind of writing finds that his instructor encourages him to do something more like the second kind, he sometimes thinks, "He wants us to make our writing flowery." *Flowery* is the standard adjective; it has been used for many years by students too lazy or too unskilled to put substance into their own writing. Actually, no matter how figuratively we use the word, there is nothing flowery in the second passage. It is vigorous and simple and, indeed, about as unflowery as anything could be.

3. A theme should have *unity*. Every sentence should in some way support the thesis. Every fact, every idea, every illustration (every element in the substance) should relate to the central purpose of the theme. Anything on a different subject should be discarded, no matter how interesting it may be.

Unless you have a clear thesis, it will be difficult or impossible to give a theme unity. The surest guard against the lack of unity is to know what your thesis is and then hold off distraction and interruption as you bring the total energy of your mind to developing that thesis.

4. A theme should have *coherence.* Its parts should fit together; the relation between them should be clear.

Even a short theme on a simple subject will have separate parts that make up the whole. These divisions of the subject, dealt with in the separate sentences and paragraphs, should clearly combine into the whole theme. When the writer leaves one division (sentence or paragraph) and goes to another, he should be sure he takes his reader with him.

Though unity and coherence are closely related, they are not the same. Unity is chiefly a quality of thought; coherence is chiefly a quality of expression. Unity is gained by discarding all irrelevant ideas, facts, and illustrations; coherence is gained by showing the bearing of, the relation between, the relevant ideas, facts, and illustrations that remain. (But thought and expression are so closely related that in practice it is difficult to separate them and difficult sometimes to distinguish between unity and coherence.)

5. A theme should have *proportion.* Important ideas, facts, and illustrations should be emphasized by length, by position, or by language. Less important elements should be subordinated; unimportant ones should be omitted.

If, for example, you were writing about your education up to the time you came to college (a pretty big subject but one that illustrates the point), you would not give a sentence or two to your high-school years and several paragraphs to the piano lessons that began and ended when you were eleven years old. To be sure, you might write your theme on the piano and you. That would be your subject, then, and if your high-school education came in at all, it would be as something subordinate. Thus correct proportion, like unity and coherence, depends on thesis.

6. A theme should be written in *clear and effective language.* The words should be exact, should give the precise

meaning you intend. They should be organized into clear and effective sentences and paragraphs. And, of course, there should be no mistakes in grammar, punctuation, and spelling.

7. A theme should have a *good title*. Though this point is far less important than the others, you should give it some thought. Find titles that catch interest, that give a picture, that arouse curiosity by suggesting—but not explaining— something in the theme.

Here are some better-than-average titles from student themes: "I Stooped to Conquer"; "Chemistry and I"; "Money, Money, Money"; "I Don't Agree." Contrast these with such unimaginative titles on the same subjects as "An Interesting Experience" ("I Stooped to Conquer"); "A Difficult Subject" ("Chemistry and I"); "A Problem" ("Money, Money, Money"); "Why Our Football Team Should Not Accept an Invitation to Play in the Sugar Bowl" ("I Don't Agree").

The title is the name given to the whole theme; it is not part of the introductory material. If your title is "Placement Tests," for example, do not start out with "They are often given to entering freshmen." Repeat the words "placement tests" or start out in some other way. Though you can be sure the reader has read the title, start out as though he had not.

APPLYING THIS CHECKLIST TO A THEME

With these seven characteristics in mind, read the following theme. (To permit concentration on other points in the checklist, we have removed misspellings, faulty punctuation, and gross mistakes in grammar.)

WHY I JOINED A FRATERNITY

(1) My father was opposed to the idea that I should join a fraternity. He said they are a waste of time and also a waste of money. However, he said that I must make my own decisions and that I have to lead my own life. That is one good thing about my father.

(2) I believe that "frats," as they are called, are valuable for many different reasons. First of all, they help you to form friendships in college. It stands to reason that friendships are an ex-

tremely valuable part of college life. In my opinion, a life when you don't have friends is a life that you would not want to live.

(3) If you do not live at home you have to eat and sleep somewhere. This costs money, probably just as much or more than a fraternity.

(4) Another point concerns study hours. The fraternities have study hours and make you hit those books for your classes. Some of them don't, but the one I am pledging does. In college you have more homework than you have in high school. I think some of the professors pile it on too fast, but anyway the fraternities help you to study because they have quiet hours.

(5) So there are several advantages to fraternities. I had many friends when I was in high school but I didn't know anyone when I first came here. I would hate to look forward to four long years of college without the good friends I have found already at Alpha Beta, which in my opinion is the best fraternity on the campus, as the scholastic and also the athletic records prove.

Fortunately for our purposes, this theme is very poor, and we may expect the scholastic records of Alpha Beta to take a tumble. Though your own writing, let us hope, is much better than this, yours in less glaring form may show some of the same defects. So let us look at it in detail, using the numbering in the checklist.

1. Has the theme a central purpose, a thesis? Obviously not, though there are several possible ones. Much of the author's trouble comes precisely because he has not found his thesis. He may think he has one because he is writing on why he wants to join a fraternity, but if he had read the section on thesis carefully he would see that at most he is only fumbling toward one.

2. Does the theme have substance? Again, obviously not. It would be difficult, in fact, deliberately to say so little in so many words. The theme needs specific reference to the student's own life. Why is the important point about the friendship to be found in fraternities treated so inadequately? Surely the writer must have had some experience he can share with the reader to make his writing meaningful. What about the night when he was homesick and a fraternity brother came into his room and asked a few questions about

a mathematics test? Has he forgotten how, after they talked awhile, he began to feel much better?

3. One of the most serious defects of this theme is its lack of unity. It is a jumble of four subjects which are weakly connected, if connected at all: (1) the divergent views of father and son; (2) the advantages of belonging to a fraternity; (3) the question of whether college assignments are too heavy; and (4) the superiority of Alpha Beta fraternity. Though unity would not necessarily require that three of these subjects be eliminated, the writer should make them support the remaining one rather than compete with it and distract from it, as they do here.

4. A theme so lacking in unity cannot be coherent. The author cannot make things seem to hang together when they have little relation to one another. Even the limited material the student has found, moreover, is in poor order: the point about fraternities and friendship is touched on in the second paragraph, dropped, and then returned to in the last paragraph.

5. Such an undeveloped theme as this can have no proportion, no emphasis. The material is so poorly thought out and so scattered that there is nothing to give proportion to, nothing to emphasize. The padding in places is the opposite of emphasis; the first sentence in paragraph 4 and the first in paragraph 5, for instance, add nothing at all.

6. The language is at best commonplace and awkward, and sometimes it is muddy. There is no reason to say that the father was opposed *to the idea* that the son join a fraternity. The father was opposed to his son's joining one. If the point is to be brought in at all, it should be brought in straight: "My father was opposed to my joining a fraternity" or "My father didn't want me to join a fraternity." And, after stumbling through all those *that*'s in the first paragraph, what is the reader to see as the good thing about the father?

Some of the sentences do not make clear, sensible statements. The first sentence in paragraph 3 is unintentionally humorous because it implies that a man who lives at home does not need to eat and sleep. The next sentence makes the remarkable disclosure that eating and sleeping cost just as much as or more than a fraternity.

7. The title is commonplace and is not even appropriate to the whole theme.

Now study the following theme, which, though not so good that it is going to crowd any classics off the shelf, is much better than the first one. Check it against the list above.

I Found Friendship

Before I came here to college last fall I had heard many arguments about fraternities and some harsh words said against them. But since I have taken the plunge and joined, I have discovered that, no matter what these organizations may be for other people, my fraternity gives me just the thing I most needed, friendship.

At home on the farm where I grew up I was used to being with my brother and my two sisters, and at first when I came here I was lonely and a little homesick. I hated to eat by myself all the time, with the din of a restaurant around me at every meal and often people standing waiting to take my place. Now instead of feeling hurried and hearing dishes and trays clattering and banging, I listen to the friendly conversation of my fraternity brothers. Before and after meals we go over subjects like the football team, our instructors, the dance next Saturday night, and even the international situation. Always there are people to talk to about everything that is going on. It reminds me of home, not in the subjects we talk about but in the friendliness in the air.

The friends I have made at the fraternity help me with my work. I had been having a lot of trouble with my course in modern European history until one of the brothers, a junior who plans to be a teacher himself, spent a couple of hours explaining things to me. Now I think I understand what was really happening in France in the days of Louis XIV and the bearing of that period upon the revolution that followed. Sometimes I get together with my friends who are also studying Spanish; we help each other by working at our assignments in a group. We ask questions of one another and study together for tests. I am getting better grades and I believe I am learning what I never knew before—how to study.

I would have things to be grateful for, however, even if my

15

grades hadn't got better. I have been working and living with friends, and I have grown, I think, to *be* a friend.

The second writer may well have more natural ability than the first, but we can't explain the difference between them as a matter of ability only. The second writer has *used* his ability and written about as well as he can. Almost certainly, the first writer has not used his. He has gone through some of the motions, but he has not, properly speaking, done any writing at all. One of the likely reasons for his failure will be indicated in the following section.

THE THREE STAGES IN WRITING

Think of writing as something you do in three rather distinct stages. The first of these is the thinking and planning stage, in which you should do little, perhaps no, actual writing. You should find your thesis and you may make an outline (outlining will be discussed in the next chapter), and you may write down some notes, but you will not be writing the composition. You will be getting ready to write it.

Some of the work of planning may not seem like work at all. Perhaps as you wait for a bus your mind plays over last summer and the experience at the hotel desk referred to a few pages back, or you think about it as you drop off to sleep. Even though the thinking you do is quite unorganized, it may be immensely useful. In it you may remember an example that is better than the first one you thought of; you may recall something which at first you had not remembered, something which will help make your experience come alive to the reader. Throughout the day and for as many days as possible, you will let your mind work around the subject so that you will not sit down to the writing job "cold."

The second stage is writing the first draft. Do not look for inspiration to come to you. It seldom comes to those who wait. *Make* it come by writing the theme at one sitting and with no interruptions. You should write rather rapidly; do not interrupt yourself even to look up in a dictionary the meaning or spelling of a word about which you are unsure. Certainly you should not interrupt yourself halfway through to turn on the radio for the basketball scores. Remember, too, that letting your mind wander to other subjects between sentences is interruption, even though you stay at your desk with pencil in hand. The most pernicious interruptions are those you cannot see, the ones that steal over you without your even being aware of them.

The third stage is rewriting—rewriting, not merely revising. Rewriting may mean throwing out a first paragraph which, you have come to see, does nothing except tell the reader that you are about to begin. It may mean adding a new paragraph or several paragraphs halfway through the theme because you see that you left an important point undeveloped. Even if you are a very skillful writer, it means polishing awkward sentences and clarifying obscure ones. It means finding a good word for a poor one and then, still later, finding the best word instead of merely a good one.

These are only some of the things you may do in rewriting. Everything you learn in this course and everything your good judgment suggests should come into play to make your final draft something very different from your first one.

For some people the process is not at all like this. Instead of thinking about the subject beforehand, they seem almost to try *not* to think about it. Then, when they can postpone the task no longer, they sit down and start the motions of writing. But they spend half their time staring at the paper, looking up the spellings of doubtful words, and breaking off to talk to someone. After three or four hours of this kind of activity, they may feel ready to quit, the job at last done. Perhaps they copy what they have written—not to improve it but merely to make it legible.

No method (only it is not really method but lack of method) could be worse, more certain to invite failure. To repeat: allow plenty of time for the subject to develop in your mind, then write the first draft at one sitting and with no interruption, and finally rewrite thoroughly. If you have thought sufficiently about your subject ahead of time, you will know what your thesis is; you will have found all sorts of things in your experience that can be used to give your writing substance; you will have put the material into a preliminary organization to give the theme unity, coherence, and proportion. If you then push your first draft through without dawdling, you will experience a sense of achievement that gives vitality and precision to your style and a concentration that helps further to tighten and clarify the organization. If you next regard your first draft as only the raw material out of which you can refine the finished product, and if you go on to rewrite and revise thoroughly, you will achieve a quality that may surprise you. The first draft of professional writers is often quite crude; if you rewrite and revise as often as the professionals do, you will be astonished at how good your own writing becomes.

EXERCISE 1

How can the following areas be cut down to subjects suitable for treatment in a five-hundred-word theme?

1. American writers and the Nobel prize for literature
2. The inadequacies of our American public schools
3. Capitalism vs. socialism
4. Television
5. Modern music
6. The history of slavery
7. Athletics and the university
8. Franklin D. Roosevelt and the New Deal
9. Teaching as a career
10. The importance of one's family life

EXERCISE 2

Discuss the two passages below, especially for their substance or lack of it.

A. One of the most important things a college student has to learn is how to study. Many students waste a great deal of time because they do not know how to concentrate. They do not use good judgment about studying, and so they do not get good results. This failure to use good judgment is very unfortunate and by all means should be avoided.

B. The college student must learn how to concentrate. He may be able to read the *Reader's Digest* and listen to the radio at the same time, but he cannot expect to learn his history and English with anything less than complete concentration. Effective study requires far more than turning off the radio, however; it requires turning off a hundred competing thoughts—about money, about tomorrow's date, about next Saturday's game. Most of us have good enough minds to get through college, but few of us have such a surplus of intelligence that we can master a page of economics when our minds are debating whether we should go down to the corner to get a coke.

EXERCISE 3

Here are two student themes on the same subject. Though one is much better than the other, examine them both for failures they show in the seven basic characteristics of a good theme.

LEGALIZED MURDER

I do not believe in capital punishment. I never have and do not think I ever will.

Most people think that mercy killing is wrong. They feel that no one has the right to take another person's life, no matter how much suffering could be prevented. The act of mercifully putting a pain-racked human being out of his misery is too much like God's work. These same people feel that if someone commits a crime such as murder, kidnapping, etc., he should pay the price, the forfeit of his life. Yet aren't these people also sick?

Let us take a sample case. John commits the terrible crime of murder. He willfully shot down a man in cold blood. He has no remorse, no regrets. He wanted money and killed for it. What makes it even more horrible is that if he had it to do over again, he would. This man is certainly a menace to society and should be put out of the way. In this I heartily agree. But is he a normal person? No, he is not.

He is not normal and he is not well. He may be in the best of physical health but his mind is sick, sick perhaps with resentment, hate, or a number of things that could prevent him from knowing right from wrong. Just as society would not kill the deformed, sick in body, neither should it kill the murderer, sick in mind and soul.

I have heard the argument that the condemned man was as sane as you and I. Would you and I react the same way he did? Would we commit murder even in anger? When we get in a rage do we not lose our sense of our reasoning? Yet we would not murder even if we would like to. Then we find that he is not the same as we are mentally, therefore not altogether sane.

People say that the death penalty puts fear into the hearts of wrongdoers so that they will think twice before they commit the major crimes. If this were true wouldn't the states that do not have capital punishment have more murders, rapes, and kidnappings than the ones that do? I am sure you will find they do not.

All through history people have been put to death for different reasons. In the time of the French Revolution it was rank, religion in the time of Moses, and political beliefs when the Czars of Russia fell. Who has the right to say you die or live except when it comes to self-protection?

War is another example of legalized murder. The fact that it is legal does not mean that it is the right thing to do. War is something that also must be ended.

If a person has done something bad enough to be exiled from society, imprison him for life; never let him take a breath of free air again, but do not resort to legalized murder.

Capital Punishment

An insignificant looking man, clad in black trousers with a long slit in the left leg, a white shirt open at the collar, and felt slippers, is half walking, half letting himself be pushed by the two burly guards at his side. In the bleak corridor framed by prison cells he is walking his last mile. He is fully deserving of his fate. He killed an attendant in the last of a long series of gasoline station holdups.

What will be the immediate results of this execution? Probably the executioner and the witnesses won't sleep too well that night. The tabloids will print the story in full morbid detail, and their readers, while pretending to be filled with horror, will enjoy every word.

The advocates of capital punishment claim that an execution every once in a while is beneficial, for it keeps the beast in man at bay. They claim that to obey the law people must fear the punishment consequent upon the transgression of the law. If this be so, then why not follow it to its logical conclusion? Why lock our prisoners in jail? Why not have a whipping procession down Fifth Avenue every day during rush hours? Why execute murderers painlessly and in private? Why not beat them to a bloody pulp in Yankee Stadium? Tickets would be at a premium and we could use the proceeds to balance the budget.

The fact is that constant contact with cruelty tends to brutalize a person. Instead of being shocked we begin to accept brutality as the norm. In those parts of the Orient where a constant state of war or famine is prevalent, the life of an individual is held in little regard. If the olfactory nerves are exposed to the most nauseating odor for any length of time, they will no longer be sensitive to it. The same appears to be true about our moral sense.

It is evident from the wave of kidnappings that followed the execution of two kidnappers in St. Louis that fear of punishment is not an effective deterrent to crime.

If society must be protected from its malevolent members, this purpose can easily be achieved by placing them in penal institutions—for life if necessary.

Murder is the gravest of crimes. It cannot be condoned because society as a whole rather than a single person commits this crime. It could be argued that though it is for the benefit of society, under no circumstance has man the right to kill his fellow man. Surely in such instances, where society not only doesn't benefit but is sometimes harmed, there can be no excuse for legalized murder—call it capital punishment if you wish.

2
Outlines

Should you make a formal written outline of your subject before you begin to write about it? There is no hard and fast answer, because writers and subjects differ so much. One writer may carry his material so clearly organized in his mind that formal outlining is unnecessary; another cannot "see" his subject until he sees it outlined. One writer finds that an outline helps bring structure out of something that was shapeless; another finds that it makes for rigidity and the appearance rather than the fact of organization. Furthermore, subjects differ in the degree to which they require the support of a written outline. A 500-word personal essay, "First Impressions of College," might not need one; a 3,000-word research paper on the life of the architect who built the college library certainly would.

There is an obvious danger in not outlining. If you start without a plan and simply trust to thinking of things as you go along, you are inviting trouble. Your theme may be mixed up because when you are almost through you think of something that should have come early. It may be badly out of proportion because you wrote so much on your second point that you do not have time for a third one, which turns out to be just as important. Making an outline often helps you not only to arrange your material in the right order and proportion but also to evaluate it. When you see things in black and white, you can judge them better.

Still, no matter how much you rely on an outline, do not let yourself become its slave. An outline is a somewhat mechanical thing, with items set down in one-two-three order.

You make an outline so that you will know for sure what these items are. You need not treat all of them at equal length simply because they have an equal place in the outline. Nor are you obliged to salute the reader with "First," "Second," and "Third" at the beginning of each section. Make your plan and follow it, but feel free to give emphasis, to shift proportions, and to include examples. Do not let your outline keep your theme from being as lively and interesting as you can make it. Remember that, just as a good painter studies anatomy but does not allow the skeleton to show through his painting of the body, so the writer should study the structure of his material but not allow it to make a display of itself.

KINDS OF OUTLINES

There are two kinds of outlines. The first is the paragraph outline. In it, each paragraph is summarized in one sentence. There are no subdivisions.

The second kind of outline is the analytical. It may be either an analytical sentence outline, in which each division of the thought is expressed in a complete sentence, or an analytical topic outline, in which each division of the thought is expressed in a noun or phrase.

Subdivisions are the essence of the analytical sentence and the analytical topic outline. The subject is first divided into two or more main divisions; each of these main divisions is next divided into two or more subdivisions; then each of these subdivisions may be further divided—and the process can be continued (though probably it should not be) until the most minute points are listed.

To illustrate outlining, we shall make a paragraph outline of the material in this chapter up to this point and follow it with an analytical sentence and then an analytical topic outline of the same material. (Because these are illustrations, we have carried the subdividing further than ordinarily should be done for material so short as this.)

Paragraph outline

1. The value of outlining varies, depending on writer and subject.
2. Failure to outline may injure the organization of the material.
3. The outline should not be allowed to constrict the writer.
4. The paragraph outline is the first kind.
5. The analytical, either sentence or topic, is the second kind.
6. Subdivisions are the essence of the analytical outline.

Analytical sentence outline

I. Should the writer outline his subject?
   A. The need for an outline varies.
      1. Writers differ in their needs.
      2. Subjects differ also.
   B. Outlining has definite value.
      1. It helps the writer see the best order.
      2. It helps him give correct proportion.
      3. It helps him evaluate his ideas.
   C. The writer needs to observe certain cautions.
      1. Outlining is mechanical.
      2. The writer must use his freedom.
         a. He is free to give emphasis.
         b. He is free to shift proportion.
         c. He is free to include examples.
      3. The form of the outline should not be evident in the theme itself.
II. There are two types of outlines.
   A. The paragraph outline summarizes each paragraph.
      1. It does so in complete sentences.
      2. It makes no subdivisions.
   B. The analytical outline divides the material into divisions and subdivisions.
      1. In the analytical sentence outline, these divisions and subdivisions are expressed in sentences.
      2. In the analytical topic outline, they are expressed in nouns or phrases.

Analytical topic outline

I. The question of outlining
   A. Varying needs
      1. of writers
      2. of subjects

    B. The values
      1. order
      2. proportion
      3. evaluation of material
    C. Warning
      1. against mechanical ordering
      2. against losing freedom
        a. in emphasis
        b. in proportion
        c. in finding examples
      3. against allowing form of outline to be evident in theme
II. The types
    A. Paragraph outline
      1. complete sentences
      2. no subdivisions
    B. Analytical (subdivision) outline
      1. sentence outline in complete sentences
      2. topic outline in nouns or phrases

Notice that the subdivisions are the same in the sentence and the topic outlines. There should be no difference between the two kinds of analytical outline except that one is expressed in sentences, the other in nouns and phrases. Notice also that there are always two or more divisions, never only one. If there is an A there must be at least a B; if there is a 1 there must be at least a 2.

The following numbering and indentation system must be used:

I.
  A.
    1.
      a.
        1)
          a)

Though an outline this elaborate might be made of a chapter, it is unlikely that the writer of a theme would be helped by carrying the subdivisions so far. The outline should not lay claim to a complexity that the writing itself does not possess.

One other point: the outline need not be completely symmetrical. A good section might look like this:

II.
    A.
    B.
        1.
        2.
        3.
    C.
        1.
        2.

This would mean that the writer had divided a main division (II) into three subdivisions (A, B, C). B, he saw, had three parts, C had two, but A, though important enough to be lined up with B and C, was not being divided.

The construction of an outline, especially an analytical sentence outline, is an exercise in clear thinking. It has value in reading as well as in writing. It helps the writer give structure to his material and it helps the reader discover the structure that is there. Making an outline requires that you see the chief divisions and their relation to one another and to the whole, then the subdivisions and their relation to one another and to the division and back to the whole. We may think of things in nature—a tree, for example, or the United States as a geographical unit; we may think of an experience, a trip from Ohio to California last summer; or we may think of an idea, the concept of freedom, or something simpler, such as joining a fraternity. Each of these is a whole. Each of them as a whole has major divisions. Each division has subdivisions. To see them in orderly relation is a large part of writing well—and reading well. It is, indeed, a large part of thinking well.

EXERCISE 1

Make an analytical sentence outline of the following essay. Then compare your outline with the one in the book. Do *not* refer to the outline in the book until you have completed your own outline.

BACH

It is not easy to appreciate great artists. It demands a kind of self-surrender which many of us are unwilling to make; we must allow ourselves to be dominated by another, a larger soul. Also, it takes time, much time, before we can visit and grow acquainted with all their important works. We could spend years on one composer alone; on one playwright; on one painter.

But there is another difficulty in such appreciation. This is the problem of historical sympathy. It is fairly easy to understand a creative artist who lives in our own spiritual climate, or in some atmosphere which more or less resembles it. Thus, we find it quite simple to read Dickens or Flaubert, because the world they inhabited is not so far away from us; much of it, indeed, is still with us in fact or in memory. But it is really hard to feel at home in the work of an artist who lived in an age very different from our own, with a different religion, a different social structure, and different psychological and artistic ideals. We may agree that he is still a great artist—in so far as he speaks to, and for, all humanity—but we shall surely misinterpret much of his personality and overlook some of the work he himself thought most interesting and important, unless we think ourselves back into his particular spiritual world. This can be done, but it needs a considerable effort; fortunately, it is a fructifying and educative effort.

What do you see when you look at a range of mountains—the chain of the Rockies from Denver, or the Swiss Alps from Berne? What do you see when you look at a forest—the wooded Vermont hills, or the Big Horn forest in Wyoming? You see the mountains as grand, something more than beautiful, noble and magnificent, God's footstool. You see the forest as a sweep of rich and splendid color, an uprush of the earth's own energy, nature not yet spoiled and made petty by the inroads of man.

Yes, but two or three hundred years ago you would not have seen the mountains or the forest with those eyes and with that spirit. You *could* not have so seen them, without a tremendous and very exceptional effort. You would have looked at the forest with distaste and a little horror, seeing it very much as we nowadays would look at a tropical swamp full of crawling snakes and decaying vegetation; it would have seemed disorderly and barbarous, a senseless upsurge of meaningless fertility. At most you might, if you had been rich, have conjectured that it would have been a good place for a hunting party, but normally you would have turned away with revulsion. As for the mountains, they would have filled you with real loathing: negative and hostile words would have come into your mind automatically: words like *barren* and *horrid,* words like *monstrous, chaotic, savage.* You would have felt about them as the visitor to Yellowstone feels about those sinister valleys filled with foul vapors and gulfs of boiling mud. If you had had to cross them, you would have done so with anxiety and alarm; as for the notion that anyone would wish to sit and contemplate them, or to feel his spirit enriched by wandering among them, or (most ridiculous of all) to *climb* them—that would have seemed to you either impossible or insane.

Two or three hundred years ago the spiritual atmosphere was widely different from ours. We can think ourselves back into it, but we must first realize that it was different, and then admit that it also was a valid way of looking at the world, with virtues and perceptions from which we are debarred. After that, we can try to define its ideals—and then, only then satisfactorily, appreciate the art it produced.

I speak from experience. For nearly forty years I have been playing the piano and listening to music. But it is only in the last twenty that I have come to understand the work of Johann Sebastian Bach. All through my teens and twenties I thought he was a dry old stick who had written some peculiarly difficult puzzles for the piano and organ, and some tediously monotonously religious utterances for the choir. Now I think he was the greatest composer who ever lived. This change in view was not simply a matter of growing up and getting more sense. No, it sprang from a new understanding of the age in which Bach lived. He worked in the seventeenth and eighteenth centuries—the period which has been called the age of baroque. I never understood the ideals of that period until I traveled in France, Germany, and Austria, and—quite unexpectedly—found myself overwhelmed by the power and magnificence of baroque architecture. The palace of Versailles, the Church of the Theatines in Munich, and scores of other noble and splendid buildings, struck me as creations of the human spirit far superior to anything that we can build today. From that I went on to the appreciation of baroque sculpture, and learned to admire the astonishing technique of Bernini—and not only his technique but the intensity of his feeling; both technique and feeling struck me as something beyond anything I had ever experienced. Thereafter it was easy to understand the great baroque painters and etchers—Rembrandt, Rubens, Callot, and a dozen more. And so, perhaps because visual impressions are more direct and powerful than aural impressions, I came the long way round toward an understanding of the baroque composers, and of their greatest master, Bach.

Suppose we try to hear Bach's music as he and his friends heard it, to elicit from it the ideals which governed him as he composed. These are the ideals, the dominant creative ideals, of the baroque age.

The first of these ideals was *tradition*. Bach and his contemporaries did not believe anything new was likely to be good, or even interesting. They thought that the newer and stranger it was, the worse it would probably turn out to be. This does not mean that they cultivated laborious repetition and copying in the manner of so many Far Eastern artists: no, they felt that any creator would surely produce novelties and ought to strive for originality, *but* they held that the most satisfactory creator would build on the work of others and prolong his own apprenticeship. Steady development was their ideal, rather than explosive newness. Again and again Bach said so, in terms which surprise us so much that we might think them insincere: they are not. When he was asked about his music, he did not imply that he had a genius for it, or was possessed by the spirit of melody. When Goethe heard a recital of Bach's organ works, he said, "It is as though eternal harmony were conversing with itself, as it may have happened in God's bosom shortly before He created the world." But when Bach was asked about his organ playing, he said, "You have only to hit the right notes at the right time, and the instrument plays itself." Many a music critic has looked at Bach's production with amazement, and spoken of it as something superhuman. What did Bach say himself? He said, *Ich habe fleissig sein müssen; wer es gleichfalls ist, wird eben so weit kommen.*—"I had to be diligent. Anyone who works as hard will get as far." If you had complimented Bach on the construction of one of his great organ fugues, he would have reacted like an architect who is praised because his buildings don't fall down and kill people.

Tradition means learning and teaching. So Bach learned, all through his early life, and taught, all through his later life. When he was young, he copied out in his own hand dozens and dozens of compositions by elder musicians in order to learn their art. When he was eighteen or so, he walked (or hitchhiked) two hundred and thirty miles to hear the famous organist Buxtehude; he had four weeks leave from his church to do so, and he stayed four months. After his style matured, he went on teaching others. He taught all his children, and made several of them into fine musicians. He taught his second wife. He taught many neighbors and younger colleagues. We are apt to think that music must be an outpouring of the solitary soul (as in Beethoven's last quartets), but the preludes and fugues of Bach are something else; they are works through which a great soul teaches innumerable lesser spirits.

The second ideal of Bach's epoch was *symmetry*. As I look out of my window I see a large apartment building. It has a tower on one side, not on the other; its frontage is stepped back, its rear elevation is irregular, just off straight; it has two grotesque water tanks on the top, and a crowd of TV masts. It looks a little clumsy to me. It would have looked grotesque, almost obscene, to Bach. The buildings of that age were absolutely symmetrical, and their aim was to combine grandeur and richness with an all-ordering harmony. (Think of St. Peter's at Rome.) It is because of his passion for symmetry that Bach was able to express an enormous range of human emotions within a single ordered pattern, the fugue. We feel that, but nowadays we find it terribly hard to understand the connection in Bach's mind between music and mathematics. For instance he took his own name and turned it into numbers: B, the second letter of the alphabet, means 2; A means 1; C, 3; H, 8; the total is 14. Invert 14, and you have 41, which is J. S. Bach, numerically converted. So, in the composition Bach dictated on his deathbed, "Before thy throne I now appear," the first line contains 14 notes, and the whole melody, 41 notes. That is only one of many such symbolic utterances throughout Bach's works.

Something quite beyond the scope of any contemporary composer in orderly ingenuity is shown in Bach's *Goldberg Variations:* one single tune, with thirty variations. This problem "did not seem difficult enough for Bach": although he kept the same bass line, he determined to show the divine variety of music by building every kind of transformation upon it. Apart from all the other variations, Bach produced nine different canons upon this single bass line, one in every third variation, working up the gamut from one to nine, and throwing in an inversion at the fifth. And, apart from its ingenuity, this is all music.

One further ideal of the baroque age was *control.* It was the era of decorum. It was the epoch of authority. Outbursts of emotion were indecent; laughter and tears were repressed or sublimated. Hence the heroines of Racine's tragedies, though flaming with passion and seething with rage, still speak in perfectly arranged sentences and rigidly ordered couplets. Hence Bach's preludes and toccatas are often boldly spontaneous and occasionally almost shapeless, plunging through every key and almost every rhythm, and then—not with a sense of loss, but with a sense of relief—the music returns to the control of the intellect and the will, as expressed by the fugue which follows and transcends the prelude. (Notice that although Chopin used to play Bach's preludes and fugues before each concert of his own, he himself, less disciplined, could compose only a set of preludes.)

In spite of his admiration for these ideals, Bach felt that, like all systems, they were too small for the soul of a great artist. In theory he observed them, and allowed them to dictate much of his work, but in practice, again and again, he moved beyond them. His predecessors and some of his followers—good composers too—did little more than what could have been predicted. But genius is unpredictable. Like Rembrandt, Bach is more than a baroque artist. After establishing the laws of his work, he went beyond them. His noblest composition, the B-minor Mass, is neither Protestant nor Catholic; it is baroque and more than baroque. It is nearly universal. Through it, as through most of his greatest music, Bach tells us that the way from the individual to the universal is through the understanding of tradition; the path to freedom lies through the acceptance, then the transcendence, of law.   —GILBERT HIGHET

Analytical sentence outline

Thesis: We can fully appreciate Bach only by understanding the ideals of his age which he expressed—and transcended.
   I. It is difficult to appreciate a great artist.
      A. It is difficult even when the artist is of our own period.

        1. It demands a kind of surrender.

        2. It demands much time.

    B. It is especially difficult when the artist lives in and expresses an age greatly different from our own.

        1. The different feeling about mountains and forests illustrates the difference between Bach's age and our own.

        2. The difference also shows itself in architecture and painting.

II. The ideals of his age governed Bach as a composer.

    A. Bach and his age believed in tradition.

        1. They believed that the artist should build on the work of his predecessors.

        2. This emphasis on tradition explains why Bach throughout his life was a pupil or teacher.

    B. Bach and his age valued symmetry.

        1. This feeling is seen in the architecture of Bach's time.

        2. The feeling led Bach to see connections between music, mathematics, and order.

    C. Bach and his age believed in control.

        1. The ideal of the age is illustrated by Racine's heroines.

        2. It shows itself in the relief with which the tumult of Bach's preludes and toccatas returns in the fugue to the control of the mind.

III. Bach transcended his age.

    A. He accepted and expressed its ideals.

    B. He also moved beyond them, so that his work is nearly universal.

EXERCISE 2

Make an analytical topic and a paragraph outline of the essay on Bach.

EXERCISE 3

Using the first chapter of this book or a piece of writing assigned by the instructor, make first a paragraph outline, then an analytical sentence outline, and then an analytical topic outline. (You may be tempted to make the topic before the sentence outline, but you will profit more from the assignment if you follow the suggested order.)

EXERCISE 4

Point out the errors in the following outline.

SHOULD EIGHTEEN-YEAR-OLDS BE ALLOWED TO VOTE?

I. Introduction: importance of the subject.
   1. Many people favor
   2. Some do not
II. They are required to serve in time of war.
   A. World War II
   B. The Korean War
   C. Today
      1. The draft
      2. Enlistment
III. Reasons why they should not be allowed to vote.
   A. Physical
      1. Men
      2. Women
   B. Mental
      1. Men
      2. Women
   C. Moral
      1. Men
      2. Women
   D. Women mature younger than men.
IV. Reasons why they should be allowed to vote.
   A. To develop responsibility
      1. They will feel it is their government.
   B. They may be called on to fight.
   C. Today people are better educated.
      1. Improved schools
      2. Television
   D. Voting will make them more mature.
      1. They are allowed to vote in Georgia.
         a. Georgia is one of the most progressive states in the South.
V. Summary and Conclusion

3

Three Cardinal Virtues

It is amazing how many people think of good English as merely "correct" English—correct in that the words are not misspelled, the difference between *who* and *whom* is observed, the infinitive is not split, the word *ain't* never climbs out of limbo, and so on. Good writing is, however, vastly more than the avoidance of errors, and both the challenge and the enjoyment of writing lie in seeing this truth.

Correctness is part of good writing, to be sure, and large sections of this book will be devoted to the matter of acceptable forms and usage, a subject much larger than spelling, and *who* or *whom*, and *isn't* instead of *ain't*. But this kind of acceptability is only a part of the whole, and not the larger or more interesting part.

CLARITY

The first of the cardinal virtues of writing is clarity. Without clarity, writing can never be good and with clarity it can never be wholly bad. The sentence "Jim and me are going to Pittsburgh tomorrow" disturbs the eye and ear, but at least we know what it means, and that is something—a good deal, in fact. The sentence "The complex world of today was achieved through the medium of trial and error, but this failure was very conducive to the development and advancement of our civilization" means little or nothing. No one, and the writer most of all, can know what is meant.

Some ideas, of course, like that of going to Pittsburgh or asking the person next to you at dinner to pass the salt, are so simple that the problem of clarity is not likely to occur. As soon as you get into more difficult areas, however, you will be challenged by clarity, as every writer is. What is democracy? Why did the French Revolution break out when it did? Why is language important in formulating thought as well as in expressing it? What are the advantages or disadvantages of living in a dormitory rather than commuting between home and college? What, in making the decision whether to establish a branch office, is the significance of the productive capacity of the firm you will work for after you graduate? When we get into subjects like these, clarity may not come easily; the most experienced and talented writer may have to work hard to get it.

How does he get it? Or rather, how do you get it?

Many sections of this book discuss clarity even if the word does not appear. The chapters or sections on logic, diction, and wordiness are among those that deal with it. The sections on dangling modifiers, reference of pronouns, and punctuation deal with it, too. Punctuation is a system devised primarily to aid in making the sentence clear, and the rules about reference and about modifiers are made for the same reason. Clarity is the goal behind the preceding chapter, too; the chief if not the only reason for making an outline is to see and present the material clearly. Much of the first chapter, too, is written to help you achieve clarity. If the writer knows his thesis, he will be greatly helped in writing clearly, and if he does not know it, he will be insuperably handicapped. If he gets substance into his writing, he will make it more interesting and forceful, and he will also make it clearer. Any weakness in unity and coherence and proportion will muddy the thought, and if the choice of words is poor, nothing else can be good. So all of the first six basic characteristics of a good theme—and perhaps even the seventh, too—have something to do with clarity.

A chief reason for dividing the writing into three stages is to achieve this quality. If a writer allows his mind to work around and through a subject, he has a good chance to see it clearly. If he writes the first draft without interruptions, he is less likely to show breaks in his thinking. And if he rewrites thoroughly, he gives himself an opportunity to eliminate obscurities which a first draft, by even the most experienced writers, is likely to show.

The absence of clarity

It will help to see the problem if you look at the following passage from a book, *Science in the Cause of Man*.

As for profit, considerations other than profit are already being pressed upon the great corporations by society through government regulatory agencies. The self-perpetuating management is understandably wary of such invasion of its prerogatives. In the present ascendance of its reputation, however, it should be more concerned about its performance than its prerogatives. What is most to be asked of the corporate enterprise system is the vigorous promotion of technological progress. This, in fact, is the primary purpose served by profit in the industrial system today; as a kind of involuntary savings, extracted beforehand from the thriftless consumer, retained corporate earnings have furnished the principal capital for industrial expansion throughout the past fifty years. —GERARD PIEL

The first thing to notice about this writing is its almost total lack of verbs that show action. As the author demonstrates, it is possible to write prose almost without verbs that show action, but it is not possible to write good prose without them. It has never been done and it cannot be done. The author uses participles and passives and the verb *to be,* but only one action verb in the active voice ("have furnished"). Out of a hundred and thirteen words, only one quickens for a moment the inert prose.

The second thing to notice is the abstract and general quality of the nouns. Though the subject requires a more abstract vocabulary than some, a more skillful writer would not allow the abstraction this passage suffers from. Except perhaps for "invasion," the nouns simply have no body, and the writer seems actually to go out of his way to choose, not merely the abstract term, but the vaguest one he can find, like "considerations" in the first sentence.

The failure to use verbs that show action and concrete and

specific nouns is not the only source of obscurity. The first phrase, "As for profit," does nothing and should have been omitted. Why does the author write, "In the present ascendance of its reputation . . . [corporate management] should be more concerned about its performance than its prerogatives"? Does he believe that if its reputation were different it should be *less* concerned about its performance? Why are "involuntary savings" "a kind of involuntary savings"? Why aren't they simply "involuntary savings"? How can they be extracted "beforehand" from the consumer? Since no business can make a profit from the consumer until he becomes a consumer by purchasing the product, the extraction cannot be "beforehand." And since some consumers need and can afford the things they buy, why didn't the writer find a better adjective than "thriftless," with its suggestion of extravagance, or why didn't he see that here he needed no adjective at all?

Finally, it is far from clear why "the vigorous promotion of technological progress" is "most to be asked" of "the corporate enterprise system" (apparently to be asked "by society through government regulatory agencies") if this is just what it is already doing, as the last sentence suggests. The writer may very well mean something here, but it is impossible to tell just what. The writing is muddy, and a difficult subject has been confused, not clarified. A failure in thinking has preceded a failure in writing.

In the following passage on the imbalance of the American economy, wealth in the private sector of the economy, poverty in the public, an economist writes with complete clarity:

The family which takes its mauve and cerise, air-conditioned, power-steered, and power-braked automobile out for a tour passes through cities that are badly paved, made hideous by litter, blighted buildings, billboards, and posts for wires that should long since have been put underground. They pass on into a countryside that has been rendered largely invisible by commercial art. (The goods which the latter advertise have an absolute priority in our value system. Such aesthetic considerations as a view of the countryside accordingly come second. On such matters we are consistent.) They picnic on exquisitely packaged food from a portable icebox by a polluted stream and go on to spend the night at a park which is a menace to public health and morals. Just before dozing off on an air mattress, beneath a nylon tent, amid the stench of decaying refuse, they may reflect vaguely on the curious unevenness of their blessings. Is this, indeed, the American genius? —JOHN KENNETH GALBRAITH

Though the superior clarity of the second passage comes partly from action verbs and concrete nouns, the real explanation must lie deeper. Like all the virtues of writing, clarity is the product of good thinking. No rules, not even such good ones as writing out a thesis sentence, will automatically bring it. The writer must think about his material at every stage of its writing; he must make it clear to himself before he can make it clear to someone else.

FULLNESS

After clarity (and assuming correctness), the second cardinal virtue of writing is fullness. The writer has to say something and he has to say enough. The enough in life is often more than just a little; the enough in writing is usually more than a simple paragraph or two.

The term *fullness* as we use it in this chapter is much the same as the term *substance* used in the first chapter. The quality in writing which the two words seek to define is so important that, varying the approach, we shall turn to it again and again in this book.

Let us assume that, after assigning a chapter in the textbook on the French Revolution and spending several class meetings on the subject, your history professor gives you an examination which includes a thirty-minute essay question on the causes of the revolution and you turn in this as an answer: "The French Revolution broke out because of the contrast between the luxury of the court and the aristocracy on the one side and the poverty of the peasantry on the other."

The answer is accurate so far as it goes, and it is written in correct and clear English. It is, indeed, an acceptable thesis sentence. But it is not a good answer.

We exaggerate, of course; no student who comes to college would turn in so small an answer to so large a question. But many themes and examinations and oral answers in class are defective, really worthless, because they lack fullness, detail, elaboration, or (going back to Chapter 1) substance.

If a history professor were to be satisfied with answers like the one above, he would not assign a chapter and spend several class meetings on the subject. He would read off the sentence above or one like it, tell the class to memorize it, and go on. He could cover world history in an hour or two. But no one would learn any history.

If a composition lacks fullness, the explanation may lie in the writer's ignorance: he simply may not know enough about his subject. If this is so, obviously the cure does not lie in this book and class. But ignorance is not always the cause of empty writing. The writer may really know a good deal about the subject but not have learned to show what he knows. His difficulty then is not ignorance but control of language.

Padding

We will better understand what fullness is if we understand what it is not. Most emphatically it is *not* padding of any kind. It is, indeed, quite incompatible with padding. Fullness is idea, fact, illustration. It is given by words that *do* something. Padding tries—and fails—to give the appearance of fullness by bringing in irrelevant material or by treating the material with words that clutter up the thought instead of developing it.

Had we introduced the subject of this section by explaining that the word "fullness" is akin to the Latin *plenus,* we would have been padding. Sometimes to know the history of a word adds to one's understanding of a subject, but here it would have added nothing. It would have been an intrusion of the irrelevant that did nothing except give the false appearance of fullness. Our student who answered the history question could have started with this sentence: "In regard to the causes of the French Revolution it is apparent that some of the causes were relatively important and some of them were not so important, as is usually the case in historical developments of any sort. For instance, in the last election in this country, some of the issues were more important than others." Written in this way, the answer would indeed be a longer one, but it would not be a full one, and the professor would have to believe that the student knew nothing about the subject.

If the writer takes fifty words to say something that could be said in twenty but says it with a force and interest that twenty words could not give, we do not call it padding. This is, of course, fullness. If, however, he takes fifty words to say something that could be said just as well or better in twenty (or even forty-nine), this is indeed padding. The good writer will be just as interested in finding what he can take out of his writing to improve it as in finding what he can add.

Kept short because they are examples, here are some obvious instances of verbal padding:

1. Are you involved in studying Economics 2? (instead of "Are you studying Economics 2?")
2. His age may be a determining factor as to whether he is employed. (Instead of "His age may determine whether he is employed.")
3. The greatest advantage obtained in my experience as an only child was that of having my parents' undivided attention and care, in regard to my having no competition in striving for my parents' favor. (Instead of "The greatest advantage in my being an only child lay in having the undivided attention of my parents.")
4. The predictions based on the poll proved to be completely wrong because the basis for sampling was apparently insufficiently broad in scope. (Instead of "The predictions based on the poll proved completely wrong because the basis for sampling was apparently too narrow.")

Here are some other examples of verbal padding. How would you correct them?

40

1. He was suffering from a case of high blood pressure.
2. Many calls similar in nature to this one were made.
3. If in America people had not been fortunate enough to be blessed with the glorious right to choose their own religion, it is certain that my grandparents would not have come to this country.
4. It is difficult to believe that there are still some people who disapprove of higher education for women.

"Thin" writing and "full" writing

The following paragraphs show the contrast between writing that is thin and undeveloped and writing that has some fullness. Notice that fullness is not necessarily gained by using more words: actually the paragraphs are the same length and the better one is filled out solely because the words are better.

A. Winter is all right, of course, but after a while I get tired of it and don't mind when spring comes along. Then I like to get out of the city and enjoy the beauties of nature.

B. I like the first snow of winter but not the last. In March I have had enough of snow. In March I want to push out of the crust and see the world coming to life again.

In the next example, the better, filled-out sentence is actually shorter than the other:

A. There seems to be no doubt but that the invention of the hydrogen bomb has confronted civilization with one of the most serious crises it has ever faced and perhaps the most serious. (Thirty-three words)

B. The hydrogen bomb may destroy modern civilization as the barbarians almost destroyed Roman civilization—and do it more thoroughly and more permanently. (Twenty-two words)

We must never forget, however, that proper development of the thought depends on the writer's having sufficient understanding of his subject. Our hypothetical student struggling with the causes of the French Revolution cannot write a good answer unless he knows something! Improved diction helps, but it is no substitute for knowledge. Read the two passages that follow to see how knowledge may bring a fullness impossible without it.

A. Corn is the principal crop in the United States. We grow a great deal of it, and feed most of it to cattle and other farm animals. We grow so much of it because the climate of our country is suitable. The climate of most countries is not so favorable as ours happens to be.

B. This country produced 3,131,009,000 bushels of corn as long ago as 1950—more than all our other grain crops combined and more than the corn crops of the rest of the world. This basic food of livestock requires a climate such as no other country possesses in equal measure: a continental climate with hot nights and heavy rainfall, especially in July, and a growing season of close to 150 days. Most of the world's temperate zone plains lack something that corn needs. The nights are too cool in Canada, the growing season too short in most of the Soviet Union, the rainfall too little in much of the Argentine. Other countries grow corn, but only the United States has a corn belt—the flat, fertile, well-watered, and well-heated plain that begins at Columbus, Ohio, and stretches with hardly an interruption nine hundred miles to central Nebraska.

SINCERITY

In an analysis of the causes of the French Revolution it would be difficult, assuming you were not bluffing, to be insincere. In most subjects, however, and especially in writing about yourself, sincerity must never be taken for granted. It is very easy to be a little insincere! It is very easy indeed to tell yourself and then in a theme to tell your reader that you are happier in your family life than you truthfully are, or that you have come to college to broaden your mind when the real reason is that you have come to make more money or to find a husband. It is easy to use words simply because they sound nice, not because they mean something to you.

No English professor would want you to care less for your parents or to place money ahead of more important things in life. A good deal of his effort, indeed, may be expended in exploring the world of values with you. Using some of the essays and stories of our time or some of the classics of the past, you and he will look at big and sometimes controversial subjects, and he will be pleased if you decide, for example, that there are at least two or three things you want out of life more than money. But he will not be pleased if you just tell him so because you think you ought to feel that way or because you think he expects you to. You might be amazed to know how easily he can tell the difference. That is an integral part of his training—to know the difference between the word that is genuine and the word that postures and pretends.

To see what we mean by this quality, think for a moment of two other arts. Sincerity is a prime quality of good acting: no amount of training can make an actor good unless he feels the role—unless, as we say, he lives it. It is a quality in playing the violin, too, and technical skill will leave an audience cold if the music does not come out of the musician as well as out of his instrument.

Even with impersonal and apparently simple subjects like describing a tree or a restaurant, sincerity comes into play. Does the writer describe the tree as he sees it—or as he remembers someone else to have described it or as he thinks he should see it? Is he using his eye to see a unique picture, his own and no one else's, or is he just seeing the generalized idea of a tree? And is he finding the words that say what he sees or the stereotyped words that say what everyone sees—what he sees or what he thinks he is expected to see?

When a novelist writes, "The voice was like steel, and Mr. Cobb's voice became equally icy," we have to believe that there has been a failure in sincerity. The author could not have felt *steel*, he could not have felt *ice*, and use the words as he does. Like an uncommitted actor, he is just going through the motions. When another novelist tells us that "Lorene turned clear around to serenely frown on him severely," we have to believe there has been a similar failure. The author uses the words because he thinks they sound nice, not because he can possibly mean anything by them, can possibly have felt them, been in them, when he wrote

43

them. (If you have any doubts about this, try to "serenely frown severely"!)

Sincerity is much more than honesty, honesty in the sense of not trying to bluff or otherwise mislead. Honesty in this sense is relatively easy, but sincerity is never so. It requires that you look deep into yourself and your subject to see what *you* find there.

When you look, you must not think that everything mean or foolish or unhappy is true and all you have to do to be sincere is to be a pessimist. The times in which we live are so cynical that this error is widespread: many people think that only bad things are likely to be true and that the others are mirages or rationalizations of some sort. If they really think this, they are blind; and if they only pretend to think it, they themselves are insincere.

You will understand, of course, that sincerity does not mean wearing one's heart on his sleeve. Nor does it mean solemnity and taking over the burdens of the world. In real life it is precisely the sentimental person or the solemn or sanctimonious person who may be least sincere. Light-heartedness in real life does not denote insincerity or even superficiality. If this is true about people, it is equally true about the way they write.

These, then, are the cardinal virtues of good writing—clarity, fullness, and sincerity. If it has them and has correctness too, writing will be good (though perhaps not good enough, since there are other virtues, too); without them, it cannot be good at all. The task of the writer is to discover the truth as he sees it and then to share this truth with his reader. He cannot share unless he discovers. Thus writing is intimately involved in living. It is, of course, something that one *does;* but it is also, it is not too much to say, something that one *is.*

EXERCISE

As precisely as you can, explain why each of the following passages is defective in one or another of the three qualities of good writing discussed in this chapter.

44

1. "Under the selective surveillance of the law of conspicuous waste there grows up a code of accredited canons of consumption, the effect of which is to hold the consumer up to a standard of expensiveness and wastefulness in the consumption of goods and in his employment of time and effort." —THORSTEIN VEBLEN

2. There is nothing in the world half so fascinating or thrilling as the feeling of rain trickling down the sides of your face.

3. All we need to say about the subject of sincerity is that it is being true to what one believes.

4. It is evident that in this day and age individuals are better educated than they were in the past ages, especially in respect to their being in attendance in school more years in their lives than was the case at one time.

5. Unknown to the busy haunts of men, the little valley lay quiet and peaceful, protected, like a child by an adoring mother, by the watchful hill that hovered above it.

6. The propagation of the species has been of the utmost significance to mankind for centuries. With this idea in mind—though it is unlikely that my parents embraced such a thought—I was heralded into this world on April seventeenth, eighteen years ago.

7. The impact of *The Grapes of Wrath* lies in the eventual hopelessness people can endure provided they have some hope in a better future.

8. "In fact, even in the marriage relationship itself some degree of individuality tends to be maintained through the differentiation of marital roles. Indeed we might say that sound marriages will attain maximum identification while maintaining at least a minimum differentiation of personalities." —HARRIET R. MOWRER

9. ". . . [H]is one defense was only the thought of Lorene and payday, warming him like a good stiff drink, a fire at which he could warm himself against this heat of hatred that was slowly freezing him." —JAMES JONES

10. "This is a beautiful time to live in. The middle-aged are young. The old, middle-aged. And the young are more than ever a pleasure to look at." —PEPSI-COLA ADVERTISEMENT

11. The youth of today faces many environmental problems, and is confronted with the rapid changes taking place about him. Such problems consist of the climate and location of his country, the type of industry found there, and the educational phase of his life.

12. Donne's poem lends itself to a religious nature and in an abstract way ties love and life together as a unit to the spiritual welfare of man.

13. Democracy consists of interpersonal relationships of a nature mutually beneficial to all individuals concerned.

14. "Happy, happy man! His time has come to own the 'car of cars' . . . and there he goes for the first thrilling ride at the wheel.

"But what an *additional* thrill he would have if he could look down the long, long road that car will travel before it comes to its final stop!

"For then he would know, beyond peradventure, that he has just taken possession of one of the mechanical masterpieces of all time!" —CADILLAC ADVERTISEMENT

15. ". . . [T]he present lasts far longer than it used to. For we've made time slow down . . . curbed the old despot's destructive disposition by learning to postpone, almost indefinitely, the damage he can do. The things we use and enjoy most—cars, clothes, furniture, home—now change far less in a year than they used to change in a day."

—AMERICAN CYANAMID COMPANY ADVERTISEMENT

4

Good Thinking: Induction, Deduction, Principal Fallacies

One of the best compliments a person can receive is to be told that he thinks straight. A prime objective of a college education is to help him earn that compliment. It is particularly one of the objectives of this course because, even if writing is good in the choice of words, sentence structure, and mechanics, it is not good if it shows mistakes in thinking. Of what value is it to communicate thought if the thought itself is confused and illogical?

THE PROCESSES OF THINKING

Our lives are made up of an almost infinite number of experiences. Thinking is essentially seeing the relationships among these experiences—classifying them, finding the patterns that exist among them, and then using that knowledge to control such of them as can be controlled. Our ability to master our environment depends ultimately on our ability to perceive and use these patterns.

The statement of a pattern of experience is called a *generalization*. Put simply, thinking consists of the processes (1) of finding generalizations and (2) of using them. We call the first process *induction*, the second *deduction*. Actually, these processes enter into almost everything we do, though we seldom think of them as processes.

The process of making an induction and then moving on to deduction has never been described more clearly than by Thomas Henry Huxley:

Suppose you go into a fruiterer's shop, wanting an apple. You take up one, and on biting it you find it is sour; you look at it and see that it is hard and green. You take up another one, and that too is hard, green, and sour. The shopman offers you a third; but before biting it you examine it and find that it is hard and green, and you immediately say that you will not have it, as it must be sour like those that you have already tried.

Nothing can be more simple than that, you think; but if you will take the trouble to analyze and trace out into its logical elements what has been done by the mind, you will be greatly surprised. In the first place you have performed the operation of induction. You found that in two experiences hardness and greenness in apples go together with sourness. It was so in the first case, and it was confirmed by the second. True, it is a very small basis, but still it is enough to make an induction from; you generalize the facts, and you expect to find sourness in apples where you get hardness and greenness. You found upon that a general law that all hard and green apples are sour; and that, so far as it goes, is a perfect induction. Well, having got your natural law in this way, when you are offered another apple which you find is hard and green, you say, "All hard and green apples are sour; this apple is hard and green; therefore this apple is sour." That train of reasoning is what logicians call a syllogism and has all its various parts and terms—its major premise, its minor premise, and its conclusion. And by the help of further reasoning, which if drawn out would have to be exhibited in two or three other syllogisms, you arrive at your final determination, "I will not have that apple." So that, you see, you have in the first place, established a law by induction, and upon that you have founded a deduction and reasoned out the special conclusion of the particular case.

In everyday experience, the inductive-deductive process commonly works in a chain. We generalize, for example, either from our own experience or from that of others, that dark clouds usually "mean" rain. Working with this generalization, we note that the morning sky is heavily overcast, and so we conclude, by deduction, that it will rain today. Now we work with another generalization, one so obvious that we seem never to have had to reach it by induction (though we did): that when it rains, a person not protected by proper clothing gets wet. So now we conclude that if it rains today (as we have concluded it will) and if we are not protected by proper clothing, we will get wet. At this point we bring in still another generalization: that anyone who gets wet has a good chance of catching cold. Having established this chain of reasoning between dark clouds, clothing, and colds, we put on rubbers and raincoat or take an umbrella with us.

Of course, if our original generalization is not true, we may find ourselves walking around all day with our raincoat draped over an arm or trailing our umbrella—as many Eastern visitors to certain parts of the West Coast have found, for there morning clouds typically do not "mean" rain but burn off by the middle of the day.

Note, too, that our generalization must be only that dark clouds *usually* betoken rain. That they do so is not a certainty. We are learning that, even in the physical world, there is no such thing as an absolutely *certain* generalization, but only generalizations which are more or less dependable. All knowledge is *probable* only, even though we have constantly to act as though our generalizations are certain. The awareness that this is true even in the physical world should make us conscious of the tentative nature of our generalizations about human nature and behavior, where the inductive process is much more difficult.

In everyday activities such as those described above, we go through the reasoning process without being aware that we are doing so because the situations are relatively simple. In fact, we get so used to the comfort of easy solutions that we often attempt to apply them in more complex situations, with results that can be disastrous. It is one thing to be caught with an unneeded raincoat because dark morning clouds actually "mean" rain only three times out of five and not always, as we easily assume; it is something quite different to conclude that because the Russians "retreated" in the Cuban crisis of 1962, they will always retreat if we are only firm.

Science made its great progress after it developed the natural processes of induction and deduction into a rigorous discipline and so greatly increased the probability of the generalizations reached. The psychological and social sciences are attempting to bring the same rigor to thinking about human behavior. Since the human organization is much more complex than physical organization, it is not likely that our generalizations about human behavior will ever be as reliable as those about physical phenomena. Yet apparently our only hope of survival lies in learning more about ourselves. It is the obligation of every educated person to know all he can about *how* we know, and to use that knowledge. It is your obligation to show in all your writing a decent respect for the basic laws of thinking.

INDUCTION

Induction becomes a conscious thinking process when it is controlled—when the observer sets out to collect a certain type of evidence. Its most highly controlled form is the science laboratory, where trial and error can speed up the process of observation. The scientist uses induction to reveal cause and effect, as in the discovery of the organism that causes a disease. The pollster uses induction—with much less chance of a reasonably certain resulting generalization—when he attempts to predict the outcome of an election.

The reliability of any generalization depends on a number of things:

(1) **Pertinence of the evidence** Trial-and-error procedures in science are usually effective in ruling out evidence that is not relevant. Edison, for example, could rule out wood as a possible conductor of electricity and have no doubts about his decision. We sometimes have more trouble when we deal with generalizations about people. It is true that, in deciding whether a prizefighter is skillful or not, we note his speed, his footwork, his punching power, and so on; and we are not tempted to include the fact that he is a divorced man, if he is. But it is not so easy for us to rule out the fact of divorce, to be sure that it is irrelevant, when we are generalizing about a candidate for political office. Our generalizations

about foreign peoples are often impaired by irrelevant evidence, as is indicated by such epithets as "shopkeepers" and "frog eaters," epithets that have a basis in fact (the French *do* eat frogs) but not in relevant fact. Sometimes, especially when we leave the area of the physical sciences, we honestly do not know whether some evidence is relevant to the generalization or not. This does not alter the fact that the reliability of a generalization depends in part on the pertinence of the evidence.

(2) **Objectivity of the observer**   Scientists know that it is difficult not to find what one sets out to find. This is one of the reasons for the rule that a scientific discovery, to be valid, should be susceptible of "discovery" by other scientists working independently with the procedures set up by the discoverer. In the arena of human relations, objectivity is much more difficult, of course. It is not easy for most Republicans to see virtues in Democrats, "conservatives" in "liberals," union members in management. Even when we are not subjected to propaganda, it is difficult for us to make objective observations of people whose habits, customs, religion, and beliefs are different from our own.

(3) **Sufficiency of the evidence**   "A college education is of no use in business. My uncle was president of his company and he never went to college." How much evidence must we have before we are justified in making a generalization? The answer is not very comforting: It depends. The more evidence we have in support of a generalization, however, the more we can rely on it. If somebody makes the assertion that people with an I. Q. of less than 90 cannot do successful college work, whether or not we should believe the assertion will depend in part on how extensive the research behind the statement has been. Gathering evidence is often hard work, and the temptation is to quit before we have enough. Yielding to this temptation leads to what is called "hasty generalization"—the lazy man's way of thinking.

(4) **Honesty of observation**   *All* the evidence must be considered, not just that which will support a desired gener-

alization. It is all too easy to reach such generalizations as "Shiftlessness is the cause of poverty" and "Women make poor drivers" by noting the instances that support the generalization and ignoring those that do not.

(5) **Careful use of authority** Obviously, nobody can himself gather the evidence for more than a few of the many generalizations by which he must live. This means that we must take somebody else's word for most of what we know. But whose word shall we accept? Who shall be our authority?

It is easy to tell, usually, whose word we should *not* accept. We should *not* accept the word of those without training and experience in the area of the generalization. We know we should not take Aunt Emma's word about labor relations, though she may make some very emphatic statements about the unreasonable demands of workers. We know we should listen to the batting champion when he talks about the fine points of hitting a baseball but can safely ignore what he says about the medicinal merits of shaving creams. We must inquire, too, whether our authority is giving his best generalizations. Consciously or unconsciously, politicians usually reflect the desires of their constituents. The skilled physician in the employ of a tobacco firm tends to see the relation between cigarette smoking and lung cancer in a different light than the physician not so employed.

Even when self-interest is in no way involved, authorities sometimes disagree—about the best methods of teaching children to read, for instance, or about how much economic aid we should give foreign countries today. We must try to judge between authorities, but there is no criterion by which we can know with certainty whom to rely upon.

Two specious authorities we need to be especially on guard against. One is the authority of the printed word. Many of us accept the printed word as gospel, as if the fact of being printed made something true. No generalization could be more dangerous. The printed word—even these words!—must be subjected to the same scrutiny as all other authority. We must always ask who wrote the word and whether he is qualified to be considered an authority in this area.

The second specious authority is "common sense," the common sense that once insisted that the world was flat. We can trust the part of our common sense that arises from our own experience only when we have subjected that experience to the rigorous thought processes we are discussing. Our experience with Slobovians may have been unfortunate; we have known only three Slobovians and they have all tried to cheat us, we think. Common sense makes a hasty generalization and tells us to distrust Slobovians. Rigorous thinking tells us that our evidence is much too limited to warrant any such generalization.

Most common sense is inherited as part of our culture. It is a bewildering mixture of wisdom, superstition, and folly. Common sense long assured man that he could not fly, that witches cast spells, that women are inferior, and that poverty and war are inevitable parts of human existence. Common sense has a long record of fallibility.

Learning to evaluate authority has at least two by-products: respect for good authority, and proper humility. Most of us have little trouble respecting the authority of our physician and being humble about our own knowledge of medicine—perhaps because we realize that our very life may depend on our respecting his authority. It is not so easy to feel this respect and this humility when the issue is less crucial or at least less immediate. Too often we "know what we think" about our relations with foreign nations, managing the national debt, or solving the race problems without first having listened to those who have the training and experience needed to think well about these subjects. The self-respecting person must walk on his own two feet, of course. But only a fool chooses to try to find his way by his own (often necessarily dim) light. Learn to use also the flares that others have lighted.

DEDUCTION

Deduction is the process by which we can put generalizations to work. Let us return for a moment to Huxley's example of the bitter apples. Without the ability to *deduce* from our generalization that all hard, green apples are bitter, we could go on biting such apples and making a wry face to the end of our days. Thus deduction saves us from the tyranny of repeated experience.

The deduction from the green apples or the threatening clouds occurs—like most of our deduction—in such simple situations that we are usually not aware of the process. Yet such processes do exist. It is the province of *formal logic* to explore the forms which the processes take. By becoming familiar with these forms, we can analyze our thinking in situations that are not so simple.

Formal logic is a highly complicated subject, and this is not the place to discuss it in detail. Here we shall concern ourselves only with one of the most common and useful logical forms, the *categorical syllogism.* Let us put the thinking about the green apples in this syllogistic form:

> Major premise: All hard, green apples are bitter.
> Minor premise: This apple is hard and green.
> Conclusion: This apple is bitter.

Note that the syllogism does not *prove* that hard, green apples are bitter, nor that "this" apple is hard and green. It merely points out the *implication* of these two premises. We could rephrase as follows: *If* it is true that all hard, green apples are bitter, and *if* this apple is hard and green, then the deductive form lets us be sure that this apple is bitter.

Now look at this syllogism:

> Major premise: All Spaniards are six feet tall.
> Minor premise: Señor Alvarez is a Spaniard.
> Conclusion: Señor Alvarez is six feet tall.

The man stands up to be measured and we discover that he is barely five feet tall. Since the syllogism is in proper form, we know that one or the other premise must be untrue.

54

We know that Señor Alvarez is indeed a Spaniard, and so we also know that the major premise must be untrue: not *all* Spaniards are six feet tall. Thus the syllogism, properly used, can force us to become aware of untrue premises (generalizations) and to revise them—in other words, to bring them into line with reality.

Here is another syllogism:

> Major premise: All Slobovians are cowards.
> Minor premise: Jan Pulac is a Slobovian.
> Conclusion: Jan Pulac is a coward.

But we have seen Jan Pulac prove himself a brave man and we know he is a Slobovian. We *know*, therefore, that our generalization that all Slobovians are cowards is untrue. Substitute the name of any people you will for "Slobovians" and the implication for foreign relations becomes obvious. Substitute the name of any racial, religious, or other group and the domestic implications are obvious, too.

We can set up the syllogism with a negative major premise:

> Major premise: No Slobovian will fight.
> Minor premise: Jan Pulac is a Slobovian.
> Conclusion: Jan Pulac will not fight.

So we pick a fight with Mr. Pulac and end up with a black eye and a generalization revised—the hard way.

The syllogisms above have been in proper form. They are what logicians call *valid* syllogisms: their conclusions follow from their premises. But look at this one:

> Major premise: Some college professors are absent-minded.
> Minor premise: Professor Jones is a college professor.
> Conclusion: Professor Jones is absent-minded.

Note that the major premise states, not that *all* college professors are absent-minded, but that *some* are. We have no way of knowing whether Professor Jones is included in this group or in the group (which must exist) of college professors who are *not* absent-minded. Therefore the *form* of the syllogism is not correct: logicians would call this an *invalid* syllogism. (We would be justified in concluding from the premises that Professor Jones *may* be absent-minded—that is, *may* be one of the *some*—but this tells us nothing about him.)

We need to repeat the very important fact that a syllogism can be valid (that is, in proper form) and yet have a false conclusion if one or both of the premises are false.

Normally, of course, we don't encounter syllogisms as such. One value of knowing the proper syllogistic form lies in being able to apply it to statements such as the following: "Like the Communists, John Smith believes in a shorter work week." Here one of two syllogisms is implied:

1. Major premise: All those who believe in a shorter work week are Communists.
   Minor premise: John Smith believes in a shorter work week.
   Conclusion: John Smith is a Communist.

This is a valid syllogism. But is the conclusion true? We don't know John Smith, let us assume, but we *do* know Joe Brown, who believes in a shorter work week and who, we know, is *not* a Communist. So we can substitute the name of Joe Brown for John Smith in the syllogism and thereby *know* that the major premise is untrue. We still don't know whether John Smith is or is not a Communist; we *do* know that we cannot decide the matter on the basis of the statement given us.

2. Major premise: Some people who believe in a shorter work week are Communists.
   Minor premise: John Smith believes in a shorter work week.
   Conclusion: John Smith is a Communist.

The syllogism is invalid. Thus we have no way of knowing from it whether or not John Smith is a Communist.

If you are interested in seeing statements of this type used on an especially wide and reckless scale, go into the newspaper files of the early 1950's and read about the activities of Senator Joseph M. McCarthy. But of course you don't have to go back to the 1950's. Perhaps you will find examples in the paper published this morning.

FALLACIES IN LOGIC

Here are some of the more serious and more common failures in thinking—fallacies in logic, as they are called.

Composition and division *Composition* is assuming that what is true of a part is also true of the whole. Obviously, this is merely generalizing from too little evidence—what we have already called "hasty generalization." It is an especially dangerous fallacy. A person who, having been cheated by one member of the human race, concluded that all members of the human race are cheaters would be forced to lead a dismal life indeed. *Division* is the fallacy of assuming that what is true of the whole is also true of every part. We can see it in the thinking of some Europeans that all Americans are rich.

The mechanism of both these fallacies is such that, if we once let them operate, they tend to condition our perception of evidence that would reveal the fallacy. Thus many people see the same action as "aggressiveness" if the actor is Jewish and "initiative" if he is non-Jewish. A Scotchman is stingy; a New Englander is thrifty. And so on.

Begging the question Begging the question is the fallacy of assuming as the premise of an argument the very conclusion which one wishes to prove. It is also called reasoning in a circle.

Consider this statement: "All young men and women should continue their education after graduation from high school because it is in the national interest of the United States, especially in this period of intense competition with the Soviet Union, that all persons carry their education beyond the secondary level." Here the conclusion about education beyond high school is also the premise upon which it is based. The wording changes triumphantly from "After graduation from high school" to "beyond the secondary level," but the argument ends where it began: as an unsupported statement of opinion that people should go to college.

Or think of this argument: "It's time we stopped throwing our money away on foreign aid. We have problems of our own: unemployment, race relations, education, juvenile delinquency, and we'd better be spending our time and money on them." The question is begged, obviously, by the words "throwing our money away." The question is whether we *are* throwing our money away, and nothing that follows is addressed to that question.

Begging the question is a technique we use to prevent a question's being examined. We use it, ordinarily without being aware of it, when we don't really want to examine into a matter but want to feel that we have done so. If we are unscrupulous, we use it to try to deceive others.

Non sequitur   (It does not follow.)   A *non sequitur* is a conclusion based on insufficient premises or premises that ignore relevant data. Here is an example: "The sales in this territory have gone down. Jones is the new salesman in this territory. Therefore, Jones is a poor salesman." (Note that while this *looks* like a syllogism, it is not in proper syllogistic form.) Other possible relevant premises are here ignored: a general business slump, a change in the sales potential in this particular territory, temporary overstocking in the territory, and so on.

Cause and effect happen in time, of course, and one common type of *non sequitur* occurs when the time element is considered to the exclusion of all other possible elements. This particular fallacy is called *post hoc, ergo propter hoc* (after this, therefore because of this). Often the time relationship between cause and effect is very clear and is, furthermore, a reliable indicator of cause. This is true of green apples and stomachache, of staying up late and being sleepy the next day, and so on. This is so often true, in fact, that it leads us into the fallacy of thinking that time relationship is *always* a reliable indicator of cause.

A few weeks after the election in 1932 of Franklin D. Roosevelt, Adolf Hitler seized power in Germany. To assume that a causal, a cause-and-effect, relation existed between these two events—to assume, that is, that Hitler seized power because Roosevelt was elected (or that Eisenhower's election in 1952 caused the death of Stalin in 1953)—would be an egregious example of the *post hoc* fallacy.

Many superstitions rest on this fallacy. Readers of Mark Twain's classic will recall how Huckleberry Finn explains his misfortunes. One morning he turns over the saltcellar at breakfast and that evening, sure enough, there in his room he finds his father, whom he fears so much. One day he brings in a snakeskin and many days later, sure enough, he and Jim miss their turn into the Ohio at Cairo and drift by in the fog at night. Turning over the saltcellar and bringing in the snakeskin came first, and so they must have caused the disaster that followed. The people of the Hebrides Islands are said to believe that body lice make a man healthy. Over many generations they have observed that healthy people have lice and very sick people do not. Lice, therefore, must make a man healthy. Everyone in the Hebrides had them most of the time, but when a man got sick and his body became hot, the lice left. Quite possibly the lice caused the fever, but they were believed to cause the health, and cause and effect were completely confused.

Ignoring the issue   Ignoring the issue is, like begging the question, a way of keeping the issue from being examined. Here, instead of making the conclusion a part of the premise, we simply ignore the issue by introducing another. The lawyer who brings his defendant's wife and children into the courtroom is trying to make the jury (and audience) drown the issue in a sea of sympathy. If a candidate for political office campaigns on the basis of his war record and his devotion to his family, he is ignoring the issues. Politicians who come out resoundingly for God, motherhood, and country are throwing up smoke screens to hide the real questions on which men are divided and on which they must make decisions.

A particularly virulent form of ignoring the issue is *argumentum ad hominem* (argument to the man). In this fallacy, not the man's ideas but the man himself is attacked. Instead of arguing that a person's ideas about college football are unsound for this or for that reason, his opponent calls him stupid or disloyal.

False dilemma   A false dilemma exists when we are asked to make an *either/or* decision though more than two choices are possible. During the Korean War, for example, it was sometimes argued that we had to choose *either* total war (nuclear war) *or* submission to Communism. Women sometimes are told they must choose *either* a home *or* a career. The "two horns" of dilemmas like these do not present all the possible choices. Not always, of course, but often we have a third choice, and perhaps many choices.

Equivocation   Equivocation is using the same term in different meanings in the same argument. In Robert Penn Warren's novel *All the King's Men,* Governor Stark ("the Boss") makes the following remarks:

"Dirt's a funny thing," the Boss said. "Come to think of it, there ain't a thing but dirt on this green God's globe except what's under water, and that's dirt too. It's dirt makes the grass grow. A diamond ain't a thing in the world but a piece of dirt that got awful hot. And God-a-Mighty picked up a handful of dirt and blew on it and made you and me and George Washington and mankind blessed in faculty and apprehension. It all depends on what you do with the dirt. That right?"

Governor Stark is attempting to justify the use of bribery and blackmail in politics. He accepts *dirt,* his opponents' name for them, and then goes on to point out how valuable dirt is. In effect he is saying that literal dirt (soil) justifies figurative dirt (bribery and blackmail). In other words, soil justifies crime. The argument shows up in its absurdity when the word *dirt* is stripped of its equivocation.

THE LIMITATIONS OF LOGIC

Unfortunately, the recognition of fallacies in logic is much more difficult in real life than in the examples given in a book like this. A student who argues that he should not "waste" his time studying history because as an accountant he is going to work with the present, not the past, is clearly begging the question, but in real life, errors in thought sometimes are more hidden; and intelligent men may disagree over whether they are errors at all, as in the following statement:

Since history does not repeat itself and since even the most erudite men do not agree about what its lessons are, its study may wisely be left to be a subordinate one in the student's education.

We are not the least concerned with arguing the truth or falsity, the wisdom or foolishness, of this statement. The only point here is that its truth or falsity is not self-evident, and men can and do disagree profoundly about such statements.

A similar difficulty arises in dealing with the *post hoc* fallacy, because a relation in time may indeed indicate a relation in cause and effect. No educated mind would make the Roosevelt-Hitler mistake or the ones that Huck Finn makes. But what, to use a simple example, are you to think if you eat some peanuts in the afternoon and suffer a stomachache that night? What, to use an example not so simple, are economists to think if the Federal Reserve Board raises the interest rate and unemployment then goes up? Perhaps something else you ate caused the upset; perhaps it was not food at all but nervous tension. Perhaps not the rise in the interest rate but a change in tariff policies in the nations in the European Common Market caused the rise in unemployment. But perhaps, after all, it was the peanuts. And perhaps, after all, it was the rise in the interest rate. Often we cannot be completely sure of cause-and-effect relations, and sometimes we cannot be sure at all.

Logic can explain the fallacy of *ignoring the issue* and using the *ad hominem* argument, but it can give no assurance that we know what the issue is. The choice in a political campaign, for example, involves policies and laws, but it also involves men, and the experience, ability, and integrity of the candidates is a legitimate subject for debate. Again, not all dilemmas are false ones. Sometimes a man or a nation really has only two choices, and a commitment either to one or to the other must be made. Finally, some equivocations are as subtle as the one about dirt is obvious.

The study of induction, the syllogism, and the chief fallacies should help one think straight, but this study is no certain shortcut to good thinking. There are no certain shortcuts. The problems in real life about which we think and talk and write are always more complex (and more interesting) than the problem of whether Professor Jones has been proved to be absent-minded.

EXERCISE 1

Criticize the editorial from the New York *Mirror* (June 3, 1963) which is reprinted here. Discuss the quality of its thinking and identify such things as insufficient or missing evidence and logical fallacies.

UNCLE'S PAYROLL TAX

While President Kennedy talks of reducing the income tax, a key member of his party—Rep. Wilbur D. Mills (D.–Ark.), chairman of the House Ways and Means Committee—wants to increase the Federal payroll tax.

That is what the Social Security tax really is. It's not an insurance premium—merely a special tax to support a government program. You can pay it for 40 or 50 years and still get no benefits in your old age if you don't happen to qualify under the rules.

This is a payroll tax that's getting steeper and steeper.

It began in the '30s as 1% (with employers paying a matching amount) on the first $3000 of a year's pay. The maximum payment was thus $30. Over the years, with the inevitable election-year tinkering by Congress, the percentage has risen to a current 3⅝% on a salary base now broadened to $4800. The maximum payment now is $174. (And, of course, that is duplicated by the employer.)

Now along comes Rep. Mills with a proposal to extend the taxable salary base to $5400. Employes making that much or more would thus pay an additional $21.75.

Mills' main objective is to ward off the prospect of deficits in the program's "trust funds," but part of the increase he proposes would also be translated into higher benefits in various categories.

And so it goes—up, up, up.

Some political dopesters think the Mills gambit has a bearing on the Kennedy medicare program, which would operate under Social Security. But Mills' suggestion could scarcely help in that direction. It only points up the fact that still another hefty increase in the Social Security tax would be necessary to handle medicare.

What the Mills proposal does, in any case, is to emphasize the staggering burden that Social Security is becoming. Even if Congress does no further tinkering (which is most unlikely), the rate schedule is now pegged for an increase to 4⅛% in 1966 and to 4⅝% in 1968.

Remembering that the employer pays a matching amount, this will mean a total Social Security tax of nearly 10% in 1968 on whatever salary base applies at the time. That kind of money could buy a pretty good retirement policy that would be genuine insurance—truly **security.**

This is a thought that is bound to occur to more and more people as Social Security approaches the overload point—the point at which it could crumble under its own weight.

EXERCISE 2

The two quotations that follow are from articles carried by the Associated Press and printed in the Philadelphia *Bulletin* of February 17 and February 18, 1959. They were written by D. Sripati Chandrasekhar, who was identified as "a distinguished Indian observer."

(1) As proof of the efficiency of China in the utilization of food: "There are literally no flies, no rats, no dogs, and no sparrows in China."

(2) "Pocket handkerchief" farming was not yielding enough because "Intensive cultivation, use of abundant fertilizers, and mechanization were impossible on tiny plots."

Let us assume that you know little about farming and nothing about China, but as a citizen you feel some responsibility to keep informed about other countries. Would you be able to make any judgment at all of the reliability of such statements?

EXERCISE 3

The statements below or statements very much like them have been made and repeated widely. Explain why the thinking expressed in them is faulty, if you believe it is. When you think it will help, first set the idea up in a syllogism.

1. You can't believe anything in the newspapers.
2. The development of the atom bomb by the United States shows the superiority of American to European universities.
3. The reports of what happened in the Nazi concentration camps must have been exaggerated, because they are too horrible to believe.
4. We should have more aircraft carriers, because what is good for the Navy is good for the country.
5. The modern woman is happier than her grandmother because she has a functional kitchen.
6. There can't be anything much wrong with a man who likes dogs.
7. Life begins at forty.
8. Clothes make the man.
9. Nothing is good or bad but thinking makes it so.
10. Women are weaker than men.
11. Our ability to produce more steel than any other nation guarantees us victory if another war should come.
12. I am the master of my fate.
13. The love of money is the root of all evil.
14. The defense always catches up with the offense and therefore we do not need to be greatly troubled about the hydrogen bomb.
15. We have always had wars and so we shall always have them.
16. Warrington should be elected President because, like the immortal Abraham Lincoln, he was born in poverty and has, therefore, a deep sympathy for the underprivileged people of our country.
17. The fact that we have so much crime in our city proves that we should return to the use of capital punishment.
18. Since this is a free country, the college should allow the elective system to operate in the selection of courses. It is undemocratic to require students to take certain courses.
19. The life expectancy in this country has been practically

64

doubled (from about thirty-five to about seventy) in the last century. It is likely, therefore, that within another century most people will live to be a hundred and forty.

20. Advertising strengthens democracy by encouraging the buyer's freedom of choice.

21. Vote for Joe Doaks. The polls show that he is going to win.

22. Smoke Parliboros—a man's cigarette.

23. Hitler could not cross the twenty-mile wide English channel. This shows that he was no threat to the United States.

24. George Washington warned this nation against entangling alliances. The United States, therefore, should withdraw its forces from Europe.

25. The reason Latin and Greek should be dropped from the curriculum is that they have no value today.

26. Look before you leap.

27. He who hesitates is lost.

28. Absence makes the heart grow fonder.

29. Out of sight, out of mind.

30. Statistics prove. . . .

31. History repeats itself.

32. Human nature does not change.

33. Love conquers all.

34. When in Rome, do as the Romans do.

35. He must be a Communist because he is opposed to loyalty oaths and so are Communists.

36. There are two sides to every question.

37. It stands to reason that the white race is superior because it has contributed most to civilization.

38. If you work for a living, then you are in business. Therefore what helps business helps you.

39. If you want to live on a shady street, you ought to want to live in a shady neighborhood.

40. Women are more emotional than men.

5

The Paragraph

Every whole thing, if it is a true whole, consists of parts in significant relation to one another and to the whole. In student writing, the theme is this whole. Usually the paragraph is the largest of these parts.

PARAGRAPH LENGTH

A paragraph should be as long as it needs to be to express its part of the whole idea. Paragraphs range from a single word to a score or more of sentences and many hundreds of words. A quick examination of a good book or magazine will show, however, that not many paragraphs, except in dialogue in novels and short stories, are less than two sentences and not many are more than ten or twelve.

If the writer begins a new paragraph every time he begins a new sentence, obviously the paragraph break means nothing except to signal a sentence break. Sentence and paragraph will have become the same, and the writer will simply have lost one of the means by which he can show the division and the organization of his thought, the "parts in significant relation to one another and to the whole." Ordinarily, therefore, the paragraph should be longer than one sentence.

On the other hand, if a paragraph runs to many sentences, it begins to approximate the theme or chapter section and thus to lose its role by being too long, just as the one-sentence paragraph tends to lose its role by being too short. Very long paragraphs, moreover, make the page look rather uninviting. A ten or twelve-sentence paragraph, accordingly, should be thought of as quite long, though not necessarily too long, and most writers should seldom go beyond four or five sentences.

UNITY IN THE PARAGRAPH

We have already seen that the theme should have unity, that "every sentence in it should in some way support its thesis," that "every fact, every idea, every illustration should relate" to its central purpose. The paragraph must have unity too. Everything in it must contribute to that part of the whole which the paragraph expresses. The theme has the unity of the whole thing; the paragraph has the unity of the part. The paragraph must deal with one part within this whole and it must show that part in relation to the whole.

The following paragraph from *The Sea Around Us* is an excellent example of paragraph unity. Rachel Carson states her topic in the first sentence. She announces, that is to say, what part in the whole chapter this paragraph is to play. Every sentence that follows develops this topic; and nothing extraneous is allowed to enter the paragraph.

Eventually the whales, as though to divide the sea's food resources among them, became separated into three groups: the plankton-eaters, the fish-eaters, and the squid-eaters. The plankton-eating whales can exist only where there are dense masses of small shrimp or copepods to supply their enormous food requirements. This limits them, except for scattered areas, to arctic and antarctic waters and the high temperate latitudes. Fish-eating whales may find food over a somewhat wider range of ocean, but they are restricted to places where there are enormous populations of schooling fish. The blue water of the tropics and of the open ocean basins offers little to either of these groups. But that immense, square-headed, formidably toothed whale known as the cachalot or sperm whale discovered long ago what men have known for only a short time—that hundreds of fathoms below the almost untenanted surface waters of these regions there is an abundant animal life. The sperm whale has taken these deep waters for his hunting grounds; his quarry is the deep-water population of squids, including the giant squid Architeuthis, which lives pelagically at depths of 1500 feet or more. The head of the sperm whale is often marked with long stripes, which consist of a great number of circular scars made by the suckers of the squid. From this evidence we can imagine the battles that go on, in the darkness of the deep water, between these two huge creatures—the sperm whale with its 70-ton bulk, the squid with a body as long as 30 feet, and writhing, grasping arms extending the total length of the animal to perhaps 50 feet.

Here, on a very different subject, is another tightly unified paragraph, the last paragraph in George Orwell's essay on Charles Dickens:

When one reads any strongly individual piece of writing, one has the impression of seeing a face somewhere behind the page. It is not necessarily the actual face of the writer. I feel this very strongly with Swift, with Defoe, with Fielding, Stendhal, Thackeray, Flaubert, though in several cases I do not know what these people looked like and do not want to know. What one sees is the face that the writer *ought* to have. Well, in the case of Dickens I see a face that is not quite the face of Dickens's photographs, though it resembles it. It is the face of a man of about forty, with a small beard and a high colour. He is laughing, with a touch of anger in his laughter, but no triumph, no malignity. It is the face of a man who is always fighting against something, but who fights in the open and is not frightened, the face of a man who is *generously angry*—in other words, of a nineteenth-century liberal, a free intelligence, a type hated with equal hatred by all the smelly little orthodoxies which are now contending for our souls.

In contrast with these two paragraphs, look at the one that follows to see the damage done by a failure in unity:

About four hundred years ago Francis Bacon, *the youngest son of Sir Nicholas Bacon,* proposed to take all knowledge for his province, but today a man can master only one small specialty, so great has been the growth of knowledge. Today a man cannot even master a restricted field like mathematics or biology or English literature. He may have a sound general knowledge of many subjects, *and he needs to reconcile—and his college should help him to reconcile—the claims of general culture and of specialization,* but he will have a complete knowledge only of something as small as the ecology of insects in New England or the problem of dating Shakespeare's plays. Even the most brilliant mathematician must be careful in a meeting of a learned society not to get into one of the sessions outside his specialty, where he might be as helpless to follow the discussion as a student in high-school algebra suddenly transferred to a college course in integral calculus. Since Bacon's day, *and Bacon was pretty surely the greatest man of his time except Shakespeare,* man collectively has amassed so much knowledge that man individually knows almost none of it.

The italicized portions violate the unity of the paragraph and should be eliminated. The first of them gives information which is irrelevant. The second introduces something about alleviating the problem before the writer has finished stating what the problem is. The third is poor because the paragraph is not about Bacon at all—except that Bacon proposed to take all knowledge for his province, a point already made and in no way strengthened or clarified by the later statement. A rereading with the italicized portions omitted will disclose how much easier it now is to see the author's meaning.

COHERENCE IN THE PARAGRAPH

Just as unity is a quality of the paragraph as well as of the whole theme, so is coherence. Whatever the unit, the relation between the parts that combine to make this unit must be clear.

Incoherence sometimes comes from putting things down in the wrong order, but usually it comes from the omission of a necessary connecting thought. The writer sees a connection but sometimes, as in the paragraph that follows, even the most attentive reader cannot see it or can see it only through a blur.

History warns us that civilization is a very fragile organism. Like plants and animals, it can die. We all know the fear that gnaws at us today, the fear that war and the hydrogen bomb may destroy civilization. It was not the hydrogen bomb which fifteen hundred years ago convulsed the Roman world. If Western civilization had not already been profoundly sick, the barbarians could not have broken in and taken over. The Romans, not the barbarians, destroyed Rome.

The individual sentences here are satisfactory, but something is clearly wrong with the paragraph as a whole—so wrong, in fact, that it is difficult to see what the writer is trying to say: that other things besides war can destroy a civilization. The paragraph lacks coherence, and the reason it lacks it is that some of the necessary connections in the thought have not been stated. The following paragraph, with the new material italicized (though ordinarily, of course, it would not be) is much better:

History warns us that civilization is a very fragile organism. *Like biological organisms, like plants and animals, it can get sick.* Like plants and animals, it can die. We all know the fear that gnaws at us today, the fear that war and the hydrogen bomb may destroy civilization. *Without minimizing this fear, let us also remember that other things can attack civilizations—that other things have attacked and destroyed other civilizations.* It was not the hydrogen bomb which fifteen hundred years ago convulsed the Roman world. *Actually, it was not war and the conquest of the barbarians either, for* if Western civilization had not already been profoundly sick, the barbarians, *poorly armed and poorly trained and comparatively small in numbers,* could not have broken in and taken over. The Romans, not the barbarians, destroyed Rome.

EXAMPLES OF PARAGRAPH COHERENCE

The following paragraphs show some of the ways to keep the parts of paragraphs unmistakably related:

A. (1) The may-apple is commonly seen in clumps growing about a foot high under trees. (2) Its large leaves nearly conceal the single flower borne by each plant. (3) This flower matures into a fruit, the so-called apple. (4) Strangely enough—and not so commonly known—though the apple is edible, all the rest of the plant, root and leaves, is highly poisonous.

Comment: The sentences are connected as follows: *May-apple* in (1) is referred to by *its* in (2); *flower* in (2) is referred to as *this flower* in (3); and *apple* in (3) is referred to again in (4).

The paragraph, though a simple series of descriptive facts that require no elaborate organization, gains some further coherence from the repetition of the word *commonly* in

(1) and (4), and by the phrase *strangely enough*, which serves as a contrasting connection between (4) and the first three sentences.

B. The climatic variation of the Soviet Union is much less than might be expected. *Although* the country is nearly three times as large as the United States, it has scarcely the variation of Texas between Amarillo and Brownsville. It has, *for instance*, no extensive subtropical area like Florida and parts of California, Arizona, and Texas. The so-called subtropical area in the Crimea and near Batum covers only a few hundred square miles, *and* it is, *moreover*, far more subject to freezing than the warmer parts of this country. The citrus area in the Soviet Union has *in fact* a winter temperature not like Los Angeles' *but* almost like Seattle's.

Comment: The coherence of this paragraph is aided by the use of the connecting and transitional words and phrases, which are italicized. Without them the paragraph would read as follows:

The climatic variation of the Soviet Union is much less than might be expected. The Soviet Union is nearly three times as large as the United States. It scarcely has the variation of Texas between Amarillo and Brownsville. It has no extensive subtropical area like Florida and parts of California, Arizona, and Texas. The so-called subtropical area in the Crimea and near Batum covers only a few hundred square miles. It is far more subject to freezing than the warmer parts of this country. The citrus area in the Soviet Union has a winter temperature not like Los Angeles'. It is almost like Seattle's.

The inferiority of the second paragraph comes partly from the monotonous sentence structure which the omission of the connecting words leads to. It also comes directly from the omission of the words and phrases that serve to bind one sentence to another.

C. (1) The explanation of this traditional attitude towards the function of government and the liberty of the citizen is not to be found in any inherent virtues or defects of the Americans themselves. (2) It is to be found, first, in the circumstances of their history, which have enabled them, until comparatively recent times at least, to get on very well with a minimum of governmental regulation; and, secondly, in their traditional democratic political philosophy, which, as formulated in the eighteenth century, was based on the assumption, among others, that the best form of government is the one that governs least. (3) What, then, were these peculiar circumstances of American history, and how was this historical experience rationalized in the traditional democratic political philosophy?   —CARL BECKER

Comment: Coherence is obtained here in a variety of ways. In (1) the words *this traditional attitude* make a connection of the present paragraph with preceding material, not quoted here. Sentences (1) and (2) are connected by contrast and repetition: *is not to be found* in (1) and *is to be found* in (2). A further connection is made by carrying over the subject: *the explanation of this traditional attitude* in (1) is referred to again in *it,* the first word of (2). *Americans* in (1) is referred to by *their* (twice) and *them* in (2). The third sentence repeats the two parts of the second, but turns them into question form: *circumstances of their history* appears as *these . . . circumstances of American history,* and *traditional democratic political philosophy* is repeated unchanged. The paragraph ends with a question that leads on to the next paragraph.

The author here repeats more words than one would ordinarily expect, but he is clearly justified because he manages to keep straight and clear material that is rather difficult and necessarily abstract. (Compare the method here with that in A above, a very simple paragraph.)

Though we can generalize about them, unity and coherence cannot be imposed by rule. They arise out of the writer's involvement in his subject and his awareness of his reader. They are most likely to be lost when he has allowed his thought to be broken into by the wandering of his mind. Thus while concentration will not assure unity and coherence, it will greatly help, and lack of concentration will assure their absence.

On transitional aids to unity and coherence, see also 23.

FIRST AND LAST PARAGRAPHS

It is the first paragraph that usually gives most trouble. A writer, like an automobile, needs to get warmed up, and sometimes he is tempted to use the first paragraph merely for this purpose—to tell the reader what he is going to do once he gets started in the second paragraph. The writer, true enough, needs to *introduce* his subject; he does not need, however, to take a paragraph to announce that he is going to introduce it. He does not need, for instance, to build his first paragraph around the idea that erosion is a very serious problem about which the American people do not think enough and then move on, in the second paragraph, to the point that in his section of the country erosion is every day destroying the equivalent of an eighty-acre farm. He should throw away the first paragraph and start with the eighty-acre farm floating down the Mississippi. That can be introduction enough!

The easy thing to do with the first paragraph is to start out with the thesis of the theme. This the writer should seldom do. In fact, he should seldom state his thesis in any part of the composition. Usually the thesis sentence, like the outline, is best felt and not seen.

The thesis of George Orwell's essay "Shooting an Elephant" is that in taking away the freedom of colonial peoples, the citizens of the imperial power lose their own freedom. Instead of beginning with this, Orwell writes: "In Moulmein, in Lower Burma, I was hated by large numbers of people—the only time in my life that I have been important enough for this to happen to me." This is in no way the thesis of the essay; it could, indeed, prepare the way for a thesis quite different from Orwell's. But it is a good opening sentence. It catches the attention. And it begins the picture of hostility and fear which lie behind the thesis and which the reader must feel if he is to grasp the thesis. So it is functional as well as interesting.

The last paragraph of a theme is sometimes wasted in much the same way as the opening paragraph. Sometimes it is used, not to tell the reader something, but to remind him that he has already been told something. The writer, it is true, needs to *conclude* his subject; but he does not need to take a paragraph to say that he has concluded it. Nothing weakens a theme more than an unnecessary ending—the theme, to return to the erosion example, that makes its point and then goes on with another paragraph to the effect that, now that we have seen and thought about what a serious problem erosion is, we should think about it some more and see what we can do about it.

TOPIC SENTENCES

A paragraph usually contains a topic sentence that states or suggests, as its name indicates, the topic or central idea, which the other sentences develop in greater detail. It gives coherence to the rest of the paragraph. Sometimes it is to the paragraph what the thesis is to the theme, with this difference, that the thesis is usually not stated and the topic sentence usually is. The topic sentence is frequently but not always the first sentence in the paragraph. Occasionally it is found at the end of a paragraph or even in the middle, and sometimes, not often, it is only implied. The illustrative numbered paragraphs on pages 76–80 may be studied for topic sentences. In paragraph 1, the topic sentence is the first sentence; in paragraph 2, it is the part of the first sentence beginning "in its original form. . . ."

The topic sentences state the thought for the other sentences to expand, so much so that with little change the topic sentences of a theme might make a good paragraph outline— but not a good analytic outline. The topic sentences pull the other sentences together and help give the paragraph unity and coherence.

Interesting though the individual sentences in the following paragraph are, something is wrong:

In Greenland and Antarctica are ice deserts where nothing lives and the only sound is the wind; in the Amazon valley are rain forests where growth is so rank from heat and moisture that the jungle is as hostile to man as the permanent ice of the polar regions. In parts of the Himalayas, over six hundred inches of rain fall every year, and in other places in the world, among them Death Valley in California, a child several years old might think raindrops something like the fairies he hears about but never sees. In places the earth towers nearly six miles into the skies, and sometimes a table-flat prairie stretches a thousand miles over the horizon.

The paragraph is invertebrate, so to speak. It needs something to give it structure, to pull it together. It needs a topic sentence, perhaps the one that follows—which, as a matter of fact, was originally written for it.

The earth has a variety in climates, topography, and resources which the Psalmist, though he felt the wonder of creation so vividly, could not imagine. In Greenland. . . .

DEVELOPING THE PARAGRAPH

If you have organized your material in your mind, you can be fairly sure that you will write topic sentences. Fortunately, they are a natural as well as a necessary way of composing the paragraph. Most of you have written them in the past, and it would probably be a mistake to go about doing something self-consciously that you already do naturally. What you cannot be sure of is that you develop your topic sentences adequately. Most inexperienced writers do not. Some of them, in fact, write a succession of topic sentences, all in one or two paragraphs, and then wonder why they have so much trouble writing the required number of words and why the theme sounds so much like an outline. It *is* an outline, a paragraph outline. The topic sentences are there but they are undeveloped. The skeleton is there, but it has been given no flesh and blood.

Let us illustrate this point by taking one thought—the weakness of the United Nations as it was originally organized—and developing it in ten different ways. You will profit from these examples if you study them as exercises; you will not profit if you believe that from now on you should write paragraphs deliberately developed by one or another of the methods illustrated here. The best paragraphs are often combinations of several methods, and you should not, except for exercise, self-consciously develop a paragraph by a set method. Your own feeling for the subject ought to suggest the method or combination of methods most appropriate.

But for exercise, let us go to the idea about the United Nations. "The United Nations organization is weak." What can we do with this bare statement? What can we do, first of all, to put edge and challenge and interest into the topic sentence, and what can we then do to produce a well-developed paragraph? Here are ten possibilities.

1. A paragraph may be developed by *actual example.* In this method the writer makes his point by giving one or more instances that support it. This is probably the simplest, the most common, and often the best method of paragraph development.

The United Nations, as organized at San Francisco in 1945, was unable to resolve the problems of the post-war world, and certainly it did not bring peace or the hope of peace. It did not ease the tension between the United States and the Soviet Union. It did not prevent aggression against Poland, Bulgaria, Rumania, Hungary, and Czechoslovakia. In Greece and China it did not prevent war, thinly disguised as civil war, between the member nations. It was not even able to provide a governor for the tiny Free Territory of Trieste or command obedience in Palestine.

2. A paragraph may be developed by *fictitious example.* Although a fictitious example might seem much less convincing than an actual example, the following paragraph will show how effective, if it is handled well, this method can be.

It might develop in the forge of necessity, but in its original form the United Nations was not government, and it could not function as government. The veto exercised by the major powers meant that no action could be taken against a major power. The United Nations might take action against Mexico if Mexico attacked the United States or against Finland if Finland attacked the Soviet Union, but it could not take action against the United

States or the Soviet Union if one of them attacked a smaller nation. In other words, the United Nations could act where action was not needed; it could not act where action *was* needed.

3. A paragraph may be developed by *comparison*. In this method the writer makes note of certain similarities between his subject and another of the same sort.

Like the Articles of Confederation, which governed the thirteen American "nations" before their union in 1789, the United Nations was a loose confederation of sovereign states. Just as Virginia, Delaware, and eleven other American "nations" realized in 1781 that consultation was necessary and agreement desirable, so in 1945 the United States and Holland and the other nations of the world, large and small, recognized that they too must consult and, if possible, agree. But 1781 left all the most meaningful decisions where they had been before, in the hands of the member states, which remained, therefore, essentially sovereign and independent; and 1945 did precisely the same thing on a world scale.

4. A paragraph may be developed by *contrast*. This method is the same as comparison except that the difference between the two subjects instead of the similarity is emphasized.

The Constitution of the United States established a nation from the surrendered power of the thirteen smaller nations. These smaller units retained their boundaries as states, and some of the functions of government remained in their hands, but other functions were surrendered beyond recall. Above the previously independent small nations was the new nation, the federal nation, capable, if necessary, of enforcing its larger will against the component parts. But the Charter of the United Nations required the member nations to surrender none of their functions; no new federal world nation was established, and no larger will could be enforced against the component parts.

5. A paragraph may be developed by *analogy*. As with comparison, the writer makes note of certain similarities between two subjects, but with analogy the two subjects are not of the same sort. If a writer showed a similarity between driving in Los Angeles and in Detroit, he would make a com-

parison. If he showed a similarity between driving in Los Angeles and juggling three balls in the air, he would make an analogy.

The attempt to confine the torrent of national passions within the framework of the United Nations was like an attempt to confine a flooding river behind a levee. As a temporary measure, the levee will help keep the river from sweeping away the homes of New Orleans; but remorselessly, if the hinterland is uncontrolled, erosion will build up the river's bed, and the threat will remain, the more dangerous for being delayed. The ultimate protection against floods in New Orleans lies in a wooded hillside in Tennessee, in an earthen dam against a tiny rivulet in Montana, and in alfalfa where corn grew before on a farm in Ohio. In the same way, the ultimate protection against the flood of national passions lies in the world's hinterland, too—in an organization and a justice which can be felt in a thatched village in central Africa or a metallurgy plant along the Ruhr.

6. A paragraph may be developed by *definition* of a key term. Even when the term is quite familiar to the reader, as is the term *government* in the paragraph below, it may be useful to define it.

Whatever it might someday be, the United Nations in 1945 was certainly not government. Government is not debate, however much debate may be necessary; and it is not the airing of grievances, however legitimate. It is not the making of resolutions, however wise; nor the expression of ideals, however noble. Government is power to make law and enforce law. Government is power to determine policy and to effect policy. Government is power, and without power there can be no government.

7. A paragraph may be developed by *restatement*. The same point is made by putting it into different words. If restatement is handled successfully, the effect is not of repetition and wordiness but rather of emphasis and clarity.

The United Nations was given a job without a tool, a function without a capacity, an ideal without a basis. It was asked to stop war by nations that had kept in their own hands the power to make war. It was asked to make peace by nations that had kept in their own hands the power to unmake peace.

8. A paragraph may be developed by *analysis*. In using this method, the writer separates a whole into its component parts so that they can be studied separately.

The Charter of the United Nations established a loose organization of sovereign states. It provided for an Assembly in which each member nation, regardless of size, had one vote. It provided for a Security Council in which the five major powers—China, France, Great Britain, the Soviet Union, and the United States—were always represented, each with one vote and the power to veto, and in which four smaller nations, elected for one-year terms by the Assembly, were also represented, though without the power to veto. Neither the Assembly nor the Security Council had the power to tax, and any army which the United Nations might establish would have to be provided by voluntary contributions from the member states and subject to their recall.

9. A paragraph may be developed by *induction*. In this method the writer brings in facts which will lead to a generalization. In the paragraph below, facts such as the inability to tax are used to lead to the generalization, implied, not stated, that such inabilities always make a government weak.

The inherent weakness of the United Nations lay in factors other than the much-publicized veto enjoyed by the great powers, important though the veto was in preventing action where action was most needed. The inherent weakness lay in the retention of sovereignty by the member nations—the small states just as much as the great powers. Since the nations were sovereign, the United Nations was not sovereign: the United Nations could not tax, though its members might give it money; it could not raise an army, though its members might lend it troops; it could not make law, though its members might agree to enforce its recommendations. The power to tax, the power to raise an army, and the power to make law remained where power had always been—with the still sovereign nations.

10. A paragraph may be developed by arguing from *cause to effect* or from *effect to cause*. In this kind of paragraph the writer shows a causal relation between one thing and another.

The unwillingness of the separate and sovereign nations to surrender their power meant, inevitably, that the original United Nations had no power. For no power had been surrendered to it. The major decisions, the decisions which make war and peace, the decisions which make political justice or political injustice, the decisions which make economic health or economic strangulation, remained where they had always been—with the source of power and the cause of world impotence, the still sovereign nation.

No study of paragraph development can be complete, because every paragraph is unique in its structure. Only a very rigid person, moreover, would insist on the feasibility of always distinguishing sharply between different methods of development. Often a variety of methods should be used, and the line of separation between one method and another may be thin and dubious—as it is, indeed, in some of the examples above.

Even if you write well now, the probability is that you can learn to do much more than you do now to develop your paragraphs and thus to make your writing less an outline and more a true composition. A study of the ten preceding examples should help you, but only if you remember that methods of development are just a means to an end. This book should long since have made you realize, if you did not realize it before, that you cannot be a good writer until you have studied the technique of writing, but also you cannot be a good writer if you become the slave of technique and think about it when you should be thinking about something else—your subject and your reader.

EXERCISE 1

Here are the opening sentences of ten paragraphs each of which makes some kind of judgment about college education. So far as you can tell, which of the methods illustrated above will these paragraphs follow? Using these methods and these opening sentences, write a paragraph for each of them.

1. I had grown pretty complacent in high school. Good grades came easily, and no one else with any speed was heavy enough to play fullback.

2. Sally may have been the most popular girl in high school, but the competition is stiffer now. In high school she may have got good grades partly because she could smile so sweetly, but in college the professors are less susceptible.

3. College is more like high school than I had expected it to be. The professors still have to pressure the students into doing their work, and the students still watch the clock to see when the hour will end.

4. Though they are not totally different, of course, I am impressed by how unlike college and high school are. In my high school, at least, the instructor had to be a policeman almost as much as a teacher, but in college I have yet to hear a professor raise his voice except in enthusiasm for his subject.

5. Going to college is like climbing a mountain instead of a hill. The view from the top is said to be finer, but the ascent is not easy, and sometimes the air is pretty thin.

6. College is not driving a smart convertible down fraternity row, although television has tried to make it seem so. For most of us, college is being broke much of the time, drinking black coffee at two o'clock in the morning before an examination, and wondering what it (not the curriculum but the universe) is all about.

7. Going to college is partly going back—going back to Plato and Sophocles, going back to the origins of man and life and the earth itself, and going back to one's own childhood to see what a man is and wants to be.

8. College consists essentially of three parts—the students, the books, and the bridge between them, the professors.

9. The idea that going to college will increase one's earning power may have some validity, but it is a mistake to make this hope the only or even the chief motivation for going. College graduates do not always make more money than their contemporaries who stopped after high school, and the idea that making money should be the chief purpose in life is precisely one that a college education ought to dissipate.

10. It is always expensive to go to college because, if nothing else, the student is giving up the job he might otherwise be holding. This fact and the fact that no law compels him to go or the college to accept him combine to make a certain seriousness of purpose much easier to come by than in high school.

EXERCISE 2

As specifically as you can, point out the failures in unity and coherence in the following paragraph:

The central theme of *A Farewell to Arms* is a rather trite one. It is the Romeo and Juliet story with its tragic ending. In certain respects I felt that this enduring love story through the war was somewhat preposterous. However, it was so artistically done in that Hemingway style that it could not be surpassed in its theme, nor could any other author probably ever employ such a theme with equal success. As in *The Sun Also Rises*, we also find death and waste pervading *A Farewell to Arms*. The vividness with which Hemingway portrays the horrors of war takes the men through many years of numerous wars. In addition, it gives a preview of what could happen should we live through such painful years.

EXERCISE 3

Develop each of the following topic sentences into a paragraph, using whatever methods seem desirable. You may develop a similar idea if one of those given does not appeal to you. For instance, in the first sentence you might substitute New York (state or city) for California; in the second sentence you might compare men and women in some other quality than judgment. Even though you retain the thought, you are not required to retain the wording given here. In an article on the United States, the editors of *Fortune* began a paragraph on the variety of California with this sentence: "The great Golden State is a good deal like the amazing elephant encountered by the blind men." The idea is essentially the same as in the first sentence below.

1. California is a state of extraordinary variety.
2. Women have better judgment than men.
3. Even though they are metropolises only ninety miles apart, New York and Philadelphia are very different.
4. Take it from a waiter—the word *please* has disappeared from the vocabulary of modern women.
5. The modern girl, torn between marriage and a career, is like a March day that can't decide whether it's summer or winter.

6. Whatever I am, I am no genius.

7. To listen to him talk was like listening to a television commercial.

8. Reading the book was like visiting a new country.

9. The first thing we need to do is to define _____.

10. I want to spend my next vacation in _____.

EXERCISE 4

Study the following paragraphs and be prepared to discuss their merits and weaknesses. What are the topic sentences? Are the paragraphs properly developed, with sufficient detail and with no part out of proportion? Are they unified and coherent?

1. Something good can be said about every weed, optimistic people tell us. But they are wrong: nothing good can be said about crabgrass. It cannot be eaten, as the leaves of dandelions can, which make such fine salad greens. It has no herbal or medicinal value, as plantain leaves are said to have against poison ivy. It does not occupy ground that would otherwise be barren and subject to erosion. It has no attractive flowers or leaves. It is a lazy plant, waiting to flourish until hot weather has made the desirable grasses shrink back; then, when these well-behaved residents of our yards are taking life with a little green assurance, but not working hard, along comes the onslaught of the crabgrass. It quickly pushes out the better perennial grasses and makes a place for itself. It clogs lawnmowers, gets thoroughly cursed, goes to seed prolifically, and, at the first adversity of frost, dies. But even in death it is unlovely, for its remains lie as big ugly brown spots through the entire winter. Before the optimists start glowing about nature, they should consider crabgrass.

2. Who has, like me, mowed in August a lawn full of crabgrass? Anyone who has will sympathize when he sees a sweating figure pushing the mower a few feet at a time, then pulling it back and shoving it again desperately into the matted grass. Crabgrass comes to the lawn late but makes up for a slow start by its frenzied growth in hot weather. Crabgrass lacks beauty and it does not make good salad greens or stop erosion. All it does is die when fall comes and leave but a patch behind. My dislike for crabgrass is about as strong as it can be.

EXERCISE 5

Write three good-sized paragraphs (each one about a hundred to a hundred and fifty words long). Make the first paragraph about a childhood impression or experience, the second about some problem or interest in a course you are now taking, and the third about something you plan to do in the future. The paragraphs are not expected to be in any way related. Do not use subjects that are too large. Underline the topic sentence of each of your paragraphs. Be prepared to show how the coherence within each paragraph is strengthened by the use of transitional words and other devices.

6

The Word

Jonathan Swift, himself the author of some of the best prose in the English language, once described good style as "proper words in proper places." In the earlier chapters of this book, and especially the last one, we have been concerned chiefly with proper places. In this chapter we shall be concerned chiefly with proper words. That is to say, we shall be concerned with diction, the selection of words for correctness and effectiveness.

APPROPRIATE USAGE

What if, in an examination or a research paper, you referred to "that guy Napoleon who got licked at Waterloo" or "that fellow Edgar Allan Poe, who was always getting plastered"? The question is rhetorical because of course you would not. But why not?

Many people would answer, "Because it isn't good English," and dismiss the subject with those words. Then, if pressed for a fuller explanation, they might answer, "It just wouldn't sound right."

You might use such words among friends, however, in a review session in a dormitory room? Yes, but that is different, you feel. In your room in the dormitory it would be all right to speak that way.

Does all this mean that you use good English with your professors but with your friends you use poor English? Or does it perhaps mean that something other than the simple distinction between good English and bad English is involved? Does it not mean that one kind of English is appropriate on one occasion and a different kind on another occasion?

If we say that someone is well dressed, we do not necessarily mean that he is wearing formal clothes. A man who came to class in a tuxedo would be at least as badly dressed as one who went to a banquet in his shirt sleeves. One is well dressed only if appropriately dressed, and appropriateness varies greatly from the camping site to the classroom to the formal dining hall.

A comparable idea of appropriateness is involved in diction, in the choice of words. There are occasions when language needs to be somewhat formal—never stiff, but rather formal, nevertheless: in a letter of application, for instance, or a technical or scientific paper. There are other occasions when it should be quite informal—never slovenly, but informal, nevertheless: in a letter to a close friend, a light-hearted speech at a dormitory dinner, or a human-interest story in the college paper.

So, though all English should be good English and all words should be the right words, what makes good English, what makes the word the right word, will depend on the occasion. By using the concept of appropriateness, we avoid the quite untenable notion that it is all right to use poor English sometimes, especially with our friends. Instead, we say that we should try to speak and write good English always, and with our friends at least as much as with other people, but that good English will range widely from informality to formality.

Suppose a man writes the personnel director of a company a letter of application in a style like this:

I'd like to pick up a little extra cash this coming summer so my dad won't have to foot the whole bill for putting me through college.

Everyone, and especially the personnel director as he tosses the letter in the wastebasket, will think the language much too informal. On the other hand, suppose a man is always talking to people in a style like this:

Next summer I should like to earn some money to reduce the expense to my father in sending me to college.

Everyone will think the language rather formal, especially for conversation with one's friends.

And yet neither passage is poor in itself. The first is acceptable informal or colloquial English. The second is acceptable formal English. Both fall within the range of good English, provided they are appropriate to the occasion. Both passages fall within the range of good writing, but each could be pushed outside the range. We could make one so slangy that it should not be used at all, no matter how informal the occasion:

Yours truly is going to stash some cash so the old man won't have to ante up.

Similarly, we could make the other so stiff and pompous that it would not be good, no matter how formal the occasion:

I would welcome an opportunity to effect an improvement in my financial status with the object of reducing my father's pecuniary responsibility in rendering possible my career at college.

Formal language is the language of scholarly magazines and books. Informal language—and remember it is to be thought of as different, not as inferior—is the language of talk and of writing that seeks to approach talk. This textbook, for example, is written in moderately formal language; the language you use with your friends is presumably much more informal. The research paper you write on slavery in ancient Athens ought to be formal; the theme you write on a personal experience should be so informal that it approximates good conversation.

On the formal level one would say, "Much thought has gone into the resolution"; in speech and informal writing, high-level colloquial language would be proper: "A lot of thought has gone into our work." On an informal level one might say, "I'm very happy to be going to Europe" or even "I'm mighty happy to be going to Europe," in contrast with the more formal "I am extremely happy"; or "I've got to save some money" in contrast with "I must save" (moderately formal) or "It is imperative that I save" (very formal). *Alibi* meaning an excuse ("What's his alibi?") or the word *enthused* stand on a lower level than the easy, homelike naturalness of such an American colloquialism as *around* (for *about*) in "He left around noon." Not to be confused with the colloquial level are those illiterate depths where we may hear *knowed* and *irregardless* and *gent*, words not to be used by educated people at any time.

You should not think that writing must be either formal or informal in an absolute sense. For one thing, degrees of formality and informality blend into each other imperceptibly. For another, a juxtaposition of the formal and the informal is often good. Even slang may sometimes be juxtaposed against formality. This blending or juxtaposing is one of the reasons why the comparison to clothing has only limited validity. In dress, a man could not mix a tuxedo with flaming red sox and tennis shoes, but in writing he can do something very much like that:

At a time of profound and chronic crisis throughout the world, when above all other times we should have sent an enlightened and public-spirited representative to Washington to join in making the decisions that will make or unmake our children's world, we have got ourselves a lemon.

Most of the sentence is rather formal in both diction and structure, but it changes abruptly at the end with the slang *lemon* and the quite informal *we have got ourselves*. Only a very rigid person would object to this sudden shift in tone. Indeed, the shift has its value and therefore its justification: the jarring contrast in language emphasizes the jarring contrast between what the congressman should be and what he is.

In most of your writing as a student you will probably be wise to use a moderately formal style—one that, in following the common practices of written rather than spoken English, is easy to read, that is free from heaviness or stiffness, and that sometimes makes use of expressions from familiar speech. Lincoln was an expert in the use of colloquialisms; so was Franklin D. Roosevelt, who suggested that a certain braggart editor was "touched in the head." A phrase like "get on the good side of" is fitting in a theme about college life: "Joe spent half the semester trying to get on the good side of the dean"; it would be inappropriate in a term paper in a literature class to say, "Claudius tried to get on the good side of Hamlet."

In writing assignments for this course and others, you will probably find yourself trying various levels of formality and informality. You may want to experiment deliberately in some way your instructor suggests, or like this: if your style is rather stiff, try giving yourself subjects that encourage you to use language that reads like easy talk; if your style leans toward carelessness, write most of the time on subjects that require a more formal choice of words.

WORDS NOT IN STANDARD USAGE

A good many words do not belong to the generally acceptable vocabulary which we call standard English. These words you should not use except under rather special circumstances. They are likely to be as objectionable in informal as in formal English. Besides profanity and obscenity, the most important groupings of these words follow.

Slang Slang originally was the specialized language of criminals and other outcasts who wished to hide the meaning of what they were saying. It still has something of this function. The beatnik or the teen-ager may not need to hide his meaning from others, but to be able to do so gives him a sense of superiority. Whatever the source, however, today the term *slang* is applied to a diction that is outside standard usage and preferred to it because the slang is thought to be more forceful or simply more in vogue. Examples are *goofy*, *put on the dog*, *it's the berries*, *pad* (meaning *apartment*), *way out* (meaning *unusual*), and *real cool* (meaning almost anything favorable).

Slang expressions sometimes get taken into standard English—get made respectable, so to speak. The noun *cant*, for example, once slang, is now not only acceptable in standard English, but is a rather sophisticated and literary word. *Hard-boiled*, as in "a hard-boiled answer," might not be appropriate even today in formal writing, but it would certainly be acceptable in speech or in informal writing. Other slang expressions simply disappear. Perhaps older professors remember them, but students and young professors may not even have heard of *ishkabibble, banana oil,* and *the cat's pajamas.* The world can suffer their disappearance with considerable equanimity.

Most slang is trite and vague, but sometimes it is expressive. There is no adequate substitute for words like *knockout, hepcat,* and *beatnik,* and even in somewhat formal writing, as has already been pointed out, a good writer may sometimes use slang, as E. B. White does when he says, "To reject the book because of the immaturity of the author and the bugs in the logic is to throw away a bottle of good wine because it contains bits of the cork." ("Walden—1954")

The fact that so much slang is unintelligible or barely intelligible to so many people at the time it is current and unintelligible to nearly everyone a few years later is one of the two good reasons for not using it unless you have very good control of language. The other is that, whether rightly or not, the person who uses much slang is thought of as badly educated.

In writing, quotation marks ordinarily should not be used with slang. See **39 i (3).**

Provincialisms Provincialisms (or localisms) are words or phrases that are used in one section of the country but not in others. Examples are *piece* meaning *distance, reckon* meaning *think, you all* meaning the plural of *you,* and *little old* as a vague term of affection. (In Texas "a little old woman"—as in "I've got a date tonight with a little old woman"—is as likely as not to be a tall, good-looking blonde of about twenty.) Though provincialisms, like accents, help give color to our national life and though the injunction to avoid them can never be emphatic, you will want to learn to address a general, not a provincial, public. At least in your more formal writing, you should eliminate provincialisms.

Archaic and obsolete words   Examples of words which, though once used, are no longer in standard usage are *eftsoons, mayhap, perchance, quoth,* and *prithee.* One may regret having to caution against using provincialisms, but not against using archaic words. To use them is always bad. Sometimes a writer will say something like *quoth* or *prithee,* thinking it amusing. He will be alone in his opinion.

Foreign words   Sometimes a foreign word or phrase gets adopted into the language, as *chauffeur* and *atom* and thousands of other words have been, so that they are no longer felt to be foreign. And sometimes a foreign word or phrase, though still felt to be foreign, says something for which there is no exact equivalent in English: *Weltschmerz* and *gaucherie* are examples. Usually, however, the use of foreign words and phrases in place of English suggests affectation and insecurity. The person who says *bien entendu* when he means "of course" or *entre nous* when he means "just between us" is impressing his readers not with his learning but with his pretentiousness. Never use a foreign word to show off. Never use it if an English word says the same thing.

Euphemisms   Euphemisms are words that seek to cover up or at least to soften something felt to be vulgar or unpleasant. We smile at the euphemisms of another day—*nether limbs* for *legs,* for example—but we often use them in contemporary English. People today may say *plump* when they mean *fat, perspire* when they mean *sweat,* and *pass away* when they mean *die.*

Much writing that is pretentious and obscure has a euphemistic motive. Here is a notice that appeared in a Washington hotel: "In order to substantiate our desire to accommodate our guests we would appreciate your cooperation to anticipate your credit requirements before departure." (Cited by Charles Morton in the *Atlantic Monthly.*) In English this means "If you wish to cash a check, please let us know before leaving." Apparently by writing this way the management thought to cover up something they felt to be indelicate—that their patrons might run out of cash.

Though no certain rule can be laid down, in general it is good to avoid euphemisms and to write directly and honestly about the subject. Shakespeare did not choose the obvious euphemism when he made "To grunt and sweat under a weary life" a great line of poetry, and the pathos of death is not ameliorated by calling it something else.

DENOTATION AND CONNOTATION

The direct meaning of a word is its denotation; the associations around it are its connotation. Although *father, dad,* and *the old man* have exactly the same denotation (a male parent), we have very different feelings when we hear or use them: *dad* is likely to have familiar and affectionate associations, *the old man* disrespectful ones. When Prohibition was repealed in 1933, the word *saloon* did not come back with alcohol. Instead, *tavern* was used, a word having the same denotation but a very different connotation. The leaders of our party are *statesmen* and *men of vision* but our opponents are only *politicians* and *visionaries,* and in war our forces are *brave* but the enemy is *reckless.*

The careful writer does not confuse *economic* and *economical,* a difference in denotation; and he discriminates between *economical* and *thrifty* and *parsimonious,* differences primarily in connotation. He knows that things that are bought and sold may be *luxurious* but only nature is likely to be *luxuriant,* and then only if she is especially abundant, so that a house may be *luxurious* and the vegetation around it may be *luxuriant,* and he is sensitive to the connotative difference between *luxuriant, abundant, rich, opulent, lush,* and *teeming.* (He doesn't call a woman's hair *teeming* simply because the dictionary gives this word as a synonym for *luxuriant!*)

The associations of some words make them appropriate mainly for sports: *on the ropes, down for the count;* others are connected with business: *to contact* someone. Some words are favorable, others contemptuous: your classmates may call you a *serious student* or a *grind,* depending on the feeling they have for you. If someone respects your work he will speak of your *business* or *profession;* if he does not, he will call it your *racket.* The connotations of *womanly* and *womanish* are so different that one is complimentary and the other insulting.

A good dictionary or a book like Roget's *Thesaurus* will help with connotation, but the books can never be so precise about connotation as about denotation. Your own sensitivity must help you to choose between *complacent* and *satisfied,* between *learning* and *pedantry,* and between *smirk* and *smile.*

TONE

When we talk we sometimes express our meaning even more by the tone of our voices than by the words themselves. If we say "Good morning," our tone can be so surly that the words actually mean something like "I'm not at all pleased to see you this morning." If we say "That's fine," tone can make the words mean "That's terrible." Or we can take a simple, factual statement like "The mayor has now decided to do something" and make the mayor look like a statesman or a bungler, depending on how we say it. Iago's line in Shakespeare's *Othello* "You are—a senator" is rather flat unless given the right tone, and then it is a devastating sneer. His "I like not that" is commonplace, but tone can make it sinister.

This great vocal resource, supplemented by facial expression and gesture, the writer obviously does not have. The speaker has words, tone, facial expression, gesture. The writer has only words. If he is a dramatist, he may legitimately count on help from his actor, construct the line for his actor, as Shakespeare did; but in all other kinds of writing, he must make words do it all.

How does he do it? How does he get tone into his writing?

Let us go back to the mayor deciding to do something and let us report his action in two very different tones. (Neither of these accounts is to be thought of as a newspaper report. Journalistic writing is usually as nearly toneless as it can be made, and though newspapers often color the news, as we say, they do it in less obvious ways than these passages show.)

One report might be something like this:

After vacillating for as long as he could and taking refuge in the supposed ambiguities of the state constitution, the mayor has finally yielded to pressure and agreed to try to do something.

Another might be something like this:

After careful examination of the constitutional and other issues involved, the mayor, responding to the people's wishes, has announced that he will take immediate action.

Besides vacillating, the mayor could *waver, hesitate, procrastinate, fidget in uncertainty,* and do many other things that would suggest confusion and delay. Besides yielding, he could *back down* or *surrender.* And of course he might make a *thorough study* rather than a *careful examination* and take *vigorous measures* instead of *immediate action.* The possible variations are innumerable.

The great difference in the two passages obviously lies in the choice of words. The connotations of *vacillating* are unfavorable, those of *careful examination* favorable. To *take refuge* suggests timidity or dishonesty, and the impression is reinforced by the word *supposed;* but for the mayor to be aware of a constitutional issue, as the second writer indicates he is, is admirable. To *yield* suggests weakness, of course, but to *respond* suggests something a democratic leader should always do. The effect of *pressure* is quite different from that of *people's wishes,* and the words *announced* and *take immediate action* suggest decisiveness as *agreed to try to do something* suggest weakness and incompetence. The difference in tone between these two passages, then, is brought about by the selection of words of one connotation or another.

The second method of setting tone is by selection of facts. In writing about almost anything, even in describing a bare room, there are more facts than the writer can use. He must always make a selection, and in doing so he gives his writing one tone or another. Thus the first writer might bring in the fact that the chief advocate for the action the mayor agreed to take was a ward leader who served two years for income tax evasion—the same man "whose connection with known gambling elements in the city has never been satisfactorily explained." The second writer might not think this relevant and so might not mention it but instead bring in the point that the mayor had delayed taking action until he had received a favorable opinion from the state's attorney general. Even small details often make a big difference: the inclusion or omission of the fact that the mayor wiped his brow or chain-smoked cigarettes may affect the tone of the whole report.

A moral problem is involved here. The fact that the mayor's action can be written about in two such different ways, the fact that no objective test will show that one of them is fair and the other is not, and the fact that neither, it is assumed, tells an actual falsehood—all this does not mean that the writer is free to write either way. He is free to write only in accord with his convictions and with his responsibility to truth. If he believes the mayor is a weak and dishonest incompetent, he cannot write as he can if he believes the mayor an able and honest executive. The writer must give his writing the tone he desires, but that tone must reflect the truth as he sees it.

We have illustrated this subject by reporting something in a tone of contempt in contrast with one of respect, but tone can express every attitude and every emotion, as you will realize if you think what you can do with your own voice. Thus the writer can do what the speaker does, but he will probably have to work harder to do it.

Remember that you want to get and keep a natural tone —for example, of irony or nostalgia or objectivity. Avoid such poses as using a series of wisecracks for humor.

GENERAL AND SPECIFIC

Content words (nouns, verbs, adjectives, and adverbs) are either general or specific. The word *tree* is specific compared with *plant,* because a tree is a kind of plant; but it is general compared with *maple,* because a maple is a kind of tree. *Walk* is specific compared with *move,* because walking is a kind of moving; but it is general compared with *strut,* because strutting is a kind of walking. Notice how the thought grows progressively more specific in this series: *animal—mammal—dog—fox terrier—my fox terrier.*

You need both general and specific words. If you wished to describe the forest cover of America before Europeans came, you would probably say something like "The eastern two-fifths of America was covered by trees." You would need the general noun. But if you were describing the backyard of the farm where you grew up, you would make your writing more vivid if you wrote about the big Norway maple you played under, not the "big tree." You might say "People seldom walk today" because you mean all kinds of people walking in all kinds of ways. You might also say "John walked into the room" if there was nothing distinctive about the way he did it. But sometimes people don't just walk. They *strut* or *march* or *amble* or *stumble* or something else. Because you were writing about many women and trying to describe none of them, you might write "American women spend much thought and money trying to stay thin," but if you were describing an individual woman you should remember that besides the rather general *thin,* she might be *slender, slim, sylphlike, lean, slight, spare, lanky, rake-thin, haggard, gaunt,* or *scrawny.*

General words can be weak and vague when used as substitutes for the real things we could say if we were willing to work out our ideas and impressions. "Tom's letter was unpleasant" is a poor substitute for something specific. Was the letter bitter, crude, violent, frightening, sad, contemptuous, threatening? Did it anger you? Did it end your friendship? Did it berate you for failing to wrap the Christmas present securely? Did it tell you it would be a long time before he would try to get tickets for you again?

ABSTRACT AND CONCRETE

For the writer, no distinction between words is more important than that between concrete and abstract. A concrete noun is a sense word; it refers to something we can see or hear or touch or smell or taste. An abstract noun refers to something we cannot see, hear, touch, smell, or taste—to something we cannot know directly through our senses. Instead, it refers to an idea or a quality or a concept, like *literature* or *democracy.* We can see and touch a book, but we cannot see and touch literature; we can see and touch a ballot, but democracy we can only know through our minds.

Just as we need general nouns, so we need abstract nouns. We could not get far in working with ideas if we had no words like *literature* and *democracy.* But precisely as you should search for the more specific word when it is appropriate, so you should search for the more concrete word when *it* is appropriate. Even when—or especially when—you are writing about abstract and difficult subjects (the meaning of democracy, the value of literature), search for the concrete words that will give the writing flesh and blood. And in writing on simpler subjects, do not be satisfied with a vague and abstract term like *trouble* in "Mary Robinson had trouble with her vegetable garden" when you can make the reader see what happened: "Mary Robinson's garden was a failure. Her tomatoes, hit by the blight, turned gray and black, and fell off the vines; her bean plants, eaten by beetles, turned brown and died."

The great writers of the world are masters of concrete diction. Though Shakespeare is constantly dealing with abstractions like *government, love,* and *sorrow,* he translates the abstraction into the concrete language of familiar life, so that if he is writing about corruption he describes it as a "blister"; if he is writing about jealousy he makes it a "green-eyed monster." He does not write abstractly about a world that is losing

97

its sense of values; instead, he writes concretely about "an unweeded garden that goes to seed." He does not write abstractly about guilt that can never be expiated; instead, he writes concretely that "all the perfumes of Arabia will not sweeten this little hand."

The Bible is another mine of concrete language. The idea that the possession of material wealth is an obstacle to salvation is expressed in the concrete language of the camel and the eye of the needle; the idea of order and responsibility in the moral life in "As ye sow, so shall ye reap"; and the coming of peace after war in beating "swords into ploughshares."

LITERAL AND FIGURATIVE

We may express ourselves either literally or figuratively. Literal language speaks directly, in matter-of-fact statements: "George had three servings of turkey"; figurative language speaks indirectly and involves a comparison of some sort: "George ate like a horse." The most important figures of speech are the simile and the metaphor. In both of them the writer notes a similarity between two things that are otherwise dissimilar. A simile makes the likeness explicit, usually by *like* or *as* (The gossip was like a net that strangled him). A metaphor makes the likeness implicit, omitting *like* or *as* (He was strangled in the net of gossip). In one of Wordsworth's sonnets Milton's soul was "like a star," a simile, and in one of Shakespeare's, love "is a star," a metaphor.

The words *specific, concrete,* and *figurative* are often confused. Concrete language, as the examples from Shakespeare and the Bible indicate, is often also figurative, but concrete language is not necessarily figurative, as the description of Mary Robinson's garden shows. Similarly, figurative language is usually, indeed practically always, concrete, as the comparisons to a horse, to nets, and to a star all show; but it is not *necessarily* concrete: we almost never compare one thing to something that we do not know with our senses, but it is possible to do so, as Shelley does when he compares the skylark to "an unbodied joy."

In both sentences "The farm has a good many acres that are virtual swamp" and "The student was sunk in a swamp of discouragement," the word *swamp* is concrete, not abstract, because a swamp can be known with one or more of the senses. In both sentences it is specific, not general, compared with *poor-quality land* or *unusable acreage*. In the first sentence it is literal, because an actual swamp is meant; in the second it is figurative, because a mental state is meant and likened to an actual or literal swamp.

Consider the passage (III, iv, 42–44) in which Hamlet tells his mother that she is guilty of an act that

> takes off the rose
> From the fair forehead of an innocent love
> And sets a blister there.

The word *rose* is concrete because a rose is something that can be known through one or more of our senses. It is also fairly specific. At least it is specific compared with *plant* or *flower*, though it is general compared with *tea rose*. It is also figurative, because Hamlet obviously is not talking about a flower at all but about something the flower suggests. What about the nouns *forehead, love,* and *blister?* Is each of them specific? concrete? figurative?

Far from being an artificial literary device, the figure of speech answers a universal need. Slang is full of figures, sometimes very expressive ones, as when someone is called a *heel*. Sportswriters use almost as many metaphors as poets do, and some of their figures, before they become stale, are picturesque, as was the term "four horsemen" when applied to a football backfield that spread terror in the opponent.

Figures of speech should be fitting in tone and bear no incongruous suggestions. The figure here is fitting: "After the sun came out, the field had a wet, metallic gleam." Here it is not: "After the sun came out, the field gleamed like a wet tin can." Careless and mixed figures have long been the source of unconscious humor:

As the fire blazed higher and closer, we stood frozen with fear.
I love this cherry tree; it is the apple of my eye.

I liked the story about the swimming pool, but it could have been
boiled down somewhat.

When the poet put a bullet through his head, he made a hole in
Spanish literature that was never filled.

Even experienced writers can get themselves into trouble
when they start using words as stereotypes instead of thinking of what they mean. Someone in the *Saturday Review*
once wrote: "The critics of Hollywood rushed into print to
announce that movies had 'come of age' and that, if the
American industry did not keep its ear to the ground, it
would surely fall on its face." The *New Yorker* quoted this
and added: "Unless it kept a stiff upper lip."

TRITENESS

Figures of speech should be fresh as well as appropriate.
But they age very quickly. Expressions like *quick as lightning, thin as a rail,* and *grow like a weed,* though acceptable
and natural in daily talk, are usually flat in writing. Never
good are such overused and pretentious phrases as *acid test,
arms of Morpheus, innocent as a lamb, mother nature,* and
staff of life.

Triteness—stale, hackneyed language—is objectionable
whether a figure of speech is involved or not. *Last but not
least* was good once, but now it is like a typewriter ribbon
that needs changing. *Sigh of relief, too funny for words,* and
many other expressions have also grown stale. Many of these
phrases, to be sure, are excellent composition—that is why
they passed into the language. But they are *somebody else's*
composition, not your own—and that is why you should try
not to use them. Because your thinking can never be exactly
the same as anyone else's, you can never express your thinking in somebody else's language. If your language is trite,
your reader will think you are letting somebody else do your
thinking for you—and he will be right.

The way to avoid triteness, obviously, is (1) to be sincere
and natural and to work hard to find words that express your
ideas and feelings and not someone else's, (2) to be some-

what sparing in the use of proverbs, familiar literary tags, and phrases from poems you have read in school, and (3) to observe the practice of good writers.

A word of caution should be given, however. Many trite phrases are not inappropriate in ordinary conversation (*fat as a pig*, for instance, or *flat as a pancake*), where we cannot take such care in the choice of words as we should in writing. Do not be so afraid of using trite language that you lose freedom of expression. Remember that none of us can avoid triteness altogether. The effort to avoid it should not be allowed to make your style strained and artificial. Many familiar phrases, moreover, do not grow tired and trite. They age, but they age gracefully. As Joseph Wood Krutch has said, "That honesty is the best policy is a platitude to which it is sometimes necessary to call attention, and when it is there is no better way of stating the platitude than by means of the cliché." It would be sad to think we could not call a man a *true friend* because others have said it before, or not say of someone else that he gave us *the cold shoulder*. These are simple and natural ways of expressing ourselves. They wear well.

Occasionally trite phrases can be turned to good advantage by an addition or change of words: ". . . while he [the football player] was not dumber than an ox he was not any smarter."—JAMES THURBER. "Here I am, just a dreamer, and there they are, captains of industry, or, at any rate, second lieutenants."—ROBERT BENCHLEY.

A LIST OF TRITE EXPRESSIONS

The following list gives a sampling from the vast store of these trite phrases (called also *hackneyed phrases, clichés,* and *stereotypes*). The groupings are not rigid; many phrases could be placed under more than one heading.

Hackneyed personifications

Jack Frost	Lady Luck
Mother Nature	the Grim Reaper

Stale literary scraps

to be or not to be

sadder but wiser

where angels fear to tread

music hath charms

trip the light fantastic

best laid plans of mice and men

lightly turns to thoughts of love

gone with the wind

more in sorrow than in anger

primrose path

Inseparable adjectives and nouns

sickening thud (also: dull, sickening thud)

gridiron warriors (and many similar phrases on the sports page)

wedded bliss

ripe old age

besetting sin

gala affair

checkered career

crushing blow

Trite figures of speech

dull as dishwater

slow as molasses

pretty as a peach

vale of life

nipped in the bud

wise as an owl

Hackneyed slang and wisecracks

dumb as an ox

that's for the birds

out like a light

way out

and how!

don't do anything I wouldn't do

what-have-you ("I like Mother's

cakes, pies, or what-have-you.")

Elegant variation

Bard of Avon (= Shakespeare)

feathered songsters (= birds)

distaff side (= female side)

filthy lucre (= money)

fair sex (= women)

staff of life (= bread)

Hackneyed and high-flown words

I am financially embarrassed.

His name shall never be effaced from my memory.

He has gone to his rest.

They were united in the bonds of holy matrimony.

His employment was terminated.

He fell into the arms of Morpheus.

Other overused combinations

as chance would have it	strong, silent man
I point with pride	easier said than done
reigns supreme	needs no introduction
last but not least	better late than never
here to stay	grand and glorious

IDIOM AND IDIOMS

The term *idiom* sometimes refers to the normal word order of a language. Thus it is English idiom to put the adjective before the noun it modifies and to say "The large house was sold today," not "The house large. . . ." In idiomatic English we say "The farmer plows his field," not "The farmer his field plows." In this sense of the word, idiom is especially important in English because we sometimes show meaning through word order. We show the difference between the idea that *the boy chased the dog* and the idea that *the dog chased the boy* by word order rather than by word endings. Word order in English, accordingly, is comparatively fixed. See **28a.**

The term *idiom* is also used to denote an expression natural to a language and peculiar to it. Sometimes idioms that violate conventions of grammar are sanctioned by long-established usage: *who do you take me for?* is an example. Sometimes they defy logic but again are sanctioned by long-established usage: I *took sick* and he *caught a cold* are examples.

English idioms may give a foreigner studying the language much trouble. How is he to determine what *ups and downs* means and, once having learned, how is he to remember, except by effort, that it is always *ups and downs* and never *downs and ups?* Would knowing what *turn* means and what *down* means help him to know that *turn down* means to *refuse?* Or knowing what *take* and *up* mean separately help him to know that in *take up his offer* they mean to *accept?* Idioms like *strike a bargain* and *hang fire* must sometimes drive him toward despair. They come naturally, however, to the writer whose native tongue is English. Except for some prepositions (see 17e) they seldom give trouble. As a resource about which we hardly need to think, idioms help make writing pithy and interesting.

RECAPITULATION

Let us summarize by saying that it is always the writer's responsibility to use the precise word, the right word, the best word. We might say, indeed, that the only proper word is the best one. And nothing, not even the dictionary, can tell you what the best word is, and no computer is going to come out with the answers to your problems. In a world in which doing things by rote seems to be increasing all the time, rote will not take over here.

We may say this, however: (1) The proper word will be one appropriate to the writing as a whole; it will belong to the level of usage the writer seeks to maintain. (2) It will be in standard usage; the writer should use slang, provincialisms, archaisms, foreign words, and euphemisms cautiously, if at all. (3) It will be correct in denotation and right in connotation. (4) It will express the tone appropriate to the subject and the writer's approach. (5) It will usually be specific as opposed to general, and concrete as opposed to abstract; and sometimes it will be figurative. (6) It will usually not be trite, because, in general, trite writing seems (and is) insincere. (7) It will respect, whether they are logical or not, the established constructions of the language.

EXERCISE 1

Write two different paragraphs treating the same subject. Make one fairly formal in language, the other rather colloquial. Possible subjects for this assignment are a description of the registration procedure or orientation program for freshmen at your college, a visit to the dean, or a criticism of a play or motion picture you have seen recently.

EXERCISE 2

What kinds of usage are illustrated in each of the following? When, if ever, might each be used?

A. 1. Get out of here!
   2. Avaunt!
   3. Shoo!
   4. Beat it!
   5. Leave at once!
B. 1. He is henpecked.
   2. His wife uses him as a doormat.
   3. She keeps him under her thumb.
   4. She is the dominant partner.
   5. She has usurped his masculine prerogatives.
C. 1. It is imperative that we examine the curriculum.
   2. We must examine the curriculum.
   3. We've got to examine the curriculum.
   4. We need to examine the curriculum.
   5. It is incumbent upon us to examine the curriculum.

EXERCISE 3

Make a list of ten slang expressions popular among your friends and explain what they mean. Which of them do you think are likely to disappear and which if any seem original and useful enough to remain in the language?

EXERCISE 4

Find five foreign words or phrases (other than legal terms) that say something for which there is no wholly satisfactory English expression.

EXERCISE 5

Analyze the differences in connotation in the words in the following series. If you find differences in denotation as well as connotation, distinguish between the connotative and the denotative differences.

1. evil person, scoundrel, pest, louse, reprobate
2. woman, lady, co-ed, babe, dame

3. patriot, public-spirited man, flag-waver, loyal citizen, chauvinist
4. countenance, face, map, mug, visage
5. falsehood, story, lie, fabrication, misrepresentation
6. contend, fight, struggle, vie, strive
7. vituperation, billingsgate, abuse, invective, obloquy
8. satisfied, contented, smug, complacent
9. penniless, broke, financially embarrassed, bankrupt, pinched
10. anger, irritation, ire, rage, fury

EXERCISE 6

In the following passage, for each italicized word find three words that are more specific or more concrete. If possible, use only single words, not phrases.

She *walked* down the street, looking at the *merchandise* in the windows. It wasn't often, she thought, that a May day was so *hot* or that the *flowers* had looked so *unattractive* when she left her home in the morning. But she kept thinking about her own situation, her father's *disease*, and the warning of the doctor that he needed a *better* climate. She had tried so long to *assume* the whole burden. She had tried so long to *economize*. She had tried so long to forget her youthful *thoughts*. She was going . . . she was going . . . she was going to buy herself some new shoes.

EXERCISE 7

For their lack of concreteness and other qualities of good diction discussed in this chapter, show why each of the following sentences is poor. Can you think of the well-known originals of these wretched paraphrases? Because of their triteness, the writer probably should not use these originals, but except for triteness they are much better than the paraphrases. Why?

1. It is inadvisable in a period of crisis to effect a sudden change in governmental personnel.
2. It is unwise to disturb an equilibrium, particularly if to do so might force a sudden change from a relatively tolerable environment to one relatively intolerable.
3. A modicum of anticipatory action sometimes forestalls the need for much more extensive action at a later date.

4. The object of very tender sentiments on my part bears a certain resemblance, figuratively speaking, to a rose.
5. In terms of the amassing of fluid capital, a reduction in cash expenditures exercises the same general effect as an increase in the individual's earning capacity.
6. Preliminary actions of one character inevitably result in successive reactions of a fixed nature.
7. A certain restraint and privacy is conducive to satisfactory interpersonal relationships.
8. Individuals whose judgment is poor often adopt a precipitate course of action that individuals whose judgment is better would not be favorably disposed to attempt to effectuate even though the latter would be given by their very natures a better opportunity to succeed in the referred-to undertaking.
9. Whether the animate or the inanimate condition is preferable is the subject of deliberation.
10. A visual withdrawal facilitates a withdrawal conceptually.

EXERCISE 8

The following sentences show poor diction. Where are they defective?

1. Today we are living in the jet age, where time is of the essence.
2. It is only recently that I have learned to appreciate the finer things of life.
3. Displays for the book fair will be furnished by publishers and authors, and artists will round out the program.
4. A new car is an expensive proposition.
5. This situation is in a great measure due to the group of publicity agents whose job is the manufacturing of stars because more often than not they assume the momentous task of convincing the people that a certain talentless personality, entertainmentwise, has something to offer.
6. I think it could be recommended to start widening many of the highways which lead to this fair city.
7. After Peggy took us on a short tour of her spacious but tastefully furnished home, she graciously served tea and insisted that we sample her favorite culinary specialty of homemade cookies.

8. Operation "Voter Registration" is working in the frame of reference of voter apathy.
9. By this time I had reached the ripe old age of eleven.
10. Dad was born in Russia and Mother stems from Poland.
11. The solution as to what should be done about the migrant labor problem in this country has the same complexities as the Russian problem with the serfs many years ago.
12. Her father watched her trudge rapidly up the stairs.
13. Thoughtlessness was one of Ronnie's strongest weaknesses.
14. This woman pitifully became an inlet for alcohol, which she thought would be an outlet for her troubles.
15. It is important that we think of objectives in terms of specific goals.
16. All in all, characterwise this novel was a poor representation of respectable personages.
17. I realized I was turning down the veritable one chance in a million.
18. In four short years I hoped to be graduated into the wide, wide world.
19. A trustworthy person makes a valuable friend and is possibly the most valued asset one can possess.
20. Unemployment is not diminishing. We have not yet learned how to deal with this problem area.

EXERCISE 9

Which of the figures of speech in the following exercise are inappropriate, incongruous, confused, or trite? Which are good?

1. Finally, with America's intervention, the backbone of Hitler's dream of world power was broken.
2. Like a jackal waiting to pull down the stricken deer, Judge Brach has the club he needs.
3. If you don't stop shearing the sheep that lays the golden egg, you are going to pump the well dry.
4. The keystone that is set in place by a stable family life is the basic stepping-stone to a child in building a good adult life.
5. The carpenters have been hard at work this week and are rapidly licking the new candy store into shape.
6. At a party, she blazes like a chandelier.

7. Betty's mind is as pure as the driven snow.
8. Last night I heard that one of my favorite old teachers had kicked the bucket.
9. You knew it was time to be careful when Nancy's voice became velvet.
10. Before the car had gone fifty feet it was swallowed up in the fog.
11. The sunset looked like a boiled lobster.
12. There in the west was the new moon, a tiny grin in the sky.
13. After I've heard her talk about the people we know, I feel as if snails were crawling over me.
14. The speaker waddled across the platform like a duck.
15. After the fire on the mountainside, we went back and saw the black, charred skeletons of the great trees we had loved.
16. Running into Bud at the party was like finding a worm in an apple.
17. The snowcapped mountains seemed to be rolling the whites of their eyes at the passing clouds.
18. The arm of the law became the handmaid of the government.
19. The brains and muscle of the gigantic task were headed by one man.
20. In time I hope that her heart will become receptive to the seeds I have planted in her mind.
21. In pursuing my college career I have been going through one hurdle after another.
22. The buffalo, after galloping a few miles on the threshold of death's door, finally escaped.
23. The snow made everything outside look as fresh as a daisy.
24. Her face was all puckers and creases, like a shrivelled red apple.
25. When he put on his new overcoat he looked as fresh as a new-laid egg.
26. Outside India, people believed that Gandhi was washed up politically and had dried up his sources of world sympathy.
27. My mother was the kindest and most uncomplaining person I have ever known. She was as patient as a cigar-store Indian.
28. One reason Napoleon sold Louisiana to the United States was that he thought with America spread out to such a great extent, the Union would quickly fold.

29. I am by no means satisfied with my procrastination, but until I can locate the seed propagating this attitude with such fecundity I must be content to war with this aggressor.
30. Dave's heart pounded suddenly against the backs of his eyes.
31. My education was the liberty I had to read indiscriminately and all the time, with my eyes hanging out.
32. The *Monitor* was built in such a short time that her faults could not be ironed out.
33. When he looked directly at anyone, his eyes became like two pieces of flint turned suddenly up in dug earth.
34. [About a man trying to get his car out of a snowdrift]: An abrupt, outraged sense of injustice and impossibility—as if he were trying to turn a doorknob with soapy hands—swept over him.
35. He was glad he was no bigger, he was thinking, as he wormed his mole-like way through the passage.

7

Vocabulary and the Dictionary

BUILDING YOUR VOCABULARY

You already know that if your vocabulary is small you will have trouble expressing your own thoughts and understanding the thoughts of others. Perhaps you took a vocabulary test to be admitted to college; you may have to take another to get a job or to be admitted to a professional school after you graduate. Such tests are widely used because the extent and accuracy of a person's vocabulary are among the best indications of his general ability. In other words, the correlation between vocabulary and ability is high.

Be constantly on the watch for new words and for new uses of old words. When you attend lectures in botany or economics or the history of the drama or read books for the courses, you will meet terms like *calyx* and *laissez-faire* and *miracle play*. To hear them or read them in action, so to speak, as a part of something you are studying, is the best way to learn new words. It is a much better way than finding lists of unusual words and memorizing them on the chance that sometime you might need them.

Use a dictionary. Look up words as soon as you come to them. Find out not only meanings but also etymologies. Where does the word come from and what do its root parts mean? Etymologies will help you remember meanings and make connections between words. What, for example, is the root part that connects *Anglophile, philology,* and *hemophilia?* Etymology sometimes will also help you see more deeply into the meaning of a word. What, for example, is the etymology of the word *atonement?* of *extravagant?* of *pre-*

posterous? of *illustrate?* We can use each of these words with more precision if we know its etymology.

Notice that many prefixes and suffixes appear again and again. Learning how they are used will often give you a good clue to the meanings of new words that contain them. Here are a few illustrations:

Prefixes

circum– (meaning *around*) circumstance, circumnavigate, circumlocution

anti– (meaning *against*) antisocial, antislavery, anticlimax

mono– (meaning *one, alone*) monomaniac, monotone, monopoly

Suffixes

–able: venerable, usable, peaceable

–tion: distinction, examination, fruition

–ness: sweetness, naughtiness, richness

Keep a list of new words in a page of your notebook. You might begin with this chapter. For example, are you sure of *prefix* and *suffix?* However much fun it may be to search out words like *esurient* and *suberose* and *desuetude* in order to puzzle your roommate, you had better give most of your attention to words that you meet in reading, in lectures, and in conversation.

Be alert not only to words you have never seen before but also to familiar words that you see in unfamiliar uses. Probably the greatest expansion in your vocabulary should result from your becoming better acquainted with words you have already seen at least occasionally. You know about *investing* money in a business; do you know what is meant by *investing* a city? A common twentieth-century word is *ideology;* you have seen it, of course, and probably used it, but do you know exactly what it means and how it differs from *idea?* Perhaps you have heard of a *nominal* friendship or an *integral* relationship, but are you sure what the italicized words mean?

T. S. Eliot has said of an older Boston society that it was "quite uncivilized but refined beyond the point of civilization." Of course you recognize *refined* and *uncivilized* and indeed have used them. Are you sure you know them though? Do you know their various shades of meaning so well that you understand what Eliot is saying? Before you get through college you may hear both the dean of women and an English professor use the word *genteel*. If you are observant you may see that they use the word quite differently, one of them to praise, the other to condemn. Will you understand how each of them may use the word correctly and yet use it so differently? Will you see that one's attitude toward life itself may be involved in this difference?

Increasing your vocabulary thus involves studying exact and subtle shades of meaning. It involves not only adding new words like *nomenclature* and *demotic* but also deepening your knowledge of words you already know, like *civilized* and *refined* and *genteel*.

USING YOUR VOCABULARY WISELY

Do not abuse the vocabulary you work to acquire. Use the words that express your meaning best and remember that the shortest, simplest, and most familiar words are often the best ones. Needless to say, you should never use words to show off. Say that you *know* something, not that you are *cognizant* of it; that you were *forced* to do something, not *constrained* to do it. Say that the man *died* in the *fire*, not that he *expired* in the *conflagration*. Say please do this as *quickly* as you *can*, not as *expeditiously* as *possible*.

When, on the other hand, you need a particular word, even if it is somewhat uncommon, like *fetish* or *antiphonal*, do not hesitate to use it. At times in this book we have used fairly difficult words when we might have used easier, better-known ones. We have used them because we have thought them the best words in the context.

This word *context* will illustrate the point. Since it is a somewhat unusual word, why did we write "in the context" instead of "for that particular sentence" or "under the circumstances"? The answer is that no everyday word or phrase expresses the meaning as well as *context* does. Words do not mean very much by themselves; they get meaning by being woven together into a pattern where every word affects every other word. *Context* suggests this pattern of interdependence, and no other simple word will do it as well.

Out of the enormous wealth of the English language, then, look for the best word and, when you believe you have found it, use it. Do not be afraid to try out words that are new to you; it is better to make mistakes while trying than not to try at all. The chief caution, to repeat, is this: Do not use words merely to impress your reader; do not use them to show off. Do not get the false idea that you are writing well by saying, unless to mimic him, that so-and-so is "replete with pseudo-erudition" when all you mean is that he is full of sham learning. Do not be like the colonel in a United States Army camp who issued an order to "reduce the volume and verbosity of electrically transmitted messages" when all he meant was to cut down on telephone calls and telegrams. Words are the coin of thought. They are too precious to use for ostentation or any other inferior purpose.

USING A DICTIONARY

A good desk-size dictionary is the most important reference book you can own. To try to go through college without one would be to impose a real handicap on yourself. You should choose one of the following:

Webster's *Seventh New Collegiate Dictionary*. Springfield, Massachusetts: G. & C. Merriam Co.

Webster's *New World Dictionary*. Cleveland, Ohio: World Publishing Co.

American College Dictionary, text ed. New York: Harper & Brothers.

Standard College Dictionary. New York: Funk & Wagnalls Co.

Though you probably will not buy one, you will rather often need to consult one of the unabridged dictionaries:

Webster's *Third New International Dictionary*. Springfield, Massachusetts: G. & C. Merriam Co.

New Standard Dictionary. New York: Funk & Wagnalls Co.

The *Third New International,* published in 1962, has more than 450,000 entries. Of this number, 100,000 are new words or include new meanings of old words—a statistic that indicates not that the second edition, published in 1934, missed words but that the English language is growing and changing almost as fast as other things in our civilization.

Especially if you should go on to do advanced work, you will need also to consult the great twelve-volume *Oxford English Dictionary.* (In an earlier edition, this was called the *New English Dictionary.* It is sometimes referred to as N. E. D., O. E. D., the *Oxford,* or *Murray's.*) It is especially useful for the student of word history, and it makes fascinating reading for anyone. Read the complete entry for almost any word and you will see what we mean.

You can go to a desk-size dictionary for information about many things:

1. The meaning of a word   As you can see in the treatment of the word *strong* in the *Seventh New Collegiate Dictionary,* the dictionary uses several methods to clarify the meaning of a word. It uses synonyms and sometimes compares and contrasts a group of synonyms in the effort to achieve a precision that will differentiate the word from all others in the language. In the dictionary cited here, the oldest meaning of the word is listed first; in some dictionaries what is assumed to be the most common meaning is listed first.

2. The spelling of a word   People go to a dictionary most frequently to see how to spell a word. (Many a theme and term paper, it may be said in passing, would have looked better had the student done so more often.) If two spellings are listed, like *theater* and *theatre,* each is acceptable.

3. The pronunciation of a word   The pronunciation of a word is usually indicated by respelling the word with diacritical marks and symbols. Since every dictionary uses a slightly different scheme to show pronunciation, you should study the discussion of pronunciation in the preface and in the pronunciation keys of your dictionary.

angle bracket **12.1**	**⁴save** \(,)sāv\ *conj* **1 :** were it not : ONLY — used with *that* **2 :** BUT, EXCEPT — used before a word often taken to be the subject of a clause ⟨no one knows about it ~ she⟩ **3 :** UNLESS ⟨~ they could be plucked asunder, all my quest were but in vain —Alfred Tenny- son⟩
author quoted **12.2.1**	**scar·a·bae·us** \,skar-ə-'bē-əs\ *n* [L] **1** *pl* **scar·a·bae·us·es** or **scar·a·baei** \-'bē-,ī\ **:** a large black or nearly black dung beetle ⟨*Scarabaeus sacer*⟩ **2 :** a stone or faience beetle used in ancient Egypt as a talisman, ornament, and a symbol of the resurrection
binomial **13.1**	**scar·a·mouch** or **scar·a·mouche** \'skar-ə-,müsh, -,müch, -,maüch\ *n* [F *Scaramouche*, fr. It *Scaramuccia*] **1** ⟨*cap*⟩**:** a stock character in the Italian commedia dell' arte drawn to burlesque the Spanish don and characterized by boastfulness and poltroonery **2 a :** a cow- ardly buffoon **b :** RASCAL, SCAMP
boldface type **1.1, 19.1**	
capitalization label **5.1**	**sce·nog·ra·phy** \sē-'näg-rə-fē\ *n* [Gk *skēnographia* painting of scenery, fr. *skēnē* + *-graphia* -graphy] **:** the art of perspective representation applied to the painting of stage scenery (as by the Greeks)
centered period **1.6**	**sceptic** *var of* SKEPTIC
cognate cross-reference **1.7.3**	**schiz-** or **schizo-** *comb form* [NL, fr. Gk *schizo-*, fr. *schizein* to split] **1 :** split : cleft ⟨*schizo*carp⟩ **2 :** characterized by or in- volving cleavage ⟨*schizo*genesis⟩ **3 :** schizophrenia ⟨*schizo*thymia⟩
comb form **3.3, 18.**	**scho·las·ti·cism** \ska-'las-tə,siz-əm\ *n* **1** *cap* **a**⟨**:** a philosophical movement dominant in western Christian civilization from the 9th until the 17th century and combining a fixed religious dogma with the mystical and intuitional tradition of patristic philosophy esp. of St. Augustine and later with Aristotelianism⟩ **b :** NEO- SCHOLASTICISM **2 :** close adherence to the traditional teachings or methods of a school or sect
definition	**¹scru·ple** \'skrü-pəl\ *n* [ME *scriple*, fr. L *scrupulus* a unit of weight, fr. *scrupulus* small sharp stone] **1**⟨— see MEASURE table⟩ **2 :** a minute part or quantity : IOTA
directional cross-reference **15.1**	**²sculpture** *vb* **sculp·tur·ing** \'skəlp-chə-riŋ, 'skəlp-shriŋ\ *vt* **1 a :** to form an image or representation of from solid material (as wood or stone) **b :** to carve or otherwise form into a three- dimensional work of art **2 :** to change (the form of the earth's surface) by erosion ~ *vi* **:** to work as a sculptor
double hyphen **1.6.1**	**sea-maid** \'sē-,mād\ or **sea-maid·en** \-,mād-²n\ *n* **:** MERMAID; *also* **:** a goddess or nymph of the sea
equal variant **1.7.1**	**se·clude** \si-'klüd\ *vt* [ME *secluden* to keep away, fr. L *secludere* to separate, seclude, fr. *se-* apart + *claudere* to close — more at SECEDE, CLOSE] **1 a :** to confine in a retired or inaccessible place **b :** to remove or separate from intercourse or outside influence **:** ISOLATE **2** *obs* **:** to exclude or expel from a privilege, rank, or dignity : DEBAR **3 :** to shut off : SCREEN
etymology **7.**	**¹sec·ond·hand** \,sek-ən-'\ *adj* **1 :** received from or through an intermediary **:** BORROWED **2 a :** acquired after being used by another **:** not new ⟨~ books⟩ **b :** dealing in secondhand merchan- dise (a ~ bookstore)
functional label **3.1**	**²secondhand** \,sek-ən-'\ *adv* **:** at second hand : INDIRECTLY
	secretary-general *n, pl* **secretaries-general :** a principal admin- istrative officer
homographs **1.4.1**	**²seer** \'si(ə)r\ *n, pl* **seers** or **seer** [Hindi *ser*] **1 :** any of various Indian units of weight; *esp* **:** a unit equal to 2.057 pounds **2 :** an Afghan unit of weight equal to 15.6 pounds
hyphened compound **1.1**	**²seethe** *n* **:** a state of seething : EBULLITION
inflectional forms **4.1, 4.2**	**¹seg·ment** \'seg-mənt\ *n, often attrib* [L *segmentum*, fr. *secare* to cut — more at SAW] **1 a :** a piece or separate fragment of something **:** PORTION **b** (1) **:** a portion cut off from a geometrical figure by a line or plane; *esp* **:** the part of a circular area bounded by a chord and an arc of that circle or so much of the area as is cut off by the chord (2) **:** the part of a sphere cut off by a plane or included be- tween two parallel planes (3) **:** the finite part of a line between two points in the line **2 :** one of the constituent parts into which a body, entity, or quantity naturally divides **:** DIVISION **syn** see PART — **seg·men·tary** \'seg-mən,ter-ē\ *adj*
lightface type **1.1**	
lowercase **5.1**	**selling race** *n* **:** a claiming race in which the winning horse is put up for auction
main entry **1.1, 19.1**	**se·man·tics** \si-'mant-iks\ *n pl but sing or pl in constr* **1 :** the study of meanings: **a :** the historical and psychological study and the classification of changes in the signification of words or forms viewed as factors in linguistic development **b** (1) **:** SEMIOTIC (2) **:** a branch of semiotic dealing with the relations between signs and what they refer to and including theories of denotation, extension, naming, and truth **2 :** GENERAL SEMANTICS **3 a :** the meaning or relationship of meanings of a sign or set of signs; *esp* **:** connotative meaning **b :** the exploitation of connotation and ambiguity (as in propaganda)
often attrib **6.**	
open compound **1.1, 2.6**	**semi-** \,sem-i, 'sem-, -,ī\ *prefix* [ME, fr. L; akin to OHG *sāmi-* half, Gk *hēmi-*] **1 a :** precisely half of: (1) **:** forming a bisection of ⟨*semi*ellipse⟩ ⟨*semi*oval⟩ (2) **:** being a usu. vertically bisected form of (a specified architectural feature) ⟨*semi*arch⟩ ⟨*semi*dome⟩ **b :** half in quantity or value **:** half of or occurring halfway through a specified period of time ⟨*semi*annual⟩ ⟨*semi*centenary⟩ — compare BI- **2 :** to some extent **:** pa . incompletely ⟨*semi*civilized⟩ ⟨*semi*-independent⟩ ⟨*semi*dry⟩ — . npare DEMI-, HEMI- **3 a :** par- tial **:** incomplete ⟨*semi*consciousne.s⟩ ⟨*semi*darkness⟩ **b :** having some of the characteristics of ⟨*semi*porcelain⟩ **c :** quasi ⟨*semi*- governmental⟩ ⟨*semi*monastic⟩
pl but sing in constr **4.3**	
prefix **3.3, 18.1**	

CHART

Notes of Webster's Seventh New Collegiate Dictionary, beginning on page 7a.)

stato·blast \'stat-ə-,blast\ *n* [ISV] **1** : a bud in a freshwater bryozoan that overwinters in a chitinous envelope and develops into a new individual in spring **2** : GEMMULE — primary stress **2.2**

stat·ol·a·try \stət-'äl-ə-trē\ *n* : advocacy of a highly centralized and all-powerful national government — pronunciation **2.**

stead·ing \'sted-ʰn, 'stēd-, -iŋ\ *n* [ME *steding*, fr. *stede* place, farm] **1** : a small farm **2** (*chiefly Scot*): the service buildings or area of a farm — regional label **8.3.4**

²steer *vb* [ME *steren*, fr. OE *stīeran;* akin to OE *stēor-* steering oar, Gk *stauros* stake, cross, *stylos* pillar, Skt *sthavira, sthūra* stout, thick, L *stare* to stand — more at STAND] *vt* **1** : to direct the course of; *specif* : to guide by mechanical means (as a rudder) **2** : to set and hold to (a course) ~ *vi* **1** : to direct the course (as of a ship or automobile) **2** : to pursue a course of action **3** : to be subject to guidance or direction (an automobile that ~*s* well) *syn see* GUIDE — (**steer·able** \'stir-ə-bəl\ *adj* — **steer·er** *n*)(— **steer clear** (: to keep entirely away — often used with *of*) — run-on entry (derivative) **16.1** / run-on entry (phrasal) **16.2**

stel·late \'stel-,āt\ *adj* : resembling a star (as in shape) : RADIATED (a ~ leaf) — **stel·late·ly** *adv*

³stint *n, pl* stints (*also* stint) [ME *stynte*] : any of several small sandpipers — secondary stress **2.2**

²stipple *n* : production of gradation of light and shade in graphic art by stippling small points, larger dots, or longer strokes;(*also*): an effect produced by or as if by stippling — secondary variant **1.7.2**

¹stom·ach \'stəm-ak, -ik\ *n, often attrib* [ME *stomak*, fr. MF *estomac*, fr. L *stomachus* gullet, esophagus, stomach, fr. Gk *stomachos*, fr. *stoma* mouth; akin to MBret *staffu* mouth, Av *staman-*] (1) **a** : a dilatation of the alimentary canal of a vertebrate communicating anteriorly with the esophagus and posteriorly with the duodenum **b** : an analogous cavity in an invertebrate animal ((c): the part of the body that contains the stomach (BELLY, ABDOMEN) **2 a** : desire for food caused by hunger : APPETITE **b** : INCLINATION, DESIRE **3** (*obs*) **a** : SPIRIT, VALOR **b** : PRIDE **c** : SPLEEN, RESENTMENT — sense divider **11.4.2** / sense letter **11.2** / sense number **11.1** / sense capitals **15.0, 15.2**

¹strike \'strīk\ *vb* struck \'strək\ struck *also* strick·en \'strik-ən\ strik·ing \'strī-kiŋ\ [ME *striken*, fr. OE *strican* to stroke, go; akin to OHG *strīhhan* to stroke, L *stringere* to touch lightly, *striga, stria* furrow] *vi* **1** : to take a course : GO **2** : to deliver or aim a blow or thrust **3** : HIT **4** : DELETE, CANCEL **5** : to lower a flag usu. in surrender **6 a** : to be indicated by a clock, bell, or chime **b** : to make known the time by sounding **7** : PIERCE, PENETRATE **8 a** : to engage in battle **b** : to make a military attack **9** : to become ignited **10** : to discover something **11 a** : to pull on a fishing rod in order to set the hook **b** (*of a fish*): to seize the bait **12** : DART, SHOOT **13 a** *of a plant cutting* : to take root **b** *of a seed* : GERMINATE **14** : to make an impression **15** : to stop work in order to force an employer to comply with demands **16** : to make a beginning **17** : to thrust oneself forward **18** : to work diligently : STRIVE (~) *vt* **1 a** : to strike at : HIT **b** : to drive or remove by or as if by a blow **c** : to attack or seize with a sharp blow (as of fangs or claws) (*struck by a snake*) **d** : INFLICT **e** : to produce (by or as if by a blow or stroke **f** : to separate by a sharp blow (~) off flints) **2 a** : to haul down(: LOWER) **b** (:) to dismantle and take away — status label **8.** / subject label **9.1** / swung dash (boldface) **3.2** / swung dash (lightface) **12.1** / symbolic colon **10.**

strin·gent \'strin-jənt\ *adj* [L *stringent-, stringens*, prp. of *stringere* to bind tight] **1** : TIGHT, CONSTRICTED **2** : marked by rigor, strictness, or severity esp. with regard to rule or standard **3** : marked by money scarcity and credit strictness (*syn see* RIGID)— **strin·gent·ly** *adv*

strong \'stroŋ\ *adj* **stron·ger** \'stroŋ-gər\ **stron·gest** \'stroŋ-gəst\ [ME, fr. OE *strang;* akin to OHG *strengi* strong, L *stringere* to bind tight — more at STRAIN] **1** : having or marked by great physical power : ROBUST **2** : having moral or intellectual power **3** : having great resources (as of wealth) **4** : of a specified number (an army ten thousand ~) **5** : effective or efficient esp. in a specified direction **6** : FORCEFUL, COGENT **7** : not mild or weak : INTENSE: as **a** : rich in some active agent (as a flavor or extract) (~ beer) **b** *of a color* : high in chroma — synonymous cross-reference **15.2** / synonymy cross-reference **17.2**

syn STRONG, STOUT, STURDY, STALWART, TOUGH, TENACIOUS mean showing power to resist or to endure. STRONG may imply power derived from muscular vigor, large size, structural soundness, intellectual or spiritual resources; STOUT suggests an ability to endure stress, pain, or hard use without giving way; STURDY implies strength derived from vigorous growth, determination of spirit, solidity of construction; STALWART suggests an unshakable dependability and connotes great physical strength; TOUGH implies great firmness and resiliency; TENACIOUS suggests strength in seizing, retaining, clinging to, or holding together — synonymy paragraph **17.1**

stron·tia \'strän-ch(ē-)ə, 'strän(t)-ē-ə\ *n* [NL, fr. obs. E *strontian*, fr. *Strontian*, village in (Scotland)] **1** : a white solid monoxide SrO of strontium resembling lime and baryta **2** : strontium hydroxide Sr(OH)₂ — uppercase / usage note **14.**

sty·loid \'stī(ə)l-,öid\ *adj* : resembling a style : STYLIFORM (— used esp. of slender pointed skeletal processes (as on the temporal bone or ulna)) — verbal illustration **12.1**

sub·ac·id \-'as-əd\ *adj* [L *subacidus*, fr. *sub-* + *acidus* acid] **1** : moderately acid (~ fruit juices) **2** : rather tart (~ prose) — **sub·ac·id·ly** *adv* — **sub·ac·id·ness** *n*

²sun *vb* (sunned; sun·ning) *vt* : to expose to or as if to the rays of the sun ~ *vi* : to sun oneself — verb principal parts **4.5, 4.6**

4. The derivation of a word   As you look up the meaning of a word, it is good practice to note its derivation. Knowing the derivation of a word often adds to the precision and fullness of one's understanding of the word. Sometimes history, sociology, and human nature itself are revealed in these derivations. The word *pagan*, for example, will suggest into what parts of the Roman world Christianity was slowest to penetrate. The word *clown* will give you a short but eloquent lecture on the snobberies of city people when they look at their cousins from the country. The word *silly* will tell you something about human cynicism.

5. Grammatical information   A dictionary gives information about the plurals of nouns and the principal parts of verbs when they are irregular or when they present difficulties in spelling or pronunciation. It does not give the plural of *boy*, for example, but it does of *man*. The regular verb *talk* is given in only its first principal part, but the irregular verb *speak* is given in its three principal parts: *speak, spoke, spoken.* In some dictionaries the second and third principal parts of regular verbs are also given if, like *study,* they show a change in spelling: *study, studied, studying.* The dictionary indicates the traditional grammatical classification (parts of speech) of all words.

6. Synonyms   The English language is especially rich in synonyms, two or more words with much the same meaning but nicely differentiated. Since good writing depends so much on finding not the approximate word but the precise word, not the merely acceptable word but the best word, you should consult the dictionary whenever you are in doubt about the choice of words. Notice, with the words *strike, strong,* and others on pages 116–117, what a wealth of choice the English language gives the writer and how the dictionary can help him find the word that best expresses his meaning.

7. The status of a word   Either after the derivation or after the definition of a word, the dictionary sometimes labels it if there is anything unusual about its status: whether it is obsolete, archaic, dialectal, colloquial, slang, British, Southern, chiefly medical, chiefly musical, and so on.

The dictionary does not lay down the law. How could it? By what authority could any body of men, no matter how well educated, prescribe the way we should spell and pronounce our words and give meaning to them? The dictionary simply records. It tells us what people do, not what they should do. For example, it spells the verb *separate s-e-p-a-r-a-t-e,* not because a board of editors decided it should be spelled this way and not even because the Latin derivation of the word indicates this spelling. The only reason the dictionary spells it this way is that people spell it this way—not all people, to be sure, and certainly not all students, but most people, most educated people at any rate, and all books, magazines, and newspapers.

To record actual usage is an immensely difficult undertaking and one that can never be completed because the language is a living thing. When Webster's *Third New International Dictionary* was published (in 1962), scholars were already gathering information for a later edition, because the English language, which has changed so much in the past, will continue to change in the future.

EXERCISE 1

Some of the sentences below make vigorous and accurate use of fairly unusual words. The diction of others is pretentious and ineffective. Which sentences show good diction, which poor? You are to assume that the sentences are written, not spoken, and that they are addressed to educated adults.

1. After performing his ablutions, he retired for the night.
2. Mr. Jones argued that the statistics were true but completely irrelevant.
3. The university's responsibility to impart knowledge to students transcends in importance its responsibility to entertain them with winning football teams.

4. Kept alive by the student fee, the literary magazine has become a subsidized expression of mediocrity.

5. The specialist questioned whether schizophrenic personalities were becoming more numerous in modern society; he said that we were merely becoming more aware of them.

6. He is an unabashed and unmitigated opportunist, without a single conviction except that he wants to get ahead.

7. The emoluments of professional classes have shown a stationary tendency during the last six months.

8. We are asked to refrain from smoking in the library.

9. Elaborate classification, so dear to the heart of pedants, is often quite useless.

10. The divisive tendencies in all societal organizations are studied in sociology.

11. It is questionable whether the iniquity of Babylon or Rome was any greater than that of parts of contemporary Paris and New York.

12. His familiarity with this type of test gave him an adventitious advantage.

13. His philosophic writings were a futile though valiant attempt to explain the dichotomy between subjective and objective.

14. I shall endeavor to get to New York in the next two or three weeks.

15. Eliot's "Prufrock" tells the tragedy not of passion but velleity.

16. His novels can have only the most meretricious and ephemeral appeal.

17. He resides in Media, a suburb of Philadelphia.

18. I have had a lingering protuberance on my arm that is causing me not a little concern.

19. This car is one of greater vintage than the others here.

20. The new bank is one of the most impressive edifices ever erected in our city.

EXERCISE 2

Look up the meaning and derivation of each of the following words:

bowdlerize	enormous
disaster	enthusiasm

gerrymander
irony
nice
pandemonium
sarcasm

scruple
sinister
subterfuge
supercilious
urbane

EXERCISE 3

Look up the pronunciation of the following words. If more than one pronunciation is listed, try to determine which is the more prevalent in your section of the country.

decadence
economics
exquisite
fascist
Hades
inquiry

mischievous
preferable
research
schism
transport (noun)
transport (verb)

EXERCISE 4

What is the meaning of each of the following prefixes? List three words using each of them.

bi–
dis–
fore–
mal–
neo–

pre–
pro–
sub–
trans–
un–

EXERCISE 5

List three words using each of the following suffixes:

–ly
–dom
–hood
–ward
–less
–ship

–ous
–ish (when used
    in adjectives,
    as in *mannish*)
–ment
–ism

EXERCISE 6

Consult a dictionary for the sources and original meanings of these words:

bus	nostril
buxom	philanthropy
cab	puppy
dehydrate	serenade
lord	skunk

EXERCISE 7

Most of the sentences below show a mistake in diction. Consult a dictionary to see whether the italicized word is used correctly. Then indicate, when a word is not correct, a word that is correct for the context.

1. Scandal magazines often *blaspheme* movie celebrities.
2. Tact has not been my most *domineering* trait.
3. Now that he had got away from the farm, he realized he was most *ambivalent* about it.
4. I think I would like a more *enervating* climate, something like Colorado's, with its low humidity.
5. When I learned that I was to be a counselor at the camp, my first reaction was a *frightening* one as I thought of the responsibility.
6. The very fact that the words are put into the mouth of Polonius *implies* some criticism of them.
7. I know that I will have to weed out the *impertinent* facts.
8. I was *literally* knocked down when he mentioned it again.
9. In *The Castle of Otranto* our *plausibility* is strained to the breaking point.
10. A fraternity should provide an environment in which good *mannerisms* may be observed.
11. No contemporary account bears more *unmistakenly* the stamp of authenticity.
12. Hamlet finds himself in a situation from which he cannot *extradite* himself.
13. Murder is, I suppose it is safe to say, one of the more *amoral* acts human beings commit.
14. The *barbarism* of these *savages* fills me with outrage.

15. I have had enough of the nauseating sweet smell of ether that is *synonymous with* hospitals.
16. Agriculture in Japan is very *intense* compared with ours.
17. In our climate, the English holly is an *exotic*.
18. Once you have seen it, you will never forget the *enormity* of the Grand Canyon.
19. In this passage, Chaucer's Parson is speaking about the *transitive* quality of female charms.
20. It is hoped that the dam will *impound* enough water to take care of our needs for many years.

EXERCISE 8

Use a dictionary, preferably an unabridged dictionary, to distinguish between these words that are often confused, and for each pair write two sentences bringing out the difference between the two words.

contemptible and contemptuous
incidents and incidence
incredible and incredulous
amoral and immoral
pleasantness and pleasantry
tragic and pathetic
wit and humor
enervate and invigorate
poetry and verse
irony and sarcasm

docility and humility
intense and intensive
ingenious and ingenuous
obscene and vulgar
aggravate and infuriate
sensuous and sensual
ascetic and aesthetic
virtue and virtuosity
practicable and practical
imaginary and imaginative

EXERCISE 9

Use a dictionary, preferably an unabridged dictionary, to determine shades of difference in meaning between these words, and for each pair write two sentences bringing out the difference between the two words.

juvenile and puerile
infantile and childish
illusion and delusion
ideal and idealistic
chagrined and mortified
credulous and gullible

shout and yell
cringe and cower
fertility and fecundity
sardonic and caustic
arid and dry (when used to describe things other than land)

innocence and naiveté
prolix and verbose
priggish and prudish
trivial and frivolous
pleasure and happiness
sadness and melancholy
decadence and degeneration

harmony and compatibility
iniquity and corruption
cogent and forceful
spurious and false
bestiality and brutality
suppress and repress
hearty and cordial

II

*Types, Models,
and Writing Assignments*

II

A

Writing About Yourself

Greek philosophers told the student searching for wisdom that he must find himself. "Know thyself" stands with "Nothing in excess" as one of the two chief commands of Greek thought.

How easy to know the self, some of us may think today, and also how relatively unimportant. How much more difficult, and also how much more important, to know others and also to know things—the atom, perhaps, or the stars, or something in between.

Clearly the Greeks did not think understanding the self either unimportant or easy, or they would not have emphasized it as they did. But even they failed to realize the difficulty of doing so, for they did not know how much of the self lies, like an iceberg, beneath the surface of consciousness. Nevertheless, they saw the importance of trying to know. They saw that to the extent we do know, we make ourselves able to understand others. They saw that it is impossible to understand very much about life unless we understand also the core from which we must start—ourselves.

Because of the importance of taking periodic stock of one's self, perhaps especially in transitional periods like one's first weeks in college, and also to assist the instructor in getting to know the students in his class, one of your first assignments is likely to be a theme about yourself.

Put yourself in the instructor's place for a moment. He has perhaps twenty-five students in your class, and other classes besides yours. Each of his many students is someone he probably has never seen before. He needs to know what kind of people all of them are—their backgrounds, their interests, their strengths and weaknesses. He needs to transfer them from names in a roll book to the status of human beings, each one an individual with ideas and feelings and experiences that are worth expressing if they can be discovered and given shape.

You might reflect on the instructor's problem. It is difficult in a few weeks to get to know a hundred people through their writing. It is especially difficult if their writing is vague and unrevealing. The responsibility is yours—to make your writing not vague and unrevealing, to make it something so expressive of yourself that only you could have written it.

Suppose in your first theme you turn in something like this:

I am a fairly average young man, and my life up to now has been rather uneventful. I was born eighteen years ago in a little town in Ohio, where my father started to practice medicine. I was the first of three children, and my younger brother and my sister and I have a close bond, even though we have had a few of the usual squabbles of growing up together.

I went through grade school without getting into any trouble, but in high school I began to get very conceited. I wanted to play football more than anything else, and when, as a sophomore, I made the team I got the biggest thrill of my life. I thought I was good enough to get by without studying, however, so I would spend all my evenings at the drugstore or looking at television.

In my junior year I flunked geometry, and my father was more exasperated with me than I like to remember. By going to summer school I gained back my eligibility, but I had to give up a fishing trip two of my best friends were taking. I felt pretty bad about this, but it taught me a lesson, and in my senior year my grades were above average.

Now I am coming to college and I am not going to let anything, even football, keep me from getting good grades. I believe I owe it to my father and mother to do the best work I can. They are making a sacrifice in sending me to college, and I intend to repay them by hard work.

This writing has some good qualities. It is straightforward, direct, unpretentious. Unfortunately, however, it is not very revealing. Its purpose is to tell something about the young man, and it tells very little. Phrases like "fairly average," "rather uneventful," "close bond," and "usual squabbles" do not give sufficient information. They do not individualize the writer. Nor, since every student would say the same thing, does the resolution to work hard in college individualize him. Try to imagine the blur of fifty or a hundred such themes, the complete indistinction of so many "fairly average" young men or women who tell little about themselves except that they, like everyone else in the class, have gone through grade school and high school and have now come to college determined to work hard.

Two faces seen a block away look very much alike. Distance blurs them so that much of the difference between them is lost. Your job as a writer is to move up on your subject, yourself, so that the difference will not be lost, so that the person you write about will become a person and not an indistinct figure a block away.

Suppose, for instance, you discuss one of your characteristics. Do you have a streak of laziness that you are—or maybe are not—struggling against? If so, you might tell the history of this laziness, the trouble it has cost you, and the efforts, if any, you are making to overcome it. How has it affected your schoolwork, your enjoyment of life, your relations with other people, your development as a person? If you make a full statement, with an abundance of illustrative detail (if you practice what is said in Chapter 1 about substance and in Chapter 3 about fullness) you will write something your instructor will read with interest—and he will notice that, oddly enough, you really are not so lazy after all, for you have taken the trouble to compose a theme that is original and expressive of yourself.

Have you always been excited by music or by chemistry? Are you a born and thoroughgoing hero-worshiper? Are you a bookworm, a relentless arguer, an aspiring poet? Do you have trouble writing? Are you shy? Are you a cynic? Have you become uncertain about your basic beliefs? Are you—? But the possibilities are limitless. Whatever you are, you are not like anyone else among the more than three billion people of the earth. However "normal" you may be, however "average," you are not like the man or woman next to you. You are your own unique self. Your task, especially in your first theme, is to help the instructor—and perhaps you too—to get to know that self better.

The following theme covers more ground than is ordinarily advisable in so short a composition, but the author avoids a mere listing of outward events in his life and gives, instead, a vivid sense of himself and his personality.

BIG MOUTH FROM KANSAS

I have been on time just once in my life. I arrived on this earth when my parents expected me, and I protested vigorously. I have been protesting ever since then; and I have always been late.

To wit: I was three when I walked, seven before I began to read, ten before I could write properly, almost eleven before I decided my thumb was not a suitable substitute for corn-on-the-cob, and nearly fourteen before somebody informed me that the angel Gabriel was not responsible for my existence. To counterbalance this retarded development, all I could offer was a big mouth, a rebellious recalcitrance, and a consuming zeal for knowledge once I was shown that something was worth learning.

I suppose one could classify me as a standard product of Kansas. I have breathed politics ever since I can remember. At five years I knew Washington died at Mt. Vernon in the odor of sanctity, Lincoln was the first American saint, and outside of the Republican Party there was no salvation. Indeed, all Democrats were infidels, and Franklin Roosevelt was anathema to God-fearing Christians.

But if this impresses you with our provincialism, there are things that outweigh any disadvantages a small town may seem to inflict upon its citizens. For instance, the Plains give one an early sense of freedom and independence. One is impressed with a sense of decency, honor, and responsibility seemingly anachronistic in these times.

Law and order are held in great reverence, and the Constitution receives as much awe as the King James Bible. My land is almost free of the political and social nostrums of the coasts, and it is truly the stronghold of Puritanism. Not that any of these are absent in the East, but they strike one with the force of a thunderhead once he crosses the Mississippi.

The space and the people have molded my character and my thinking to a degree that would be impossible to eradicate. These factors, with some reading and some travel, have made me what I am. I like tall elm trees that are like avaricious old men, with sharply etched fingers grasping for the sky. I like the feel of thick carpets under my feet, and a golden haze illuminating a sleepy morning. I like white cottages surrounded by greenest grass with roses, peonies, or the delicate lavender iris to command the passer-by. I like sauerkraut. I like the look of children at Christmas and the long beards on old men. I like to walk up stairs and over bridges. I like good jokes and good friends. The two are inseparable.

I don't like people who want to be tender apple blossoms. I don't care for metaphysics taken too seriously, for man does not live by logic alone. I don't like the seven years' itch, because I had an itch for seven years and it nearly drove me crazy. I hate to stand at movies, and I detest the childish Bohemianism of our supposed intellectuals. I don't like tragic muses or a lack of a sense of humor. I loathe all tight clothing and old meanies that take candy from children or happiness from anybody. I dislike cement plants because I worked in one.

I want a wife. I want a whole barnful of children. I want an ample income and lots of books and music. I want to travel occasionally. I want to write and be able to put nuance and shading into words. I want to be happy.

And will I? Probably not.

—STUDENT THEME BY DON L. STEWART

In the following theme, a student who is a little older than most college students looks back at his freshman year.

RETROSPECT

For most students, the freshman year of college is one of emotional stress, nervous tensions, problems of adjustment, and sometimes failure. Freshmen are perhaps more free from direct supervision than they have ever been before, but at the same time are expected to give up voluntarily so large a part of this new freedom that they are actually less free—if they expect to pass. Decisions have to be made, often speedily, with Mom and Dad not always around for help and advice. Freshmen discover—or are deliberately exposed to—so many new, strange, and powerful ideas that some of them lose their ideals, ethical and religious values; others, fortunately, find strength in the conflict and their beliefs become more firmly held. Whatever the outcome, however, the first year of college is, and is expected to be, one of confusion, doubt, question, and change.

My first freshman year changed me a great deal and, I'm afraid, the change wasn't for the better. I became frustrated under the work load, and no one was around to push me into making the effort necessary to bear it. I was far enough away from home for the change to be a complete one, and I could not, or did not want to, adjust to it. I became disillusioned with course material; the subject I was majoring in didn't look attractive once I began to study it, and my other or "General Education" courses didn't impress me as worthwhile either. As a result, I left school on the verge of flunking out.

That was five years ago. Now I'm nearing the end of my second freshman year, and, in comparing the two, I find differences so great that it could well have been two different people I was looking at rather than the same person doing the same thing at an interval of five years. My grades are a full point higher and some of them are more than that. My classmates refuse to believe that two or three hours of review or brush-up studying will prepare me for an exam; they wonder how I can possibly manage to go to a basketball game the night before a test, or spend all day Saturday working on my boat. On my part, I find that I can be somewhat detached and amused—though sympathetic—over their frantic cramming, worrying, and breathless scurrying around in what is called "campus life."

Am I suffering from an inflated ego? I don't think so. Many of my classmates are my equal or superior intellectually, and few will finish this year the way that I finished five years ago. I'm hardly able to brag about throwing away a year of my life.

Yet there are differences between me and the average freshman, differences that I think are quite pronounced and important, and which have led me to develop some ideas about college life. Right away you might say, "Well, you're older; you're twenty-four instead of eighteen." True, but isn't this explanation a little too simple? Just how, and where, and why does age make the difference?

When I graduated from high school I didn't particularly want to go to college—except that I thought it might be fun. Everyone else was doing it, weren't they? My parents picked the school, and, after looking over my supposed talents and aptitudes, a course of study. Then they gave me a gentle shove. It was the path of least resistance, so I followed it.

This was a big mistake, and one that many people make—people who go to college because they don't know what else to do. College isn't the place to find out. It is not a proving ground where a student can hop from course to course, testing each to see which he likes best. Neither is college a place to go to acquire status. High school is the place for a general education, including a large part of the growing up process; college is for advanced training in a specific area. If a person hasn't found his niche by the time he has graduated from high school, he should look for it somewhere other than at college, which isn't—or at least wasn't—designed to fulfill this function.

I am convinced, through my own experience, that it would be a very good thing if more men and women would take a break between their secondary and their higher education. It would give them a time to think, to make up their minds, to find out if college is really what *they* want and why, and, for the men, a chance to rid themselves of their military obligation so that they could look forward to an uninterrupted future. Of course it has been argued that "Once you're out of school and earning money, you won't want to go back." This may be true for some, but is this bad? College requires a dedication to the principle of sacrificing present wants for future improvements, and the people who would rather be earning money are probably those who wouldn't make a great success of college if they did go.

My four years away from school gave me a chance to come to *my own* conclusions about my future. It also served another and equally important purpose. Career servicemen (enlisted) are often contemptuous of college students, and I have heard statements like "Students talk so much about life that they don't have a chance to live it." Remarks like this, stemming as they do from the fact that enlisted men are supervised by officers who are college graduates, obviously are distorted. Like other misstatements, however, they have some basis in truth.

The world of the classroom, the lecture, the discussion, the book, and the study desk is not the real world. It is a reflection, and a reflection, no matter how clear, cannot show life as it really is with the clarity and impact of personal experience. How very much richer and more meaningful learning is when you can directly equate it with something you have known, something you have seen or done. A student may learn many things, but almost always from the insulated viewpoint of an observer, someone on the outside looking in, rather than from the vital, feeling one of a participant. I may not be an expert on world affairs, but I have had the taste of life—and death—that can bring the world of books alive. Now they have a meaning they could not have had before. I not only think; now I also *remember*.

Finally, my four years away from school have given me a chance to think about God, life, society, right and wrong, and many of the other concepts that so often bewilder the freshman. Over the course of these years, through the countless hours in port watches, and in the light of wider experience, I have had the chance to develop my attitudes and my ideas slowly and naturally. The average student doesn't get the chance to do this kind of thinking. He's under too much pressure; he just doesn't have time. New and often radical ideas are thrown at him so fast that he can't possibly do justice to them. He skims over their surface and rejects them outright or accepts them in their entirety without examining them.

All this represents a purely personal opinion and I may be wrong. Statistics do bear me out to some extent, however; veterans and other older students are more successful in college than younger students because, as I see it, they go to college to complete their education, not their growing up.

—STUDENT THEME BY ROBERT W. MOORE

ASSIGNMENTS

I. Choose the trait of character that seems to reveal most about yourself. Show how this trait developed and how it has affected your life.

II. Think of an experience which taught you something important about yourself or about your relations with other people. Describe the experience and show as fully as you can what you learned from it.

III. Think of the person outside your family who has had the greatest influence on you. What, as nearly as you can define it, has this influence been? How has it actually shown itself in your interests, activities, or beliefs?

IV. How has your family life given or failed to give what a child should have in growing up to maturity?

V. Write a theme on one of the following subjects or a similar one.

1. I've been seeing a psychiatrist
2. Stop the world; I want to get off
3. I grew up with a silver spoon
4. I come from the slums
5. I made the right (or the wrong) decision
6. What made me want to be a _____ (farmer, scientist, nurse, accountant, etc.)
7. On being the oldest child (or the youngest, or prettiest, or most spoiled)
8. I was never the same after that
9. What it means to be in a minority group
10. My parents gave me everything but understanding

B

Using Illustration

As the sections on substance (page 10) and fullness (pages 38–42) have brought out, all writing needs illustrative detail. Usually your illustrations, though frequent, will be fairly brief. Sometimes, however, you may find it useful to expand the illustration to considerable length. To help you learn how to do so is the purpose of this assignment.

Before looking at a passage that has much illustration, let us look at one that has none:

The motivation experienced by the scientist is sometimes the desire to solve a practical problem of some sort. Sometimes, however, practical considerations do not enter the scientist's mind and he is motivated only by the pure desire to know and to understand.

Writing like this may be satisfactory at times, especially to introduce a subject or to conclude it. It is too abstract, however, too lacking in illustrative detail, to be used throughout a composition. The next passage, an illustration developed at considerable length, is surely more interesting. Probably it is more understandable too, for an idea is seldom really explained and understood until it is illustrated.

Science is founded upon curiosity—upon "idle" curiosity about "useless" things. The scientist wants to know. Like the child, he wants to know just for the sake of knowing.

Not all science, it is true, develops out of this idle curiosity about useless knowledge. Sometimes the scientist is looking for something to serve a useful purpose, a vaccine against smallpox, for instance—or an explosive to destroy the world! But the basic work in science is rarely done to serve such a purpose. It may have a useful result (it usually does), but it does not have a utilitarian purpose. The scientist's purpose, like the child's, is simply to know.

Consider radio, television, radar, and other uses of electromagnetic waves. The technology that made them possible goes back to certain abstruse mathematical speculations by Clerk Maxwell and other physicists in the nineteenth century. Maxwell had no interest in knowing something useful. He only wanted to know.

It is easy to imagine someone taking him to task for wasting his time. "Why don't you do something useful," an impatient father might have asked, "instead of wasting precious time with a lot of useless mathematical equations? With your ability you could do something worthwhile, like inventing better textile machinery. You could make a lot of money out of it. And you could help England keep her markets and provide better clothing for people at cheaper prices. Even if you have no interest in making money, you ought to recognize a duty to help your country and to improve living standards throughout the world."

So Maxwell might have been talked to, but if he was, he did not heed the argument—either the selfish one to make a lot of money or the patriotic one to help his country or the humanitarian one to serve mankind. But out of his "idle" and "useless" speculations came radio and television—and radar, which saved his country in 1940 by enabling British fighter planes to track down the night bombers of the Nazis.

If you are going to use an illustration, obviously you need a good one, like this about Clerk Maxwell, especially when you are using it at some length. Perhaps you believe that people worry too much about the future. You may have noticed that most of the misfortunes they anticipate do not happen and that the misfortunes which do come to them they did not anticipate. What event in your experience or observation illustrates this truth? Do you know a man who worried about losing his job and never lost it but instead lost his health? Can you use his experience, as the other writer used Clerk Maxwell's? Do you know of someone who was bitterly disappointed when his company transferred him from the glamorous fullness of life in New York City to the anticipated emptiness of life in the branch office hundreds of miles away—and found the transfer the best stroke of luck he ever had?

Perhaps you want to write on the subject that money cannot buy happiness. Surely you know of someone's experience to illustrate it. Perhaps you want to write about the qualities of a good sergeant or a good camp director. You can and should draw on your own knowledge of sergeants or camp directors to illustrate these qualities in action.

Whether the subject is worry, or money and happiness, or the qualities of a good camp director, or any other topic, the writer who takes a specific instance of the point he wants to make and develops the instance in some detail may not need to do much else. If presented clearly and forcefully, the facts speak for themselves, and the reader will have the truth impressed upon his mind as no amount of abstraction could impress it.

Where should you go for your illustrations? The answer is simple: to your own experience if possible. You can write with an interest and force that nothing else is likely to supply if you write about things that have happened to you. If you must depart from your own immediate experience, go as little distant from it as possible; in other words, go to the lives of friends or relatives or associates who are close enough to you so that you know the details by having been able to share what has happened to them. If you have shared the experience, it is, in the larger sense of the word, a part of your own experience. Of course, like the writer of the material on Maxwell, you may have to go outside your own experience for the most telling illustration, and you should not hesitate to do so when it will strengthen your writing. But do not do it until after you have searched through what you yourself have experienced or observed.

The illustration need not be unusual or spectacular to be effective. Note how the author of the following excerpt makes use of an incident that is common to all of us—a "trivial" incident, she herself calls it. She uses, too, an illustration drawn from her knowledge of research that others have done. When you want to find the right illustrative material, search your mind for what you have read and heard; but search your memory, too, for those "trivial" things you have experienced, for they may turn out to be the best illustrations of all.

We cannot hope to work out, here, an all-covering answer to the old question of why, even with the best intentions, we so often do what we ought not to do and leave undone what ought to be done. But neither can we ignore that question. The least we can do is to note once more that powers and limitations are oddly bundled together in our human make-up. The least we can do is to take stock of certain reasons why we get our lives into a muddle, feel pulled two ways at once, defend half truths as whole truths, deceive ourselves and defend our self-deceptions to the last ditch.

Every one of us is a self-with-problems—psychological problems. Either to ignore these or to talk as though we could get rid of them if we just had enough backbone is to remain at their mercy—and to remain cruelly obtuse in the judgments we pass upon other people. To know them for what they are is, in some measure at least, to escape their tyranny.

. . . [A] dog not only cannot walk and scratch at once but has an inner mechanism which prevents his *wanting* to do both at once. He may do them in such quick succession—stopping to scratch and then walking on—that it looks to a human observer as though the wish to walk must so hold over in the dog's consciousness that the need to scratch would be experienced emotionally as a nuisance and an interruption. Analysis of the dog's nervous system, however, suggests that such is not the case. While he is scratching he is not disturbed because he is not walking; he has simply swung from one total channelized experience to another—and when he swings back, he swings back *whole*.

We human beings live in a world of mutual exclusives far more complex than the dog's mutual exclusives of walking and scratching. We cannot spend the same five-dollar bill on something we ourselves want and on something we want to give to a friend, or simultaneously be a good listener at a dinner party and pour out all the opinions and anecdotes that crowd to our own lips, or be both a person of independent judgment and a person of unquestioning loyalty to the political party that is ours by family tradition. Our life is full of mutual exclusives, but we do not have the dog's automatic provision for doing one thing or another and remaining *whole* in the process. Because we lack that provision we are capable of unique individuality; but we are also subject to long hesitations and indecisions, to feelings of doubt and guilt, to regrets and self-condemnations, and to self-justifications that easily become self-deceptions.

On a certain evening a friend drops by to ask us to go for a ride. We want to go. Standing on the porch talking, we realize both how beautiful the evening is and how tired we are. Yet there are two arguments against our going: we have brought home from the office work that should be done by morning, and with that work as a reason we have already turned down another friend who invited us to go to the movies. We hesitate . . . and say, "I wish I could, but I can't." Then, just as we are feeling firm in that decision, a breeze brings a whiff of honeysuckle . . . and one part of our mind is reclaimed by the evening's beauty. At last we say, "Well . . . if we aren't too long, I can sit up and do my work later." That seems a reasonable solution—or so we tell ourselves—and our other friend will be at the movies by now and will not see us out by the river. We feel a little guilty, vaguely dishonest . . . but, after all, we did not *want* to go anywhere earlier in the evening. We really did intend to work . . . we were not so tired then . . . and, anyway, a movie would take a lot more time than just a short ride. . . .

So we go, and the river is as beautiful as we thought it would be. Yet we are not relaxed in our enjoyment. The memory of our other friend nags at us. Moreover, the work we left at home has come along as a sort of mental stowaway. Even as the moon is rising, half our mind is on that work. We become restless . . . wanting to be on our way. But we do not feel we have a right to suggest starting back; if we are going to be a kill-joy, we might better have stayed home in the first place.

Slowly, at last, we do drive back, far later than we intended—so late that when our friend suggests stopping at a diner it does not seem worth while to protest. We won't get any work done anyway. In the diner, however, we come abruptly face to face with the friend with whom we did not go to the movies . . . and at that point we begin to feel that there is a lot to be said for a dog's life.

Trivial as such an incident may seem in our world of mammoth tragedies, it still partakes of the nature of those larger conflicts that most deeply disturb us. It shows us behaving in a way that goes counter to the private image we cherish of ourselves, so that we feel guilty and somehow tarnished; it threatens us at the always vulnerable point of our social linkages. Thus we have simultaneously exposed ourselves to self-condemnation, to condemnation by another individual, and to a kind of abstract condemnation by the rules of social fairness—the *mores*. —BONARO W. OVERSTREET

Here is an example of writing that makes much use of illustration drawn not from personal experience but from research.

In all the world of living things, it is doubtful whether there is a more delicately balanced relationship than that of island life to its environment. This environment is a remarkably uniform one. In the midst of a great ocean, ruled by currents and winds that rarely shift their course, climate changes little. There are few natural enemies, perhaps none at all. The harsh struggle for existence that is the normal lot of continental life is softened on the islands. When this gentle pattern of life is abruptly changed, the island creatures have little ability to make the adjustments necessary for survival.

Ernst Mayr tells of a steamer wrecked off Lord Howe Island east of Australia in 1918. Its rats swam ashore. In two years they had so nearly exterminated the native birds that an islander wrote, "This paradise of birds has become a wilderness, and the quietness of death reigns where all was melody."

On Tristan da Cunha almost all of the unique land birds that had evolved there in the course of the ages were exterminated by hogs and rats. The native fauna of the island of Tahiti is losing ground against the horde of alien species that man has introduced. The Hawaiian Islands, which have lost their native plants and animals faster than almost any other area in the world, are a classic example of the results of interfering with natural balances. Certain relations of animal to plant, and of plant to soil, had grown up through the centuries. When man came in and rudely disturbed this balance, he set off a whole series of chain reactions.

Vancouver brought cattle and goats to the Hawaiian Islands, and the resulting damage to forests and other vegetation was enormous. Many plant introductions were as bad. A plant known as the pamakani was brought in many years ago, according to report, by a Captain Makee for his beautiful gardens on the island of Maui. The pamakani, which has light, wind-borne seeds, quickly escaped from the captain's gardens, ruined the pasture lands on Maui, and proceeded to hop from island to island. The CCC boys were at one time put to work to clear it out of the Honouliuli Forest Reserve, but as fast as they destroyed it, the seeds of new plants arrived on the wind. Lantana was another plant brought in as an ornamental species. Now it covers thousands of acres with a thorny, scrambling growth—despite large sums of money spent to import parasitic insects to control it.

—RACHEL L. CARSON

ASSIGNMENTS

I. Write a theme on one of the following subjects, using illustration as a chief means of developing the idea.

1. The qualities of a good student
2. The dangers of conformity
3. The pleasures of reading
4. Money can't buy everything
5. Status and the university
6. Man proposes; God disposes
7. A little learning is a dangerous thing
8. For want of a nail
9. Pride goes before a fall
10. We don't speak the same language

II. Choose one of the following statements with which you do *not* agree. Limiting yourself to one paragraph of not more than five or six sentences, give an illustration based on your own experience or observation to show the incorrectness or weakness of the statement.

1. Women are more vain than men
2. Men are braver than women
3. The Army will make a man of him
4. Small towns are less corrupt than big cities
5. Travel makes a man wise
6. People who know books do not know life
7. A dog is a man's best friend
8. In a big city you don't even know your neighbors
9. Television commercials are delightful
10. Absence makes the heart grow fonder

C

Explaining a Process

Hardly a day passes without our explaining how to do something: how to perform an experiment in chemistry, how to be a better high jumper, how to pick out a good pair of shoes, how to play chess, how to plan a trip to Europe. And if we have been lost at night on a strange highway, we know the value of clear directions and the exasperation that comes when they are not clear.

Explanations should be written in concrete, specific language. They should not refer to the *instrument* or *tool* when the writer means a *wrench*. They should not talk about the *piece* when they mean the *pawn*. They should say that Florence is five or six hours by train from Rome rather than (so helpfully!) "It isn't too far."

In writing explanations, remember the experience and knowledge of the reader. Avoid technical language when you are addressing a reader without technical training. Define any technical words you must use if there is possibility of misunderstanding. Choose your terms to fit your audience. For instance, you should define the term *arpeggio* if you are addressing nonmusical readers but not if you are addressing musicians. The term *duodenary* could be used in a mathematics journal, but either it should not be used at all or if used it should be explained in a magazine of general circulation.

You will want to use illustration or comparison when appropriate: our understanding of the unfamiliar is always aided by references to the familiar. We move into new territory of the mind by seeing how it is similar to and different from what we already know.

You should present all the important facts, of course, but don't smother the reader. Do not confuse him either by the omission of things he needs to know or by the inclusion of things he does not need to know. Present the material in a series of orderly steps, so that the reader can move from one step in the process to the next. As far as possible, give the reasons for each step; the reader will follow directions more readily if he understands not only what they are but also the reasons for them and where they are leading.

Warn the reader of things not to do; tell him of dangers in the process, of places where he may go wrong. For instance, in giving directions for planting gladioli, you might gain emphasis by repetition: "Put the plants where they will have full sun. Do not expect them to do well where they have even partial shade."

These precepts can be followed in explaining any process, whether the directions are bare and strictly functional, like explaining registration procedure to next year's freshmen, or whether they are more imaginative because you are trying to give pleasure and understanding as well as information. As in all writing, clarity is essential, but it need not keep you from seeking other qualities in your writing when they are appropriate.

In the following essay, the student succeeds in making the process not only clear but interesting. Despite the subject, she even suggests something of her own personality.

Cake and Tea

The fitful spatter of rain against the window pane followed by spurts of wind from the northeast keeps coming between me and my book. I look up, and the bare branches of trees wave back and forth, black against a thick gray sky. I try again to read, and hear the uneven scutter of rain and wind. It's a day for tea and pound cake and a fire blazing noisily in the hearth.

The kitchen shades are drawn, and the fluorescent light is bright as sunshine. I light the oven, set the thermostat at 300, and bring out pans and bowls and spoons from cupboards and drawers with a clatter. Then I prop the cookbook, open to the recipe, in front of me.

First I sift some flour, and measure two and three-quarters cups. Then I add one and one-half teaspoons of baking powder, and sift again into a bowl, which I set aside for later use.

Now the arm-work begins. Into another bowl I measure one-half cup of vegetable shortening, one-quarter cup of butter, three-quarters teaspoon of salt, one-half teaspoon of mace, and one-half teaspoon of grated lemon rind, and cream them together until the mixture is soft and fluffy. Then I measure one and one-quarter cups of sugar and add this—a tablespoon or two at a time—to the shortening mixture, creaming like mad after each addition.

Naturally, I have forgotten to remove the three eggs from the refrigerator long enough ahead of time to let them warm up to room temperature, but I add them anyway—one at a time—beating thoroughly after adding each one, about seventy-five strokes to each egg.

The milk comes next—two-thirds of a cup, and I barely have enough. I dump a little of the flour mixture into the egg mixture, and stir it in carefully. Then a little milk, and more stirring; now flour, and stir; milk, stir; and end up with flour, stirring until the batter is smooth and completely free of unsightly lumps—or any lumps at all.

I should have got out that 9 × 5 × 3-inch pan and lined it with paper, but I didn't, so I do that now. Then I pour the lovely pale yellow smooth-as-cream batter into the pan, and scrape down the sides of the bowl, leaving just enough on the spoon for a taste.

The oven has preheated to 300 degrees long since, and so I turn the knob to "Bake," put in the pan, shut the oven door, set my timer to ring at the end of one hour, and go back into the living room to build that blazing fire in the hearth.

In no time at all—what with trips to the basement for kindling wood, heaving logs about, and burning up several books of paper matches—the timer bell tells me it's time to set the oven thermostat to 325, and the timer to ring at the end of fifty more minutes.

Now I must make the tea—in my best pewter pot, of course. The tea tray gets a fresh doily, and everything is ready but the cake, which has ten more minutes to go. I take a quick look. It's browning lightly on top and shrinking daintily away from the sides of the pan, just as it should.

When the timer bell finally rings, I remove the cake from the oven, run a spatula gently around the sides of the cake, then lay a cake-cooling rack upside down on the pan, and turn rack, pan and all over. The cake drops from the pan without a murmur. I remove the paper from the bottom of the cake, and while I wait for the cake to cool, I take a quick look at the outdoors. It can't be true—the rain has stopped, and the sun is blinding.

—STUDENT THEME BY RACHEL SUTTER

Part of the material which follows illustrates skillful explanation of a process. The excerpt can also be studied as persuasion of the most useful kind.

You know you have to read "between the lines" to get the most out of anything. I want to persuade you to do something equally important in the course of your reading. I want to persuade you to "write between the lines." Unless you do, you are not likely to do the most efficient kind of reading.

I contend, quite bluntly, that marking up a book is not an act of mutilation but of love.

You shouldn't mark up a book which isn't yours. Librarians (or your friends) who lend you books expect you to keep them clean, and you should. If you decide that I am right about the usefulness of marking books, you will have to buy them. Most of the world's great books are available today, in reprint editions, at less than a dollar.

There are two ways in which one can own a book. The first is the property right you establish by paying for it, just as you pay for clothes and furniture. But this act of purchase is only the prelude to possession. Full ownership comes only when you have made it a part of yourself, and the best way to make yourself a part of it is by writing in it. An illustration may make the point clear. You buy a beefsteak and transfer it from the butcher's icebox to your own. But you do not own the beefsteak in the most important sense until you consume it and get it into your bloodstream. I am arguing that books, too, must be absorbed in your bloodstream to do you any good.

Confusion about what it means to *own* a book leads people to a false reverence for paper, binding, and type—a respect for the physical thing—the craft of the printer rather than the genius of the author. They forget that it is possible for a man to acquire the idea, to possess the beauty, which a great book contains, without staking his claim by pasting his bookplate inside the cover. Having a fine library doesn't prove that its owner has a mind en-

146

riched by books; it proves nothing more than that he, his father, or his wife, was rich enough to buy them.

There are three kinds of book owners. The first has all the standard sets and best-sellers—unread, untouched. (This deluded individual owns woodpulp and ink, not books.) The second has a great many books—a few of them read through, most of them dipped into, but all of them as clean and shiny as the day they were bought. (This person would probably like to make books his own, but is restrained by a false respect for their physical appearance.) The third has a few books or many—every one of them dog-eared and dilapidated, shaken and loosened by continual use, marked and scribbled in from front to back. (This man owns books.)

Is it false respect, you may ask, to preserve intact and unblemished a beautifully printed book, an elegantly bound edition? Of course not. I'd no more scribble all over a first edition of *Paradise Lost* than I'd give my baby a set of crayons and an original Rembrandt! I wouldn't mark up a painting or a statue. Its soul, so to speak, is inseparable from its body. And the beauty of a rare edition or of a richly manufactured volume is like that of a painting or a statue.

But the soul of a book *can* be separated from its body. A book is more like the score of a piece of music than it is like a painting. No great musician confuses a symphony with the printed sheets of music. Arturo Toscanini reveres Brahms, but Toscanini's score of the C-minor Symphony is so thoroughly marked up that no one but the maestro himself can read it. The reason why a great conductor makes notations on his musical scores—marks them up again and again each time he returns to study them—is the reason why you should mark your books. If your respect for magnificent binding or typography gets in the way, buy yourself a cheap edition and pay your respects to the author.

Why is marking up a book indispensable to reading? First, it keeps you awake. (And I don't mean merely conscious; I mean wide awake.) In the second place, reading, if it is active, is thinking, and thinking tends to express itself in words, spoken or written. The marked book is usually the thought-through book. Finally, writing helps you remember the thoughts you had, or the thoughts the author expressed. Let me develop these three points.

If reading is to accomplish anything more than passing time, it must be active. You can't let your eyes glide across the lines of a book and come up with an understanding of what you have read. Now an ordinary piece of light fiction, like, say, *Gone with the Wind,* doesn't require the most active kind of reading. The books you read for pleasure can be read in a state of relaxation, and nothing is lost. But a great book, rich in ideas and beauty, a book that raises and tries to answer great fundamental questions, demands the most active reading of which you are capable. You don't absorb the ideas of John Dewey the way you absorb the crooning of Mr. Vallee. You have to reach for them. That you cannot do while you're asleep. . . .

But, you may ask, why is writing necessary? Well, the physical act of writing, with your own hand, brings words and sentences more sharply before your mind and preserves them better in your memory. To set down your reaction to important words and sentences you have read, and the questions they have raised in your mind, is to preserve those reactions and sharpen those questions.

Even if you wrote on a scratch pad, and threw the paper away when you had finished writing, your grasp of the book would be surer. But you don't have to throw the paper away. The margins (top and bottom, as well as side), the end-papers, the very space between the lines, are all available. They aren't sacred. And, best of all, your marks and notes become an integral part of the book and stay there forever. You can pick up the book the following week or year, and there are all your points of agreement, disagreement, doubt, and inquiry. It's like resuming an interrupted conversation with the advantage of being able to pick up where you left off.

And that is exactly what reading a book should be: a conversation between you and the author. Presumably he knows more about the subject than you do; naturally, you'll have the proper humility as you approach him. But don't let anybody tell you that a reader is supposed to be solely on the receiving end. Understanding is a two-way operation; learning doesn't consist in being an empty receptacle. The learner has to question himself and question the teacher. He even has to argue with the teacher, once he understands what the teacher is saying. And marking a book is literally an expression of your differences, or agreements of opinion, with the author.

There are all kinds of devices for marking a book intelligently and fruitfully. Here's the way I do it:

1. *Underlining:* of major points, of important or forceful statements.

2. *Vertical lines at the margin:* to emphasize a statement already underlined.

3. *Star, asterisk, or other doo-dad at the margin:* to be used sparingly, to emphasize the ten or twenty most important statements in the book. (You may want to fold the bottom corner of each page on which you use such marks. It won't hurt the sturdy paper on which most modern books are printed, and you will be able to take the book off the shelf at any time and, by opening it at the folded-corner page, refresh your recollection of the book.)

4. *Numbers in the margin:* to indicate the sequence of points the author makes in developing a single argument.

5. *Numbers of other pages in the margin:* to indicate where else in the book the author made points relevant to the point marked; to tie up the ideas in a book, which, though they may be separated by many pages, belong together.

6. *Circling of key words or phrases.*

7. *Writing in the margin, or at the top or bottom of the page, for the sake of:* recording questions (and perhaps answers) which a passage raised in your mind; reducing a complicated discussion to a simple statement; recording the sequence of major points right through the book. I use the end-papers at the back of the book to make a personal index of the author's points in the order of their appearance.

The front end-papers are, to me, the most important. Some people reserve them for a fancy bookplate. I reserve them for fancy thinking. After I have finished reading the book and making my personal index on the back end-papers, I turn to the front and try to outline the book, not page by page, or point by point (I've already done that at the back), but as an integrated structure, with a basic unity and an order of parts. This outline is, to me, the measure of my understanding of the work.

If you're a die-hard anti-book-marker, you may object that the margins, the space between the lines, and the end-papers don't give you room enough. All right. How about using a scratch pad slightly smaller than the page-size of the book—so that the edges of the sheets won't protrude? Make your index, outlines, and even your notes on the pad, and then insert these sheets permanently inside the front and back covers of the book.

Or, you may say that this business of marking books is going to slow up your reading. It probably will. That's one of the reasons for doing it. Most of us have been taken in by the notion that speed of reading is a measure of our intelligence. There is no such thing as the right speed for intelligent reading. Some things should be read quickly and effortlessly, and some should be read slowly and even laboriously. The sign of intelligence in reading is the ability to read different things differently according to their worth. In the case of good books, the point is not to see how many of them you can get through, but rather how many can get through you—how many you can make your own. A few friends are better than a thousand acquaintances. If this be your aim, as it should be, you will not be impatient if it takes more time and effort to read a great book than it does a newspaper. . . . —MORTIMER J. ADLER

ASSIGNMENTS

I. In a short theme write simple, factual directions for one of the following subjects or a similar subject within your knowledge.

1. How to plant a tree
2. How to equip a boat
3. How to make a salad
4. How to choose a campsite
5. How to cut out a dress
6. How to grow African violets
7. How to develop vocal muscles
8. How to drive from Washington, D. C., to Boston

II. The following subjects offer more room for imagination and personal feeling, including possibly humor.

1. How to break a habit
2. How to lose a suitor
3. How to be the life of the party
4. How to fail an examination
5. How to ruin a vacation
6. How to impress the dean
7. How to be a pest without really trying
8. How to age your car
9. How to blow your horn
10. How to enjoy life without money
11. How to study in a dormitory
12. How to find enough time

D
Defining Terms

When someone uses the word *definition,* your first thought is probably of the brief and severe statements found in dictionaries. The dictionary definition does three things: (1) it *names* something; (2) it tells us what *kind* of object or idea is being defined; and (3) it tells us how this object or idea *differs* from others of the same kind. Technically these three parts are called (1) the *term,* (2) the *class* or *genus,* and (3) the *differentiae.* For example, a hammer (name or term) is an instrument (kind of thing, class, or genus) that differs from other instruments in its appearance and structure (it has a head fixed crosswise on a handle) and in what it does (it is used for such purposes as driving nails).

You should not think of the bare, factual statements of the dictionaries as the only kind of definition. Many definitions in books and magazines run to several pages. Their purpose is to explain an idea or to present an attitude. If a writer takes a page to define *student cafeteria,* it is not because the reader needs the kind of information he goes to a dictionary for. It is because in defining the term in his own individual way, the writer is able to show what he thinks about cafeterias and perhaps about other things, such as student behavior and college life. Thus definitions of this sort give explanations that are fuller than a dictionary has space for, and they make comparisons and often give examples. They usually avoid the clipped language of the dictionary, and they are not carefully divided into the three parts mentioned in the preceding paragraph. Often they are humorous. Above all, they permit the writer to reveal himself, as the dictionary definition does not.

Good subjects for these fuller definitions are familiar student terms like *examination, date, chemistry, library, allowance.* Since this type of definition depends largely on personal experience and personal attitudes, you should feel free to introduce your own feelings and ideas. Your definition may take any mood, of course—serious or humorous, sympathetic or sad or sarcastic or indignant—that seems to you best.

Definitions of such abstract words as *education, liberty, democracy, justice, sincerity* are useful but often very difficult to make. Except in the physical sciences like chemistry and biology, men are often so far apart in their thinking they cannot even agree about what the issues of disagreement are. Yet sometimes two people can hardly understand each other until they have defined an abstraction: if by *happiness* you mean having an interesting job and I mean lying on the sand and loafing, we are so far apart that we cannot have a sensible discussion of happiness until we define—though not necessarily agree on—our terms.

Sometimes important practical actions follow from the definitions we give to words. Before we establish an educational system, for instance, we should be sure we know what we want—what we mean by the term *education.* The hiring of teachers, the building of schoolhouses, the choice of courses, and indeed every specific decision relating to education will depend on what we mean by the term. What applies to a complicated matter such as an educational system applies in lesser degree to all our communications that involve generalizations.

The following suggestions should help you in defining words, especially abstract words. First of all, think of the purpose for which you are defining. Is it to inform, to contrast, to distinguish, to amuse, to arouse? Is it, for example, to contrast the term *democracy* with *republicanism,* or is it to renew the reader's convictions about the value of democracy? Is it to let off steam about having stood in registration lines all day, or is it to propose a solution to the problem of registration?

Second, think of related terms, terms similar to *education,* if that is what you are writing about, or terms different from but often confused with it. Think of *going to school, reading books, reading the best books, earning credits, acquiring information, training for a profession, developing the mind, expanding one's awareness.* Distinguish the word *education* from these related terms. Certainly you would not be satisfied with a definition of *education* that went no further than *attendance at school.* Would a person whose schooling stopped at the eighth grade necessarily be uneducated? Would a person who had graduated from college necessarily have an education along with his diploma? If he graduated from college *summa cum laude?* If he had a doctor's degree?

Third, think of illustrations or typical examples. What people seem to you genuinely educated? Why? What qualities do they show? What activities, interests, and attitudes distinguish them from people who are not educated? In what ways, as specifically as possible, have they profited from their education?

In the definition that follows, note that the author first tells what the subject is not and then tells what it is.

It is easier to say what loyalty is not than to say what it is. It is not conformity. It is not passive acquiescence in the status quo. It is not preference for everything American over everything foreign. It is not an ostrich-like ignorance of other countries and other institutions. It is not the indulgence in ceremony—a flag salute, an oath of allegiance, a fervid verbal declaration. It is not a particular creed, a particular version of history, a particular body of economic practices, a particular philosophy.

It is a tradition, an ideal, and a principle. It is a willingness to subordinate every private advantage for the larger good. It is an appreciation of the rich and diverse contributions that can come from the most varied sources. It is allegiance to the traditions that have guided our greatest statesmen and inspired our most eloquent poets—the traditions of freedom, equality, democracy, tolerance, the tradition of the higher law, of experimentation, cooperation, and pluralism. It is the realization that America was born of revolt, flourished on dissent, became great through experimentation.

Independence was an act of revolution: republicanism was something new under the sun; the federal system was a vast experimental laboratory. Physically Americans were pioneers; in the realm of social and economic institutions, too, their tradition has been one of pioneering. From the beginning, intellectual and spiritual diversity have been as characteristic of America as racial and linguistic. The most distinctively American philosophies have been transcendentalism—which is the philosophy of the Higher Law—and pragmatism—which is the philosophy of experimentation and pluralism. These two principles are the very core of Americanism: the principle of the Higher Law, or of obedience to the dictates of conscience rather than of statutes, and the principle of pragmatism, or the rejection of a single good and of the notion of a finished universe. From the beginning Americans have known that there were new worlds to conquer, new truths to be discovered. Every effort to confine Americanism to a single pattern, to constrain it to a single formula, is disloyalty to everything that is valid in Americanism.   —HENRY STEELE COMMAGER

The following essay (originally an address given at the University of Notre Dame), is an example of definition developed at length and used to state a position. The subject is similar to the preceding one and the point of view is not very different. The first is an example of definition as a part of something else; the second is an example of a whole essay developed largely by definition.

THE HARD KIND OF PATRIOTISM

It is not easy to be a patriot these days—not because it is difficult to love one's country. The difficulty lies with loving one's country in the right way.

The love itself is profound and instinctive, rooted in our childhood discovery of all the infinite delights of being alive—for me, the vast skies, the spring green of the corn, the fall colors and winter snow of the Illinois prairie; for all of us, the shining Christmas trees, the colored mesas and bright flowers of the desert, the rocky shores and pounding seas "way down East," the aspens showering autumn gold on the slopes of the Rockies.

It doesn't matter what your picture is. For all of us, it is "home," the place where we spent the endless, dream-filled days of childhood, the place that still nourishes our secret, life-giving imagination, the place we love as we love bread, as we love the earliest image of maternal care, as we love life itself. In doing so, we love what has largely made us what we are. The difficulty is, as I have said, to love it in the right way.

I think the complexity of modern technological society makes the loving difficult for everybody, but here in America we have some quite special problems, which come not from our complex present but from our historical inheritance.

Some states emerge from some pre-existing tribal unity, some grow up within an already established culture, and some are forged by conquest, with victor and vanquished settling down to a new synthesis.

None of these routes was followed by America. Our people have come from every "tribal" group; they have largely had to create their own civilization as they went along to absorb a continent. They have never been conquered or had any sort of synthesis imposed upon them. Their community had, in fact, a unique beginning—it was from the moment of its birth a land "dedicated to a proposition"—that men are born equal, that government is a government of laws, not men, and exists to serve them, that "life, liberty, and the pursuit of happiness" are man's inalienable right.

But consider the consequences of this astonishing start. We are Americans because we belong to a certain ideal, visionary type of political and social order. We can't point back to a long, shared civilization. It is true, most of us have Europe and the West behind us. But not all—and, anyway, it is a concept of the West that we create rather than inherit. And no one is standing on our necks keeping us down and together.

The result is a community, surely, whose instinctive, rooted, taken-for-granted unity has to be all the more dynamic. If we are not dedicated to our fundamental propositions, then the natural cement in our society may not be enough to take the strain.

I would agree that there are substitutes. When a President said that "the business of America is business," he told us something about the degree to which a standard of living can do stand-in duty for a way of life. But the question, "What manner of people are we?" cannot be everlastingly answered in terms of two-car families or split-level homes.

America is much more than an economic or geographical fact. It is a political and moral fact—the first community in which men set out in principle to institutionalize freedom, responsible government, and human equality. And we love it for this audacity! How easy it is, contemplating this vision, to see in it—as Jefferson or Lincoln saw in it—"The last, best hope of man." To be a nation founded on an ideal in one sense makes our love of country a more vital force than any instinctive pieties of blood and soil.

But it also demands a more complex and discriminating love. Will the fabric hold if the ideal fades? If the effort to realize our citizens' birthright of freedom and equality is not constantly renewed, on what can we fall back? As a going concern, we can no doubt survive many shocks and shames. It was Adam Smith who remarked that "There is a great deal of ruin in every state." But can we survive, as a confident and growing community, if the essentially liberal thrust of our origins is forgotten, if we equate liberty with passive noninterference, if we exclude large minorities from our standards of equality, if income becomes a substitute for idealism, consumption for dedication, privilege for neighborly good will?

Well, you may say, "Why be so concerned; after all, one of the most forceful elements of our free society is precisely our discontent with our own shortcomings. Because we are free, because we are not the victims of censorship and manipulated news, because no dictatorial government imposes on us its version of the truth, we are at liberty to speak up against our shortcomings. We don't confuse silence with success. We know that 'between the idea and the reality . . . falls the shadow,' and we are determined to chase away that shadow in the uncompromising light of truth."

But *are we?* It is at this point that our patriotism, our love of country, has to be a discriminating, not a blind force. All too often, voices are raised, in the name of some superpatriotism, to still all criticism and to denounce honest divergencies as the next thing to treason. We have risen up from the pit of McCarthy's time, when honest men could lose their jobs for questioning whether there were 381 known Communists in the State Department. But the intolerant spirit which equates responsible criticisms with "selling the country short" or "being soft on communism" or "undermining the American way of life" is still abroad.

I can give you no comfort in suggesting there is an easy way around this type of criticism. Our position today *is* equivocal. We *are* in one sense a very conservative people—for no nation in history has had so much to conserve. Suggestions that everything is not perfect and that things must be changed *do* arouse the suspicion that something *I* cherish and *I* value may be modified. Even Aristotle complained that "everyone thinks chiefly of his own, hardly ever of the public interest." And our instinct is to preserve what we have, and then to give the instinct a colored wrapping of patriotism.

This is in part what the great Dr. Johnson meant when he said: "Patriotism is the last refuge of a scoundrel." To defend every abuse, every self-interest, every encrusted position of privilege in the name of love of country—when in fact it is only love of the status quo—that indeed is the lie in the soul to which any conservative society is prone.

We do not escape it—but with us, an extra edge of hypocrisy attaches to the confusion. For our basic reason for being a state is our attempt to build a dynamic and equal society of free men. Societies based on blood ties can perhaps safely confuse conservatism and patriotism. People with long backward-looking traditions can perhaps do so. Countries under the heel of dictators must do so. But if the world's first experiment in the open society uses patriotism as a cloak for inaction or reaction, then it will cease to be open—and then, as a social organism, it will lose its fundamental reason for existence.

Do not, therefore, regard the critics as questionable patriots. What were Washington and Jefferson and Adams but profound critics of the colonial status quo? Our society can stand a large dose of constructive criticism just because it is so solid and has so much to conserve. It is only if keen and lively minds constantly compare the ideal and the reality and see the shadow—the shadow of self-righteousness, of suburban sprawl, of racial discrimination, of interminable strikes—it is only then that the shadow can be dispelled and the unique brightness of our national experiment can be seen and loved.

The patriots are those who love America enough to wish to see her as a model to mankind. This is not treachery. This—as every parent, every teacher, every friend must know—is the truest and noblest affection. No patriots so defaced America as those who, in the name of Americanism, launched a witch-hunt which became a byword around the world. We have survived it. We shall survive John Birchism and all the rest of the superpatriots—but only at the price of perpetual and truly patriotic vigilance.

This discriminating and vigilant patriotism is all the more necessary because the world at large is one in which a simple, direct, inward-looking nationalism is not enough.

We face in Communist hostility and expansionism a formidable force, whether Mr. Khrushchev and Mr. Mao Tse-tung pull together or apart. They disagree so far only on whether capitalism should be peacefully or violently buried. They are both for the funeral. So long as this fundamental objective remains, we must regard the Communist Bloc as a whole with extreme wariness.

Even if the Communists are divided and confused everywhere—even if they have scored of late none of the victories in Africa, East Asia, and the Middle East our doomsayers predicted—still the Communist Bloc is aggressive and powerful and determined to grow more so. Taken individually, the European states are all outnumbered. Even America has only a margin of superiority over the tough, austere Soviet Union. Even if the Russian forces in Cuba are not going to conquer the Americas, still their presence in this hemisphere endangers the peace.

So we have sensibly concluded in the NATO Alliance that our separate sovereignties and nationalisms must be transcended in a common, overwhelming union of deterrent strength. Together our weight keeps the balance of power firmly down on our side, and it removes from each state the temptation of playing off one state against another and weakening the overall power in order to strengthen its own. This is the first reason for transcending narrow nationalism.

The second follows from our economic interdependence. The Atlantic world has taken 70 per cent of world trade and absorbed 70 per cent of its own investments for the last seventy years. We are an interwoven international economy. Bank rates in Britain affect investments in New York. Restrictions here affect carpet makers in Belgium. French farmers affect everybody. We can only avoid the mismanagement of this community if we pursue joint policies. My friend Jean Monnet has outlined the essential list: expansion of demand, currency stability, investment overseas, trade with the developing nations, reserves for world trade. Without joint policies here, we could easily slip back to the debacle of the period between the great civil wars of Europe of 1914 and 1939.

In this context, separate, divisive nationalism is not patriotism. It cannot be patriotism to enlarge a country's illusory sense of potency and influence, and reduce its security and economic viability. True patriotism demands that, in some essential categories, purely national solutions be left behind in the interest of the nation itself. It is this effort to transcend narrow nationalism that marked the supremely successful Marshall Plan. It marks the great enterprise of European unification—after so many tribal wars. It could mark the building of an Atlantic partnership as a secure nucleus of world order.

So our vision must be of the open society fulfilling itself in an open world. This we can love. This gives our country its universal validity. This is a patriotism which sets no limits to the capacity of our country to act as the organizing principle of wider and wider associations, until in some way not yet foreseen we can embrace the family of man.

And here our patriotism encounters its last ambiguity. There are misguided patriots who feel we pay too much attention to other nations, that we are somehow enfeebled by respecting world opinion. Well, "a decent respect for the opinions of mankind" was the very first order of business when the Republic was created; the Declaration of Independence was written, not to proclaim our separation, but to explain it and win other nations to our cause. The founding fathers did not think it was "soft" or "un-American" to respect the opinions of others, and today for a man to love his country truly, he must also know how to love mankind. The change springs from many causes. The two appalling wars of this century, culminating in the atom bomb, have taught all men the impossibility of war. Horace may have said: "It is sweet and fitting to die for one's country." But to be snuffed out in the one brief blast of an atomic explosion bears no relation to the courage and clarity of the old limited ideal.

Nor is this a simple shrinking from annihilation. It is something much deeper—a growing sense of our solidarity as a human species on a planet made one and vulnerable by our science and technology.

For, on this shrunken globe, men can no longer live as strangers. Men can war against each other as hostile neighbors, as we are determined not to do; or they can coexist in frigid isolation, as we are doing. But our prayer is that men everywhere will learn, finally, to live as brothers, to respect each other's differences, to heal each other's wounds, to promote each other's progress, and to benefit from each other's knowledge. If the evangelical virtue of charity can be translated into political terms, aren't these our goals?

Aristotle said that the end of politics must be the good of man. Man's greatest good and greatest present need is, then, to establish world peace. Without it, the democratic enterprise—one might even say the human enterprise—will be utterly, fatally doomed. War under modern conditions is bereft of even that dubious logic it may have had in the past. With the development of modern technology, "victory" in war has become a mockery. What victory —victory for what or for whom?

Perhaps younger people are especially sensitive to this growing conviction that nowadays all wars are civil wars and all killing is fratricide. The movement takes many forms—multilateral diplomacy through the United Nations, the search for world peace through world law, the universal desire for nuclear disarmament, the sense of sacrifice and service in the Peace Corps, the growing revulsion against Jim Crowism, the belief that dignity rests in man as such and that all must be treated as ends, not means.

But whatever its form, I believe that, far from being in any sense an enemy to patriotism, it is a new expression of the respect for life from which all true love springs. We can truly begin to perceive the meaning of our great propositions—of liberty and equality—if we see them as part of the patrimony of all men. We shall not love our corner of the planet less for loving the planet too, and resisting with all our skill and passion the dangers that would reduce it to smoldering ashes.

I can, therefore, wish no more for the profound patriotism of Americans than that they add to it a new dedication to the world-wide brotherhood of which they are a part and that, together with their love of America, there will grow a wider love which seeks to transform our earthly city, with all its races and peoples, all its creeds and aspirations, into Saint Augustine's "Heavenly city where truth reigns, love is the law, and whose extent is eternity."   —ADLAI E. STEVENSON

ASSIGNMENTS

I. A student in another country has seen a catalogue from your school. He is puzzled by the following words and would like them defined. Choose one of them for a definition of two or three paragraphs. You may bring in personal feeling and humor if you wish, but write a definition, not a personal essay and not a letter. Your purpose is to clarify something that is puzzling this person.

cafeteria	grade-point average
debate club	laboratory
dormitory	liberal arts
faculty	prerequisites
fraternity	probation

II. In your own words and without using a dictionary, give one-sentence definitions of any five of the terms listed under I. Let your definitions have the three parts described on page 151.

III. The following terms are often used inaccurately. Choose one of them and write two definitions: first, a definition that gives the loose and thoughtless notion of the word, and, second, a definition that is in your opinion a good one.

classical music	good taste
jazz	fashion
courage	modern painting
radical	modern poetry
conservative	luxury
liberal	respectability
progress	sentimental

IV. Using definition and illustration, write an essay making a distinction between two of the following terms.

education and training	evergreen and conifer
sincerity and tactlessness	relaxation and indulgence
courage and recklessness	freedom and license
conviction and prejudice	knowledge and wisdom
conservative and reactionary	humor and wit
instrument and tool	the pretty and the beautiful
engine and machine	flag-waving and patriotism
discipline and repression	suburbia and exurbia

V. Write two good-sized paragraphs defining the same term but expressing two conflicting attitudes toward it. *Capitalism, marriage, suburb, television,* and *campus politics* are examples of terms about which you may be able to express opposing views.

VI. Write two good-sized paragraphs defining the same term for two different purposes. In one, your purpose should be primarily to inform or explain and in the other to entertain or persuade. For example, you might take a term like *keeping up with the Joneses* and imagine yourself defining it for a foreigner or a child, and then take the same term and define it for people who already know its meaning. Some other possibilities (but the list could be endless) are *tranquilizers, education, sophistication, efficiency.*

E

Writing Summaries

A writer sometimes needs to summarize in comparatively brief form material which originally appeared at much greater length. The condensations of novels and articles in the numerous digest magazines are, perhaps unhappily, a familiar example. A secretary's report of a meeting and a student's notes on a lecture are other examples. Business, government, the armed services, and indeed all large organizations rely heavily on the summary, because the man who makes the decision often cannot study the whole material on which it must be based; he relies on summaries that have been prepared for him.

A summary is a relatively brief statement of what has been written or spoken. Usually the writer will have no reason to introduce his own ideas, and if he does introduce them, he will make perfectly clear the difference between his and those in the original. His primary—and often his only—role is to understand and compress. And most certainly he cannot compress until he has understood.

Though writing a summary thus requires no originality, the task is not easy. It makes the severest test of the ability to read (or listen) accurately. It is likely to show how often, either through inattention or through prejudice and other presuppositions, we distort what we read and in effect write our own ideas into the material while we read the words—but not the thought—of another person. It is likely to show what bad readers, part of the time at any rate, most of us are, even those of us who like to think of ourselves as well educated. Because, then, the preparation of a summary helps develop skill in reading as well as in writing, this assignment has a special importance.

Assuming that the writer of the summary has read the material accurately, his problem is selection. The original author has expounded his thought in ten thousand words, let us say. If he has done his work well, none of those words are surplus; all add to the richness and detail necessary for complete understanding; all are part of the substance. And yet the second writer must summarize those ten thousand in one thousand words, perhaps, or in one hundred, or even fifty. How does he do it?

He can do it only by the exercise of a judgment which distinguishes between the more important and the less important, between the central and the peripheral, between the essential and the incidental, between the principle and its illustration. If we think of "first things" as meaning "most important things," the adage "first things first" has a special value for the writer of a summary: he has no space for anything but first things. He must see what is the heart of the matter and spend no words on anything else.

When you write a summary, bear two points particularly in mind. First, write the summary in your own language, without quotation or paraphrase. Second, summarize not parts but the whole. Nothing would be more mistaken, for example, than to turn each paragraph into a sentence. Everything in some of the original paragraphs may be illustrative. The points they illustrate would appear in the summary; the illustrations, naturally, would not. The whole core of the thought may be lodged in a single paragraph or two. The well-made summary, therefore, might present this core almost as fully as did the original. In any event, the summary, like the original, should make us see the thought not in isolated parts but as a unified whole.

The six hundred words of this chapter up to this point may be summarized in fewer than fifty as follows:

A summary compresses the original statement without criticizing it. It requires accurate reading and sound judgment that distinguishes between the relative importance of different parts of the original. In language appropriate to a brief treatment, it translates the original thought not as fragmentary parts but as an organic whole.

The four thousand words of the United States Constitution without amendments may be summarized in about two hundred and fifty words as follows:

The Constitution establishes a national government of three branches: (1) the legislative, called the Congress, consisting of a Senate, in which each state has two members, and a House of Representatives, in which a state's membership is based on its population; (2) the executive, headed by a President elected by an electoral college, to which each state sends as many delegates as it has members of Congress; and (3) a federal court system headed by a Supreme Court.

All bills must be passed by a majority vote of each branch of Congress and signed by the President. If the President vetoes a bill, it becomes law only if passed by a two-thirds vote of both branches of Congress. In addition to its legislative functions, the Senate confirms major appointments and, by a two-thirds vote, ratifies treaties.

The Congress has power to declare war, to maintain an army and navy, to collect taxes, to maintain a currency, and to regulate commerce with foreign nations and among the states. The President administers the laws. He is commander-in-chief of the army and navy and he conducts foreign affairs. The federal courts interpret the laws and judge cases involving federal questions.

The Constitution may be amended by a two-thirds vote of both branches of Congress and a three-fourths vote of the states.

A *précis* is similar to a summary in compressing the thought of something that had been stated at some length. It differs from a summary in these respects: First, the précis follows the order and proportion of the material in the original, whereas the writer of the summary is free to change the order and proportion if he wishes to do so. Second, the précis follows the language of the original so far as this is possible in brief compass; the writer of the summary should not do so.

Third, the précis states only the thought of the original; the writer of the summary is free to interpret the material and comment on it if he makes clear that he is doing so.

The Gettysburg Address follows and then a précis of slightly less than half the number of words in the original:

Fourscore and seven years ago our fathers brought forth on this continent a new nation, conceived in liberty, and dedicated to the proposition that all men are created equal. Now we are engaged in a great civil war, testing whether that nation, or any nation so conceived and so dedicated, can long endure. We are met on a great battlefield of that war. We have come to dedicate a portion of that field as a final resting place for those who here gave their lives that that nation might live. It is altogether fitting and proper that we should do this. But, in a larger sense, we cannot dedicate—we cannot consecrate—we cannot hallow—this ground. The brave men, living and dead, who struggled here, have consecrated it, far above our poor power to add or detract. The world will little note, nor long remember, what we say here, but it can never forget what they did here. It is for us the living, rather, to be dedicated here to the unfinished work which they who fought here have thus far so nobly advanced. It is rather for us to be here dedicated to the great task remaining before us,— that from these honored dead we take increased devotion to that cause for which they gave the last full measure of devotion— that we here highly resolve that these dead shall not have died in vain—that this nation, under God, shall have a new birth of freedom—and that government of the people, by the people, for the people, shall not perish from the earth.

Eighty-seven years ago our fathers founded a nation whose ideals were liberty and equality. This war is a test of whether a nation conceived in accordance with ideals like these and dedicated to them can endure. We have come to dedicate this resting-place to those who gave their lives that the nation might live, and it is proper that we should do this, but in truth we cannot dedicate this ground because the brave men who fought here have already done so. Rather it is for us to be dedicated to the task remaining before us. It is for us to resolve that these men shall not have died in vain and that government of, by, and for the people shall not perish.

166

Because the summary and précis take their thought from someone else and because the summary (and to a less extent, the précis) requires that the wording be stripped to the barest essentials, you will not find them helpful in developing your own ideas and in giving you practice in illustrating and in other ways filling them out. In a world in which we must all do much reading, however, and in which many of us do much misreading, writing the summary or précis has great value. It may teach us, indeed, that we still have to learn how to read.

ASSIGNMENTS

I. Write a 100-word summary of Chapter 1 in this book.

II. Write a 500-word summary of an essay in a book of readings or a magazine.

III. Write a 500-word summary of a novel or a play.

IV. Write a 500-word précis of a short story.

V. Write a 150-word summary and a 500-word précis of Gilbert Highet's essay on Bach (pages 27–31).

F

Writing a Contrast or Comparison

If you came back from a trip to Wyoming, you would probably tell your friends who had not been there about the Teton Mountains or the Red Desert by a comparison (emphasizing the similarities) or a contrast (emphasizing the differences) with the kind of country they know. If a new instructor has characteristics that remind you of an old acquaintance, you will think of likenesses between them. If a house is being built that seems to be a radical departure from anything else in the neighborhood, you will consider the points of difference. If you are fortunate enough to have two jobs open to you this coming summer, you will compare their advantages and disadvantages before you decide which one to take. And you may already have found that comparisons and contrasts are often used in essay examinations in college.

You will never need to write a pure comparison (why compare two pieces of thread of the same length and from the same spool?) or a pure contrast (why contrast a bicycle with a pound of coffee?). You will combine comparison and contrast, though in different proportions, depending on your subject and purpose.

If two things are often associated, though perhaps superficially and even mistakenly, you should probably emphasize contrast; if the two things are not often associated, you should probably emphasize comparison. For example, because they are both in California, Los Angeles and San Francisco are likely to be associated, at least in the minds of people who live east of the Sierra Nevada. Though you should not ignore the similarities, you should probably emphasize the differences between the two cities—in history, in culture, in climate and vegetation. On the other hand, the same association does not exist between San Francisco and New York. Though not ignoring the differences, you should probably emphasize their similarities in their each possessing a great ocean port, in their varied cultural resources, and in their cosmopolitan atmosphere. In other words, you will probably emphasize comparison when the similarity between two things lies beneath the surface and contrast when it is the difference between them that is hidden.

The most interesting themes will be those that bring out unexpected points. The differences between a metropolis like Chicago and a small corn-belt town in central Illinois would furnish material for a clear but rather obvious contrast. In the eyes of those of its many residents who call Chicago an overgrown village, there must be similarities as well as differences, however. The writer who points them out will make both city and town more understandable, not so much by the contrast, which is obvious, as by the comparison, which is not. The difference between Stephen Dedalus in Joyce's novel *A Portrait of the Artist as a Young Man* and Antigone in the play by Sophocles are obvious enough. But perhaps there are similarities, too, in their intransigent idealism and other qualities. Perhaps the similarities, just because they are less obvious, are worth emphasizing instead of the differences. Conversely, the similarity, except in social position, between Tom Sawyer and Huckleberry Finn is clear enough. It is the difference in the minds of these two boys that is interesting and worth examining.

A good contrast shows us that things that look similar (*Look* and *Life,* for instance) have significant differences. A good comparison shows us that things that look different (such as a tree and a flower) have significant similarities. Together they help us see both the unity and the variety in all things.

Avoid laboring all the obvious points. You will not fascinate the reader by telling him that football is played by eleven men in contrast with the nine in baseball, but you may win his interest if you explain in some detail the very different role of teamwork in the two sports. Your reader's mind will not be enriched if you tell him that the novels of Scott and Stevenson are similar in their Scotch background, but he may learn something if you show him how Scott describes and Stevenson ignores the social and economic problems of the periods in which their stories of romantic adventure take place.

The temptation in writing a contrast or comparison is to treat one of the parts (New York, say) for several paragraphs and then, about half way through, turn to the other (San Francisco), bringing them together only in the last paragraph or two. This is *not* the way to do it. If you should wish to write about the comparative advantages or disadvantages of going to a large university or to a small college, you might divide your subject into three divisions: the comparative costs of going to each, the quality of the academic training each of them gives, and the social advantages of one compared with the other. Do *not* analyze the large university in each of these three divisions and then turn to the small college and take the divisions up again. In a paragraph or whatever you need, discuss university and college *together* for cost, and then move on to your next division, again discussing university and college *together*. If you will look at the contrast between a plant and an animal which follows, you will notice that the authors do not first describe a plant and then an animal. The two objects are looked at simultaneously. This is what you should do in this assignment—and also for examination questions which involve contrast or comparison.

A CONTRAST

In this passage, the authors, wishing to make clear the organization of a plant, contrast its characteristics with those of an animal.

Naturally, the organization of a plant is very different from that of an animal—a mouse, let us say. A mouse has nerves and sense-organs and muscles and a busy little brain, but what should a plant want with these things? It has no food to seek, and that is the chief thing that an animal does with its brain. Indeed, if a plant could walk about, it would have to tear up its roots at every step! It sits still and spreads its leaves towards the light, and its roots into the soil. It lacks the complicated digestive apparatus of a mouse, for the mouse consumes energy-yielding fuels that have to be adjusted before they can be fitted into his tiny body. But the plant has no need to consume fuels; it contents itself with the elementary molecules that it finds in the air and soil. It does not rush about from place to place and has no muscles that toil strenuously; therefore it has no need of a heart-pump and violently pulsing blood; the slow, steady ooze of sap, upwards and downwards along the stem, suffices to keep its parts in communication with each other, and is quick enough for its slow, dignified chemical interchanges. Nevertheless, it should not be thought that the organization of a plant is simple. It has a very great variety of specialized tissues, struts and girders, pipes, living laboratories, storehouses of various kinds, but they are planned and specialized altogether differently from the tissues of a mouse.

—H. G. WELLS, JULIAN HUXLEY, AND G. P. WELLS

A COMPARISON

In the following paragraph, the author makes his point by comparing the difficulties of our day and the difficulties of other periods in history.

At the present moment a discussion is raging as to the future of civilization in the novel circumstances of rapid scientific and technological advance. The evils of the future have been diagnosed in various ways, the loss of religious faith, the malignant use of material power, the degradation attending a differential birth rate favouring the lower types of humanity, the suppression of aesthetic creativeness. Without doubt, these are all evils, dangerous and threatening. But they are not new. From the dawn of history, mankind has always been losing its religious faith, has always suffered from the malignant use of material power, has always suffered from the infertility of its best intellectual types, has always witnessed the periodical decadence of art. In the reign of the Egyptian king, Tutankhamen, there was raging a desperate religious struggle between Modernists and Fundamentalists; the cave pictures exhibit a phase of delicate aesthetic

171

achievement as superseded by a period of comparative vulgarity; the religious leaders, the great thinkers, the great poets and authors, the whole clerical caste in the Middle Ages, have been notably infertile; finally, if we attend to what actually has happened in the past, and disregard romantic visions of democracies, aristocracies, kings, generals, armies, and merchants, material power has generally been wielded with blindness, obstinacy and selfishness, often with brutal malignancy. And yet, mankind has progressed. Even if you take a tiny oasis of peculiar excellence, the type of modern man who would have most chance of happiness in ancient Greece at its best period is probably (as now) an average professional heavy-weight boxer, and not an average Greek scholar from Oxford or Germany. Indeed, the main use of the Oxford scholar would have been his capability of writing an ode in glorification of the boxer. Nothing does more harm in unnerving men for their duties in the present than the attention devoted to the points of excellence in the past as compared with the average failure of the present day.

—ALFRED NORTH WHITEHEAD

The passage that follows is an excerpt from an essay by Matthew Arnold in which he examines two concepts of the good life. Notice how the writer makes each of them clearer by contrasting it with the other.

. . . Let me go back for a moment to Bishop Wilson, who says: "First, never go against the best light you have; secondly, take care that your light be not darkness." We [the people of Great Britain at the time Arnold wrote, a century ago] show, as a nation, laudable energy and persistence in walking according to the best light we have, but are not quite careful enough, perhaps, to see that our light be not darkness. This is only another version of the old story that energy is our strong point and favourable characteristic, rather than intelligence. But we may give to this idea a more general form still, in which it will have a yet larger range of application. We may regard this energy driving at practice, this paramount sense of the obligation of duty, self-control, and work, this earnestness in going manfully with the best light we have, as one force. And we may regard the intelligence driving at those ideas which are, after all, the basis of right practice, the ardent sense for all the new and changing combinations of them which man's development brings with it, the indomitable impulse to know and adjust them perfectly, as another force. And these two forces we may regard as in some sense rivals,—rivals not by the necessity of their own nature, but as exhibited in man and his history—and rivals dividing the empire of the world between them. And to give these forces names from the two races of men who have supplied the most signal and splendid manifestations of them, we may call them respectively the forces of Hebraism and Hellenism. Hebraism and Hellenism—between these two points of influence moves our world. At one time it feels more powerfully the attraction of one of them, at another time of the other; and it ought to be, though it never is, evenly and happily balanced between them.

The final aim of both Hellenism and Hebraism, as of all great spiritual disciplines, is no doubt the same: man's perfection or salvation. The very language which they both of them use in schooling us to reach this aim is often identical. Even when their language indicates by variation—sometimes a broad variation, often a but slight and subtle variation—the different courses of thought which are uppermost in each discipline, even then the unity of the final end and aim is still apparent. To employ the actual words of that discipline with which we ourselves are all of us most familiar, and the words of which, therefore, come most home to us, that final end and aim is "that we might be partakers of the divine nature." These are the words of a Hebrew apostle, but of Hellenism and Hebraism alike this is, I say, the aim. . . .

Still, they pursue this aim by very different courses. The uppermost idea with Hellenism is to see things as they really are; the uppermost idea with Hebraism is conduct and obedience. Nothing can do away with this ineffaceable difference. The Greek quarrel with the body and its desires is that they hinder right thinking; the Hebrew quarrel with them is that they hinder right acting. "He that keepeth the law, happy is he"; "Blessed is the man that feareth the Eternal, that delighteth greatly in his commandments"—that is the Hebrew notion of felicity; and, pursued with passion and tenacity, this notion would not let the Hebrew rest till, as is well known, he had at last got out of the law a network of prescriptions to enwrap his whole life, to govern every moment of it, every impulse, every action. The Greek notion of felicity, on the other hand, is perfectly conveyed in these words of a great French moralist: "C'est le bonheur des hommes,"—

when? when they abhor that which is evil?—no; when they exercise themselves in the law of the Lord day and night?—no; when they die daily?—no; when they walk about the New Jerusalem with palms in their hands?—no; but when they think aright, when their thought hits: "quand ils pensent juste." At the bottom of both the Greek and the Hebrew notion is the desire, native in man, for reason and the will of God, the feeling after the universal order—in a word, the love of God. But, while Hebraism seizes upon certain plain, capital intimations of the universal order, and rivets itself, one may say, with unequalled grandeur of earnestness and intensity on the study and observance of them, the bent of Hellenism is to follow, with flexible activity, the whole play of the universal order, to be apprehensive of missing any part of it, of sacrificing one part to another, to slip away from resting on this or that intimation of it, however capital. An unclouded clearness of mind, an unimpeded play of thought, is what this bent drives at. The governing idea of Hellenism is *spontaneity of consciousness;* that of Hebraism, *strictness of conscience.* . . .   —MATTHEW ARNOLD

ASSIGNMENTS

I. Compare or contrast two occupations. Use one of the following or another of your choice:

1. Being a waiter and being a clerk
2. Farming and ranching
3. Bookkeeping and accounting
4. Medicine and dentistry
5. Being a stenographer and being a secretary

II. Contrast your expectations before an event with reality. The following are suggested subjects:

1. Reaching maturity
2. Falling in love
3. A teacher or course
4. A trip or holiday
5. An interview with the dean or someone else in authority

III. Compare or contrast the two parts in one of the following pairs in order to show the essential quality of each member of the pair:

1. Two composers (for example, Haydn and Mozart)
2. Two authors (for example, Golding and Salinger)
3. Two works of art (for example, Beethoven's third and fifth symphonies)
4. Two newspapers or two somewhat similar magazines
5. Two somewhat similar television programs

IV. By comparing or contrasting two games or sports such as the following, show the qualities of mind or body they require and the kind of interest they appeal to. Do not compare rules except as they may show the qualities of each game.

1. Checkers and chess
2. Baseball and football (or hockey or cricket)
3. Two card games
4. Billiards and pool
5. Hunting and fishing

V. Contrast two products or services which are in competition with each other and show which of them, in your judgment, is superior. Here are some suggestions:

1. Ford and Chevrolet (or an American car and a foreign car)
2. Travel by air and by train (or by bus)
3. RCA and Philco television
4. Canned and frozen foods
5. Automatic and hand shifting

VI. Write a theme comparing or contrasting two geographical areas such as the following:

1. Dallas and Fort Worth
2. St. Louis and Kansas City
3. Toronto and Montreal
4. North Dakota and South Dakota
5. Glacier Park and Yellowstone
6. The north woods of Maine and Wisconsin
7. The corn belt and the wheat belt
8. My home town and a neighboring town
9. The neighborhood I live in and another in my town
10. A summer in the mountains and a summer on the shore

Note: Assignment IV on page 161 may also be used for assignments in contrast and comparison.

G

Writing an Analysis

Suppose a reporter for the college paper wishes to write an article on the prospects of the school's baseball team. He will examine the pitching, the fielding, the hitting, the reserve strength, and whatever else he considers significant. In other words, he will make an analysis. He will take a whole subject (the baseball team) and divide it into its important parts so that they can be examined separately. That is what an analysis is: the separating of a whole into the parts that compose it. These parts may be physical—the various parts of the nervous system of the body, for example—or they may be conceptual—for example, the various motives that prompted you to go on to college.

Most of the writing you do involves some analysis. It would be difficult or impossible to write a contrast or comparison, for example, without making an analysis too, and it is unlikely that a definition would be pure definition, with no analysis. Writing a theme of analysis, therefore, may not be very different from writing other themes, except that this time you consciously go about separating a whole into the parts that compose it.

Not all subjects are so easy to analyze as the strength or weakness of the baseball team. It takes no remarkable insight to see that pitching is one element in baseball and hitting another. But if you are analyzing the national economy in order to determine the outlook for employment in an industry or on the farm, you may need to make a trip to the library. You will certainly need to do some careful thinking about the subject.

See that the parts of your analysis are consistent with one another. Find the proper basis for division of the subject and then follow it consistently. Preparing a theme on the qualities of a good teacher, you might begin by deciding on the following as the main parts of your subject: a good teacher must be intelligent and well informed; he must be objective and fair; he must be friendly; and he must be given the most modern equipment. As you think the subject over, you will realize that the fourth point is not a quality at all; it is inconsistent with the first three and must be dropped.

Similarly, an agronomist might classify the soils of this country according to the moisture they receive. Classifications like *arid* or *semiarid* or *subhumid* would be consistent with one another. Or he might approach them quite differently and classify the soils as forest or grassland in their formation. *Coniferous forest* would be consistent with this second classification but not with the one based on moisture, because *coniferous forest* would be a division of *forest soil.*

Make clear exactly what your subject is. If you are writing on part of a larger subject, let the reader know just what you are including and what you are leaving out. For example, if you are writing about advertising work on a country weekly, show that you are considering only this aspect of country newspapers. If you are analyzing the economic forces that lead to international conflict, be sure you understand—and your reader understands—that you are not considering psychological and other noneconomic forces.

Do not overlook some essential element of your subject. No one would write about a baseball team and ignore its pitching, or about a symphony orchestra and ignore its violin section, but with more complex subjects the writer may fall into just such an error. To write about the value of extracurricular activities without discussing the experience they give in working with other people would be like writing about the advantages of airplane travel and neglecting to say anything about speed.

Do not overdevelop some parts of the analysis at the expense of others that are equally or more important. To return to our conveniently simple and transparent example: to give four or five paragraphs to pitching and fielding and a scant sentence or so to hitting would make a badly balanced article on the prospects of the baseball team. On the other hand, if the writer knew enough he might very well limit his analysis to the defensive strength of the team (its pitching and field-ing) and perhaps write another analysis of its offensive strength. Consciously and clearly limiting the subject is something entirely different from carelessly or ignorantly distorting it.

Notice the informal but effective analysis in the student theme "Adjustment to College," which follows. The subject of adjustment is divided into three kinds of adjustment: (1) in social life; (2) in the small problems of daily living; (3) in academic work. Each of these is further divided; work, for instance, is divided into two related but distinct parts: (a) studying and (b) thinking. Underlying this threefold di-vision but never confusing it is another, the twofold division between high school and college.

The analysis, then, is fairly complex. And yet the writing is light and pleasing to read. The author sees her subject so clearly that she can write an analysis that does not read like an expanded outline. The theme illustrates the most impor-tant point to remember in this assignment: that you should show the parts in clear and natural relation to one another and to the whole.

Adjustment to College

It is a sudden change, this change from being a child in June to an adult in September. I suppose I must have done a lot of growing—or "maturing"—during those three months of summer that slipped away so quickly. Certainly the university assumes that I have.

I was not really a child last June, perhaps, but most of the time my parents and teachers combined to treat me like one. My teachers told me what to think; the school office told me what to do; Mother saw that I had orange juice and green, leafy vege-tables; and Father slipped me a five-dollar bill when I needed one. At times I felt like quite a young lady, but no one treated me like one. I was watched. I was coddled. I was protected.

Now it is scarcely three months later and everything is different. I am not watched, not coddled, not protected.

Moving from high school to university means so many changes, so many kinds of adjustment, so many new freedoms and responsibilities. And all within three months!

There is the change involving associations with other girls and with men. I don't think I realized it at the time, but in high school I had very little choice in selecting my friends. I moved within a circle, the circle made by class, church, and neighborhood. Mother never told me that Jane must be my best friend, but every circumstance worked to make my best friend a girl like Jane and not very different from me. Father never told me that Bob rather than Jerry should take me to the prom, but Bob and Jerry were pretty much alike except that Bob was tall and played basketball and Jerry was shorter and played football.

Here it is different. A hundred girls live in my dormitory, and they come from as far away as New Mexico. Some of them are the daughters of wealthy men, but the girl in the room next to mine is the daughter of a truck driver and she must earn every dollar her education costs her. And I've certainly found out that the world consists of more than Episcopalians and Presbyterians. So there is no circle, or if there is one, it is very large indeed. For this university, I have already discovered, is not a tight little island like our high school but a big and varied world.

There is change involving daily living, even in such things as what to eat and what to wear. If in the cafeteria I pass up the green, leafy vegetables there is no mother to frown. If I spend my money too fast, there is no father in the next room to scold me—and slip me a five-dollar bill.

But the biggest change involves studying and thinking. In high school I was told when to study and what. Someone was always at my elbow to give me a steer. In the university I am on my own. If I think I can learn history by rolling over in bed and missing the lecture, the university would not collapse in fury as the high school almost did. It would just—so I understand— flunk me.

More than a change in studying is involved, however. There is a change in thinking too. In high school we were always told to think for ourselves, but it often seemed we had to think for ourselves the way the teachers already thought. In the university I find the instructors aren't so sure they know all the answers.

I have already heard the question "Well, what do *you* think?" asked a dozen times. I believe university teachers are wise enough to remember that if it took them perhaps forty years to form the right opinions, we students should not be expected to do so in eighteen years.

So I am not told whom to like; I can skip the little circle and look around. I am not told what to eat; I can skip the cabbage and take more potatoes. I am not told when to study; I can skip the class almost as easily as I skip the cabbage. And I am not told what to think; I can't skip the Stevenson essay in English class, but I don't have to like it especially just because the instructor does.

I like this freedom, this necessity to make an adjustment. Being an adult has come rather suddenly, but I am enjoying it.

—STUDENT THEME BY SUSAN ANDREWS

In the following analysis, the writer takes a whole (the idea of moral decay in the period between World War I and World War II) and examines some of its causes and manifestations. (The paragraph may also be studied as an example of illustration.)

If the Ku Klux Klan in America, or the Croix de Feu in France, or Mosley's handful of Fascists in Britain, used violence, not everybody was outraged. The ravings of Huey Long or Father Coughlin were not without appeal. Skill in propaganda was admired, whether it was national advertising to frighten or cajole the public into buying, or the obscene ravings of a political demagogue. There was a cynicism about the uses of language that boded ill for representative government and its complete dependence on reason and the word. It was an era of double-talk. Arguments were more and more examined, not for their validity, but for the motive behind them and the identity of the person who must have paid to have them spread. Communication was degenerating into ventriloquism, supported by the mass media of radio and movie screen. The common processes of self-government were thought of primarily, if not exclusively, in terms of "salesmanship." Above all, "abstractions" like justice, right, wrong, had an increasingly hollow ring. Society was increasingly anti-intellectual, and increasingly victimized by mountebanks. The moral issues which Wilson had called on his generation to face now sounded unconvincing. Americans found it difficult to believe that Mussolini's brutal Fascism could be fundamentally wrong, if it was really true that at last in Italy "the trains ran on time." The French upper classes read Mussolini's writings—which really were more intelligible than Hitler's—with deep interest. Men felt a growing sense of relief that what their fathers called "morals" were really "mores" and could be studied disinterestedly in sociology, anthropology, and the other "social sciences," sciences that were descriptive and not properly normative at all, sciences that dealt with shifting "values." T. S. Eliot's poem *The Wasteland* was not an inaccurate picture of Christendom during the Long Armistice. In that Wasteland there was no power of the human spirit strong enough to stop Japan from seizing Manchuria, or Italy from raping Ethiopia, or Hitler from making one "last territorial demand" after another. There were a dislike of principles or ideas, a fascination with whatever seemed to succeed, a great deal of boredom, sensation-mongering, and fatalism. Hitler, who was neither genius nor statesman, was temperamentally enough like a good medium in a trance to sense the vacuum in the Wasteland. —STRINGFELLOW BARR

ASSIGNMENTS

I. Write a theme on one of the following subjects or on a similar subject.

1. The snob appeal in advertising
2. The qualities of a good teacher
3. The composition of an orchestra
4. The reasons for studying a foreign language
5. I prefer Iowa
6. Why restaurant meals are expensive
7. The cost of going to college
8. The structure of a corporation (or other business firm)
9. Why men fear marriage
10. Causes of accidents
11. Why _____ was not elected.
12. How automobile driving reveals character
13. Why the team lost so many games
14. Student feeling about convocations
15. Why our local newspaper leaves more than a little to be desired

II. Choose a candidate for political office whom you do not favor and analyze the appeal he makes to voters. What fears and hopes does he appeal to? Or to what economic, racial, and religious groups?

III. Analyze an argument about foreign policy, educational philosophy, or some other important subject. Choose an argument which (1) expresses a conclusion you yourself agree with, and (2) rests on one or more logical fallacies. Expose the shoddiness of the argument. (Remember that it is comparatively easy to see the fallacies on the other side but it is difficult, and at least as important, to see those on our side.)

IV. In about five hundred words, analyze your feelings, and the reasons for them, on one of these occasions:

1. When I failed in a crisis
2. When I was hired (or fired)
3. When I heard some very good (or very bad) news
4. When I faced up to the fact that I wasn't going to be _____ (a major league ballplayer, Broadway actress, President of the United States, or something else)
5. When I tried to rationalize my bad behavior

H

Writing a Theme of Persuasion

In analysis, the purpose is to secure the reader's understanding of a subject; in persuasion, the purpose is to win his support. Analysis tries to make the reader see; persuasion tries to make him believe.

In reality, of course, the two types of writing are closely related. Often they are found together. An intelligent action must be based on understanding, and understanding requires some kind of analysis. Certainly a writer cannot persuade if his analysis insults his reader's intelligence.

Just as persuasion is based on analysis, so analysis leads to persuasion. With some subjects—the analysis in the last chapter of the baseball team's prospects will serve as example—the analysis may simply satisfy curiosity, but with many subjects analysis will suggest some kind of action. For instance, no matter how objective it might be, an examination of the prospects for industrial prosperity would probably suggest action by government, labor, or management that the writer thought his analysis showed the need for.

The chief problem in writing effective persuasion is to convince the reader that the analysis is sound. If the reader finds confusion and ignorance where he is looking for logic and knowledge, the writing will backfire; instead of persuading those who disagree, it may even cause those who already agree to waver.

The best way to persuade the reader of the soundness of an analysis and the need to act on it in a certain way is to present an honest, clear argument of a kind that you yourself would respect. Let us look at the steps you should take in doing this.

First, select a subject that you know something about and believe in. You cannot expect to win conviction if you do not have it yourself. You might write an excellent theme, to be sure, on a subject about which you were puzzled or undecided, but not a theme of persuasion.

Second, formulate your proposition—for instance, that your school needs a new dormitory. If possible, formulate the proposition even more pointedly than this—that your school needs a new dormitory more urgently than it needs the proposed stadium.

Third, study the whole subject carefully. Talk to others or read about it. Find out what the facts are and remember that even a minor factual error will tend to discredit the whole argument.

Fourth, examine points of view and arguments that are opposed to yours. If you do not examine them, you are likely to write beside the point and fail to persuade simply because you have not dealt with the right questions. Suppose, for example, your argument for a new dormitory is that living and sleeping seven days and nights a week under decent conditions instead of in a rooming house populated by termites is more important than having a team that people watch two hours a week a few times in the fall. Your argument, though true, may be insufficient to persuade those who worry about new taxes. Your task, then, is to persuade them if you can that a dormitory would pay for itself—would be, as the financiers say, self-liquidating.

Fifth, decide on the main lines of your argument and organize the evidence which supports your position. Do you need to define any of your terms? Are you avoiding fallacies in logic? Have you arranged your points in the most convincing order?

Sixth, because you want to win the respect of your reader, avoid name-calling, which is the resort of the desperate and unscrupulous; avoid prejudice, which will keep you from doing straight thinking; avoid trying to trick the reader. If you think someone else's idea dangerously mistaken, you will be more persuasive if you explain why it is mistaken and why it is dangerous than if you try the shortcut of applying ugly names to the man who holds it. Above all, try to remember that only one of your two aims is to try to persuade. The other is to find and share the truth.

One final point: the fact that you should avoid name-calling and other forms of prejudice does not mean that you must write without feeling. If you believe in something strongly, your belief will have an emotional as well as an intellectual quality which will get into your words and enrich them. The great examples of persuasion—Lincoln's Cooper Union address, for instance—were written by men who not only understood their subjects but felt strongly about them too.

The following student essay is an example of persuasion on a familiar subject.

School Spirit

Of course we need more school spirit around this place. Doesn't everyone say so?

But what do we mean by school spirit? Do we only mean going out on Saturday afternoons and cheering ourselves hoarse while we watch our simon-pure amateurs get trounced again by the subsidized mercenaries from out of state? Does school spirit mean nothing but pride in a football team that numbers less than one percent of the student body?

Don't we have some other things to cheer for? Maybe school spirit should get into the classroom and the library and the Union as well as the stadium. Maybe we should start cheering not with noise but with quiet appreciation for some of the things we have here.

Our faculty is well-trained and conscientious. It knows more than we know—usually very much more. It is eager to pass its knowledge on to us.

Our student body is all right too. It doesn't seem to contain an average quota of football players, but it has plenty of leaders for the business and professional world of tomorrow. At least the record shows the high intellectual calibre of our students in the past, and there is no reason to think the calibre is declining now. With over half of this year's freshman class from the top quintile of their graduating classes in high school, we don't seem to be throwing the gates open to very many morons yet.

Finally, what about our maligned co-eds? Is it really true that the pretty girls go to State and the others come here? Or is it just a wise-crack, beginning to wear out? Open your eyes and stop dreaming about that grass on the other side of the street.

So let's stop thinking of school spirit as nothing more than cheering for the team. Let's not get complacent about how good we are, but let's not be apologetic either. Even our severest critics would have to admit we are better in some things than we are in football. —STUDENT THEME BY DAVID ROYCE

In the two following excerpts, notice the emotional force of the writing, as well as the thoughtful and logical appeal they make to the mind.

Some have suggested that the United States would be safe if it were to keep ahead of other countries in the development and production of atomic weapons. It is not certain that this country could succeed in this attempt over any great length of time and certainly not for all time, for others will surely come abreast of us—and perhaps in less time than we think. But let us look more closely at the suggestion. Supposing that the United States remains ahead of other countries in number or effectiveness of bombs, what good does it do us? Do we plan to attack other countries at a favorable moment? Following such an attack, it would be necessary to occupy the countries with our armies in order to prevent the manufacture of bombs in the future. Some 7 per cent of the world's population would have to keep its feet on the necks of the rest of the world's peoples. It does not seem likely that we would choose this role voluntarily. . . .

Later, when other countries secure enough atomic bombs to destroy the cities and other appropriate targets of this country, we would be in a position to destroy their cities, and it would do us no good whatever to have bombs enough to destroy those targets more than once. Extra bombs would be useless once sufficient numbers were available to destroy all large military targets of any possible enemy. If our hypothetical enemy had sufficient bombs to destroy our military targets, in what way could we keep ahead of this enemy? Atomic bombs are different. Enough can be made to destroy completely all possible targets and kill the inhabitants of all major cities of any country. It is then impossible to destroy them twice or to kill people twice. Eventually, therefore, we cannot hope to keep ahead of other countries in an atomic war. —HAROLD C. UREY

ON HUNTING

One late autumn day a friend of mine was driving slowly through a little dirt backroad, possessing his soul in peace and having a look at the golden autumnal glory of things. There were numbers of fat and frisky squirrels to be watched and enjoyed, wood-smoke and apples to be smelled, and the tonic *beadle-beadle!* of blue jays to be heard ringing through the November oak woods. A sweet day, this; and my old friend, having that disposition to appreciate the earth and be glad for it—which is in theory the disposition of us all—was of a mind to take the never-returning splendor to his heart. What he took, instead, was a rifle bullet. It came from nowhere in particular—*crack! crump!*—through the car window. It ended his day, and days.

He had neglected, being a meditative fellow notoriously cut off from wholesome and red-blooded concerns, to notice that the hunting season was under way. He had not realized that that time was here when in rural regions safety is to be secured only by huddling in the cellar, and when a reasonably decent-minded philosopher, having sought that sanctuary, may test his self-control by pondering upon what is going on outdoors and then seeing whether he can retain his supper.

A less abstracted man, to be sure, could scarcely have failed to notice the evidences of the fall festival outdoors. The indications, after all, are abundant. There is the sudden increase, for instance, in stray cattle. Their puzzled wanderings around the highways let us know of the cutting of stock-fences by tool-bearing huntsmen who have realized it is much easier to sever a fence than to break it down by climbing over it or to bash it in, say, by carrying a battering ram. Or again, there are the characteristic vestigial posters to be seen on trees. It is not ordinarily possible to read their lettering, for this has usually been obscured or obliterated by a blast of shot; but even the moderately alert and knowledgeable of us are aware of what such a poster *has* said. It has said POSTED; and it has been tacked to its tree, with painstaking labor, by some simple-hearted citizen in anticipation of the hunting season. The obliteration of the lettering by shell-fire lets us know that that season, in all its target-loving and pranksome exuberance, has in fact begun. Or, again and yet again, what averagely alert observer can miss the emptied whiskey bottles, strewn colorfully along the forest-paths where ordinarily are found only the cleft imprints of the hoofs of deer? Or who, not already deaf, can fail to hear the bangs of firing, the whistlings of trajectory, that in this season become the music of Arcady? What one of us, scanning the newspaper, can miss the spate of annual headlines: HUNTER ACCIDENTALLY KILLS PAL: THOUGHT HE WAS PORCUPINE?

That friend of mine who is gone, I am afraid, failed in alertness. In any case, perhaps, he was not a man fulfilling the stern norm we call "adjustment to cultural environment." He had a great love of animals and found a refreshment in watching them alive, in the exercise of their power; and he had never got it through his head, somehow, that it is a manlier thing and more character-building to enjoy their deaths. His old car, even before the bullet smashed through it, was a seedy sort of affair. At the end of its hood there was only a radiator cap. Never, in a moment of red-blooded enjoyment of the outdoors, had he thought to hack off the ringed tail of a killed raccoon or even the plumy little tail of a slaughtered squirrel and tie it there in token of his strength. He was a kind of namby-pamby man, I guess. Perhaps it is as well that he has left.

It can be said, of course, that not all hunters, not in fact more than a tiny minority, engage in cutting fences, littering the clean green woods with whiskey bottles, peppering away at POSTED signs, or firing their deadly weapons across roads. It can be said that no profession or pastime ought to be judged by what oafs may infest it. Do we condemn medicine because, alas, there are some M. D.'s glad and eager to perform an eight-dollar abortion in an alley? When we speak of that noble calling, the law, what we have in mind is Oliver Wendell Holmes, not the shyster pattering after the ambulance.

It can be said that most hunters observe regulations. It can be argued that, but for hunting, some kinds of animals might become overnumerous. It can be said that a hunter is helping rid the land of many creatures which are only vermin—such ones as foxes, crows, woodchucks and the like—and that sportsmen, by the fees they pay for licenses and the contributions they make to sportsmen's organizations, help in a wildlife restoration that matches or overmatches their wildlife reduction. Hunting, it can be said, is after all a thing long respected and of ancient lineage, going right back to the dawn-days of humanity and an instinct so primary as to stand as sacred. It can be held that a hunter takes his joy, not, as sentimentalists might suppose, from spilling blood, ending life, and asserting power by that means, but rather from experiences to which any killing is merely incidental: the sight and scent and relished excellence of the outdoors, the chance to watch beasts and birds at close range, the wholesome charm of exercise and recreation and camaraderie. It can be pointed out that an esteem for hunting is as general as an esteem for base-ball, for the flag, for the cross, and for mother.

All these things can be said. *Can* be said? They have been said hundreds, thousands, probably millions of times. The pages of hunting magazines burst with them, in an over-and-over repeti-tion so continuous and strenuous that it needs less than Shake-spearian insight to be struck by the muchness of the protesting.

While they can be said, they can also be questioned, by an oc-casional abnormal logician. *Is* hunting for sport a pastime from primitive times? Or is it rather the fact, as some scholarly anthro-pology may suggest, that primitive men went hunting for the stern and sole purpose of getting something to put in their bellies, and that when they did bring down a bear or bison they were apt to be so overcome by the enormity of their assault upon the animal brotherhood that they hastened to perform rites of sad apology to the victim and yet more poignant rites of propitiation to the Great Power Who Is Life-giver of All?

Are foxes vermin? There are several ecological scientists who have examined briefly into the matter—say for twenty or thirty years—and think not. *Is* it the love of the glory of outdoors, and not of the killing, that sends the huntsman forth? If it is, why in the holy name of sanity does he burden himself with that long, heavy, unnecessary object that has a butt at one end and is likely, if he isn't careful, to go *bang*? It's just the fun of exercising the *skill* of shooting, is it? Dr. Roy Abbott, a biologist, has remarked that no living bird or beast calls forth this skill more prettily than does a beer can tossed in the air.

At this level, in these terms, a dust-up over hunting can of course go on forever. It is the function of the raised dust to ob-scure the matter centrally at issue. That issue is this:

Is the sport of hunting, simply as such, a man-worthy thing or isn't it? Let it be supposed that all hunters obey all regulations.

Let it be supposed that no whiskey bottle is dropped to pollute any glen or dingle, no fence is broken, no fawn is shot, no forest is set afire, no robins are massacred in mistake for pheasants and no deer-hunters in mistake for porcupines (or possibly chipmunks), and no meditative philosopher, out to enjoy the loveliness of autumn, is ever plugged through the pericardium. The question persists: Is it a spectacle of manhood (which is to say of our distinctive humanness), when on a bracing morning we look out upon the autumn, draw an exhilarating breath, and cry "What a glorious day! How golden the light of the sun, how merry the caperings of creatures; *Gloria in excelsis Deo!* I will go out and kill something"?

We're a long, long way from Eden, our species. The ideal man that we once were, in the Christian view, or the ideal man, in any view, that it is supposed to be our dedicated dream to become . . . that ideal is very far, very difficult, and needs our utmost trying. Do we draw the closer to it when for ten or eleven months of the year we pay no attention at all to the garden of the creation into which we have been invited, and when for the remaining month or two we are concerned to draw what blood we can, to put a stop to what fellow-lives we can, and to make a smear of blood and guts where there had been living squirrels, living grouse, living deer enjoying the sometime sanctuary of the green places? *Manly?* It doesn't take a man to kill something. Any animal can do that. What it takes a *man* to do—and he is the only creature on all the earth that can do it—is to feel pity and show mercy, to feel gratitude for aliveness and give the thanks of restraint, to be so very strong, in his manhood, that he can be gentle.

Well?

If we put aside all our fear of being thought sissies, if we disregard the virile chest-thwackings of those weak and unfulfilled ones who must go killing because only in a bloody gunmanship can they assert and reassure themselves, if we just drop all the long, long pretence, and look with a grave candor into the heart of us . . . do we hesitate over an answer? We don't, I think.

In the history of our kind, we have abandoned a series of ugly pretendings. We used to pretend we thought it was perfectly all right to chop off a child's hand for petty theft. We went about slapping each other heartily on the back and assuring each other that of course it was. We used to join together in a genial general howl at the amphitheatre, sharing the wholesome entertainment of watching lions disembowel an old lady. *Corking* sport! Who but a dangerous radical or a sickly mother's-boy could deny it? We used to pretend it was fun watching the hangings, and we smothered successfully for ages any small inner voice whispering to us that perhaps really, deep down inside, it did make us feel sort of sick and funny and ashamed when the four flogged horses dashed off in four directions and ripped apart the living body of a man being drawn and quartered.

There remains the pretending about hunting to be abandoned. The time will come when it will be. ("What! Abandon the splendid manly practice of pitting bears against dogs in an arena as Sabbath diversion? Why, such a time will *never* come, Sir!") The end of hunting, of course, won't come soon. Neither did the end of bear-baiting, nor of boiling in oil, nor of slavery. Right up to our fathers' day we were shooting robins and bobolinks and hanging them up in strings in the market-place at ten cents a string. Still, the time will come. If it doesn't, it will be for only one reason. It has at last become possible for us—with an atom bomb in our one hand, a hydrogen bomb in our other—to delay a little *too* long our turning from barbarity and our facing of the quiet truths deep in our hearts. After all, with these new equipments, even just a minute or two long can make quite a difference. We may all have disappeared.   —ALAN DEVOE

ASSIGNMENTS

I. Write a theme in which you advocate something needed at your school. The following are intended only as suggestions of the kind of general subjects in which you might find material for a theme. The best subject will be one based on a need you yourself know about.

1. Improved student drama (or music)
2. A new dormitory (or other building)
3. A change in student government
4. A change in the grading system
5. What to do about intercollegiate athletics
6. An improved college newspaper
7. What to do about examinations

191

8. What to do about fraternities (or sororities)
9. Better guidance or placement help
10. The study of foreign languages

II. Write a theme in which you try to persuade someone to do something. (You need not mention the person you are trying to persuade, but you should keep him clearly in mind.) The following list should suggest a subject.

1. Why a certain town or neighborhood is a good or bad one to live in
2. Why my college is the one (or not the one) to attend
3. Why we should go to _____ on our vacation
4. Why one should or should not work for such and such a company or at such and such a job
5. Why _____ should or should not be elected mayor
6. Why one should watch or should avoid such and such a program on television
7. Why you should read such and such a book or magazine article
8. Why you should or should not be more conformist than you are
9. Why you should study French (or some other subject)
10. Why you should or should not get military service out of the way before coming to college

I

Writing a Critical Review

Is the latest musical comedy worth the price of admission? Is the current best seller worth reading? Hundreds of musical comedies, plays, and moving pictures are produced every year, and thousands of books are published. Since we cannot see or read very many of them, we need guidance to tell us which are worth our time and money. We may read the reviews in a magazine or get the opinion of a friend. In either event, we are looking for guidance; we are looking for someone in a position to criticize.

The word "criticize" comes from the Greek word *krinein*, meaning "to judge" or "to discern." It does not mean "to find fault with" any more than it means "to praise." The good critic is as sensitive to excellence as he is to its absence. A critical review of a good novel should praise it, just as the review of a poor one should point out its weaknesses. Each of them will be critical if it shows good judgment and uncritical if it does not.

A good critical review will always be in part a summary, but only in small part. The reader obviously must be given some idea of what the book (or motion picture or whatever is being reviewed) is about before he can understand a critique of its merits. The critic, however, will not meet his responsibilities if he merely gives a summary. He will deserve to be called a critic only if he helps us understand the work he is writing about and tells us something of its value. He will be a critic only if he makes judgments.

When we talk about making judgments, we mean much more than merely passing judgment. To *pass* judgment is to say a hasty and perhaps dogmatic "yes" or "no," "good" or "bad," "exciting" or "dull," and let it go at that. To *make* a judgment is to analyze and evaluate. The critic is a guide who helps us see what might otherwise escape us. Just as a person who knows tennis can analyze the fine points of the game which escape the ordinary spectator and, by pointing them out to him, increase his pleasure in the game, so the good critic can help us to see better, to read with more insight and more enjoyment.

Thus, good criticism explains. It does not merely label a book interesting or uninteresting; it explains why it is so and gives facts or quotations as evidence. The good critical review tells a reader something about the *why* and the *how* as well as the *what*. It may or may not encourage him to read a book. In any event, it seeks to help him read it more intelligently, more critically, if he does read it.

In brief, then, a good criticism will use summary only as a starting point, and it will avoid mere labeling. Instead, it will give the reader a clear notion of what the work is about, what it attempts to do, how well it does it, and what its value and interest is. It will try to help the reader or viewer make a selection and then, once the selection has been made, understand and enjoy what he reads or sees.

In spite of its value, the student critical review risks superficiality. Except for the research paper, most student themes run to about five hundred words. It is possible to review a good book with something other than superficiality in five hundred words—possible but difficult. Probably it would be wise, therefore, not to write a critical review as such about most of the reading you do this semester, especially if your syllabus includes undoubted classics. Probably it would be wise, and certainly more modest, to write about Homer's glorification of war or Stephen's rejection of his family than to attempt a critical review of the *Iliad* or *A Portrait of the Artist as a Young Man*. You might write a review of a contemporary novel like *Lord of the Flies*, but Homer and Shakespeare and even Joyce, though they will always be written about, have moved far beyond the range of the critical review as such.

The following essay is a student's review of a motion picture. Notice that though the author gives the gist of the story, the review is not a mere summary.

Soldiers Three

I have seen some pretty bad movies, but this one is worse than pretty bad. It must establish some kind of record for stupidity and dullness.

The producers announce that it was "suggested" by Rudyard Kipling's novel of the same name. Even in Hollywood, where respect for truth is considered an old-fashioned prejudice, they were ashamed to claim that this concoction was "based" on Kipling. After all, there are libel laws.

It is one of those things where it's supposed to be very funny if a man gets drunk and assaults anybody who happens to be around. This makes it very simple for producers because they don't have to think. And, of course, they don't have to be witty. That's too difficult and maybe another old-fashioned prejudice. All they have to do is to put a man on the screen (this time three men, three alleged British soldiers in an alleged India), give him a bottle, have him start weaving, and then have him start brawling. I'm supposed to roll in the aisles because it's so funny.

Well, the soldiers three do a lot of weaving and a lot of brawling. But their hearts are in the right place. They break a lot of skulls and every regulation in the army, and they drive their colonel to distraction, to despair, and almost to death. But in the crisis, they come through. They come through! They lay down their bottles, pick up their rifles, defeat a million or so Indians, and win their colonel a promotion.

So you see, it's just terribly funny. And it's so heroic too. Just think, a million or so Indians!

Next Friday I think I shall ask my escort to read me an out-of-date textbook or the *Congressional Record*. Or we might go to the library and get a newspaper from 1910 and read the obituaries.   —STUDENT THEME BY JULIA EISNER

Here is a short review that, without summarizing the book, tells us a good deal about its subject and the author's treatment of it.

"The world on the verge of its catastrophe was very brilliant," wrote Winston Churchill of the years before World War I. "Empires crowned with princes and potentates rose majestically on every side." In *The Fall of the Dynasties,* an account of the collapse of Europe's royal houses from 1905 to 1922, Edmond Taylor agrees, but only partly, with this bit of Churchillian nostalgia. Beneath all the pomp and circumstance there were undercurrents of misery and unrest that were later to gather head in the tides of war and revolution, and inundate the old dynasties.

Before 1914 social legislation was very meager. Homeless masses of people camped in the parks or slept in shifts in furnished rooms. It has been estimated that, in a glittering capital like Vienna, a third of the children were born illegitimate.

And as for the princely personages themselves, what emerges from Mr. Taylor's narrative is less the impression of regal grandeur than of tragic mediocrity in the face of the historical crises with which they were confronted. Francis Joseph of Austria was a doddering old man presiding over a patchwork empire. The Russian Czar was an inept little man, a puppet in the hands of a hysterical and power-crazy Czarina. The Sultan of Turkey, scion of the once powerful Osmanlis, was a ravaged and impotent captive of his own harem. And the Kaiser himself, who publicly affected the mask of imperial warlord and Teutonic beast of prey, was in his private life only a dull and stuffy German paterfamilias with very limited capacities of imagination. Only the British royal family had ties with its own people. The other European dynasties, having outlived their usefulness, were like dead leaves ready to be blown away by the winds of revolution.

Mr. Taylor has woven all these stories into a unified and superbly readable chronicle. He writes with unobtrusive elegance and the professional reporter's sharp eye for detail. He has a grand theme, and his performance lives up to it. The First World War was the pivotal event of our century, from which all subsequent upheavals and conflicts issued. All of us who survive, Mr. Taylor concludes, have been scarred, at least emotionally, by it.   —WILLIAM BARRETT

Here is another review which tells the reader a good deal about a book. Notice especially how it makes rather than merely passes a judgment.

Not everything's up to date yet in Afghanistan. But, according to James Michener in a factual note appended to his new novel,

Caravans, some changes have been made since 1946. These include the introduction of such aspects of Western civilization as airports, street paving, hotels and bakeries. Naturally, then, a novel set in Afghanistan before the appearance of these innovations would seem far more exotic and colorful to American readers than one focused on a recent excursion north of the Khyber Pass. Never one to overlook any element of possible sales appeal, Mr. Michener has arranged that the story of *Caravans* should take place in 1946. The news about *Caravans* is that it is about one-fifth as long as Mr. Michener's supercolossal *Hawaii,* and that it is just as readable. That this sleek combination of lively travelogue and mediocre fiction will be both popular and profitable is as certain as a change in the weather.

Mr. Michener knows how to keep a narrative rolling along. He knows how to make dramatic use of strange customs, picturesque characters and gorgeous scenery. His prose is adequately professional. If he is superficial and unconvincing in characterization, few of his enthusiastic readers will object. Probably they won't object that in *Caravans* two principal characters, on whose mysterious motivation the whole story hangs, are utterly incomprehensible.

As a guided tour to some of the most inaccessible regions of Afghanistan *Caravans* is lots of fun. Mr. Michener is fine when he describes the Dashti-i-Margo Desert with its temperature above 130 degrees; when he escorts his readers through the passes of the Hindu Kush; when he explains the ancient "karez" system of underground irrigation; when he describes a caravan of Kochi nomads—dirty, ignorant, underfed thieves but wild and free and brave, traveling thousands of miles each year with their camels, sheep, goats and donkeys; when he describes gruesome public executions.

But, as a novel, *Caravans* is implausible in plot and psychologically baffling. A young member of the United States Embassy's staff in Kabul journeys into the back of beyond to find a missing American girl who had married an Afghan engineer. Ellen Jaspar is a beautiful blonde from Dorset, Pa. She is in a state of hysterical revolt against her conventional parents, against her home town, her country, her civilization.

Trying to find something better in more primitive societies, she marries her Afghan and then deserts him in favor of a nomad chieftain, whom she deserts, in turn, in favor of a fugitive Nazi physician. Ellen is promiscuous and a serious mental case, but Mr. Michener cannot make her seem like a real human being, much less like an interesting one. He fails equally with the doctor, whose murky mind is only a dark muddle.

There's a lot of dialogue in *Caravans* and there's a laborious effort to avoid using the word "said" too often. Mr. Michener has found at least 74 other words that can be applied to human utterances, including such choice items as "fumbled," "mumbled," "reacted," "brightened," "chuckled" and "huffed."

—ORVILLE PRESCOTT

ASSIGNMENTS

I. Write a critical review of about 500 words on a motion picture, a play, or a radio or television program.

II. After consultation with your instructor, write two reviews of the same book, one about a hundred words in length and the other about five hundred.

J
Characterizing and Describing People

Most of us take shortcuts when we speak of people. We depend on vague tags like "a good guy," "a nice girl," or "an ambitious young man." Although we can hardly escape using such labels in the hurry of daily life, we should not think they really characterize anyone. When we want to know about Jack Smith and Dick Johnson, we are not going to be satisfied to learn that both are good guys. Perhaps each of them is, but how much does the tag tell us when the two men are quite different in appearance and personality? We want to know what each of them is like, what his individual qualities are. We want him identified as a separate person, as a unique person, not blurred into a vagueness in which we cannot distinguish him from the millions of other "good guys."

Whether you write at some length or whether you do it in a few quick strokes, you should look for definite facts about the person you describe and incidents that reveal his character. In order to see the value of specific information, study the following contrasting pairs of sentences:

He was intelligent but not very practical.
He was intelligent enough to make Phi Beta Kappa at the University of Michigan, but he lost his inheritance through speculation in Wall Street.

Her appearance attracted attention.
When she came into the room, conversation stopped; the men looked at her with admiration, the women, some of them at least, with envy.

He calls himself lazy, but sometimes he is quite industrious.

He calls himself lazy, but after a spell of idleness he will get out his books and work from right after dinner until two or three in the morning with hardly a break.

Fred Sharpe was a large man, but he was not in good condition.

Fred Sharpe still had the size that had made him a tackle at Penn State, but his question-mark stoop made him look shorter than he was in those days twenty years ago, and his muscles had long since turned into fat.

Again to realize the value of specific information, see how Edith Wharton might have (but never would have!) told about one of her characters: "Mr. Welland, whose health was poor, at least so he thought, was a rather ineffective old man and quite dependent on his wife and daughter."

And this is the much fuller, more specific way she did write it:

In obedience to a long-established habit, the Wellands had left the previous week for St. Augustine, where, out of regard for the supposed susceptibility of Mr. Welland's bronchial tubes, they always spent the latter part of the winter. Mr. Welland was a mild and silent man, with no opinions but with many habits. With these habits none might interfere; and one of them demanded that his wife and daughter should always go with him on his annual journey to the south. To preserve an unbroken domesticity was essential to his peace of mind; he would not have known where his hair-brushes were, or how to provide stamps for his letters, if Mrs. Welland had not been there to tell him.

Here is another example. Faulkner might have said something like "Armstid was an easy-going man to whom time meant nothing, but he did not squander his money." Like Edith Wharton, Faulkner is much fuller, much more specific:

. . . after a while Armstid said what he had come to say. He had already made two previous trips, coming in his wagon five miles and squatting and spitting for three hours beneath the shady wall of Winterbottom's barn with the timeless unhaste and indirection of his kind, in order to say it. It was to make Winterbottom an offer for a cultivator which Winterbottom wanted to sell. At last Armstid looked at the sun and offered the price which he had decided to offer while lying in bed three nights ago.

Faulkner's sketch of Armstid and Edith Wharton's of Mr. Welland appear in novels and therefore differ in form from the character sketch that might appear by itself, as in a letter of recommendation for Tom Smith or a historian's analysis of the character of Adolf Hitler. In a novel, the author may wish to portray only one facet of character; later in the novel other facets may appear, and perhaps it will not be until the last page that we see the person as the author wishes us to see him. The character sketch naturally differs in that all the understanding of the person must be given at one time and in that it is given largely through direct statement by the writer. Though the methods by which it is done may differ, however, the objective of good characterization, wherever it may appear, is to avoid the tag that does not characterize and instead to find the fact that brings the person to life.

Although your description may give an idea of your subject's appearance, remember that the reader is not likely to be much interested in appearance except as it reveals character. And in making sure that you present the main features of a person's character, do not forget that sometimes, as perhaps Edith Wharton has reminded you, things that look like trifles—small habits, simple gestures, little incidental remarks—may reveal more about someone than the things everyone notices at first. A man who makes a large (but inexpensive) display of his love for downtrodden humanity may at first impress you with his noble spirit. You may be less impressed when you observe that he always takes the most comfortable chair, always studies a plate of sandwiches to find the biggest one, and always cheerfully accepts other people's cigarettes but never offers his own. Upon reflection, you may decide that he has more than his share of selfishness and that his love of humanity is pretty much a sham. Your aim, of course, should be to penetrate the surface to discover and reveal the real man.

You will sometimes be called on to compose a second and different kind of character sketch, one on the distinguishing features of a group or a class of persons. In an examination or an essay you may be asked to characterize the American frontiersman, the plantation owner in the South before the Civil War, or an industrialist in the North after it. In the characterization of a class, you will seek general rather than individual qualities; you will study a number of individuals and decide on features that are typical of the group. You will characterize not Sarah Worm, that odious grind, but grinds in general. You will think about the traits of Miss Worm and the other grinds you have known, and you will draw the conclusion that grinds have certain characteristics in common. If you really dislike grinds, you may find that as a group they are dull, unsociable, unoriginal people, interested in grades rather than ideas, constantly engaged in their uninspired, unemotional plodding. Or you might surprise everyone by writing a character sketch that shows how the grind is misjudged, how he is a likable but shy person, and how he loves ideas and learning far too much to fritter his time away on students who know very little and aren't even bothered by their ignorance.

Here is a character sketch by a student. Notice that though it makes no explicit judgment, the writer's attitude is clear.

AUNT RAGUSA

Aunt Ragusa sits there and sits. Other people would sit there and talk or crochet or read a book or look at television, but Aunt Ragusa just sits. Once in a while she gets up and walks over to another chair and sits down in that. This is her exercise.

If my mother comes in and says, "It's been a nice summer day, Aunt Ragusa," she answers, "Yes, it has indeed." If five minutes later my father comes in and says, "It's been a miserable sticky day, Aunt Ragusa," she answers, "Yes, it has indeed."

She is, however, a woman of strong opinions. She favors a firm hand with the Russians ("I do believe they wouldn't dare to fight") and with labor unions ("I do believe they are getting too big for their trousers").

Though she has never been married and, I suspect, never been courted, she gives my sister and me plenty of advice about the opposite sex. "Now, Harris, girls appreciate a young man whose finger nails are clean."

"Yes, Aunt Ragusa," I say.

—STUDENT THEME BY HARRIS WEINBROOK

The next character sketch, also written by a student, reveals a different (but not wholly different) attitude toward its subject.

I Know Him Well

I know him well, but few people do. He is not the type of man who arouses interest or becomes the topic of conversation. He is too quiet. If most people were asked what they think of him they would probably say, "He seems like a nice man, but he isn't very sociable."

And perhaps they are right. Even when he was a child he liked to be alone walking down the paths beside the creek a few miles from his home or floating on his back and dreaming of the day he could be a sailor. And even now he sometimes rebels against social conventions. He is the only person I know who, upon becoming the least bit sleepy, will say a mumbled good night to his puzzled visitors and leave them to their own conclusions as he goes to bed. He is the only person I know who says, "The less you say, the better off you are." And he is the only person I know who abides by such a motto.

He can do so because he is convinced that he is no one and that nothing he says or does is important. Although he knows perfectly well what he wants to say, his words become jumbled. And when he applies for a job, although he is a licensed engineer and has some machinist training, far be it from him to demand anything specialized.

What pleasure is there in a trip, he will ask, what joy in a celebration? The scenery in the backyard is just as good as the scenery anywhere. Fuss and bother are a lot of nonsense. You can't fight life. Life is the same thing over and over.

Yes, the same old thing day after day. But there is one comfort. This world still offers food, sleep, and television. What more could you ask of life than a plate piled high? Food makes the world go round. And he is the man with 280 pounds to prove it.

A time comes, however, when even food cannot keep his mind

occupied. He wants to forget his job and the things he should do around the house; he wants to escape. Walking is too much exertion now that he is in his late forties, but television cowboy and mystery films will help him get away. He doesn't care whether the story is enjoyable or dull. If it's a comedy, he'll sometimes laugh until the tears flow down his cheeks. If it's so dull that no one else would endure it, that's all right too, for now it will make him sleepy and he will lose himself in a long snooze before going to bed.

He lacks the push and the confidence which spell success but that doesn't mean that he is particularly unhappy. He manages to earn enough money to go on living and he has the love of a wife whom he wooed and won in his own way.

His love story began at the age of twenty-six. (He just wasn't the kind of man who rushed into anything.) One day his girl offered him a piece of candy and, in a please-buy-me-some tone, said, "Ralph, this is my favorite candy." He heartily agreed that it was rather good, and just to prove the point, he ate the entire box of Loft's pecan butter crunch.

But beneath his strange surface this girl saw a man who was dependable, a man who would not be a great success but no failure either, a man who could be unthoughtful, maybe even selfish, yet loyal and honest. He is my father and I think she was right.   —ANONYMOUS STUDENT THEME

In the following paragraphs John Maynard Keynes, a British economist, sketches the personal qualities of President Wilson which, he believes, contributed to the failure of the peace after World War I.

The President was not a hero or a prophet; he was not even a philosopher; but a generously intentioned man, with many of the weaknesses of other human beings, and lacking that dominating intellectual equipment which would have been necessary to cope with the subtle and dangerous spellbinders whom a tremendous clash of forces and personalities had brought to the top as triumphant masters in the swift game of give and take, face to face in Council,—a game of which he had no experience at all.

We had indeed quite a wrong idea of the President. We knew him to be solitary and aloof, and believed him very strong-willed and obstinate. We did not figure him as a man of detail, but the clearness with which he had taken hold of certain main ideas would, we thought, in combination with his tenacity, enable him to sweep through cobwebs. Besides these qualities he would have the objectivity, the cultivation, and the wide knowledge of the student. The great distinction of language which had marked his famous Notes seemed to indicate a man of lofty and powerful imagination. His portraits indicated a fine presence and a commanding delivery. With all this he had attained and held with increasing authority the first position in a country where the arts of the politician are not neglected. All of which, without expecting the impossible, seemed a fine combination of qualities for the matter at hand.

The first impression of Mr. Wilson at close quarters was to impair some but not all of these illusions. His head and features were finely cut and exactly like his photographs, and the muscles of his neck and the carriage of his head were distinguished. But, like Odysseus, the President looked wiser when he was seated; and his hands, though capable and fairly strong, were wanting in sensitiveness and finesse. The first glance at the President suggested not only that, whatever else he might be, his temperament was not primarily that of the student or the scholar, but that he had not much even of that culture of the world which marks M. Clemenceau and Mr. Balfour as exquisitely cultivated gentlemen of their class and generation. But more serious than this, he was not only insensitive to his surroundings in the external sense, he was not sensitive to his environment at all. What chance could such a man have against Mr. Lloyd George's unerring, almost mediumlike, sensibility to every one immediately round him? To see the British Prime Minister watching the company, with six or seven senses not available to ordinary men, judging character, motive, and subconscious impulse, perceiving what each was thinking and even what each was going to say next, and compounding with telepathic instinct the argument or appeal best suited to the vanity, weakness, or self-interest of his immediate auditor, was to realize that the poor President would be playing blind man's buff in that party. Never could a man have stepped into the parlor a more perfect and predestined victim to the finished accomplishments of the Prime Minister. The Old World was tough in wickedness anyhow; the Old World's heart of stone might blunt the sharpest blade of the bravest knight-errant. But this blind and deaf Don Quixote was entering a cavern where the swift and glittering blade was in the hands of the adversary.

—JOHN MAYNARD KEYNES

Here is a sketch of a class, a certain kind of American lawyer.

For example, take the American lawyer turned politician. As a lawyer he has become accustomed to taking infinite pains in negotiating contracts, making abstracts, drawing wills and constructing his pleadings. There is no soft thinking here. But let that same lawyer enter the political arena and be called upon to deal with broad economic and political questions, and his thinking and pronouncements degenerate into a strange compound of moral platitudes, empty stereotypes, and romantic sentimentalities. If he "lawed" as shoddily as he "politicked," he would not last two days as a practicing attorney. In most cases however, he suffers no harm as a result of his loose political thinking, because his constituents, reared in the tradition of the frontier pulpit pounder, expect their politicians to deliver themselves of "messages" in which evil is put to rout by the forces of righteousness.

—WILLIAM G. CARLETON

So far in this chapter we have talked about character sketches, the kind of writing that gives a direct analysis of the qualities of a person. But sometimes you may wish to describe someone—to picture him so that we see him and know him through our senses. In such a theme, you may show him as the portrait painter sees him—in repose—but more likely you will describe him in action, perhaps a very simple action like coming into a room, selecting a chair, sitting down in it, and reaching over and turning on the radio. In the way people look and in the way they do things, they reveal themselves. The author does not need to tell us what they are like, for their actions do that without his comment. In a character sketch, the author would say that a young woman was nervous and troubled; in a description he would picture her as she lifted a cup and spilled coffee on herself because her hand was unsteady. The author of the description lets the facts of appearance speak for themselves.

You will find many examples of description—usually brief—in short stories and novels. The set description of the kind often assigned in college is an interesting and useful exercise in accurate observation and careful reporting of what you have seen. In a description you will want to decide on a dominant impression that you support by your choice of words and by the details you select. You will also want to make sure that you keep looking at things from some clear and consistent point of view. (For further discussion of point of view, see pages 213–214.)

In the following passage, Mark Twain lets Huck Finn describe his father. What is the dominant impression, the tone, that Mark Twain has tried to create? Notice the careful choice of words—for example, *tangled, greasy,* and *mixed-up.*

He was most fifty, and he looked it. His hair was long and tangled and greasy, and hung down, and you could see his eyes shining through like he was behind vines. It was all black, no gray; so was his long, mixed-up whiskers. There warn't no color in his face, where his face showed; it was white; not like another man's white, but a white to make a body sick, a white to make a body's flesh crawl—a tree-toad white, a fish-belly white. As for his clothes— just rags, that was all. He had one ankle resting on 'tother knee; the boot on that foot was busted, and two of his toes stuck through, and he worked them now and then. His hat was laying on the floor; an old black slouch with the top caved in, like a lid.

In the following student description, what is the dominant impression? Is it as sharply defined as in the passage from Mark Twain? Are the details well chosen? Does the description seem on the whole convincing or does it seem in any way forced and exaggerated? Point out any words that seem to you especially well selected. Do you get a notion of Jerry's traits of character?

EAGER BEAVER

I went over to Jerry's room the other night to ask him about the history test we were going to have the next day. Since he didn't answer when I called to him, I walked in. He was sitting at his desk all right, but he was asleep, leaning over with his head resting on his arm, which was sprawled out on the desk. Lying open beside his arm was his history textbook, just where it had been shoved when drowsiness overcame Jerry's very meager love of history. I called to him. He stirred faintly, opened his eyes, and looked at me in a stupefied way. Then he lifted his fat, shiny face, rubbed his eyes and his round, bulblike nose, and sat up in his chair and yawned. He ran a plump hand through his tousled blond hair and slid down on the chair and stretched, throwing wide his arms and yawning again, this time noisily, as if he really enjoyed it. He had on a short-sleeved red plaid sports shirt, badly wrinkled and puffed out somewhat above the belt of his gray cord pants. I thought he probably also had on his usual loafers, but I couldn't tell because his feet were under the desk. He lifted an arm heavily and wearily, put a hand into a shirt pocket, and pulled out a pack of cigarettes. His hand, moist and shiny like his face, gleamed under the desk lamp as he groped for a book of matches. When he lit the cigarette, he held the match in front of his face so long and stared at it in such a dazed way that I thought he was going to burn himself.

After a couple of drags on the cigarette and a few more yawns, he shoved the chair back, leaned hard on it as he got up, and said, "Come on, let's get a coke. That guy can't expect us to study all the time." —STUDENT THEME BY JOHN DI ANGELO

ASSIGNMENTS

I. Write a character sketch of someone you know well.

II. Write a sketch of one of the following subjects or a similar subject.

1. The college teacher
2. The life of the party
3. The junior executive
4. The Monday-morning quarterback
5. The sorority girl
6. The name-dropper
7. The visiting alumnus
8. The club woman
9. The sophomore
10. The know-it-all

III. After you have written the sketch of an individual in Assignment I, write a general sketch on the same subject. If you have written a sketch of your younger brother, for example, write a sketch of younger brothers as a class. If you have written a sketch of your roommate, write a sketch of the roommate as a general class, or the bookworm, the borrower, the true friend, or some other type your roommate represents.

IV. Write a description of several hundred words of a person doing something. He should be doing something quite ordinary. You should not analyze his character and state of mind, but in describing his appearance and manner you may suggest them. Here are some possibilities:

1. A professor waits for his class to assemble. (What does he do with his pencil? What does the set of his lips tell? What kind of suit does he wear?)

2. A student walks into a room, lights a cigarette. (No one just walks. How does *he* walk? No one just lights a cigarette. How does *he* light one?)

3. A man shaves himself.

4. A well-dressed woman enters a restaurant by herself.

5. A young but no longer youthful woman does her ironing.

6. A waitress watches the man she had served leave, and then picks up the tip.

7. A child, left without a baby-sitter for the first time, watches his parents drive off.

8. A young wife pours her husband a cup of coffee.

V. Take an ordinary statement like he or she *frowned, smiled, laughed, coughed,* or he or she was *young, good-looking, angry,* or he or she *ran up the steps, started to cry, reached out an arm,* and with a well-selected adjective or two or a figure of speech, or in some other way try, in a single sentence, perhaps a very short one, to individualize the person.

K

Describing a Thing or Place

A description tells what impression an object makes on our senses. The object may be an animal, a building, a scene —anything, indeed, that we are aware of through one or more of our senses. We often say that description tells what something looks like, but we must not forget that impressions come to us from all our senses, not from sight alone.

Description usually appears as part of a larger piece of writing—such as an essay, a short story, or a novel—but description of a thing or a place is worth practicing in its own right because it demands unusual exactness (and it quickly reveals inexactness) in organization, selection of material, and word choice.

Depending on the purpose for which they are written, descriptions are classed as "scientific" or "artistic." A scientific —or informational—description is objective and factual, giving precise measurements and other kinds of information. Descriptions of this kind are found in textbooks in the sciences and engineering and in magazines like *Popular Mechanics* and *Scientific American*. In this chapter we are concerned primarily with the other kind of description, which is imaginative and personal and which we rather hopefully call "artistic." This kind of description is governed by the mood of the viewer and it reflects the feeling aroused in him by the object. Details are chosen and words are selected to convey the desired impression. Whereas scientific description seeks to give information about an object, artistic description seeks to create an image of it in the reader's mind.

Though modesty and truth may keep us from calling our

words either scientific or artistic, we are always describing things. "The street is dirty," we say; "the highway coming into town is cluttered up"; "the dress is pretty"; "the campus commands a beautiful view of the surrounding countryside." Just as when we describe people, most of the time when we describe places and things, we rely on an adjective or two.

Right here we encounter a difficulty, the same kind of difficulty we meet when we try to describe people. No doubt the dress is pretty, but how much do we know when told this? We are told very little because many other dresses are also pretty. If we are told that a dress is like several million other dresses, obviously we are not told much about it.

What about "It commands a beautiful view"? In spite of the speed with which Americans are disfiguring their country, beautiful views exist in many places and in great variety. "Beautiful view" does not even tell us whether the view is of ocean, mountain, farm country, city, or something else. It tells us nothing, in fact, except that the speaker approves of what he sees.

In everyday conversation we often cannot do better, or at least not much better, than "pretty dress" and "beautiful view," just as in describing a person we may have to get along with "good guy" or "ambitious young man." In ordinary life we often do not have the time to describe persons or places and things in any other way. Sometimes, indeed, not much is called for except quick statements of liking or disliking.

This is not always true, however. Sometimes, especially in writing, you need to tell the other person more, much more, than the simple fact that you think something is pretty. Sometimes, even in conversation, you need to describe and not merely label.

How is this done? How do you make the reader see through words something you yourself have seen with your eyes, heard with your ears, or known with one of your other senses? For words to communicate ideas and information and for them to communicate sense impressions—these are two very different functions.

You should not put too much reliance on the adjective and adverb. The lazy way to describe is to pile on the adjectives and adverbs:

"It's a pretty dress."

"What do you mean pretty?"

"Well, it's really pretty—sort of pink and, well, awfully pretty."

Modifiers can do good work, of course, and sometimes the unexpected but exactly right adjective can light up a whole paragraph. The core of the sentence, however, is the noun-verb relation. If writing is really to describe, the noun and the verb will have to do most of the work.

Good descriptive writing must have sufficient detail to make us see, hear, smell, taste, or feel; and the problem of what detail to use and what not to use is crucial. What is the revealing fact, the suggestive fact, the one that will bring the picture to life? Even if you should write an extended description of a completely bare room, you as observer would have far more detail than you as writer could use. There would be a blotch on the wallpaper of this shape here and another of that shape there; there would be ink stains on the floor here and chipping of the lumber over there; the room would have a smell to it and dimensions, of course; and it would have a window, perhaps cracked, that looked down on a courtyard that had. . . . The point is that if you use your eyes and other senses, even a bare room is made up of a vast number of details—far too many for you to use. Your task is to select those that will do most to make your reader see, hear, smell, taste, and touch.

The detail you select will depend in part on the keenness of your observation. The more you take in, the wider your selection. Most of us are not good observers and we miss a great deal that is right in front of our eyes. One of the values of assignments in description, indeed, is that they encourage us to get out of the prison of ourselves and into other things. The man standing in the bus was young and healthy-looking and no doubt many passengers thought they noticed him, but how many observed the small twitching around his lips and wondered what was going on inside? Most of the passengers ride the same bus every day, but if one of the buildings along the route were suddenly carted away, how many of them would be able to describe it or perhaps even say whether it had been a restaurant or a filling station?

In selecting detail, remember that you have seen something from a certain point of view and you wish your reader to see it that way too. You are looking at the valley from the hill on which the college stands, let us say. The hill is your point of view. More exactly, you are looking at the valley from the steps of Ransome Hall, at five o'clock in the evening with the sun setting through the October foliage of the trees. This is your physical point of view. You will have a mental point of view also. The valley and everything in it will not look quite the same to the man who is happy and the man who is troubled in spirit, or to the man who has recently come to them and the man who has grown tired of them because he is so eager to get to New York and graduate school at Columbia.

Or let us say that you are in an automobile approaching one of the big cities of the United States. Here you pass a filling station, then a place that calls itself "Shoe City"—though it looks more like an ill-constructed building than a city, you think—then a place that calls itself "Toy Riot"—and why "riot" you don't have time to tell because before you know it you are passing something called "Beefburger Haven." Here too there is a physical point of view, a moving one this time, that of an automobile moving along a certain highway at a certain time of day and time of year. Even more, there is a mental point of view—that of a youthful visitor from upstate, say, to whom all this movement and all these lights are exciting and even glamorous, or that of someone to whom they are only ugly and wearisome. To change the illustration but not the point, you can describe the ocean as seen from a beach, from an airplane, from an ocean liner, from a small fishing boat: these are differences in physical point of view. And you can describe it as seen by someone who loves it (and there are many ways to love it) or as one who dislikes and fears it (and again there are many ways). These are differences in mental point of view.

You are free, of course, to choose any point of view you like. In fact, you must have some point of view. There is no value in describing something except in the precise way you, and perhaps you alone, see it. Sincerity, which is so important in other writing, is equally important in descriptive writing. It means—and this is not so easy as it may seem—being true to your own vision.

As you know, the sense of sight is the most important of the five senses that nature has given us, and modern civilization puts particular emphasis on it. The good writer will remember, however, that man does not just see. Man has four other senses with which to know the world. The good writer, accordingly, will try to make his reader hear things and smell, taste, and touch them.

In order to develop your skill in reaching the other senses and in order to develop your readiness to do so—and it is in part simply a matter of readiness, of willingness to get away from the domination of the eye—it is good practice to shut your eyes sometimes, even to imagine yourself blind, and discover how much of the world you can apprehend through the other senses and communicate through them. Even before he has tasted the food, a blind man can tell much about a restaurant: the smells, the sounds, the feel of the tablecloth and whether there are bread crumbs on it. Perhaps you can learn to do so too.

Here is a student theme which, though uneven, has some good descriptive detail. Where is the writer most successful in creating a picture? Where does he fail?

A RAINY DAY IN THE COUNTRY

It was raining. The earth was soft and wet beneath my feet as I made my way up the path which led to the house. Large slabs of stone were arranged along the pathway, and as I stepped upon them, they wobbled so beneath my feet that I was afraid I might fall. Little drops of rain clung to the grass which grew on both sides of the path.

The house, which needed to be white-washed, looked even more gray and dreary than it did in yesterday's sunlight. The light which shone through the front window, however, seemed to lend to the house a warm and inviting atmosphere.

Beyond the house there was a stream of water which was flowing rather quickly, and I watched the cool, clear water as it ran over the stones. A dog stood on the other side of the narrow stream, looking cold and wet as the raindrops sprayed from his wagging tail.

The pair of stockings which hung, forgotten, on the clothesline were drenched, and large drops fell to the ground beneath them.

The entire countryside was indeed wet and dreary, and I was glad to go into the house from which shone the inviting light.

In the following excerpt, note how the author mingles description of a place with description of people. Notice how little feeling of set description there is but how much is suggested.

The two grubby small boys with tow-colored hair who were digging among the ragweed in the front yard sat back on their heels and said, "Hello," when the tall bony man with straw-colored hair turned in at their gate. He did not pause at the gate; it had swung back, conveniently half open, long ago, and was now sunk so firmly on its broken hinges no one thought of trying to close it. He did not even glance at the small boys, much less give them good-day. He just clumped down his big square dusty shoes one after the other steadily, like a man following a plow, as if he knew the place well and knew where he was going and what he would find there. Rounding the right-hand corner of the house under the row of chinaberry trees, he walked up to the side porch where Mr. Thompson was pushing a big swing churn back and forth.

Mr. Thompson was a tough weather-beaten man with stiff black hair and a week's growth of black whiskers. He was a noisy proud man who held his neck so straight his whole face stood level with his Adam's apple, and his whiskers continued down his neck and disappeared into a black thatch under his open collar. The churn rumbled and swished like the belly of a trotting horse, and Mr. Thompson seemed somehow to be driving a horse with one hand, reining it in and urging it forward; and every now and then he turned halfway around and squirted a tremendous spit of tobacco juice out over the steps. The door stones were brown and gleaming with fresh tobacco juice. Mr. Thompson had been churning quite a while and he was tired of it. He was just fetching a mouthful of juice to squirt again when the stranger came around the corner and stopped. Mr. Thompson saw a narrow-chested man with blue eyes so pale they were almost white, looking and not looking at him from a long gaunt face, under white eyebrows.   —KATHERINE ANNE PORTER

Here is a description of a winter landscape. Notice especially the tone of the passage.

A girl in an orange-coloured shawl stood at the window of Pedlar's store and looked, through the falling snow, at the deserted road. Though she watched there without moving, her attitude, in its stillness, gave an impression of arrested flight, as if she were running toward life.

Bare, starved, desolate, the country closed in about her. The last train of the day had gone by without stopping, and the station of Pedlar's Mill was as lonely as the abandoned fields by the track. From the bleak horizon, where the flatness created an illusion of immensity, the broomsedge was spreading in a smothered fire over the melancholy brown of the landscape. Under the falling snow, which melted as soon as it touched the earth, the colour was veiled and dim; but when the sky changed the broomsedge changed with it. On clear mornings the waste places were cinnamon-red in the sunshine. Beneath scudding clouds the plumes of the bent grasses faded to ivory. During the long spring rains, a film of yellow-green stole over the burned ground. At autumn sunsets, when the red light searched the country, the broomsedge caught fire from the afterglow and blazed out in a splendour of colour. Then the meeting of earth and sky dissolved in the flaming mist of the horizon.

At these quiet seasons, the dwellers near Pedlar's Mill felt scarcely more than a tremor on the surface of life. But on stormy days, when the wind plunged like a hawk from the swollen clouds, there was a quivering in the broomsedge, as if coveys of frightened partridges were flying from the pursuer. Then the quivering would become a ripple and the ripple would swell presently into rolling waves. The straw would darken as the gust swooped down, and brighten as it sped on to the shelter of scrub pine and sassafras bushes. And while the wind bewitched the solitude, a vague restlessness would stir in the hearts of living things on the farms, of men, women, and animals. "Broomsage ain't jest wild stuff. It's a kind of fate," old Matthew Fairlamb used to say.

Thirty years ago, modern methods of farming, even methods that were modern in the benighted eighteen-nineties, had not penetrated to this thinly settled part of Virginia. The soil, impoverished by the war and the tenant system which followed the war, was still drained of its lingering fertility for the sake of the poor crops it could yield. Spring after spring, the cultivated ground appeared to shrink into the "old fields," where scrub pine or oak succeeded broomsedge and sassafras as inevitably as autumn slipped into winter. Now and then a new start would be made. Some thrifty settler, a German Catholic, perhaps, who was trying his fortunes in a staunch Protestant community, would buy a mortgaged farm for a dollar an acre, and begin to experiment with suspicious, strange-smelling fertilizers. For a season or two his patch of ground would respond to the unusual treatment and grow green with promise. Then the forlorn roads, deep in mud, and the surrounding air of failure, which was as inescapable as a drought, combined with the cutworm, the locust, and the tobacco-fly, against the human invader; and where the brief harvest had been, the perpetual broomsedge would wave.

—ELLEN GLASGOW

ASSIGNMENTS

I. Write a description of not more than fifty words of a house or other building.

II. Write descriptions of about a hundred words each of two areas of a city you know, one of them an attractive neighborhood and the other an ugly one.

III. Write two descriptions, each of them about a hundred words, of a restaurant or something else as you know it and the other of the same thing as you think a blind person might know it.

IV. Write a description of not more than twenty-five words of a garden or a tree.

V. Write a description of about three or four hundred words of a scene during a particular and limited period of time. Take an area that you can see from one place and show at one particular moment—in the snow, on a rainy summer day, at night under the street lights, after a storm, or under some other special condition.

VI. Write a description of two or three hundred words of a section of this country. You might, for example, think of yourself as describing the wooded and mountainous country of Pennsylvania to someone who lives on the treeless plains of western Kansas. Or you might describe the winter landscape of Minnesota to someone who lives in Florida.

L

Writing Narration and Narrative Incidents

Writing is conventionally classified as exposition, description, or narration. Exposition is to explain; description to picture; narration to tell some kind of story. In exposition you might give the reasons you have come to college to prepare yourself to be a high-school teacher; in description you might picture the high-school teacher who did most to influence your decision to become a teacher yourself; in narration you might relate a specific experience, perhaps the time this teacher asked you to take over his class and the sudden surprise it brought when you discovered that you enjoyed it and could do it much better than you had thought you would.

There is no reason to labor the distinction between these three kinds of writing. Much good writing is a mixture of the three kinds. Perhaps, indeed, it would be better to say there are two principal kinds of writing, exposition and narration, with description an adjunct of the other two. For practice you need to write descriptions, but description almost never stands alone. In this assignment you are asked to tell some kind of story, something you did or something someone else did, something that did happen or something that could have happened. If you do it well, you will hardly be aware—and your reader will hardly be aware—of when you are telling the story and when you are describing the persons and places in it.

In narration, then, something must take place. There must be action of some sort. Something must begin, like your taking over the class in fear and misgiving; it must develop, like your finding that you could do it more successfully than you had thought; and it must end, like your discovering what your profession was going to be.

The word *action,* though true, may be misleading, however. The interest and value of narration is almost never in the action as such. Who is interested, to be frank, in your action in taking over the class a year ago? What we want to know is what went on inside of you. Even when the action is violent, like the killing in *Noon Wine* (and you should leave such subjects to people like Katherine Anne Porter), the interest and value of the story is not at all in the killing but in what it did to the mind and spirit of the man who committed the crime.

In looking for subjects, the most important thing is to remember the value of simplicity and truth. You should not write about fighting sharks off Nassau or outwitting Communist agents in Iran or rescuing damsels from the clutches of Martian monsters in outer space. Themes on subjects like this will be phony—and dull.

Even though you realize that you should not write about Martian monsters, your impulse may be to select the most exciting incident in your own life—the time you pulled a drowning boy out of the lake or the time you returned a punt seventy-five yards to break the tie and win your school the championship. The trouble with incidents like these is that, though exciting to participate in or to observe, they are rarely interesting to read about. Their action is too quick, and the action tells too little about human nature, your own or other people's. Pulling the drowning boy out of the lake is an experience too exclusively on the purely physical level. Your experience *afterwards* might be a good narrative subject, however: what it meant to be the town's hero for a day and how, perhaps, you tried to be modest about it but hungered for every word of praise; or how you found to your surprise and chagrin that many people didn't know about it even after it was written up in the newspaper. ("Well, Jim, what you been doing? I haven't seen you since you got back from school.")

Another kind of theme you should avoid is a scattered series of events with no central purpose. Probably you should avoid the travel theme, for example—the theme that all too often turns into an account of how you got up at five o'clock on June 17, packed the bags and boxes in the car while your mother fixed lunch, and managed to leave home by 6:20; how, after driving two hours at an average speed of thirty-seven miles an hour, you stopped for breakfast at the town of Stale Springs, known as the watercress center of this area; and how, after you left town, you had just turned right onto State Highway 46 when you had a flat tire. . . . Needless to say, nothing is duller than this sort of narrative that wanders pointlessly because the writer has failed to organize the events he relates into anything meaningful.

What kind of experience, then, do you write about? Perhaps, on second thought, you can do something with the travel theme, just as, on second thought, you could do something with rescuing the drowning boy. Possibly at breakfast at Stale Springs something made you realize, perhaps more vividly than you ever had before, how pleasant small-town life can be. Or possibly the realization was of the drabness of small-town life, and therefore it brought a renewed willingness to return to the city once the trip was over.

What brought the realization, whatever it was? Was it the abundance of the vegetable garden around the restaurant instead of concrete and confusion? Or, on the contrary, was the side yard littered with last year's decay of tin cans and orange crates? Were there ketchup stains on the tablecloth? Did the bacon come with congealed fat coating it? Was the waitress's freshness like the cheerful morning when you saw her, or was it like a radio joke? Did the chairs squeak?

Here, in any event, you have a possible subject if you can work it out. Nobody cares whether you ate breakfast at 8:20 at Stale Springs or not, but if you can find the facts (like tin cans and orange crates) to create a picture and explain a state of mind, then the reader will indeed be interested. He will be able to share with you an experience of delight or disgust or whatever it may have been. He will be with you as you ate the breakfast just as he was with you when you faced the class or when you discovered you were not a hero.

This discussion implies that you should write about personal experiences. If you write several narratives, you might try writing about something that happened to someone else or something you create in your imagination, but in your first narrative themes you will be wise to write out of your own immediate experience.

In writing narration, your task is to re-create the experience, give us the feel of participating in it. You should not inform us that something happened; you should *show* it happening. The two paragraphs that follow are not good narrative because instead of showing something happening they merely give information about it:

Baby-sitters certainly earn their money. This fact was forcefully impressed upon me many times when, as a girl in high school, I used to take care of the young son of Mr. and Mrs. Johnson.

Joey was a nice little fellow at heart but so mischievous that he often gave me near heart failure. One night I was sitting while his parents were attending a dinner-dance down town. Suddenly I realized Joey was leaning way out of the window. I have never been so frightened in my life. I got him in but later that evening he locked himself in the bathroom and gave me another scare. I finally got him to bed. Later his parents returned and I was paid four dollars. I feel I certainly earned it!

This has no value as narrative because, as has been said, though we are informed that certain things have happened, we don't *see* them happening. In the following theme, in contrast, a student writer has succeeded in bringing the experience to life.

JOEY

"Joey, come down!"

The words sounded more like a plea than a command.

"Joey, come here!"

This time they were a command. The little boy turned his head to glance at me. Then, quite as if I had not spoken, he turned back to contemplate the street three storeys below.

I stared at him, and I could feel my hair starting to uncurl. From the waist down, the little boy was fine. His legs were supported by a sturdy wooden stool, *inside* the room. But the rest of his body was dangling from the window ledge, *outside* the room.

Giving up mere words, I slipped up on him. With one hand on the trapdoor of his pajamas and the other wrapped around his neck, I dragged him to safety.

"Joey, don't ever do that again! What are you trying to do, ruin my young life?"

He smiled in his own angelic way and explained, "I was just looking out the window. My mommy lets me."

I glared at him. "I'm not your mommy!"

Eventually I got him to bed. At the crucial point I did not rely on persuasion. I pulled the covers back and shoved him under in one motion. Then I turned the light off.

"I didn't wash my hands."

I should have known. I must be slipping.

The little boy scampered from his bed and into the bathroom in two seconds. Before I got there, I heard the door lock. The bathroom also had a window opening on the street three storeys below.

"Joey, honey, open the door."

The only answer was the sound of running water splattering against the basin. I tried again.

"Joey, dear, please open the door."

Still no answer and still the splashing of water. I had had enough.

"Joseph, open the door this minute or I shall tell your father!"

The splashing stopped, the lock turned, and a little face appeared.

"Oh, all right. But don't tell my father."

I knew I had taken unfair advantage of the poor kid, but a girl can take just so much. After all, it's only a dollar an hour. I gripped his hand in mine and marched him along.

"Into bed and stay there!"

This time there was no argument.

"Goodnight, Joey."

"Goodnight."

"How was Joey?" Mrs. Johnson asked me two hours later. "Did you have any trouble with him?" This was the traditional question.

With the four dollars pressed tightly in my hand, I smiled and

223

gave the traditional answer: "Oh, no, Mrs. Johnson. He was no trouble at all. In fact, he was a perfect darling."

The funny thing is that I meant most of it, too.

—STUDENT THEME BY MIRIAM RODGERS

As this theme shows, the writer of narration will usually make some use of dialogue, sometimes considerable use. As the theme also shows, the function of dialogue is twofold: first, to help carry the action forward (to get the story of Joey and the baby-sitter told); and second, to characterize the people in the story (to tell us what kind of people Joey and the girl are).

Fitzgerald's *The Great Gatsby* is, among other things, the picture of a marriage that is losing whatever value it once had to the partners, Tom and Daisy. In the following passage, coming early in the novel, Fitzgerald's task is largely through dialogue (1) to carry the action forward—that is, to show the marriage losing its value; and (2) to characterize the speakers and especially to bring out the brutality and stupidity of the husband and the triviality of the wife.

"Civilization's going to pieces," broke out Tom violently. "I've gotten to be a terrible pessimist about things. Have you read 'The Rise of the Colored Empires' by this man Goddard?"

"Why, no," I answered, rather surprised by his tone.

"Well, it's a fine book, and everybody ought to read it. The idea is if we don't look out the white race will be—will be utterly submerged. It's all scientific stuff; it's been proved."

"Tom's getting very profound," said Daisy, with an expression of unthoughtful sadness. "He reads deep books with long words in them. What was that word we—"

"Well, these books are all scientific," insisted Tom, glancing at her impatiently. "This fellow has worked out the whole thing. It's up to us, who are the dominant race, to watch out or these other races will have control of things."

"We've got to beat them down," whispered Daisy, winking ferociously toward the fervent sun.

"You ought to live in California—" began Miss Baker, but Tom interrupted her by shifting heavily in his chair.

"This idea is that we're Nordics. I am, and you are, and you are, and—" After an infinitesimal hesitation he included Daisy with a slight nod, and she winked at me again. "—And we've produced all the things that go to make civilization—oh, science and art, and all that. Do you see?"

Notice how much Fitzgerald tells us in so few words. Only he does not seem to tell us: he gives us the information and with it we tell ourselves. The facts as he gives them tell us that Tom is badly educated, pretentious, bitter, and insecure. They tell us that Daisy has a trivial mind and enjoys mocking her husband. They tell us the marriage has moved into the storm line and may flounder.

How do we know all this? Since Fitzgerald does not tell us explicitly, how do we know? Without attempting a complete analysis of the passage, let us look at several parts of it so that you may learn from Fitzgerald something about how to use dialogue to reveal character.

1. "It's all scientific stuff; it's been proved." This is the language of a man who knows nothing about science. It is the language of someone who believes that anything claiming to be scientific must be so provided it confirms him in his prejudices.

2. "It's up to us, who are the dominant race, to watch out or these other races will have control of things [become dominant]." Our domination proves our superiority, but theirs would not prove theirs. Tom is not bright enough to see that he has worked himself into a logical trap.

3. "We've got to beat them down." Daisy is not repelled by her husband's ideas. She is not being ironical. She simply refuses to take them seriously. She is trying to take nothing seriously and her husband least of all.

4. ". . . all the things that go to make civilization—oh, science and art, and all that." Tom, not at all sure what civilization is, thinks it must have something to do with art and science and "all that."

In *The Sun Also Rises*, instead of describing a man as insincere and hollow, Hemingway writes: "Mrs. Braddocks brought up somebody and introduced him as Robert Prentiss. He was from New York by way of Chicago, and was a rising new novelist. He had some sort of English accent." A moment later Prentiss asks: "Do you find Paris amusing?" When the answer is yes, he says "Really?"

This is almost all there is. Hemingway makes no explicit description and offers no explicit comment. All we have are the facts—but how convincing they are—that Prentiss is from New York by way of Chicago and has some kind of English accent and that he asks if Paris is amusing. In about fifty words Hemingway has told us a good deal about Prentiss— that he is embarrassed to be an American and that he condescends to, feels superior to, one of the great cities of the world. Prentiss is a fraud. Without making a judgment himself, Hemingway forces us to make one.

Narrative writing, then, must relate some kind of action, if nothing more than of two people eating lunch together. Usually we are not interested in the external action as such, however. We are likely to be much less interested in the eating of the lunch than in what is going on within the minds of the characters—their getting ready to fall in love, perhaps, or in some other way discover something about themselves. Thus human nature is the subject of most narrative, and the narrative writer, though he may sometimes give an account of such things as storms, as W. H. Hudson does in the following passage, is showing human nature responding to life. All through his narrative, therefore, he is characterizing. Sometimes he does it directly and in his own voice, as when Fitzgerald tells us that Tom speaks "violently." Often, however, he does it indirectly. He tells us that Tom fumbles into an "all that" and that Prentiss has some kind of English accent. He tells us these things and leaves it to us to make our judgment of them. By showing us how people talk and think and behave, he forces us to exercise our own humanity.

In the following narrative observe especially the multitude of exact, concrete details in colors, in names of objects, in sounds.

It was in sultry summer weather, and towards evening all of us boys and girls went out for a ramble on the plain, and were about a quarter of a mile from home when a blackness appeared in the southwest, and began to cover the sky in that quarter so rapidly that, taking alarm, we started homewards as fast as we could run. But the stupendous slaty-black darkness, mixed with yellow clouds of dust, gained on us, and before we got to the gate the terrified screams of wild birds reached our ears, and glancing back we saw multitudes of gulls and plover flying madly before the storm, trying to keep ahead of it. Then a swarm of big dragon-flies came like a cloud over us, and was gone in an instant, and just as we reached the gate the first big drops splashed down in the form of liquid mud. We had hardly got indoors before the tempest broke in its full fury, a blackness as of night, a blended uproar of thunder and wind, blinding flashes of lightning, and torrents of rain. Then as the first thick darkness began to pass away, we saw that the air was white with falling hailstones of an extraordinary size and appearance. They were big as fowls' eggs, but not egg-shaped; they were flat, and about half-an-inch thick, and being white, looked like little blocks of bricklets made of compressed snow. The hail continued falling until the earth was white with them, and in spite of their great size they were driven by the furious wind into drifts two or three feet deep against the walls of the buildings.

It was evening and growing dark when the storm ended, but the light next morning revealed the damage we had suffered. Pumpkins, gourds, and water-melons were cut to pieces, and most of the vegetables, including the Indian corn, were destroyed. The fruit trees, too, had suffered greatly. Forty or fifty sheep had been killed outright, and hundreds more were so much hurt that for days they went limping about or appeared stupefied from blows on the head. Three of our heifers were dead, and one horse—an old loved riding-horse with a history, old Zango. —W. H. HUDSON

Here is another example of a remembered experience. Notice how quiet it is, in contrast with the tumult which Hudson describes. And yet it is interesting.

No More Sundays

As far back as I can remember Sunday always belonged to Grandmother. Father would take my brother and me along with my mother in our freshly washed car and off we would go in the early morning to see her. We would drive through the busy city, over the massive bridge on the river, and then climb the hills.

When we finally reached Grandmother's house, she would be standing there on the porch smiling, and we would run to her and be enveloped in her arms. She always felt big and warm and made us think of flowers even in winter.

The house was always happy and a big pitcher of cold milk and a plate of cookies waited for us. We would dash into the kitchen, finish our goodies, and then run out into the big back yard.

Here, where the air was fresh and clean, we would spend hours chasing the butterflies from flower to flower. It was as if Grandmother's garden held all the flowers in the world. Then we would swing on the swings, play in the tree house, and watch the ducks in the pond. Grandmother had the very best place in the whole world.

In the late afternoon we would go back into the house and eat the feast she had prepared for us. She always baked us a cake and never scolded us for taking a second and then a third helping. Then we wiped the dishes for her. At last we would have to start home, our hands holding the bag of cookies and our cheeks warm from her kisses.

In the winter we would sit by the fireplace and drink hot chocolate. Then we would run up to the attic, almost as big as a whole apartment in the city, and play games. Sometimes we would go through the old trunks, pulling out the clothes of by-gone days and pictures of Grandmother when she was a girl. Sometimes she came up and, going through a very special trunk, she would find something that we would put in a very special place when we returned home.

Then Grandmother became ill and had to be taken to a hospital. We never really saw Grandmother after that. We would go to the hospital and all we could do was look at her through the window of her room on the third floor. She would look at us and smile as much as she could.

The hospital had a big garden but it wasn't fun like Grandmother's so we sat on the front steps and waited for our parents. In the winter we waited in the white, stiff lobby that smelled bitter and looked so sad. There were no hugs and cookies. No butterflies and feast. Just Grandmother's smile through the window.

Then there was no Grandmother at all. She was gone and so were Sundays. —STUDENT THEME BY MARLENA ROBINSON

After writing fairly simple narratives about personal experiences, especially if you have been successful with them, you may wish to try something else. Here is an example of something written out of the imagination by a student who had had no experience like that narrated here. It was suggested by the following headlines in a newspaper:

WOMAN TRIES TO COMMIT SUICIDE
Widow, despondent over husband's death,
Fails in attempt to take her life

Mom Died Too

When Pop died we kids became orphans. Of course we were all grown and married, and Mom was still living, but when Pop died, all the things that meant "Mom" to us died with him. All that was left was somebody in her image. Her voice had lost its caressing warmth and from her eyes had gone the bright tenderness that had been there before. When she spoke, it was in a monotone without timbre or resonance, and her beautiful blue eyes became opaque and hard. It would be nice to say that the light went out in Mom when Pop died because she loved him so much. I can't say it because it isn't true.

I was the only one who completely understood Mom. It was not because I was so smart, but because I was so much like her. We liked the same kind of people, we got angry at the same things, and we both felt the need of sacrifice to those who belonged to us. Nature completed the pattern by giving me the same number of children, three boys and a girl.

One morning, a couple of weeks after Pop died, the phone rang. "Eleanor?" Through its strain I recognized the voice of Uncle Jim. "Get down to the City Hospital right away. Your mother is very sick. Took some poison. The doctors are working on her. Your brothers are here now."

They let us see her after they had saved her life. We stood by her bed, my brothers and I. Desperately, I voiced the question that was in our minds. "Why, Mom? Why?"

She looked at us. Like the click of a camera, her eyes lit up for a moment, as if to take a picture of her loved ones, and as quickly they were shuttered. She turned away.

Why? Why? I had to find the answer. Everything that was important to me depended on finding out why she had done this.

For my answer I had to go all the way back to the beginning, as far back as I could remember.

Pop was an easy-going guy whose philosophy was "live and let live." He had a shrewd mind and he might have accomplished big things had it not been for his one great weakness—gambling. Yet, I don't know whether it was gambling that was his undoing or being married to the wrong kind of woman. Anyway, the combination was too much for him. He couldn't fight both.

Pop's whole life was wrapped up in cards and horses. Once in a while he would tear himself away from his daily double or inside straight and look after his family. What did it matter to us if we had holes in our shoes when Pop took us to the circus? Maybe our rent wasn't paid, but we had some swell toys. We felt Mom was being mean when she complained that she had a hard enough time feeding us without worrying about feeding the dogs Pop brought home. We grew up knowing that we couldn't depend on Pop for too much but he was our father and we loved him for the things he gave us.

Mom was a wonderful mother. She lived only for her children. Maybe she felt she had to make up for what Pop didn't give us by giving more of herself. But she wasn't right for Pop. She too was weak. It wasn't an out and out weakness like gambling. It was a more hidden kind and only those of us who have it recognize it for what it is. People called her good because she didn't complain. But wouldn't a devoted mother who loved her children so much fight for their bare need for food, clothing, and shelter? She was uncomplaining not so much because she was good as because it was easier to accept the burden of her husband's gambling than to fight against it.

We kids finally grew up, married, and had children of our own. Throughout the years there had always been the gambling, but after we left the house, taking the life and laughter with us, the sickness broke into a raging fever.

Mom, too, felt the years. Her nerves were not as strong as they had been and she was lonely. With her children gone, her work lessened, and she had too much time to brood. After thirty uncomplaining years, she started to fight with Pop. She came to my brothers and me to ask us to tell Pop to give up gambling. We knew it wouldn't do any good and we didn't want to interfere, but we felt we owed it to her. It was on one of those occasions that I spoke to him. It might have turned out all right as it had at other times, but I had my own little hell to live with and what I said that night wasn't pretty. During the argument he said to me, "Look here now, that's no way to talk to your father."

"Father?" I cried. "You call yourself a father? What did you ever do for me?"

Very quietly he answered, "I never did you any harm."

His voice and the hurt in his eyes nearly drove me crazy. I walked out of the room, tears spilling from my eyes, hating him, myself, and all the things that made me speak to him as I had. Then I heard him say to Mom, "Agnes, you're taking the children away from me, and I'll never forgive you."

A few months later he caught pneumonia. Mom and I sat together watching him under the oxygen tent.

"Eleanor," my mother said, "your father is dying."

"Yes, I know, but the only thing I feel is that it will be a release for you."

She looked at me with something close to horror. My father was dying and I felt no loss. She said nothing. In the morning he died.

Mom blamed herself because we didn't cry when Pop died. She remembered his words. She felt she had robbed a father of his children. She reasoned that because she had taken the children from their father, she had no right to them either. The doctors saved her body, but she ended her life anyway in her fashion. This was her way of atoning for the sin she thought she had committed. That is why Mom took poison.

—STUDENT THEME BY RIMA GOLDSMITH

ASSIGNMENTS

I. Write a paragraph or two on one of the following subjects or a similar subject. In this assignment you should try through simple action to reveal character and state of mind.

1. A father warns his son against an unwise marriage.
2. A student tries to persuade his father to let him leave college.
3. A woman tries to talk a policeman out of giving her a ticket.
4. A man enters a restaurant, orders coffee and doughnuts.
5. A student, examination in hand, enters a professor's office.

II. Write a narrative theme on one of the following subjects or a similar one.

1. My first job
2. The hardest money I ever earned
3. When I became aware of beauty
4. When I became aware of cruelty
5. I learned what it meant to be poor
6. The time I learned about women (or men)
7. All that glitters is not gold
8. She wasn't too sick to be dancing with another man
9. I put him in his place
10. I was afraid I would fail

III. Write a paragraph about an event as a local newspaper would report it. Then write a narrative telling how you, a participant in the event, experienced it. You might take a fire, a Sunday school picnic, an accident, a dance, a game, or almost anything else that might be reported in the newspaper.

IV. Write a paragraph about an event as a local newspaper would report it. Then write a theme telling how you, as an observer, might describe it.

M

Answering Essay-type Examination Questions

It is bad enough to do poorly on an examination because you have not studied the material. It is worse to have studied it and still do poorly.

It is your responsibility to communicate your knowledge to your instructor. You must not expect him to look directly into your mind and see what you know but have not said. If you cannot express it, the instructor must assume you do not know it. And yet, every instructor will agree, many students fail to do justice to themselves in their examinations. Their failure is at least in part a failure in communication rather than in understanding.

If you have difficulty communicating your knowledge, you need of course to develop your general writing ability. Everything in this book thus bears on the subject "Answering Essay-type Examination Questions." Since examinations, however, are written under special conditions, a few points can be made that apply particularly to them.

First, understand the question. Be sure you have read it thoroughly. This caution may seem too obvious to need stating, but you would be surprised to know how many students, especially under the stress of an examination, read words and misread meanings. Do not let yourself be in such a hurry to get started that you attempt to fly off in several directions at once—or in the wrong direction.

Second, if you are asked a "fact" question, state the fact fully and clearly; give all the information that is required—and nothing else. For example, if you are asked "What are the two chief functions of the spinal cord?" you might answer "The two chief functions of the spinal cord are (1) to exercise reflex control over the activities of the various glands and internal organs and (2) to carry messages to and from the brain." You will *not* improve your answer by adding such irrelevant information as "The spinal cord looks like a string or cord. That is why it is called the spinal *cord*. It is a bundle of nerves. Frogs, like human beings, have spinal cords. The cord is protected by the bones of the spinal column." Stick to the question and do not try to impress the instructor with the wealth of your uncalled-for information.

Third, especially with a discussion question, take enough time to formulate your answer mentally before you start writing. Take time, that is, not only to understand the question but to give your answer some organization, perhaps in rough outline form. It is physically possible to write two thousand or more words an hour. Since no instructor would expect anything like that number, you will be showing good judgment if you take time to organize your answer before starting to put it down in words. The several minutes you spend doing so may well be the most fruitful of the whole hour because they will help you write more rapidly, as well as more cogently.

Fourth, give evidence and illustrations. If you have made a general statement, you will strengthen it greatly by mentioning a fact that supports it or illustrates it. For example, if you say that Shakespeare made use of the conventions of his time, you will show that you know what you are talking about if you explain that plays with revenge as their central theme were popular and that Shakespeare wrote *Hamlet* in this convention. Or if in a test in American history you say that neither the North nor the South was fully united during the Civil War, you will improve your answer by referring to the disgruntled Copperheads of the North and to the mountain people of Virginia and the Carolinas who remained loyal to the Union. No matter how sound a generalization is, it is much more convincing if it is supported by evidence.

On the other hand, and this is the fifth point, avoid a string of facts with no generalization to explain their significance.

For example, if you are answering the question "What were the chief accomplishments of the first presidential term of Woodrow Wilson?" you will *not* be doing well if you write something like this: "Wilson was inaugurated in 1913 and called a special session of Congress. Some of the features of this session were the Clayton Anti-Trust Act, the Federal Reserve System, and a new tariff. The tariff rates were lowered. There was trouble with Mexico. Another feature was the sinking of the *Lusitania*." Although you have some useful facts here, you show no understanding of the subject. You will have given, not an answer but some information out of which an answer might have been made.

A good answer to the question might properly divide the material under two headings, the first having to do with domestic legislation, the second with foreign relations and the effort to avoid war. You might say that the domestic legislation was thorough and extensive; it attempted to curtail the power of monopoly by making a number of reforms in financial control and in the conduct of business. This point you might illustrate by discussing tariff changes, the establishment of the Federal Reserve System, and legislation to control trusts. After giving evidence like this to support your first general statement, you might follow it with a second generalization about foreign relations and their effect on the domestic program. If again you cited sufficient evidence to support this generalization, you would have made clear your understanding of this period in our history.

In other words, to summarize the last two points together, you must give the pertinent facts, but you must also show what the facts mean. You must have the facts. And you must do something with them. *Generalizations unsupported by facts are empty; facts unorganized and uninterpreted by generalizations are meaningless. Only as they are united do they make a good answer.*

Finally, since all instructors, whatever they teach, object to bad writing, take time at the end to read through your answer and correct errors in grammar, spelling, and punctuation. If you write fast, you will probably make errors, but the fear that you may do so should not be allowed to slow you down and distract your attention. Write as well as you can without worrying about such errors. Then allow yourself five minutes or more at the end of the period to go over your examination for nothing except these things.

To illustrate some of these points, let us consider four hypothetical answers to an examination question. Suppose the question is on the excerpt by Urey on pages 186–187 of this text. (Even though you have read it before, read the excerpt now before you go on. Still better, read the excerpt and answer the question before reading the four answers that follow; then compare yours with them.) "Explain why Urey believes that neither foreign conquest nor the production of atom bombs can protect this country in the future."

Student A writes:

Urey tells us how destructive the atom bomb is, and he urges that we do something about it. He thinks it is a pity that politics has kept us from doing anything about it so far.

Such an answer is obviously worthless. It reveals that the student has not understood the material; it suggests that he has not even read it and is attempting a very poor bluff.

Student B writes:

Urey says it wouldn't do us any good to conquer other countries. The atom bomb is so destructive that they would be in ruins, and so it wouldn't do us any good to own them.

This answer is no better than the first. It does not invite the suspicion that the student is bluffing, but it shows something just as bad—that he has understood only enough to distort the author's point completely.

Student C writes:

Urey doubts whether we can keep ahead of other nations in the production of atom bombs. He also says that the atom bomb is so destructive that it would not do much good to have more bombs than an enemy.

This answer is better than the first two, but it is not good. It is vague and undeveloped. While it indicates that the student does not actually misunderstand the essay, it shows that he has failed to get much out of it.

Student D writes:

Urey admits that this country now has a superiority in the production of atom bombs, but he points out that we, seven percent of the world's population, cannot conquer and hold the rest of the world to prevent other nations from catching up with us. Perhaps, without conquering other nations, we can still outproduce them, keep them from catching up with us, it has been suggested. Urey asks what good that would do us. If they had enough bombs to destroy us, what good would it do us to have twice as many bombs to destroy them twice?

This, it should go without saying, is a good answer. The student has understood Urey's argument, and he has set it down clearly.

You should have no trouble seeing what is good or bad about the following four answers to another hypothetical question, this one based on the Overstreet excerpt on pp. 139–141: "Explain what the author means by living in a world of mutual exclusives." (Again, it is good practice to write out your own answer first.) Notice how the second student brings in an illustration but apparently does not understand it and certainly fails to do anything with it. Notice how the third student apparently understands the idea but writes a relatively poor answer (though a much better one than the second student) because he has not supported and illustrated his generalization. Notice how the fourth student not only understands the idea but illustrates it. The first student's answer needs no comment.

(1) The author explains how exclusive all social groups are in relation to other groups. This exclusiveness leads to discrimination and is therefore bad.

(2) The author discusses the difference between dogs and people. She tells how she had a date once with one man after

she had turned down another man because she was so busy. Then she met this first man while she was out with the second one. She felt very embarrassed and decided dogs were happier than people because they wouldn't have problems like this one.

(3) The author explains that human beings have to make choices because they cannot do two things at once, though they often wish to do so.

(4) The author explains how man, unlike lower forms of life, is often torn between two desires, each of which, if acted upon, excludes the possibility of carrying out the other. The dog may wish to scratch and to walk, but he does not wish to do one when he wishes to do the other. In contrast, the human being may really wish to work and at the same time really wish to play, and he therefore may be divided in his mind and troubled as no dog ever is.

The nervousness that seizes many students before and during an examination can hardly be argued away in a book like this. It may be remarked, however, that if you become tense you should not think you are unusual. Rather, you should realize that your response is the normal one. Some tension, as a matter of fact, is desirable. It is nature's way of preparing the body or mind for special exertion.

Much of the panic that some students are subject to can be avoided if they will get a good night's sleep before the examination, realize that the frantic effort to memorize everything at the last minute is futile and even confusing, and understand that no one remembers everything in a course—or is expected to.

One final word, and perhaps the most important of all, should be added: The student who studies a subject only to pass an examination rarely writes a really good examination. All during the semester such a student has been taking in an assortment of facts and trying to memorize his instructor's interpretation of them merely to hand facts and interpretation back to the instructor. He can list the facts and paraphrase the interpretations, perhaps, but he cannot use them. Actually, he has not wanted to use them; he has only wanted to return them. The best examinations are written by students who want to know a subject, not merely to pass a course.

ASSIGNMENTS

I. What mistakes and what needs talked about in this section apply particularly to your preparation for examinations and your writing of them? Write two or three paragraphs of explanation.

II. If you have an examination you have written this year, analyze it and write a paragraph or two on its merits and defects.

III. Write a theme on (1) the difficulties you have had with college examinations and (2) the steps you hope to take in order to do better work.

IV. Imagine yourself the instructor and prepare a good question on Highet's essay on Bach (pp. 27–31). Try to compose a question which will test understanding, not mere memory.

V. Suppose you were given this question about Dostoyevsky's *Crime and Punishment*. (Of course you could not answer the question if you had not read the novel, but you can do this assignment whether you have read it or not.) "Though *Crime and Punishment* has many abnormal characters acting in unusual and even melodramatic situations, the novel has great imaginative relevance for all readers, including those who are in no way abnormal and those whose lives have not been unusual. In a well-developed essay with adequate illustrative detail, account for this relevance."

First, what do the words mean, especially the word *relevance* and the term *imaginative relevance?*

Second, after you are sure of the meaning of the separate words, what does the question mean? What does it call for? Can you put the question in different words and make it mean the same thing?

Third, what would you think of an answer which discussed several characters but not the principal one? Of an answer which discussed only the principal character?

Explain why this would not be a satisfactory answer:

In *Crime and Punishment*, Raskolnikov, a student, murders an old, widowed pawnbroker and her stepsister. He suffers a great deal even though he escapes arrest. He comes to love a prostitute and partly under her influence he confesses his crime. He is sentenced to serve eight years in Siberia. Another unusual and even melodramatic episode is the attempt of Raskolnikov's sister to shoot a suitor and his subsequent suicide.

Explain how this answer would be improved:

Guilt and fear are present in all men. It is not necessary to have been a murderer to experience guilt; it is not necessary to fear imprisonment to fear the world. *Crime and Punishment* is a great novel because it treats the universal subjects of guilt and fear and also love and regeneration. No one can read about its characters without reading about himself.

N
Writing Letters

Letters may be divided into three broad categories: personal, business, and social.

PERSONAL LETTERS

There was a time when personal letters were not only the principal way of keeping in touch with one's friends but, for most educated people, the principal form of literary expression. When you have a chance, read some of the letters of Lord Chesterfield to his son, of Charles Lamb, or of Edward Fitzgerald. These were all literary men, of course, and their letters are far better than average. Yet they were not different in kind from the letters that educated nonliterary people of the time tried to write.

For a number of obvious reasons (the telephone, a more complex society, and so on), the writing of personal letters does not occupy us so much as it did our ancestors in the eighteenth and nineteenth centuries. Still, the educated adult who does not write business letters, reports, and memoranda as a major part of his job will find that personal letters constitute the great bulk of his writing activity.

The good personal letter is a cross between a conversation and a theme. Today it is likely to be nearer the conversation than the theme in informality. And yet, if it is worth much, it resembles the theme in several ways: (1) It is not all small talk, but has one or more subjects about which the author has something to say. This requires some thinking, some exploration of the subject. (2) It does not ramble, as conversation does, but uses a coherent organization, though not so rigid a one as the theme. On occasion one may incorporate

Thursday, midnight

Dear Doris,

It's been a while since we had the last double date at the shore before school opened, but I've been real busy.

Everything's O.K. this year. This new dorm is twentieth-century, and I have all but six hours in my major. When my friend Jeannie from Sweetwater came over last week end, she told me we have the best-looking rooms she has seen. We had a marvelous time at the game in spite of having to bury ourselves in two blankets apiece and wear earmuffs and everything else warm that we could lay our hands on. This was actually the best game of the season, and the boy who sits in front of me in Personality Adjustment made two of the three touchdowns—quite a personality! He could teach the course. Jeannie got so excited that she spilled hot coffee over an elderly gentleman's stadium-blanket, but he was cheering Bill Johnson's touchdown so hard that he just said "Watch it, little lady!" and went on yelling. That was an afternoon-deep freeze—but worth it!

I wish you could be in that psych class. Every day we study a new case-history, and some of those people we saw last summer around the hotel would make perfect material. In fact, I'm going to write up some of them as part of my term paper, which, incidentally, I have to finish this week end even if I have to shut myself up in my room twenty-four hours straight to do it. You remember the man with his wife—the one we always called Brigitte? Now there's a problem of adjustment! And what I can say about some of the adolescents—that twelve-year-old monster with glasses who always carried a water pistol which his mother never saw but everybody else did see. Maybe I'll even write up my own case-history—"Me as I Look to Me," you know.

Well, as you can see, I'm already in the mood for writing term papers. But do take time out from whatever you're doing to let me know how you like Highbridge U. at this point. I wish you could transfer here—because we'd have such fun—both playing Bertold Brecht or something, both in the choir, and all the rest—but I know you want a school near New York because of your music. Write soon and happy days!

Hasta luego,
Karen

postscript-like material in the letter ("Back for a moment to what John told us about that Pentagon business"), but using much of this is likely to prove disconcerting. As a matter of fact, the good letter writer pays almost as much attention to transitional words and phrases as the theme writer does. And he uses the techniques we have been discussing and practicing in the preceding chapters and assignments—he explains, defines, compares and contrasts, characterizes, and so on. (3) Though the good personal letter *sounds* like conversation, it is much more economical of words than conversation.

The letter on page 242 is a not atypical letter from one college girl to another. Note these things about the letter:

1. This girl did not feel it necessary to use her address or the date in the heading, but this information usually is included.

2. The salutation of the personal letter is usually the addressee's first name, followed by a comma, not a colon.

3. The complimentary close is highly informal—you can use almost anything you want to. You sign only your first name.

4. This letter is interesting and pleasant enough, but Karen did not use the opportunity to explore her subjects more thoroughly. The personal letter gives you a chance to think things through, without being stuffy, with somebody you care something about. It should have the dimensions of the *best* conversations without the trips into side lanes that those conversations inevitably take.

BUSINESS LETTERS

Almost all business letters are concerned with sales and public relations, and these, of course, involve techniques with which we cannot here be concerned. But good business letters do not differ in language and principles of organization from other forms of good writing. The language should be your own, unencumbered by padding or trite expressions. It should be sincere, and as vivid as is appropriate. You should check for misspellings, and the grammar should be standard. Use language that is neither highly formal nor very informal, but at about the level we have tried to maintain in this book. Clarity is of prime importance, of course, but clarity is not enough—your letter should be interesting as well. It should have *shape*—a beginning, a middle, and an end. It should have unity (nothing extraneous) and coherence—the paragraphs should follow one another logically.

Type all business letters on 8½″ × 11″ white paper. (The size may vary if for a business firm.) For very short letters you may want to double space, but single spacing gives a better appearance even for short letters, which can then be typed on half-size sheets.

Maintain a margin of about an inch on the left and keep the line endings as even as possible on the right. Avoid hyphenation at the ends of lines. After proofreading and revising (as for all other writing), *retype*. Never send a business letter with strikeovers or penned corrections or insertions. If at all possible, the letter should be restricted to one page and —again, if possible—to a single subject.

The Form

Certain standard forms should be observed in all business letters. We shall illustrate these forms with special reference to the letter of application, the one kind of important business letter you are likely to use soon.

(1) *The heading* This, the address of the writer and the date, goes at the upper right-hand side of the letter. It may take one of three forms, of which the first is the most common.

Block style, no end punctuation	415 Grove Street Bloomington, Illinois March 25, 1964

Indented, no end punctuation	415 Grove Street
	    Bloomington, Illinois
	        March 25, 1964

244

Indented, end punctuation   415 Grove Street,
                      Bloomington, Illinois,
                      March 25, 1964.

(2) *The inside address*   This is the *full* name and address of the person addressed. Use the appropriate title of address —Mr., Mrs., Dr., Professor, and so on. Type the first line (all lines in block style) flush left with the margin.

Mr. Grover L. Sands, Director   *Block style*
Bear Springs Camp
Bear Springs, Michigan

Mr. Grover L. Sands, Director   *Indented, no end*
   Bear Springs Camp   *punctuation*
      Bear Springs, Michigan

Mr. Grover L. Sands, Director,   *Indented, end*
   Bear Springs Camp,   *punctuation*
      Bear Springs, Michigan.

(3) *The salutation*   Use the person's last name in the salutation, which is always set flush left with the margin: Dear Mr. Jones, Dear Mrs. Smith, etc. Use a colon after the name.

(4) *The body*   Keep the letter as short as the subject permits, as we have noted above. If a second page is necessary, type the last name and title of the addressee at the top flush left, followed by the page number (Mr. Jones, page 2).

Do not include in the letter material that can be reduced to an easily read form and typed on a separate page for enclosure. The chief function of the application *letter,* for instance, is to let the addressee gain an impression of the applicant over and above what the facts (age, training, experience, references, etc.) can tell him. These can be put in an easily read resume.

(5) *Complimentary close*   The complimentary close varies with the purpose and tone of the letter. When emphasis is on public relations and the letter is warm in tone, "Cordially" or "Cordially yours" is appropriate. "Yours truly" is usually

too formal. Closes like "Respectfully yours" and "Faithfully yours" sound like something out of the eighteenth century and should never be used. "Sincerely" or "Sincerely yours" is dignified and safe.

(6) *The signature*   Type the name you customarily use (that is, with middle name or initial or no middle name) and sign over the name.

The sample application letter illustrates the above principles.

---

415 Grove Street
Bloomington, Illinois
March 25, 1964

Mr. Grover L. Sands, Director
Bear Springs Camp
Bear Springs, Michigan

Dear Mr. Sands:

   Dr. Charles Johnson, Placement Director at Alba College, has told me of your interest in securing a counselor in music at Bear Springs Camp for the coming summer. I should like to apply for that position, and I enclose a brief summary of personal information in support of this application.
   My principal instrument is the trumpet, but I am fairly good on

---

percussion instruments, and I can play enough piano to fill in when needed. During my junior and senior years in high school I was fortunate enough to be named assistant conductor of the band, and I occasionally conducted the orchestra in rehearsal. I studied harmony while in high school, and I am taking counterpoint and fugue at Alba College. In addition, I can tutor in seventh- and eighth-grade English and history. I expect to major in English and minor in history.

I was a member of the Boy Scouts, and I belong to the 4-H Club of Baylor County. I get along well with younger boys and enjoy working with them.

My high-school grades averaged B; I made A's in all my music courses. My grades so far this year have averaged B-, and I am making A in counterpoint and B+ in fugue. I am a member of the college band.

Dr. Johnson tells me that you expect to be visiting our campus April 14. I hope I will have a chance to talk with you then. Meanwhile, I shall be glad to furnish any further information you may want.

Sincerely yours,

Thomas A. Jones

Thomas A. Jones

[Separate sheet, to be enclosed]

Personal Data

NAME	Thomas A. Jones
ADDRESS	415 Grove Street, Bloomington, Ill.
DATE AND PLACE OF BIRTH	Bloomington, Ill., June 11, 1945
EDUCATION	Bloomington High School, Diploma, 1963
	Freshman at Alba College, Bloomington, 1963–64
EXPERIENCE	Helper, Gray's Pharmacy, Bloomington, part-time, 1959–60, summer, 1960
	Clerk, Swanson's Music Shop, Bloomington, summer, 1961
	Private teacher of trumpet, summers, 1962–3
REFERENCES	Mr. Charles Le Bow, Music Director, Bloomington High School
	Mr. Oscar Pierce, teacher of English, Bloomington High School
	Reverend Horace Friedlander, First Methodist Church of Bloomington

```
                    Dr. Joseph Macredi,
                       Chairman, Department
                       of Music, Alba
                       College
PERSONAL            Height  5' 10"
                    Weight  175
                    Hobbies  Ornithology,
                       baseball
                    Health Excellent--no
                       physical defects
```

SOCIAL NOTES

The machinery of society is oiled by set forms of more or less formal communications.

1. If you have spent a weekend at the home of a classmate, you will want to thank the parents. You will use personal stationery and write in ink. The note is informal.

> 725 Wisconsin Avenue
> Pocatello, Idaho
> March 17, 1963
>
> Dear Mr. and Mrs. Saunders:
>
> I believe this sort of letter is usually called a "bread-and-butter" note. Remembering the duck, those pancakes, and all the rest of the good things this past weekend, I think it might be better to call this one a "cake" note!
>
> But the talk was just as good as the food. I'm still a Republican, I guess, but you've certainly given me something to think about.
>
> Harry has promised to visit my parents early next month. Maybe we can all get together before the end of the school year. Meanwhile, thanks for treating me like another son.
>
> Sincerely yours,
> Tom Jones

2. Should you be lucky enough to be invited to a formal affair, your invitation will probably come on a small folded paper, with the following engraved message. (In less affluent circles, it may be in ink—longhand—never typed.) The language is rigidly prescribed.

> Mr. and Mrs. James Clark request the pleasure of Mr. Thomas Jones' company at dinner on Tuesday, April the seventh, at eight-thirty o'clock.
>
> R.S.V.P.
> 462 Knightridge Road
> March the Twenty-sixth

The R.S.V.P. (French: *Répondez s'il vous plaît*) means "Please reply," and you do, on paper of about the same size, in longhand, and in ink.

> Mr. Thomas Jones accepts with pleasure the kind invitation of Mr. and Mrs. James Clark to dinner on Tuesday, April the seventh, at eight-thirty o'clock.
>
> 624 College Avenue
> March the twenty-eighth

3. For less formal occasions, the invitation is less formal and so is the reply. Both are in longhand and in ink. The language is natural, not prescribed.

ASSIGNMENT I

You have become friends with a young Frenchman who, though he spent some time in this country, was not here long enough to learn much about the country. (He knows English very well.) In his last letter he has inquired about one of the subjects listed below. Write him a letter in which you answer his question—that will be the principal, though not the only, matter of your letter.

American college life   Race prejudice in America
American political parties   Beatniks
Dating in America   Cowboys
Baseball   Farming in America

ASSIGNMENT II

Write a letter of application for a part-time or summer job—other than counseling in a summer camp.

ASSIGNMENT III

Invite Mr. and Mrs. Reginald Van Gleason to a formal dance at your country estate and write their acceptance for them.

ASSIGNMENT IV

We have not discussed "public" letters, such as letters-to-the-editor. Write such a letter on something like the need for a new system of student elections, for more courses in the classics, or for changes in the fraternity setup, and explain in a paragraph how it differs from a personal letter.

O

Writing a Research Paper

The research paper—or, as it is often called, the library paper or term paper—is a special kind of long theme based on investigation of a carefully selected subject. The investigation is carried on chiefly in books, articles, pamphlets, and newspapers. The research paper differs, therefore, from most other themes in drawing its substance primarily from library materials rather than from opinions, impressions, and experience. Writing it will be of value to you, both in advanced college courses and afterwards, for it will give you practice in methods of uncovering facts, weighing their importance, taking notes on what you find, and putting your information and ideas into clear and interesting form.

As an introduction to doing a research paper, read the following section, which gives a brief survey of the project from start to finish. It is both a quick preliminary glance at the whole process and a summary that you may find useful to refer to later as a check on your own progress.

TEN STEPS IN WRITING A RESEARCH PAPER: A BRIEF GUIDE

(1) Unless your instructor assigns your topic, find a subject of your own. Sometimes an area you have been interested in but have had no time to investigate will do very well, but often a subject that you know nothing at all about will be at least as good. Then you will have the pleasure of seeing for yourself that as you come to know about a subject you grow to like it; you will learn, in other words, that knowledge breeds interest.

(2) Do some rapid reading, taking no notes, in encyclope-

dias and other books that survey the whole area of which your subject is a part. This will enable you to get at least a rough idea of the proportions of your subject and to see what its limits may be.

(3) Make a preliminary outline and state the thesis of your paper—at least an approximate, preliminary thesis—in a sentence.

(4) Make a tentative, working list of sources (your "working bibliography"). Be sure that all the items on this list are available in the library you are going to use and that you can get hold of them fairly quickly.

(5) Start to gather material. After you have completed your first rapid survey and pretty well defined your subject, begin to read more carefully and to take notes on points that seem important. Make out a bibliography card for each source; record on it full information so that this work will not need to be repeated. Put notes in your own words whenever possible; copy the words of the source only when you think you may want to quote them. Be sure (a) that you put down the exact name of the source and the exact page and (b) that, if you quote or record facts from a source, you give the exact words or facts of the passage or, if you are summarizing, that you summarize a thought accurately.

(6) As you gather material, keep reconsidering your subject. Probably you can limit it even further than you thought when you made your preliminary outline and your first statement of thesis. In any event, you should see your subject more and more sharply as you go along.

(7) Continue to add items to your list of sources. Put aside items you find you cannot use; some of them may later prove to have material you need. Remember that you are working toward a final bibliography, which will be an important part of your paper.

(8) When you think you have completed your reading and note-taking, or have almost done so, look over all your notes and revise your outline. Then sort your note cards according to their subject under the main headings of your outline. Next, arrange the first group of cards and, after

thinking about them and deciding what facts to use and what passages to quote, start to write. Keep going; do not make style or punctuation your main concern in the first draft. After you have finished the first section of your paper, go right ahead to the second, and so on until the rough draft is completed.

(9) Read over the completed first draft. If you discover that some parts of the paper require further work or that you need to fill in gaps in the material, go to the library and get this done at once. Then sit down to write the second draft. This time, pay careful attention to everything that will make the writing of your paper good. Be especially watchful of the punctuation of such unfamiliar material as footnotes, but do not fall into the error of thinking that because this is a research paper, you may slight the qualities of good writing. The research must be good, but the writing must also be good.

(10) If the second draft is satisfactory, make your final copy. Observe all regulations about form. (For example, does your instructor ask for a title page or for an outline with the final draft? Where does he ask you to put your footnotes—at the foot of the page or at the end of the paper?) Arrange the list of sources in alphabetical order and draw up your final bibliography. Since there is more chance for error in this paper than in any other you are likely to write in this course, give your final draft an especially thorough proofreading.

Then, at long last, hand in your paper—on time! And if your instructor wishes, turn in with it your bibliography cards and note cards and rough drafts.

CHOOSING A SUBJECT

If your instructor does not assign a subject, you will want to give thought to finding a good one for yourself. The first requirement is that the subject be one in which you are interested—or can become interested. (And that is, or should be, practically everything.) It will probably be too large at first, but do not worry about that. You cannot write about such broad topics as Switzerland or Byron or farming or the American Revolution, but they all will be found to include many suitable subjects if you examine them carefully. One student who was interested in American history narrowed his subject from the whole vast record of the United States to the story of a man he had always wanted to know more about—Patrick Henry. But since even this subject was much too large, the student sought an aspect of Henry's life about which he could write a research essay. After some quick reading, he discovered that historians had wondered why Henry refused to attend the convention that adopted the American Constitution. This looked like a good trail to follow, and the student did so, finding himself with a subject of the right size, unified around a central problem that threw interesting light on Patrick Henry and on the period when the Constitution was adopted. This subject was limited enough to allow the student to be accurate and reasonably thorough.

If, after searching your mind, you still do not come up with a promising subject, go to an encyclopedia and leaf through it, or turn to a newspaper and glance over the great range of subjects suggested there. A few minutes spent with the New York *Times* on a single Sunday showed many subjects worth considering. Here are some of them: federal aid to schools, causes of automobile accidents, the Gregorian chant, Buddhism, growth of automation in industry, the climate of Guatemala, educational use of television, the Republican Party in the South, the American Federation of Musicians, Benedict Arnold's plot (and how guilty was his wife?), Dinosaur National Monument (and other national parks), efforts to save the whooping crane from extinction, history of the federal income tax, irrigation in India. Some of these subjects would need much limitation, and for others information might not be available to you. But after looking over such a varied list (itself just a skimming of the possibilities), no one should complain that he can't find a subject for research.

The following kinds of papers are usually unsatisfactory:

the technical paper in such fields as astronomy, medicine, or music; the biographical sketch, which provides little opportunity for the student to give original organization to his material; the paper depending on a single book; the paper requiring too much background (for instance, "The Influence of the Eighteenth-Century Novelists on Charles Dickens"); the paper depending on books available only in widely scattered libraries; the formless paper, composed of a series of parts not closely connected ("Customs of the Pennsylvania Dutch," for instance); or the paper on so narrow a subject that the student will have difficulty finding enough material ("Cosmetics in Ancient Egypt").

Keep in mind that your subject must involve material in the library. Not all research does. Much research is carried on in scientific laboratories. And when the polltakers wish to find out how people are going to vote in the next election, they do not go to the library but knock on front doors. However, since a major purpose of this assignment is to familiarize you with the library, your research should be based on material found there.

A LIST OF SUGGESTED TOPICS FOR RESEARCH PAPERS
(Most of these topics will need to be limited.)

The Antarctic Expedition of Captain Robert F. Scott
Are Pesticides Becoming Dangerous?
How Did Jefferson Davis Justify Secession?
Origins of the Ballet
Yeats and the Irish Theatre
A Famous Trial
The Theory that Bacon Wrote Shakespeare's Plays
Garibaldi and the Unification of Italy
The Effectiveness of Brainwashing
Importance of the Press Correspondent in the Civil War
Problems Connected with the Death of President Harding
Effectiveness of Classroom Television
The Psychological Effects of Color
Fluoridation
Second Thoughts about Hiroshima
The Rise of Mussolini

256

Why the RAF Won the Battle of Britain
Importance of the Submarine in World War I
Why ————— Was (or Was Not) Elected
The Invention of Moving Pictures (or any other important
    mechanical device)
Who Really Invented the Steamboat?
The Adoption of Prohibition in Maine (or some other state)
The League of Nations and Mussolini's Invasion of Ethiopia
Freedom of the Press in the Confederacy (or in the North)
    During the Civil War
Modern Whaling Methods
Benjamin Franklin's Effort to Gain French Support in the
    American Revolution
The Governmental Structure of the Aztec Empire
Byron's Part in the Greek War for Independence
The Quaker Attitude Toward Slavery
How the Korean War Started
Theories of the Origin of Hurricanes
How My College (or University) Was Founded
Problems Created for Cities by the Growth of Suburban Areas
Agricultural Resources of Israel
Melville and the Literary Critics of the Nineteenth Century
Formal Gardens in Colonial America
Soil Erosion in North Africa
Roman Aqueducts
England's Role in the Promulgation of the Monroe Doctrine
Coeducation in Nineteenth-Century America
Divorce in Soviet Russia
The Climate of Mars
Theories of Diet in the Eighteenth Century
Slavery in Ancient Greece
Napoleon on St. Helena
Validity of Intelligence Tests
Crops Without Soil
Goebbels' Propaganda Methods
Vocabulary and Success
Why John Hancock Signed the Declaration of Independence
Why Napoleon Retreated from Moscow
Significance of the Dead Sea Scrolls
Socialized Medicine in Great Britain
Why Lee Was Compelled to Surrender at Appomattox

The Original Plan for Washington, D.C., and the Actual
  Growth of the City
Why Were the Japanese Successful at Pearl Harbor?
What Has Been Done to Break Down the Caste System in
  India?
The Reasons for Grover Cleveland's Opposition to Bryan
Ancient Atomic Theories
The Problem of Railroads in the Confederacy

USING THE LIBRARY

After a subject has been approved by your instructor, you
should go to the library and start a *systematic* search for material. Here are the chief steps to take in discovering what
has been written on your subject and—especially important
—what is available in your own library (for you must remember that not even the largest libraries contain all books; you
may see items in the bibliography of an encyclopedia article
that are not to be found anywhere in this country).

(1) Look in the card catalogue. Every book the library
has is listed alphabetically under the *author*, the *subject*, and
the *title*. On every card are a number of essential facts, as
the illustration on page 259 will make clear.

A quick examination of this card will show that it contains
information of great practical value for anyone investigating
the Aztecs: (1) The book is sufficiently recent to take account of modern research. (2) Its length indicates that it
probably stands in a middle ground between brevity and
great detail. (3) It has a rather generous amount of illustrative material. (4) It is part of a series sponsored by a repu-
table scientific society; you can therefore place considerable
reliance on what it says. (5) It contains in its bibliography a
long list (some twenty-seven pages) of books and articles;
you can doubtless find a number of items here that you too
will want to look into. (6) The card is also filed under the
subject headings "Aztec" and "Mexico—History—To 1519";
such headings are valuable leads: you will want to look in
the card catalogue to see what other books are listed under
these subjects.

Although some cards contain less information and some more than the one we have used for illustration, all cards that seem in the least connected with your subject are worth examination. A little practice will enable you to tell a great deal about a book just by looking at the card in the library catalogue.

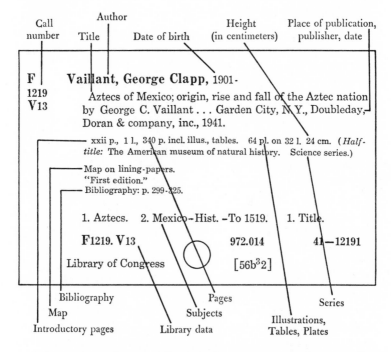

(2) Look in the periodical and newspaper indexes and in bibliographies. The most generally useful are these:

A. The *Readers' Guide to Periodical Literature*, commonly known simply as *Readers' Guide*. Articles that have appeared in most of the nontechnical magazines since 1900 are entered here, listed alphabetically by subject and author. *Readers' Guide* is published in annual volumes; monthly supplements keep it up to date. Next to the card catalogue, this is for most students one of the most helpful sources of information. Before you start to use it, read the explanation of abbreviations at the beginning of each volume.

B. The *New York Times Index*. This is published monthly. For events of any general importance since 1913, it can be used for newspapers in all parts of the country. Find in it the date of a happening and then look in whatever papers are available to you for that date.

C. A few others, somewhat more specialized:
1. The *International Index to Periodical Literature*. This lists many scholarly, technical, and foreign articles not found in *Readers' Guide*. It is very valuable for some subjects, because in general the magazines it indexes are more specialized than those listed in *Readers' Guide*.
2. *Poole's Index to Periodical Literature*. This lists articles in general periodicals by subject only, from 1802 to 1906. It corresponds to *Readers' Guide* for older articles.
3. *Book Review Digest*. This often helps you decide quickly on the worth and scope of books published since 1905.
4. Indexes in particular fields. The following are useful. For further information, consult your librarian.
   Agricultural Index
   Biography Index
   Education Index
   Granger's Index to Poetry
   Industrial Arts Index

D. *Essay and General Literature Index*. This index is a key to books in which essays and articles are collected. It includes many individual essays not listed in the card catalogue.

(3) Look in the reference room or department of your library. Here you will find reference works, some general, others rather specialized. Listed below are some of the most important.

GUIDE

Constance M. Winchell's *Guide to Reference Books* (based on an early *Guide* by Mudge). This may be a good place to begin your search. It will list the reference books most useful in your field.

ENCYCLOPEDIAS

Chambers's Encyclopedia
Encyclopedia Americana
Encyclopaedia Britannica
New International Encyclopedia

Of special encyclopedias and related reference works there are too many to name, but here are a few good and representative ones:

On agriculture	*Cyclopedia of American Agriculture*
On business	*Business Executive's Handbook*
	Encyclopedic Dictionary of Business
On education	*Cyclopedia of Education*
	Encyclopedia of Modern Education
On history	*Cambridge Ancient History*
	Cambridge Medieval History
	Cambridge Modern History
	Dictionary of American History
On literature	*Cambridge Bibliography of English Literature*
	Cambridge History of English Literature
	Cambridge History of American Literature
	Literary History of the United States
On music	*Grove's Dictionary of Music and Musicians*
On religion	*Catholic Encyclopedia*
	Encyclopedia of Religion and Ethics
	Jewish Encyclopedia
	New Schaff-Herzog Encyclopedia of Religious Knowledge

On science   *Van Nostrand's Scientific Encyclopedia*

On the social

sciences   *Encyclopedia of the Social Sciences*

DICTIONARIES

Oxford English Dictionary (also called *New English Dictionary on Historical Principles;* abbreviated as OED or NED)

Webster's Third New International Dictionary

New Standard Dictionary (Funk and Wagnalls)

There are many special dictionaries, such as Fowler's *Dictionary of Modern English Usage* and Partridge's *Dictionary of Slang and Unconventional English.* Consult the files of your library.

BIOGRAPHICAL DICTIONARIES

On living Americans   *Who's Who in America*

On Americans of the past   *Dictionary of American Biography*

On living persons, chiefly British   *Who's Who*

On British subjects of the past   *Dictionary of National Biography*

On living persons of all lands   *Current Biography* (published monthly)

YEARBOOKS

Americana Annual (annual supplement to the *Encyclopedia Americana*)

Britannica Book of the Year (annual supplement to the *Encyclopaedia Britannica*)

Information Please Almanac

New International Year Book (annual supplement to the *New International Encyclopedia*)

Statesman's Year Book

Statistical Abstract of the United States

World Almanac and Book of Facts

ASSIGNMENT I

Write about three or four sentences on a research subject you are considering. Tell something about the subject in general, show what aspects of it you might treat, and indicate how you think you might limit it. Then list at least five sources that you find in the card catalogue of your library or in the periodical indexes. (Be sure that all the items in the indexes are in your library.) For each source give the author's full name and the exact title. Your instructor may also wish you to give the library call numbers for books on your list.

FINDING THE BEST SOURCES

It is a widespread superstition that anything in print, especially if it is in a book, must be true. Many books are sound and accurate, of course, but others contain a mixture of truth and falsehood, and some are completely unreliable. Although you may feel rather unsure who the best authorities are, you have to make some kind of judgment, because you simply cannot do good research if the sources you use are poor. The problem of reliability, which sometimes plagues even the most experienced scholar, cannot be cleared up in a few paragraphs, but you may find the following advice helpful.

First, go whenever possible to primary sources as well as to secondary sources. Primary sources are original materials, such as documents, reports, and letters. Secondary sources are books and articles based on these original materials. Your own paper, if it is good enough, is a secondary source. Lincoln's letters and speeches would be primary sources; Carl Sandburg's *Abraham Lincoln: the War Years* would be secondary.

Second, try to discriminate among authors. Difficult though this is, it is not quite so difficult as it may appear on first thought. Here are some aids in making judgments about books and articles. (1) What do you know about the author? If he is writing on the history of the tariff in the United States and is a professor of economics at a leading college or university, that fact means something—though not everything. (2) Where was the article published? Publication in a good professional journal is a recommendation. (3) What do the reviewers quoted in the *Book Review Digest* say about a book? (And remember that you can use the *Digest* to lead you back to the full review if you need to.) (4) Is the book referred to with respect by other writers and included in bibliographies? (5) What can you tell from the style? Does it impress you as biased or objective? Does the author go in for name-calling when he should be quietly seeking the truth?

Third, for most subjects, consult both recent and older sources. Although for many subjects older material is valuable and sometimes definitive, you should always see what contemporary work has been done. For example, a paper on the rise of the Standard Oil Company which used only sources before 1940—and therefore neglected such an essential source as Allan Nevins' *Study in Power: John D. Rockefeller* (1953)—would show very inadequate investigation.

Fourth, do not depend on articles in popular magazines. Such articles are occasionally useful when you are first surveying your subject, but they tend to be superficial, repetitious, and often erroneous. What would you think of a physician who kept up with the research in his field, not by reading medical journals but by reading their popularizations in newspapers and digest magazines? At most, glance through popular articles quickly; then follow up your subject in better—often professional—magazines and in books.

THE WORKING BIBLIOGRAPHY

After your subject has been approved, your next step is to assemble—by means suggested in the section above called "Using the Library"—a tentative or working bibliography. A bibliography is simply a list of books, periodical articles, and possibly other sources which pertain to your subject, and the word *tentative* here means that you think they may pertain but you do not know because you have not examined them.

This tentative collection of sources will do to work with (which is why it is called your "working" bibliography), but it will certainly be changed considerably as you go along, and may be quite different from the final bibliography at the end of your finished research paper.

To set about assembling your working bibliography, provide yourself with a supply of ruled cards ($3'' \times 5''$ or $4'' \times 6''$). Record the essential information about each book or article on a separate card.

Here is a specimen bibliography card for a book (see page 259 for the library's catalogue card for this same book):

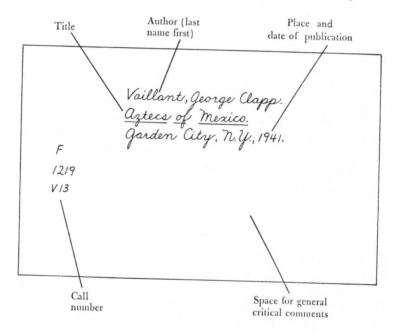

Here is a card for a periodical article:

> Frederick, John T. "Fiction of the Second World War," *College English*, XVII (Jan., 1956), 197-204.

Note that on the first card the title is underlined, as are the titles of all books. Note also that on the second card the title of the article is placed within quotation marks, the name of the periodical is underlined, the volume number (XVII) is given in Roman numerals without the word *volume*, the date is in parentheses, and the first and last pages of the article are indicated.

OUTLINING

Whether you outline for shorter themes or not, you certainly will need an outline for your research paper. In fact, you will probably need at least two outlines: a preliminary one after you have finished your first reading (of such things as encyclopedia articles) and a final one after you have finished your reading and note-taking. For the general principles of outlining, refer to pages 22–33.

Your instructor will tell you whether or not he wishes you to hand in an outline with your completed paper.

TAKING NOTES

After you have decided on a subject, made a quick survey of it and a preliminary outline, and collected your working bibliography, you are ready to start taking notes. Keep the following advice in mind.

(1) Carry with you a supply of ruled cards. These are the 3" × 5" or 4" × 6" cards mentioned above under "The Working Bibliography"; some instructors prefer that you use the smaller size for bibliography cards and the larger size for notes. Some students cut up slips of paper of these sizes, but notes on such slips are more difficult to handle than those on cards.

(2) Put only one note on each card. Then, when you have finished gathering material, you will find it easy to shuffle the cards around and arrange them in any order you need.

(3) Indicate at the bottom of the card the name of the source and the page or pages from which you are taking your note. You may use shortened titles. Thus: Vaillant, *Aztecs*, pp. 143–47. (You will have full bibliographical information about your source on the bibliography card.)

(4) When you quote directly, put quotation marks around the quoted words. Be sure to note the page numbers on which the quoted material appears in the source. Thus: Vaillant, *Aztecs*, p. 145.

(5) Be exact. Pay strict attention to punctuation and to spelling, especially the spelling of proper names. Check all note cards for accuracy while you have the sources before you. Write legibly.

(6) Use brackets for corrections and explanations inserted in a quotation. (See **38**.)

> This poem [*Hero and Leander*] was begun by Marlowe and completed by Chapman.

(7) If you wish to omit words within a quotation, use ellipses. (See **30c**.) Be sure that any omission does not distort the sense of the original.

(8) Take notes as you read when you find material that

you think you may want to use. Do not, however, copy almost everything in a book on the chance that you may use it somewhere. Part of the time you should take no notes at all, and most of the time when you do take them, you should put them in your own words.

(9) Allow a little space at the top of each card. This you can later use for labeling the card with a useful heading (sometimes called a "slug"). Cards for a paper on the Spanish conquest of Mexico, for instance, might bear such headings as "Landing in Mexico," "Personality of Cortez," and so on.

The following note card illustrates some of the advice just given. Observe that the note is partly in the student's own words and partly quoted directly. The numbers in parentheses refer to the points made above.

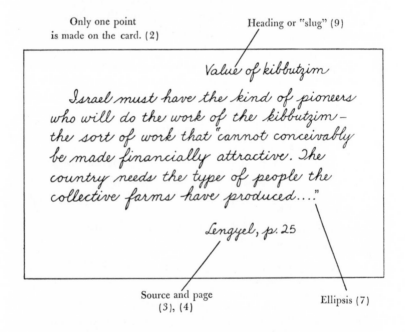

Only one point is made on the card. (2)

Heading or "slug" (9)

Value of kibbutzim

Israel must have the kind of pioneers who will do the work of the kibbutzim — the sort of work that "cannot conceivably be made financially attractive. The country needs the type of people the collective farms have produced...."

Lengyel, p. 25

Source and page (3), (4)

Ellipsis (7)

(See page 309 for the use that the student made of this card.)

USING MATERIAL FROM A SOURCE

The material you find in a book or article may be used in various ways. Since this is a practical matter of much importance and one that commonly puzzles students, let us take a passage and illustrate some of the legitimate—and one or two of the illegitimate—uses to which it may be put:

A perennial defense of football has been that it developed college spirit. However, as earlier chapters indicate, there has rarely been a dearth of college spirit. Such spirit as was generated by athletics has not always been of an admirable variety. But one thing football *did* accomplish: it broke the pattern of snobbishness based on race, religion, and wealth. Students and alumni alike recruited team candidates from all ranks and races. In 1893 the captain of the Harvard team was William H. Lewis, a Negro. American Indians from Carlisle played against the most aristocratic teams in the East. The sons of Polish immigrants shared locker rooms and training tables with Princeton Anglo-Saxons. The many jokes about the unpronounceable names of football players are only testimony to the prevalence of second-generation Americans on college teams. And because of the prestige of football heroes, such men tended to become big men in college. Perhaps football's greatest achievement is its contribution to social democracy in the colleges.

—ERNEST EARNEST

Here are some ways you might properly use this passage:

1. You might quote the whole paragraph, or almost all of it, though you probably would not want or need to do so. Usually only the essential primary sources should be quoted at such length.

2. You might quote parts of it in either of the following ways, depending on whether the quoted material runs to four lines or more:
   A. According to Earnest, college football "broke the pattern of snobbishness based on race, religion, and wealth."

269

B. According to Earnest, college football

> . . . broke the pattern of snobbishness based on race, religion, and wealth. Students and alumni alike recruited team candidates from all ranks and races. . . . And because of the prestige of football heroes, such men tended to become big men in college.

Note that the quotation under B runs to more than four lines. It is therefore indented and—if the theme is typed—given single spacing. No quotation marks are used for material set off in this way.

3. You might summarize the paragraph in your own language:

Though football has not always benefited American education, Earnest points out that it has had one good effect. Because of the prestige of the football player on the campus and because the football player often came from the wrong side of the tracks, the old snobbishness of the American college began to break down. The football player was judged on performance, not by family, and the practice of judging men in that way, once it had begun in the stadium, began to penetrate into other parts of the college.

4. You might combine summary and quotation:

Though football has often injured American education, Earnest points out that "it broke the pattern of snobbishness based on race, religion, and wealth." Because of the standing of the football player on the campus and because he often came from the wrong side of the tracks, he had to be judged by performance, not by family.

5. The passage might be used as the source of a fact:

The little that is heard of the American Indian in sports in recent years should not lead us to the wrong conclusion. There was a time, early in this century, when Indian football teams from the school at Carlisle, Pennsylvania, played with the best colleges in the East.

Of these five more or less distinct ways of making use of the passage, each is legitimate—with this important provision: that the use is acknowledged in a footnote. (Footnotes are explained in the next section.)

Learning to use printed material involves knowing what not to do, as well as what to do. Two types of misuse are especially common.

First improper use:

A frequent defense of football is that it has developed college spirit. College students have usually had sufficient spirit, however, and moreover, the spirit brought about by football has not always been desirable. Football did accomplish one thing of value, however, in that it did much to destroy snobbishness based on race, religion, and wealth. A Negro was elected captain of the Harvard football team in 1893 and the Carlisle Indians played against the most aristocratic teams of the East. The sons of immigrants played side by side with the sons of people who had come over on the Mayflower. The jokes about the unpronounceable names of football players show how many second-generation Americans made the team. Because of the prestige of football, it has contributed a great deal to the growth of social democracy in the colleges, as Earnest says.

The paragraph above deserves severe criticism, even though the name of the source (Earnest) is mentioned in passing. The paragraph is improper because it is neither summary nor quotation but an indeterminate mixture, in which the student sometimes echoes and sometimes appropriates the language of the original. The paragraph invites the charge of plagiarism, which is the stealing of someone else's words and ideas and presenting them as one's own. Close paraphrase of this sort should be contrasted with summary, the third method illustrated above, in which the language is authentically different from that used in the original.

Second improper use:

Ernest Earnest attacks the recruiting practices of colleges in their effort to build up winning football teams. Instead of drawing their students from the class of people who wanted and needed an education, the colleges brought in alleged students who could hardly speak English. Football, in fact, has contributed to the growth of socialism, he says.

The passage above, a complete travesty of the original, will illustrate an important point: to misrepresent what an author says is as dishonest as to plagiarize from him.

FOOTNOTES

Purposes of footnotes

(1) The chief use of footnotes is to indicate the source of a quotation, fact, or idea.

(2) Footnotes may be used occasionally for definition, supplementary explanation, or comment. Such footnotes usually should be held to a minimum.

    A. Definition:
        [1] *Cloth of Calicut* is the old name for calico.

    B. Explanation:
        [2] The name *Canada* was for a long time applied only to a small area around what is now the city of Quebec.

    C. Comment:
        [3] Little reliance can be placed on the geographical data in Frobisher's narratives of his voyages.

Form of footnotes

The first reference to a source requires a full description of it, in contrast with later references, which are briefer. The form of these first footnote references depends on the kind of source that is referred to.

The forms recommended here are those of the *MLA Style Sheet,* published by the Modern Language Association of America and endorsed by many scholarly journals and presses. A few entry forms not in the *MLA Style Sheet* have been added.

    A. Book with one author:
        [4] Theodore Spencer, *Shakespeare and the Nature of Man* (New York, 1942), p. 21.

Many instructors prefer to add the publisher's name in *all* references to books: (New York: Macmillan, 1942). Follow your instructor's advice consistently.

Note: When the author's *full* name has been given in the text of the paper, use this form:

> [4] *Shakespeare and the Nature of Man* (New York, 1942), p. 21.

Use the following form if both the author's full name and the title of the book have been mentioned in the text:

> [4] New York, 1942, p. 21.

B. Book with more than one author:
> [5] Henry Weinberg and William Hire, *Case Book in Abnormal Psychology* (New York, 1956), p. 136.

C. Edited book:
> [6] John C. Bushman and Ernst G. Mathews, eds., *Readings for College English,* 2nd ed. (New York, 1957), p. 24.
> [7] Francis Parkman, *The Discovery of the Great West: La Salle,* ed. William R. Taylor (New York, 1956), p. 16.

D. Translated book:
> [8] Ivan Turgenev, *Fathers and Children,* trans. Richard Hare (New York, 1948), pp. 98–101.

E. Book quoting another book:
> [9] Gelett Burgess, *Are You a Bromide?* (New York, 1906), pp. 17–18, quoted by Jacques Barzum, *Teacher in America* (Garden City, N.Y., 1955), p. 186.

F. Book with more than one volume:
> [10] Samuel R. Gardiner, *History of the Great Civil War* (London, 1893), III, 291.

Note that abbreviations for *volume* and *page* are not included.

G. Signed periodical article:
> [11] E. B. White, "Letter from the South," *New Yorker,* XXXII (April 7, 1956), 39.

Note that the title of the article is in quotation marks, the name of the periodical is in italics (underlining in handwritten or typewritten work), the volume number is in Roman numerals, and, as in footnote 10 above, no abbreviations for *volume* or *page* are used. The following alternative form is acceptable (if your instructor approves):

> [11] E. B. White, "Letter from the South," *New Yorker*, April 7, 1956, p. 39.

H. Unsigned periodical article:
> [12] "Mollet's Uncertain Future," *New Republic*, CXXXIV (April 23, 1956), 7.

I. Book review:
> [13] Arthur F. Burns, rev. of Adolf A. Berle, *The American Economic Republic* (1963), *Reporter*, XXIX (Sept. 12, 1963), 52.

J. Signed newspaper article:
> [14] Antony Lewis, "Check on Loyalty in Science to Ease," New York *Times*, April 22, 1956, Sec. 1, p. 1.

K. Unsigned newspaper article:
> [15] "Czechs' Premier and Aides Ousted," New York *Times*, Sept. 22, 1963, Sec. 1, p. 1.

L. Signed encyclopedia article:
> [16] F. W. Hodge, "Cliff-Dwellings," *Encyclopaedia Britannica* (1952), V, 810.

M. Unsigned encyclopedia article:
> [17] "Altgeld, John Peter," *Encyclopedia Americana* (1952), I, 451.

N. Bulletins, government publication:
> [18] *Education Directory, Part 3: Higher Education* (Washington, 1956), p. 128.

O. Biblical reference:
> [19] Job 26:14.
> [20] Exod. 23:10.

P. Shakespearean reference:
> [21] *Lear* III. vii. 74–77.

Q. Interview:
    [22] Dr. John Rhoads, in interview with the author, June 4, 1963.

References after the first full footnote are much shortened. There are in general two methods of making these later references; both of them are illustrated below. The first one follows the *MLA Style Sheet* and is generally now preferred because of its simplicity and clarity. The second, with its Latin words and abbreviations, is not so widely favored as it once was. Consult your instructor and use consistently the method he advises.

First method of making footnotes:

1. Theodore Spencer, *Shakespeare and the Nature of Man* (New York, 1942), p. 21.
2. Spencer, p. 37.
3. E. B. White, "Letter from the South," *New Yorker*, XXXII (April 7, 1956), 39.
4. White, p. 40.
5. Spencer, p. 89.
6. White, p. 40.
7. "Altgeld, John Peter," *Encyclopedia Americana* (1952), I, 451.
8. "Altgeld," p. 451.

Second method of making footnotes:

1. Theodore Spencer, *Shakespeare and the Nature of Man* (New York: Macmillan, 1942), p. 21.
2. Ibid., p. 37.
3. E. B. White, "Letter from the South," *New Yorker*, XXXII (April 7, 1956), 39.
4. Ibid., p. 40.
5. Spencer, op. cit., p. 89.
6. White, loc. cit.
7. "Altgeld, John Peter," *Encyclopedia Americana* (1952), I, 451.
8. Ibid. (or Idem)

If this second method looks mysterious, compare it with the first method. The references are, footnote for footnote, exactly the same.

ASSIGNMENT II

Put the following in proper footnote form: (1) A reference to page 162 of *George Washington: Leader of the People* by Clara Johnson, published in 1951 by Follett Company, Chicago, Illinois. (2) A reference to *Brave Men and Great Captains* by Ernest Dupuy and Trevor N. Dupuy (Harper and Brothers, New York), 1956, page 21. The book has 364 pages. (3) A reference to page 201 of Clara Johnson's *George Washington: Leader of the People* (Chicago, 1951, the Follett Company, publishers). (4) A reference to page 346 of an article by Strong, George B., called "Philadelphians at the Battle of Trenton," published in *Eastern Historical Review* (volume xc, number 4, April, 1961). The article runs from pages 339 to 380. (5) Another reference to page 351 of the same article. (6) Another reference to page 47 of the book by Clara Johnson mentioned above. (7) Another reference to the article by Strong, page 374. (8) A reference to the article on George Washington in volume 23 of the *Encyclopaedia Britannica*, page 384. The edition is the one published at Chicago in 1960. The author is Allan Nevins. The article runs from pages 380 to 387. (9) A reference to Henry Fielding's novel *Joseph Andrews*, published at Boston in 1961 by Houghton Mifflin Company and edited by Martin C. Battestin, professor at the University of Virginia. The reference is to page 141. The book is in one volume. (10) A reference to page 270 of *Reading Poems* by Wright Thomas and Stuart Gerry Brown, published in 1941 by Oxford University Press, New York.

Standard practices with footnotes

Follow these practices in the use of footnotes:

1. Place footnotes at the bottom of the page unless your instructor tells you otherwise.

2. Number footnotes continuously from the beginning to the end of the paper. Thus, if you have thirty-eight footnotes in the paper, the first note will be [1] and the last will be [38].

3. Place the footnote number at the end, not the beginning, of the passage to which it refers.

4. Leave a space between footnotes. If you are typing, single-space footnotes and double-space between them.

5. Do not use footnotes for matters of common knowledge. The fact that you learned from the *Encyclopaedia Britannica* that Sir Isaac Newton died in 1727 does not mean that you must footnote the information and credit the *Britannica*. The year of Newton's death is common knowledge, not in the sense that everyone knows it, but because the fact is available in many different places. You could have found it in other encyclopedias, in biographies, and even in some dictionaries.

6. Ideas as well as facts and phrases should be acknowledged if the ideas are not common knowledge.

7. If you are at any time in doubt about whether you need a footnote to give credit to a source, consult your instructor —and be sure such consultation takes place *before* you hand the paper in, not afterwards.

FINAL BIBLIOGRAPHY

The sources you have used in preparing your research paper should be listed in the final bibliography. Observe the following procedures:

1. Arrange entries in alphabetical order according to the last name of the author or, if no author is named, according to the first word of the title (disregarding *a, an,* and *the*).

2. Include all sources referred to in your footnotes and, with your instructor's consent, all others that you found useful and pertinent.

3. Do not include items from your working bibliography if you have not used them or if you found them to have no bearing on your subject. (Padding a bibliography is hazardous, as one student discovered. She was writing on the history of tennis and listed a book called *The Tennis Court Oath.* This entry made clear, first, that she knew nothing about a fa-

mous incident in the French Revolution, and second—and more important—that she had not read the book.)

4. For periodical articles, give the numbers of both the first and the last pages.

5. Use these illustrations as models unless your instructor suggests a different system:

"Altgeld, John Peter." *Encyclopedia Americana* (1952), I, 451.

"Czechs' Premier and Aides Ousted." New York *Times*, Sept. 22, 1963, Sec. 1, p. 1.

Lewis, Anthony. "Check on Loyalty in Science to Ease." New York *Times*, April 22, 1956, Sec. 1, p. 1.

"Mollet's Uncertain Future." *New Republic*, CXXXIV (April 23, 1956), 7–9.

Parkman, Francis. *The Discovery of the Great West: La Salle*, ed. William Taylor. New York: Rinehart and Company, 1956.

Spencer, Theodore. *Shakespeare and the Nature of Man.* New York: The Macmillan Company, 1942.

Weinberg, Henry, and William Hire. *Case Book in Abnormal Psychology.* New York: Alfred A. Knopf, 1956.

White, E. B. "Letter from the South." *New Yorker*, XXXII (April 7, 1956), 39–49.

ASSIGNMENT III

Make out a final bibliography based on the books and articles referred to in Assignment II, page 276.

ABBREVIATIONS AND WORDS USED IN FOOTNOTES AND BIBLIOGRAPHY

Many words and abbreviations are occasionally seen in footnotes, but most scholars now prefer to use as few such terms as possible. You may need some of the following, which are fairly common, in your own paper. At any rate, you should know what they mean when you see them.[1]

---

[1] This book follows the now common practice of not italicizing any of these words and abbreviations. (See the *MLA Style Sheet*, § 28, "Use of italics.") Many instructors, however, prefer to italicize such words and abbreviations as *passim, ibid.*, and *op. cit.*

anon.	anonymous
ca. (circa)	"about"; used for approximate dates: ca. 1853
cf. (confer)	"compare"
ed., eds.	edition, editor, edited by; editors
f., ff.	and the following page or pages: 183 ff.
ibid. (ibidem)	"in the same place"—that is, in the source named in the immediately preceding note
l., ll.	line, lines; used in references to poetry
loc. cit. (loco citato)	"in the place cited"
n.	note; used to refer to a footnote: p. 18, n.3
n.d.	no date of publication stated
op. cit. (opere citato)	"in the work cited"—that is, in a work previously referred to in a footnote
p., pp.	page, pages
passim	"here and there; in various places in a work"
sec.	section
sic	"thus, so"
trans.	translator, translated by, translation
vol.	volume

THE RESEARCH PAPER AS A PIECE OF WRITING

From note cards to the completed paper is a single process. The note cards are your raw material; the rough draft is a factory where the raw materials are worked on; and the final paper is the finished product.

One point cannot be insisted upon too strongly: writing a research paper is not primarily an exercise in footnotes and other mechanical requirements. Like all your other compositions, it is an exercise in thinking and in writing. Your instructor will examine the form of your footnotes, but he will continue to admire good writing and thinking in the body of your paper. He will examine the form of your bibliography, but he will look for evidence that you have understood the books you have used. Research is a method of finding the truth about something and making it available to others. Only through the union of good thinking and good writing can you accomplish this objective.

A SPECIMEN RESEARCH PAPER

Study the following research paper to see how well it puts into practice the advice that has been given in this chapter.

Outline

I. Parts of Israel flourish now as in Biblical times.
   A. For many centuries the land was neglected and abused.
   B. The land has been made fertile again, especially by the contributions of the kibbutzim.
II. The kibbutz has a history going back to 1909.
III. A kibbutz is a collective farm.
   A. Members join voluntarily and participate democratically.
   B. Members work and live together.
   C. Women share equally in work with men.
IV. Examples of the work of the kibbutzim can be found in various parts of Israel.
   A. Many of the kibbutzim have been strikingly successful.
   B. The kibbutzim in the Negev have met special problems.
      1. The land has been a barren desert for centuries.
      2. Hard work has been done to improve the land but much remains to do.
V. The kibbutzim have been both criticized and defended.
   A. They allow little personal privacy and no private ownership.
   B. Many people have seen them as genuinely democratic and as essential to Israel's agricultural growth.

THE KIBBUTZ AND ITS CONTRIBUTION

TO ISRAEL'S AGRICULTURE

by

Eve Twersky

English 2

March 25, 1961

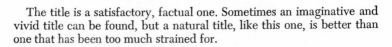

Comments for page 1

The title is a satisfactory, factual one. Sometimes an imaginative and vivid title can be found, but a natural title, like this one, is better than one that has been too much strained for.

The opening paragraph gives an interesting general view and connects the present with ancient days. The student might well have made clearer where in Israel the Jezreel Valley is.

A quotation of several lines is given single-spacing and is indented. (See page 270.)

Footnote 1 is an example of a first reference to a book.

THE KIBBUTZ AND ITS CONTRIBUTION
TO ISRAEL'S AGRICULTURE

There are vast green acres of rich, cultivated land along the coastal plains and throughout the Jezreel Valley of Israel. An observer standing on a hilltop overlooking the valley would see for many miles around the lush, fertile countryside producing in abundance wheat, barley, sesame, and vegetable crops. He would be impressed by the many citrus groves and vineyards along the coastal plain which "has become by far the most important agricultural area of the country."[1] If this observer were able to step back in time and scan the countryside of Israel in the days of the Bible, he would find little change in the appearance of its plentiful harvest. The Bible speaks of Israel's opulence:

> For the Lord thy God bringeth thee
> into a good land, a land of brooks and

---

1. Robert R. Nathan, Oscar Gass, and Daniel Creamer, Palestine: Problem and Promise (Washington, D.C., 1946), p. 118.

Comments for page 2

Footnote 2 uses standard practice with a Biblical citation, including the customary abbreviation.

Footnote 3 is a useful explanatory footnote.

waters, of fountains and depths
springing forth in valleys and hills;
a land of wheat and barley, and vines
and fig-trees and pomegranates; a land
of olive-trees and honey; a land
wherein thou shalt eat bread without
scarceness, thou shalt not lack any
thing in it. . . .[2]

Thousands of years have elapsed, however,

since the Biblical era, and during the many

post-Biblical centuries the blossoming country-

side in general, and the Jezreel Valley in

particular, had become swamplands ravaged by

war, time, disease, and man-made destruction.

Nathan, Gass, and Creamer mention the conditions

that prevailed in the valley.

Due to its exposure to raids from
"over the Jordan," The Valley of
Esdraelon[3] has been abandoned during
periods of insecurity alike in the
days of Gideon and during the early
twentieth century. Before Zionist
immigration, neglect of drainage had

---

2. Deut. 8:7-9.
3. The Valley of Esdraelon is now called
the Jezreel Valley.

The last sentence here rather skillfully brings the introductory material around to the main subject—the kibbutz.

These facts give a quick and helpful view of the history of the kibbutz.

Footnote 4 is a second reference to the book mentioned in footnote 1. Notice the shorter form of this citation.

Footnote 5 illustrates the use of footnotes for definition.

Footnote 6 is another first reference.

turned the valley into swampland in-
fested with malaria.[4]

It is only in modern times that Israel has
begun to bloom again and to produce rich crops.
The reclaiming of the desolate areas can be
attributed to the many courageous, pioneering
people who went out to the wastelands, and with
the help of modern machines, scientific knowledge, and perseverance urged the land back into
productivity. These were the people who joined
ranks to form the kibbutzim.[5]

The first kibbutz was established in 1909
on the banks of the Jordan River and was called
Degania. The goals of its members were to
reclaim the land and to colonize the country.[6]
The land upon which they built was owned by the

----

    4. Nathan, Gass, and Creamer, p. 120.
    5. Kibbutz, a Hebrew word meaning "in-
gathering," is the name used for Israel's
collective farms. Kibbutzim is the plural of
kibbutz.
    6. Murray Weingarten, Life in a Kibbutz
(New York, 1955), p. 7.

This paragraph makes useful distinctions, emphasizing the contrast with other kinds of collective farms.

Footnote 7 is a reference to a bulletin.

Jewish National Fund. With few exceptions all kibbutzim today are situated on Jewish National Fund land. In some cases the land is owned by the Palestine Jewish Colonization Association, an organization founded by Baron Edmond de Rothschild to help farmers establish agricultural settlements.[7]

A kibbutz is a collective farm system which a member joins of his own free choice--in contrast with the collective farms in some other countries. When a person decides to live on a collective farm he must relinquish his money to the treasury, since there is no individual ownership in a kibbutz. In contrast with a Moshava cooperative farm, where the land may be owned privately, a kibbutz can never own the buildings that it erects or the land that it cultivates. All property is leased to the

---

7. The Israel Economist, Annual report (Jerusalem, 1953-54), p. 66.

Notice how the note card was used in the preparation of the paper.

Ownership of land

Kibbutz not owned but leased to members for 99 years (by Jewish National Fund). Lease renewable.

Weingarten, *Life in a Kibbutz*, p. 23

Footnote 9 shows how more than one source can be mentioned in a single footnote. The second citation illustrates a reference to an article in a periodical.

kibbutz for a renewable period of ninety-nine
years.[8]

Participants in a kibbutz meet once a week
to discuss finances, current topics, and problems. Each member has the right to vote, and at
general annual meetings a committee of management is elected to serve for a period of not
more than two years.[9] Officers receive no
additional pay, services, or goods.[10]

Because the work in a kibbutz is strenuous,
the membership is composed mainly of young
people, married as well as single. Each member
is trained to the best of his ability; his
aptitude is taken into consideration; and he is
assigned to the tasks which suit him best. The
members not only work collectively but also live

---

8. Weingarten, p. 23.
9. "Colonies, Agricultural," Universal
Jewish Encyclopedia (1941), III, 270. See also
C. W. Efroymson, "Collective Agriculture in
Israel," Journal of Political Economy, LVIII
(February 1950), 30.
10. Weingarten, p. 27.

Notice how the note card was used in the preparation of the paper.

> Communal living
> "The members live in several-family houses, generally with individual rooms for married couples. The children live in separate children's houses, though in daily contact with their parents during the parents' leisure hours." Everyone comes for meals to a large dining room. All eat together. During working hours, children are cared for by trained nurses.
>
> Nathan, Gass, and Creamer, _Palestine_, p.201

Footnote 12 is a first reference to a book. The author's name is omitted because it has been given in full in the text.

collectively. They share family houses, and only married couples have their own rooms. All the children live together in a large building, and they are cared for by trained nurses while their parents work. At mealtime all are assembled in the huge community dining room.[11]

Women share the responsibility of work, and they perform the same tasks as the men in working the land, driving tractors, and raising cattle. As Horace M. Kallen states,

> The women emulate the men. . . . They insist on the equal right to . . . work and to fight, and to stand beside their men in all things. They meet the responsibilities of child-rearing by rendering them collective and delegating them to someone made a specialist in child-care.[12]

Together the young men and women who comprise the kibbutz perform the manifold tasks necessary to keep a land flourishing. They plow

---

11. Nathan, Gass, and Creamer, p. 201.
12. Utopians at Bay (New York, 1958), p. 63.

The following card shows how a long quotation was used. Note that an ellipsis marks the omission of a sentence. (This quotation is unusually long. Some of the material probably should have been put in the student's own words.)

Irrigation, Degania

"The problem of inadequate rainfall has been solved by a large pumping installation which brings water from the Jordan to all the settlements nine hundred acres. The yields of these irrigated lands are very high and make it possible for over four hundred people to live in the two villages into which Degania is now divided. There are, for instance, eight crops of clover a year. Every inch of soil is cultivated and Degania is a thriving and beautiful place." Lowdermilk, *Palestine*, p. 142

the earth and sow the seeds and put in the young

plants from which vegetables, citrus orchards,

and vineyards spring forth. On land that is

arid they lay pipes underneath the soil to draw

water from nearby rivers and springs to irrigate

it. Lowdermilk cites the Degania Kibbutz as an

excellent example of bringing water to a dry

parched area.

> The problem of inadequate rainfall has
> been solved by a large pumping instal-
> lation which brings water from the
> Jordan to all the settlement's nine
> hundred acres. The yields of these
> irrigated lands are very high and make
> it possible for over four hundred
> people to live in the two villages
> into which Degania is now divided. . . .
> Every inch of soil is cultivated and
> Degania is a thriving and beautiful
> place.[13]

Kibbutz members have gone undaunted into

swampy regions, where they have planted trees to

drain the swamps. Ginegar Kibbutz, situated in

---

13. Walter Clay Lowdermilk, Palestine, Land
of Promise (New York and London, 1944), p. 142.

The story of this kibbutz is a vivid and effective example.

the previously swamp-filled Jezreel Valley,[14] has become the Jewish National Fund's main afforestation center.

In many cases kibbutz pioneers have established kibbutzim in mountainous regions previously thought to be incapable of sustaining vegetation. An example of the determination of kibbutz members to conquer a rough and unyielding terrain is the Kiryath Anavim settlement in the mountains of Judea. The Universal Jewish Encyclopedia mentions the hardships encountered by these men and women in trying to establish their settlement. The soil in this region is so rocky that before they could begin planting, the settlers had to blast holes in the rocks to uncover the earth below. They labored arduously to plant trees in this area, and Kiryath

---

14. Nathan, Gass and Creamer, p. 201.

The paper could have been more definite here. What specifically has resulted from the reclaiming, which is still (we learn two paragraphs further on) not successful in making the Negev "a flourishing area"?

This same paragraph presents skillfully two views of the past of the Negev—an assertion that the area has always been desert contrasted with Biblical testimony that it was once fruitful.

Footnote 15 refers to the same encyclopedia article cited in foot-note 9.

Footnote 16 illustrates a reference at second hand—a book citing an-other book. Observe also that the name of the author (C. Leonard Wooley) is given in the footnote because it had not been given in full in the text. Contrast this with footnote 12 above.

Anavim, the "first successful agricultural settlement in the mountains of Judea," is now a rich producer of grapes and fruit.[15]

Perhaps a more remarkable feat in the accomplishments of the kibbutz settlers is the reclaiming of the Negev, the dry, desert-like land in the south of Israel. Although Wooley claims that the land has always been a desert throughout man's history,[16] the Bible maintains that the Negev in the days of Moses was so fruitful that a cluster of grapes from that region had to be borne on a pole by two men.[17] The first book of Samuel also attests to the richness of the south country by mentioning the spoils that were carried from it.[18]

----

15. III, 281.
16. C. Leonard Wooley, The Wilderness of Zin (Palestine Exploration Fund: 1914-15), p. 17, quoted by Lowdermilk, p. 184.
17. Num. 13:22-23.
18. I Sam. 15:9; 27:9; 30:16.

The beginning of this paragraph ("From the preceding paragraph . . .") sounds as if it might be something left over from the first draft. There are many more effective ways the paragraph could have opened, as, for example: "This was the forbidding land that faced the men and women who decided to establish a kibbutz in the Negev in 1939." What is needed, of course, is to get the paragraph started while at the same time making a smooth transition from the preceding paragraph. Perhaps you can think of a better way to do it.

Lowdermilk attributes the decay of the Negev mainly to the many Bedouin nomads who roamed the desert after the decline of the Roman Empire in 395 A.D. Despising agricultural work, they took the crops from the earth without recultivating it, and when the soil could yield no more, they moved on to other sites. The soil was so thoroughly destroyed that for many centuries the earth lay barren.[19]

From the preceding paragraph one can readily understand the enormous task that faced a group of men and women when they decided to establish a kibbutz in the Negev in 1939. They persevered, however, and attracted other hardy people, so that the Kibbutz Negbah in the Negev increased its population from 70 in 1939 to 570 in 1955. It is true that there is much more agricultural work to be done in the Negev before

---

19. Lowdermilk, pp. 191-192.

Notice how several short quotations are all clearly included in the one citation in footnote 20. There was no need to have a series of footnotes, all close together and all referring to the same place in the same book. Observe also how skillfully the student has led into the quotations, so that the combination of her words and the quoted material is a smooth blending: "They criticize its 'forced gregariousness . . . and depart in search of a more private personal life.' " Notice too the ellipsis within this sentence.

it can be considered a flourishing area. By no means can it be compared with the richly developed Jezreel Valley or the coastal plains, but as long as there are men and women who are willing to settle in arid country and who are determined to turn a desert into an orchard, there is hope for the future of the Negev.

Although the kibbutz has achieved positive results, many people in Israel do not consider it to be an ideal way of life. They criticize its "forced gregariousness . . . and depart in search of a more private personal life." They attack it "because it operates without the incentive of individual profit." Despite these criticisms, the kibbutz "has been defended as the full realization of a democratic, non-exploitative society," [20] and it is vital to the growth of agriculture in Israel. The training

_____

20. Nathan, Gass, and Creamer, p. 201.

In footnote 21, the names of the authors could have been repeated from footnote 20. Since "ibid." is so much shorter than the three names, probably it is wisely used here.

received by each member of a kibbutz is far
superior to that of the individual farmer in a
free enterprise system. Indeed, in many cases
the successful owner of a private farm has
received his previous knowledge of farming
techniques in a kibbutz. In addition, since the
settler in a kibbutz does not strive to compete
socially, his morale is much higher than that of
the profit-seeking farm laborer.[21] These two
factors are instrumental in making the collective farm a prolific producer of agricultural
crops.

Because the challenge of kibbutz life is
great, the hours long, and the work at times
tedious, only the self-sacrificing, courageous
men and women who are imbued with idealism and
a pioneering spirit find this way of life
attractive.[22] Lengyel maintains that Israel

----

21. Ibid., pp. 202-203.
22. Weingarten, p. 49.

Notice the ellipsis at the end of a sentence. Contrast this with the previous ellipsis.

"needs the type of people the collective farms have produced. . . ." He stresses the important role they play in bolstering the state's economy.[23]

Israel's kibbutzim now number 250 and boast a population of 70,000. If the growth of the collective settlements in the past is indicative of the future rate of expansion, Israel may some day be a leading producer of agricultural crops in the Middle East.

_____

23. Emil Lengyel, Israel: Problems of Nation-Building, Foreign Policy Association: Headline Series, No. 89 (New York, September-October 1951), p. 25.

The first item is an encyclopedia article. Since the author's name was not given, the article is listed alphabetically according to the title.

The second item is a periodical article. Note that numbers of first and last pages are given in the bibliographical listing, but in a footnote only the pages actually quoted or referred to are stated.

The third item is a bulletin. Note that the first important word, *Israel*, is used in the alphabetical listing rather than the article *The*.

The fourth item is a book. Note that the student has followed the *MLA Style Sheet* in omitting the publisher's name for this book (and for other books in the bibliography). Many instructors, however, want their students to learn the common practice of including the publisher's name. For example, they would prefer for the eighth item the following:

Shaw, Irwin. *Report on Israel*. New York, Simon and Schuster, 1950. Follow your instructor's advice.

The fifth item is part of a series of publications.

The seventh item has three authors. Note that only for the first author is the normal order of names reversed.

Though the eighth item, Shaw's book, is not mentioned in the paper, it is properly included here, because the student obtained useful information from it. It is a source of part of her knowledge of the subject.

BIBLIOGRAPHY

"Colonies, Agricultural." Universal Jewish Encyclopedia (1941), III, 268-288.

Efroymson, C. W. "Collective Agriculture in Israel," Journal of Political Economy, LVIII (February 1950), 30-46.

The Israel Economist, Annual Report. Jerusalem 1953-54.

Kallen, Horace M. Utopians at Bay. New York, 1958.

Lengyel, Emil. Israel: Problems of Nation-Building. Foreign Policy Association: Headline Series, No. 89, New York, September-October 1951.

Lowdermilk, Walter Clay. Palestine, Land of Promise. New York and London, 1944.

Nathan, Robert R., Oscar Gass, and Daniel Creamer. Palestine: Problem and Promise. Washington, D.C., 1946.

Shaw, Irwin. Report on Israel. New York, 1950.

Weingarten, Murray. Life in a Kibbutz. New York, 1955.

III

The Handbook

III

The Handbook

GRAMMAR

1 Words: Parts of Speech

Words are divided, on the basis of their form, meaning, and use, into classes called parts of speech. Traditionally, there are eight of these classes: nouns, pronouns, verbs, adjectives, adverbs, prepositions, conjunctions, and interjections. The uses of the eight parts are as follows:

NOUN names a person, place, thing, idea, or condition
PRONOUN takes the place of a noun and has the uses of a noun
(Nouns, pronouns, and other words used as nouns are called *substantives.*)
VERB asserts an action or condition and indicates time
ADJECTIVE modifies (that is, describes or identifies) a noun or pronoun
ADVERB modifies a verb, adjective, or adverb
PREPOSITION relates its object (a noun or other substantive) to another part of the sentence
CONJUNCTION links parts of sentences together
INTERJECTION expresses emotion (and is unconnected grammatically with other sentence parts)

A word can often be classed as one part of speech or another according to its use in a sentence. For example:

The *plow* broke the ground. (Noun)
I *plow* the hillside first. (Verb)
He broke the *plow* handle. (Adjective)

2 Word Groups: Phrases and Clauses

2a *Phrases*

A phrase is a group of related words that does not contain both a verb and a subject (a substantive about which the verb asserts something, **3a**). It is a unit that functions as if it were a single word.

The common kinds of phrases are discussed below:

(1) A **prepositional phrase** is made up of a preposition and a substantive (called the object of the preposition). It is used mainly as an adjective or adverb.

> The dog *with the collar* is Tom's. (Adjective)
> The clouds darkened *over him*. (Adverb)

(2) A **verbal phrase** is made up of a verbal (an infinitive, participle, or gerund—see **13a**) and the words attached to it:

Infinitive phrase (may be used as a noun, adjective, or adverb):

> *To choose this subject* is foolish. (Noun)
> His wish *to choose this subject* is foolish. (Adjective)
> He was eager *to choose this subject*. (Adverb)

Participial phrase (used only as an adjective):

> Anyone *choosing this subject* is foolish.

Gerund phrase (used only as a noun):

> *Choosing this subject* is foolish.

(3) An **absolute phrase** is one that is not connected grammatically with the rest of the sentence. It commonly consists of a substantive (as subject) and participle—and sometimes a complement (**3c**).

> *The weather being warm and clear,* I started out on foot.
> We sat late on the lawn, *a full moon lighting the road before us.*

Exercise 1

In the following sentences underline once each prepositional phrase and twice each verbal phrase. Circle each absolute phrase.

1. The car with the officials followed slowly behind us.
2. The King having left, Hamlet came in reading a book.
3. To play hockey well is his chief ambition.
4. Jenny had been waiting since ten o'clock, her temper rising each minute.
5. Leaning forward, he called to us.

6. Playing professional baseball is hard work.
7. He was too kind for his own good.
8. In the door stood Jerry.
9. Rubbing his eyes, he looked around.
10. To play the violin was agony for him.

Exercise 2

Write six sentences, one containing a prepositional phrase with a noun as object, one containing a prepositional phrase with a pronoun as object, one containing an infinitive phrase, one containing a participial phrase, one containing a gerund phrase, and one containing an absolute phrase.

2b *Clauses*

A clause is any group of words containing a verb and a subject. A clause may be independent (also called *principal* or *main*) or dependent (also called *subordinate*).

(1) An **independent clause** can stand alone as a separate statement. It can be punctuated as a sentence.

> He pulled the car to the curb.
> He stopped.
> We can understand hobbies; we tend to fear scholarly studies.—JACQUES BARZUN. (A sentence with two independent clauses. Each could be punctuated as a separate sentence.)

(2) A **dependent clause** cannot ordinarily stand alone as a separate, independent statement. A dependent clause usually begins with a word which indicates that the clause is dependent—a subordinating conjunction (*although, because, before, if, since, unless, until, when,* and others) or a relative pronoun (*that, which, who, whom, what, whatever, whoever,* and others). The subordinating conjunction or relative pronoun relates the dependent clause to the independent clause.

Subordinating conjunction

> *If* you hate cats, you should not become a veterinarian.
> Answer the telephone *when* it rings.

317

Relative pronoun

> A person *who* hates cats should not become a veterinarian.
> I do not want a telephone *that* rings constantly.

In many subordinate clauses the relative pronoun may or may not be stated:

With relative pronoun:

> These advantages are due to the work of a man *whom* we never saw.

Without relative pronoun:

> These advantages are due to the work of a man we never saw.

The subordinating conjunction of noun clauses may also sometimes be omitted. Indeed, sentences frequently sound more natural if the relative pronoun or the conjunction *is* omitted. Note the difference in sound of these pairs:

> She brought the book I had been looking for.
> She brought the book which I had been looking for.

> I was sure he would be late.
> I was sure that he would be late.

Dependent clauses are used in three ways—as nouns, as adjectives, and as adverbs:

> *When I start* does not matter. (Noun clause, subject of verb. A noun can be substituted: The *time* does not matter.)
> *When I start,* I will call you. (Adverb clause, modifier of verb *will call.* An adverb can be substituted: *Then* I will call you.)
> The time *when I start* is uncertain. (Adjective clause, modifier of noun *time.* An adjective can be substituted: The *starting* time is uncertain.)

Exercise 3

In the following sentences underline the italicized words whenever they make up a clause.

1. She said *we would need heat in the house.*
2. *Which one* did you pick?

3. Who was the woman *who came to the door?*
4. *What I do* is my own business.
5. We stayed in the boat *after it reached the pier.*
6. He did not understand *when to stop a joke.*
7. The bus *that stops on the left* is the one to take.
8. I still am not sure *which bus to take.*
9. Working in the garden *may be your idea of fun.*
10. *Before he reached the end of the story,* we were bored.
11. *Before reaching the end of the story,* he had bored me.
12. Throwing aside the book *I was reading,* I stood up.
13. I do not know *when you can get in.*
14. The dog looked at the door, *which was still open,* and barked.
15. Did you go to the play *that opened last night?*
16. *Unless we win this game,* we cannot pay for the stadium.
17. George insisted *that shooting frogs was sport.*
18. The old cherry tree, *which grew beside the kitchen,* is gone.
19. *That I owe you two dollars* is unfortunately true.
20. Is she the girl *I told you about?*

Exercise 4

Indicate whether each clause in Exercise 3 is used as a noun, adjective, or adverb. Put N, ADJ, or ADV in the margin.

Exercise 5

From a periodical of your own or your instructor's choice, copy ten sentences containing dependent clauses. Underline each dependent clause and indicate whether it is used as noun, adjective, or adverb.

3   The Sentence

A sentence is a word or group of related words making an independent statement and ending with a period, a question mark, or an exclamation mark.

> I live on a farm.
> Where does he live?
> What a home he has!

The sentence is the basis of English communication, and to be able to manage the sentence is essential for anyone who wishes to write or speak effectively. A sentence normally has a grammatical subject and predicate. These and other related parts (complements, modifiers, and connectives) are discussed below.

3a *The subject*

The subject is the term about which something is asserted. The subject is a substantive (a noun, pronoun, or other sentence part used as a noun).

The subject may be a single noun or pronoun.

> *Roses* bloom.
> *John* laughs.

But in most sentences the subject is more complicated.

> *These yellow roses* bloom all summer. (Here the simple subject is *roses*; the complete subject is *these yellow roses*.)

A subject that is made up of two or more substantives is called a compound subject.

> *Roses* and *chrysanthemums* bloom at different seasons.
> *The furniture, the cat,* and *I* were put in the back of the old truck.

Note: You can identify the subject by placing *who* or *what* in front of the verb. The answer will be the subject: Tom read the book. (Who read it? Tom. *Tom* is the subject.)

3b *The predicate*

The predicate is the word or group of words that says something about the subject. The core of the predicate is a verb—a word that makes an assertion.

The predicate may be a single verb.

> Roses *bloom*.
> John *laughs*.

But usually it contains other words.

These roses *bloom heavily in June.* (The verb is *bloom;* the complete predicate includes the verb and its modifiers, *heavily* and *in June.*)

A predicate that has two or more verbs making assertions about the same subject or subjects is a compound predicate.

He *selected a magazine* and *carried it to his chair.*
The boy *staggered under the load, stumbled,* and *finally fell at the foot of the steps.*

Exercise 1

In the following exercise separate the complete sentence subject from the complete sentence predicate with a slant (/).

1. The boys examined the fish carefully.
2. Flying fish do not have wings.
3 The man came back for his book today.
4. His knowledge was remarkable.
5. The holiday was celebrated all over Canada.
6. Some ancient moralists considered courage the greatest of all virtues.
7. Pleasure does not always show itself in a smile.
8. The long, lazy, sun-filled days there on the farm seemed like moments in his memory.
9. He expected the long, lazy, sun-filled days there on the farm never to come to an end.
10. To speak in haste is to speak foolishly.

Exercise 2

Underline the complete predicate in the following sentences.

1. They came at last to the fork in the river.
2. Are these your glasses?
3. Many spectators now get their baseball games by television or radio.
4. Where did the fire start?
5. The prospects of success are bleak.
6. Snow fell that night all over the Dakotas.
7. Long may the Republic live!
8. This "wide world," this "vast globe" of ours, is whirling, like a speck of mislaid dust, through space.

9. The quarterback then calmly threw the winning pass.
10. Listen to the weather report.

3c *Complements*

Some verbs need a word or group of words to complete their meaning. This completing element, called a *complement*, may be a direct object, an indirect object, a subjective complement, and, less commonly, an objective complement or a retained object.

(1) Direct object   A direct object receives the action of the verb. The direct object is always a substantive.

> The dentist pulled the *tooth*.   (Noun)
> The words pleased *him*.   (Pronoun)
> The words pleased *whoever heard them*.   (Noun clause)

(2) Indirect object   An indirect object indicates who or what receives the direct object.

> The experience taught *me* a lesson.

Lesson is the direct object. Who receives it? *Me*, the indirect object.

(3) Subjective complement   A verb may be followed by a subjective complement, which refers back to the subject and says something about it. The subjective complement may be a noun, pronoun, or adjective:

> English is a Germanic *language*.   (Noun)
> That was *she*.   (Pronoun)
> Tom seems *generous*.   (Adjective)

The subjective complement always follows such verbs as *to be, to seem,* and *to become*. Subjective complements are also called *predicate nouns* and *predicate adjectives*.

(4) Objective complement   An objective complement renames or refers to the direct object.

> We elected Tom our *secretary*.
> The frost turned the leaves *brown*.

(5) Retained object An object that follows a verb in the passive voice (**12j**) is called a retained object.

> At last we were given the *facts*.

Exercise 3

In the following sentences underline once each direct object of a verb; underline each indirect object twice; and circle each subjective complement.

1. Jessie threw the cup on the floor.
2. All morning he looked miserable.
3. Emma talked politely but gave me a scornful look.
4. The bell in the tower rang twice last night.
5. The fall from the loft hurt him.
6. After the letter came, Margaret grew angry.
7. I am the author of the letter.
8. She threw George a kiss.
9. The law is, of course, a mistake.
10. The knife is here on the shelf.

3d *Modifiers*

A modifier is a word or group of words qualifying or describing another word or making its meaning more precise. Modifiers are adjectives or adverbs—or words, phrases, or clauses used as adjectives or adverbs. The modifier of a substantive is an adjective or its equivalent; the modifier of a verb, an adjective, or an adverb is an adverb or its equivalent.

> That very bad painting on the north wall was hastily done.

That and *bad* are adjectives modifying *painting; very* is an adverb modifying *bad. On the north wall* is a phrase used as an adjective to modify *painting. North,* an adjective, modifies *wall. Hastily* is an adverb modifying the verb *was done.* For a more detailed discussion of modifiers, see **15.**

Exercise 4

Underline once each modifier that is used as an adjective, and twice each modifier used as an adverb. Mark groups of words as well as single words.

1. People sometimes have romantic eyes, but who has glamorous ears?
2. His trembling hands sought his face.
3. We caught them quickly.
4. Tom walked happily across the lawn.
5. The little store at the corner will have fresh corn.
6. Any student who does not work will have trouble.
7. We had a very strange experience on that trip.
8. Our thoughts returned again to her story.
9. It was an obviously untrue but troubling account.
10. Her grandparents' farm was on the right.

3e *Connectives: Prepositions and Conjunctions*

(1) Prepositions

A preposition is a word that relates its object (a noun or other substantive) to another part of the sentence. The preposition and its object combine to form a prepositional phrase. Each such phrase forms a unit that may be used as an adjective or adverb (and, rarely, as a substantive).

> A friend *of* mine who lives *in* Montana is expecting a visit *from* me. (Note that *of mine, in Montana,* and *from me* are prepositional phrases.)

(2) Conjunctions: coordinating and subordinating

Coordinating conjunctions (*and, but, for, or, nor, so, yet*) connect parts that are similar or equal grammatically, such as two nouns, a noun and a pronoun, or two phrases.

> a sweater *or* a jacket
> Tom *and* I
> in the air *and* on the ground

Subordinating conjunctions (*if, because, when, after,* and so on) join dependent (subordinate) clauses to other clauses. (Relative pronouns like *who, which, that* subordinate as do subordinating conjunctions.) Dependent clauses function like adjectives, adverbs, or nouns. See also **2b(2)**.

Exercise 5

In the following sentences underline each preposition once, each subordinating conjunction twice, and each relative pronoun three times.

1. While the enemy was digging in, the American army made a surprise crossing of the river.
2. First the student looked up the matter that should have come second.
3. Sometimes I wonder what he will do and where he will go after he leaves here.
4. The man in the tweed jacket looks tired but quite pleased with himself.
5. We did not realize the damage that had been done until the storm was over and the debris cleared away.

3f *Order of sentence parts: common patterns*

In English the meaning of a sentence depends largely on the order in which words appear. There is a world of difference—at least for the participants—between "The boy chased the dog" and "The dog chased the boy."

In the typical English sentence the subject comes before the predicate:

The Senate / ratifies treaties.

There are several regular patterns for the predicate:

Verb without object or subjective complement

$$\overset{\text{s}}{\text{The telephone}} \; \overset{\text{v}}{\text{rang.}}$$

Verb + object

$$\overset{\text{s}}{\text{She}} \; \overset{\text{v}}{\text{answered}} \; \overset{\text{o}}{\text{the telephone.}}$$

Verb + predicate noun

$$\overset{\text{s}}{\text{That building}} \; \overset{\text{v}}{\text{is}} \; \overset{\text{PN}}{\text{the courthouse.}}$$

Verb + predicate adjective

        S   V PA
That building is new.

Sometimes an indirect object is part of the pattern.

     S   V   IO   O
She wrote Tom a letter.

Verb without subject, object, or subjective complement

    Go!

Verb + object

     V   O
Try our pies.

Sentences beginning with there

     V   S
There are three telephones in the office.

Questions

     V   S
Were the directions clear?

The patterns may sometimes be shifted for emphasis or variety. (See **27a** and **28d.**)

3g *Types of standard sentences*

Sentences are classified grammatically on the basis of the clauses they contain.

    (1) A **simple sentence** consists of one independent clause and no dependent clauses.

    The storm is over.

    (2) A **compound sentence** consists of two or more independent clauses. It contains no dependent clauses.

    The storm is over, but the ground is still wet.
    He has lavished much learning on his task; he has not
      been satisfied with a few vague impressions.

(3) A **complex sentence** consists of one independent clause and one or more dependent clauses.

> Although the storm is over, the ground is still wet.

(4) A **compound-complex sentence** is both compound and complex; it consists of two or more independent clauses and one or more dependent clauses.

> Although the storm is over, the ground is still wet; we cannot go for a walk now.

Exercise 6

Indicate in the margin what kind of sentence each of the following is.

1. After all these years, life on the farm seemed far away.
2. When Carl thought of the creek, he remembered how he had nearly drowned there.
3. He had gone out to learn to swim, and Burney, an older boy, was giving him a lesson.
4. Suddenly in the rushing, slippery water, he slid off Burney's hands, which had been holding him up.
5. Away and down he went; he grasped in panic for something solid.
6. Later, after he had been pulled out, Burney pounded him on the back; then they both lay on the bank and laughed.
7. Would he ever really feel easy in the water again?
8. He promised himself that any children he had would learn to swim early—and he meant to keep that promise.
9. Where should he send someone who wanted swimming lessons?
10. The best place to learn is in a pool, but there is no pool near here.

Exercise 7

Write four sentences on the same subject. Make one simple, one compound, one complex, and one compound-complex.

3h *Nonpatterned and imperative sentences*

Some sentences do not contain all the grammatical parts of an independent clause and so cannot be put into any of the four standard types (3g). Even though such sentences are not typical, they are acceptable and natural, and serve a variety of purposes, of which the following are among the most common:

(1) Exclamations

What a day! Oh! Such talk!

(2) Transitions

And a final instance.
Now for some of our contemporaries.

(3) Descriptive details for drama or emphasis (italics added to identify illustration)

When the friends get to the burying-ground they hack an oblong hole a foot or two deep, dump the body in it and fling over it a little of the dried-up, lumpy earth, which is like broken brick. *No gravestone, no name, no identifying mark of any kind.*—GEORGE ORWELL

Another resource would be lost to him, another place gone: the only company he cared for in the alien, ugly little town he was losing. *Nothing but work, drudgery, constant hastening from dwelling to dwelling among the colliers and the iron-workers.*—D. H. LAWRENCE

(4) Reports of conversation

"Hello. Haven't seen you for ages. Been out of town?"
"Yes. Went East for a while. Thought I might stay but changed my mind."

(5) Answers to questions (in conversation and elsewhere)

No. Yesterday. Not at all.

(6) Imperative sentences—those making requests or giving commands (in which the subject is commonly said to be *you* understood)

Sign on the dotted line. (= You sign on the dotted line.)

Warning: Except in writing imperative sentences and in recording conversation, you should use great care with sentences of the kind illustrated above. An incomplete sentence that has been written thoughtlessly is usually very crude. See Fragments, **4.**

4 Fragments

Avoid sentence fragments—parts of sentences mistakenly written as complete sentences. Correct a fragment by giving it a subject and predicate, by attaching it to a complete sentence, or by rewriting it entirely.

Distinguish carefully between such weak, careless parts of sentences and the successful fragments used for artistic effect —to create realistic dialogue, for instance, or to give emphasis. (See **3h.**) Until you have a very sure feeling for what a sentence is, you should not write anything but standard subject-and-predicate sentences or sentences in which *you* is understood as the subject.

4a *Do not use a dependent clause as a sentence.*

Such a fragment nearly always trails along after an independent clause. Revision is usually easy: either attach the dependent clause to the main statement or turn the dependent clause into an independent clause.

> FRAGMENT This, they realized, was his home. *Where everyone was subdued and on his guard.*
>
> REVISION This, they realized, was his home, where everyone was subdued and on his guard.

> FRAGMENT "Andrea del Sarto" is a poem about a great painter. *Who loves his wife deeply but is not loved in return.*
>
> REVISION "Andrea del Sarto" is a poem about a great painter who loves his wife deeply but is not loved in return.
>
> ANOTHER REVISION "Andrea del Sarto" is a poem about a great painter. He loves his wife deeply but is not loved in return. (Here the dependent clause has been made independent.)

FRAGMENT   By the time he reached home, Lindbergh had become a national hero. *Which is something that will never happen to me.*

REVISION   By the time he reached home, Lindbergh had become a national hero. This is an experience I am never likely to have.

Exercise 1

Revise any of the following that are fragments.

1. If much research had been devoted to the problem.
2. Who is the best student?
3. Who is the best student.
4. This is the corner. Where I met you last week.
5. And such a coincidence is not likely to happen again for a long time.
6. I have not heard from her for three days. Which is a long time for her.
7. Maybe she has taken the job. That she was talking so much about.
8. Here are the horses. Which one do you want me to ride?
9. There is the new schoolhouse. Is that what she's been talking about?
10. George Van Sandt, with much talent but little experience.

4b *Do not use a word or phrase (or other group of words not a sentence) as a sentence.*

Revise by working the word or group of words into the main clause or by restating the phrase to turn it into an independent clause with subject and predicate.

FRAGMENT   The sociologist said that education of women should be adapted to their future needs. *To keep them from being frustrated.* (Infinitive phrase)

REVISION   The sociologist said that, to keep women from being frustrated, they should be given an education fitted to their future needs.

FRAGMENT   Unemployment sends some men into a panic. *Driving them to a frantic search for any kind of work.* (Participial phrase)

REVISION   Unemployment sends some men into a panic, driving them to a frantic search for any kind of work.

FRAGMENT   You might think people would resent such a talkative boy, but they do not. *The reason being Stevie's poise and appearance.* (Absolute phrase)

REVISION   You might think people would resent such a talkative boy but, because of Stevie's poise and appearance, they do not.

FRAGMENT   Then we came to the waterfall. *The most beautiful sight on our journey.* (Appositive phrase)

REVISION   Then we came to the waterfall, the most beautiful sight on our journey.

FRAGMENT   I thought she was dressed for a masquerade. *But soon changed my mind.* (Group of words without a subject)

REVISION   I thought she was dressed for a masquerade, but I soon changed my mind.

FRAGMENT   Then she went on nervously with her work. *Knitting.* (Single word used as sentence)

REVISION   Then she went on nervously with her knitting.

Exercise 2

Revise the fragments below.

1. The house has been built on the corner. Occupying a valuable piece of land.
2. Finally he was so bored that he left the house. Only to return a few minutes later.
3. He rowed in as straight a line as he could. Keeping the white house as his marker.
4. Then he took the road to the left. Home.
5. The first Indians in America lived off nature. Gathering fruit, digging roots, and hunting animals.
6. I left an *Atlantic Monthly* in the barbershop. To raise the cultural tone there.
7. The battery in the car is weak. The lights having been left on all night.
8. I bought a copy of the *Post-Dispatch.* My favorite newspaper.
9. He walked over to the library. And took out the history book he needed.
10. Today I am happy to say that I am free at last. Free to choose for myself.

5 Comma Splice (*or* Comma Fault)

Avoid careless comma splices (also called *comma faults*). The comma splice or comma fault is the error of using a comma to mark the division between two independent clauses not joined by a conjunction. The following sentences illustrate this mistake:

SPLICE   We are five miles from the city, the congestion in traffic is already apparent.

SPLICE   In the far distance George could see a large white house, this looked like his destination.

SPLICE   In searching for material for my paper, I came upon much information about production of automobiles, although this sounded interesting, I knew it would be out of place in a paper on automobile design.

SPLICE   Baseball is said to be a young man's game, some of the best players are in their middle thirties.

5a   *Revising to avoid the comma splice*

(1) Revise the comma splice by making two sentences.

SPLICE   I cannot say in which generation I would rather live, each has its advantages and disadvantages.

REVISION   I cannot say in which generation I would rather live. Each has its advantages and disadvantages.

SPLICE   The interior spiritual life of man is a web of many strands, they do not all grow together by uniform extension.

CORRECT   The interior spiritual life of man is a web of many strands. They do not all grow together by uniform extension.—A. N. WHITEHEAD

(2) Revise the comma splice by using a semicolon instead of the comma.

SPLICE   Under the impact of television and automobile, the small town has changed, its quiet and its peace have disappeared.

REVISION Under the impact of television and automobile, the small town has changed; its quiet and its peace have disappeared.

(3) Revise the comma splice by using a coordinating conjunction after the comma.

SPLICE Most of the original bird life of Hawaii has been wiped out, to find its fugitive remnants you would have to search assiduously in the most remote hills.

CORRECT Most of the original bird life of Hawaii has been wiped out, and to find its fugitive remnants. . . .—RACHEL CARSON

(4) Revise the comma splice by subordinating one of the independent clauses. This subordination will most frequently involve making one of the clauses dependent, but often other forms of subordination may be used.

SPLICE The American passenger pigeon existed in greater numbers than any other bird ever known, it is now extinct.

REVISION SUBORDINATING THE FIRST CLAUSE Although the American passenger pigeon existed in greater numbers than any other bird ever known, it is now extinct.

REVISION SUBORDINATING THE SECOND CLAUSE The American passenger pigeon, which is now extinct, once existed in greater numbers than any other bird ever known.

REVISION MAKING THE SECOND CLAUSE A PART OF THE PREDICATE The American passenger pigeon once existed in greater numbers than any other bird ever known but is now extinct.

(5) Revise the comma splice before a conjunctive adverb. Remember that a conjunctive adverb (such as *however, therefore, indeed, thus, then,* and *consequently*) is not a coordinating conjunction. To correct such a comma splice, you will usually either split the material into two sentences or use a semicolon instead of a comma.

SPLICE In earlier days, only unusual and highly intelligent men chose science as a career, therefore scientific work was carried on in a dedicated spirit.

REVISION USING SEMICOLON In earlier days, only unusual
and highly intelligent men chose science as a career; therefore scientific work was carried on in a
dedicated spirit.

REVISION INTO TWO SENTENCES In earlier days, only unusual and highly intelligent men chose science as
a career. Scientific work was therefore carried on
in a dedicated spirit.

5b *Using the comma splice*

You may—rarely—use a comma splice when you are sure it
will be appropriate. Occasionally a comma splice may help
give speed or lightness of tone, especially to a colloquial or
narrative passage in which the independent clauses are short
and similar in form.

APPROPRIATE COMMA SPLICE Then it happens! Her mind ceases
to function, her fingers grow numb, she can't remember a
note.

Observe where the comma splice is used (and where it is not
used) in these passages:

She brought no life with her; she absorbed what there was, she
was like so much blotting paper.—ALDOUS HUXLEY
Livvy said she would not smoke, she would not indeed; they
might laugh but she was an old-fashioned girl.
—ELIZABETH BOWEN

Warning: You should be sure you know what effect you are
going to produce if you use a comma splice. Unless you are
sure, do not use it.

Exercise

Revise careless comma splices in the following sentences, deciding in each instance which is probably the most effective method
of revision. Leave correct sentences unchanged.

1. This pig was different from any other we had ever seen, it was
reddish, had long ears, and was not fat.
2. Up the river on the right were two large islands thickly covered with trees, on the left was a village once inhabited by
cannibals.

3. I grumbled and felt sorry for myself, I thought the whole world was against me.
4. I don't work, in that way my vacation is not spoiled by the thought of returning to work.
5. The black soils of the Soviet Union are like North Dakota's, they are subject to drought.
6. Use your own judgment, it will probably be wrong, but take a chance.
7. It takes skill to handle fragmentary sentences, the inexperienced writer should use them rarely or never.
8. She wanted to take the left fork, her husband wanted to drive on straight ahead, and I vowed never to go hitchhiking again.
9. For rearing children, there's nothing like the country, they grow like everything around them.
10. Two points are not covered in the book, we should take them up in class.
11. The mayor was encountering unexpected opposition, he abruptly changed his tune.
12. All the gifts that we had ordered arrived without damage, but their delivery was somewhat delayed.
13. Liverpool is the second largest city in England, it is an important shipping center.
14. The stage was set to nominate Richards as the party's candidate for governor, the nomination will probably take place Saturday.
15. He did not get what he wanted, the foreman, in fact, demoted him.

6 Fused Sentences (*or* Run-Together Sentences)

Avoid fused sentences (also called *run-together sentences*). A fused sentence is two or more independent statements joined without punctuation or conjunction between them. It is thus like the comma splice but worse, because in the fused sentence not even a comma is used to separate the independent clauses. A fused sentence may be corrected in the same way as a comma splice: by subordination of one of the independent clauses or by placing between the two

335

statements a period, a semicolon, or a coordinating conjunction and a comma. Which kind of correction is best will depend on the individual sentence. The following sentences illustrate possible revisions of fused sentences.

> FUSED   You enter the city you smell the gasoline refineries.
> REVISION BY SUBORDINATION   As you enter the city, you smell the gasoline refineries.

> FUSED   We must not neglect the social effects of modern medicine think of the changes caused by the increased number of old people.
> REVISION BY MAKING TWO SENTENCES   We must not neglect the social effects of modern medicine. Think of the changes. . . .

> FUSED   They did not win the game so far as I could see, they did not even try.
> REVISION USING A SEMICOLON   They did not win the game; so far as I could see, they did not even try.

> FUSED   I knew him as soon as I saw him I did not say a word.
> REVISION USING A COMMA AND COORDINATING CONJUNCTION   I knew him as soon as I saw him, but I did not say a word.

Exercise

The following exercise contains a number of fused sentences. Rewrite them in correct form, choosing the method that seems most appropriate. Leave any correct sentences unchanged.

1. Across the field was a thick clump of bamboo in the middle of the clump was a spring.
2. An old man was sitting on a low bench making a fishing net beside him was his wife twisting the fibers to make cord for him.
3. In this region July is the wettest month, November the driest.
4. His flight to Washington came as a surprise embassy officials had expected no immediate developments.
5. Only this text is authentic the others are certain forgeries.
6. Still a small-town boy at heart, he dreamed of getting out of the city once he had made his fortune.
7. They persist in their actions in spite of every argument we have presented.

8. Ideas vary in importance sentence structure should vary in order to show emphasis and subordination in the ideas.
9. The writing was not sincere the author was showing off, blowing a loud horn to draw attention to himself.
10. In guiding a boat an old-time Mississippi River pilot had absolute authority he could land it as he saw fit he could even take it into danger against the advice of the captain.

7 Substantives: Nouns

A noun is the name of something—a person, a place, a thing, an idea, or a condition.

PERSON   His *brother* was a *friend* of *Elsa.*
PLACE   They moved from *Albany, New York,* to the *Middle West,* and then to *Laramie, Wyoming.*
THING   A *brick* was used as a *bookend* for the last *volume* of the *encyclopedia.*
IDEA OR CONDITION   The *concept* of *democracy* is new, at least as far as *history* goes.

A noun is often preceded or "signaled" by a definite article *the* or one of the indefinite articles *an* and *a.*

7a *Classes*

(1) **Common or proper**   A common noun is one that is not the name of a particular place, person, or thing. A proper noun, on the other hand, names a particular place, person, or thing.

COMMON	PROPER
street	Broadway
city	San Diego
spy	Major André
commission	Interstate Commerce Commission

(2) **Abstract or concrete**   Abstract nouns name ideas, qualities, concepts: *greatness, splendor, imagination, life, courage.* Concrete nouns name objects that can be per-

ceived by the senses: *nail, sandwich, ashtray, elephants, telephone.*

(3) **Collective** A collective noun, although singular in form, names a group of persons or things: *audience, family, team.*

7b *Forms*

Nouns have four forms—the common form for singular and plural (*boy, boys, child, children*) and the possessive for singular and plural (*boy's, boys', child's, children's*). The common form is used for subjects and objects.

7c *Uses*

Nouns are used as follows:

As subject of a verb

The *radio* is on the shelf.

As object of a verb or preposition

He tossed a *book* on the *table.*

As indirect object

The editor gave *Alvin* a dollar.

As retained object

She was given a *scolding.*

As complement, chiefly predicate noun

My grandfather is an *editor.*

As appositive

Mr. Lindquist, our *teacher,* is not here today.

As a word of direct address

Come here, *Jimmy.*

As part of an absolute construction

The *class* having ended, we left.

Exercise

Show how each italicized noun is used according to **7c.**

1. The *storm* came about *noon,* lasted nearly an hour, and brought lightning that struck a *tree* and scarred the *bark.*
2. We sent my *sister* a birthday *present,* a *box* of chocolates.
3. You will soon find out, *Fred,* that my cousin is a *student* who always has *trouble* deciding on a suitable theme *subject.*
4. The *town* of *Monterey,* when *Stevenson* visited it, had only two or three *streets,* paved with *sand.*
5. All *arrangements* having been made for the *trip,* we forgot our *anxiety* and relaxed.

8 Substantives: Pronouns

A pronoun is a word used as a substitute for a noun or other substantive. Most pronouns have an antecedent—that is, a noun or pronoun, expressed or understood, which they refer to. For example, in the sentence "The mayor says he has lost confidence in the local newspaper because it refuses to take a stand," the pronoun *he* has *mayor* as its antecedent, and the pronoun *it* has *newspaper* as its antecedent.

Some pronouns (called *indefinite*) have no antecedent. They express a substantive idea for which we have no noun: *anyone, someone, whoever,* etc.

8a *Classes*

PERSONAL   I, we, you, he, she, it, they (*We* gave *it* to *them.*)

INTERROGATIVE   who, which, what (*Who* is there?)

RELATIVE   who, what, as, which, that (This is the man *who* fell.)

INDEFINITE   all, any, anyone, both, each, either, everybody, everyone, none, one, some, etc. (*Anyone* can tell you.)

DEMONSTRATIVE   this, that, these, those (*This* is my answer to *that* question.)

REFLEXIVE OR INTENSIVE   myself, ourselves, yourself, yourselves, himself, herself, itself, themselves (Reflexive: He pinched *himself.* Intensive: He ate it *himself.*)

RECIPROCAL   each other, one another. (They looked at *one another.*)

339

8b *Person*

Person of the pronoun indicates the person speaking (first person), the person spoken to (second person), and the person spoken of (third person).

> FIRST PERSON *I* know the answer. They gave it to *me*.
> SECOND PERSON *You* know the answer.
> THIRD PERSON *He* knows the answer *they* gave *him*.

8c *Number*

Pronouns may be singular or plural. Some pronouns are always singular—for example, *I, he, she, one.* Some are always plural—for example, *we,* they, us, both, few.* Some may be either singular or plural—for example, *what, which, none.*

8d *Gender*

The gender of a pronoun indicates the sex or lack of it of the person, animal, or thing referred to. Certain pronouns are always of one gender—masculine: *he, him;* feminine: *she, her;* neuter: *it;* but most are without a specified gender: *I, you, they, one, each, anybody.*

8e *Case forms*

Case is the form a pronoun takes to indicate its grammatical use—that is, its relation to other parts of the sentence.

Personal pronouns

| | SINGULAR | | |
	First Person	*Second Person*	*Third Person*
SUBJECTIVE	I	you	he, she, it
POSSESSIVE	my, mine	your, yours	his, her, hers, its
OBJECTIVE	me	you	him, her, it

* Except when used by royalty or editorially to refer to the single person speaking or writing.

PLURAL

	First Person	Second Person	Third Person
SUBJECTIVE	we	you	they
POSSESSIVE	our, ours	your, yours	their, theirs
OBJECTIVE	us	you	them

The relative pronouns are inflected as follows:

SINGULAR AND PLURAL

SUBJECTIVE	who	which	that	what
POSSESSIVE	whose	whose, of which		
OBJECTIVE	whom	which	that	what

8f Uses

A pronoun may be used in the same ways as a noun:

As subject of a verb

He knows the way.

As object of a verb or preposition

Bill liked *her* and sent an invitation to *her*.

As indirect object

The manager gave *me* a dollar.

As complement, chiefly predicate pronoun (like a predicate noun)

This is *he*.

As appositive

The last student to come in—the *one* in the red dress—was the slowest of all.

In direct address

Look here, *you*.

As part of an absolute construction

They having left, the meeting became peaceful.

In addition, a relative pronoun introduces a dependent clause (and at the same time acts as a subject or object within the clause):

> The man *who* just spoke is my biology professor. (*Who* introduces the dependent clause *who just spoke* and is the subject of the verb *spoke*.)
> We asked *whom* he had seen. (*Whom* introduces the clause *whom he had seen* and is object of the verb *had seen*.)
> There is the tree *that* they cut down.

9 Agreement of Pronoun and Antecedent

Make a pronoun agree with its antecedent in number, person, and gender. The antecedent is the word or idea that the pronoun refers to. See 8.

9a *Number*

(1) **A pronoun agrees with its antecedent in number.** A singular antecedent requires a singular pronoun; a plural antecedent requires a plural pronoun.

> Tom is here. He just came in. (*Tom* is singular; *he* is singular to agree with its antecedent, *Tom*.)
> Jack and Marian came in. As usual, they were late. (*They* is plural to agree with its plural antecedent, *Jack* and *Marian*.)
> There is the girl who is to lead the meeting. (*Who* is singular to agree with its antecedent, *girl*.)
> The men who are doing the most work will get a chance to take the trip. (*Who* is plural to agree with its antecedent, *men*.)

(2) **When two antecedents, one singular and one plural, are joined by *or* or *nor* (*either . . . or, neither . . . nor*), the pronoun generally agrees with the nearer.**

> Neither *Jerry* nor his *sisters* could find *their* books.
> Either *Jerry* or his *sisters* will have to look for *their* books.

But with such sentences care must be taken to avoid confusion or awkwardness. Usually the sentence will sound more natural if you place the plural antecedent second:

> AWKWARD AND AMBIGUOUS   Neither the *clerks* nor the *manager* would face *his* responsibility.
>
> REPHRASED   Neither the *manager* nor the *clerks* would face *their* responsibility.

When the antecedents refer to persons of different sexes, a plural pronoun may be needed to avoid clumsiness or absurdity.

> ABSURD   Either *Mark* or his *sister* will have to tell *her* father what happened.
>
> REVISED   Either *Mark* or his *sister* will have to tell *their* father what happened. (A plural idea is here clearly the antecedent of *their*. Note that exceptions of this kind are rare.)

(3) When a pronoun refers to a collective noun, the noun, verb, and pronoun must agree in number, with either the verb or pronoun, or both, indicating what that number is.

> The *class* will have *its* final examination Friday. (The singular pronoun indicates that *class* is here treated as a unit.)
>
> The *class* should put on *their* raincoats before going out. (Here the plural pronoun indicates that *class* is thought of as a group of individuals.)
>
> The *class have* finished *their* assignment. (Here both verb and pronoun indicate that the noun is to be considered plural.)

Once the number of a collective noun has been indicated, by either verb or pronoun, that number should be kept throughout the passage.

> INCONSISTENT   The committee *is* exhausted from today's meeting. *They* must reassemble, nevertheless, for another meeting tomorrow.
>
> CONSISTENT   The committee *is* exhausted from today's meeting. *It* must reassemble, nevertheless, for another meeting tomorrow.

When you want to shift number, change the antecedent noun.

The committee is exhausted from today's meeting. The members must reassemble, nevertheless, for another meeting tomorrow. (The noun *committee* is changed to *members*.)

(4) **In formal writing, pronouns referring to the following words are nearly always singular:** *each, either, neither, one, anyone, someone, everyone, anybody, everybody, somebody, nobody.*

Anyone can join by submitting *his* application. (Not *their* application)

Neither (*or* Neither girl) sees her way clear to take the job. (Not *their* way)

Each of the committee chairmen will read *his* own report. (Not *their* own report)

Sometimes, however, a plural idea is clear and its expression inevitable:

I looked back and saw everybody waving, and I knew how much I would miss *their* friendliness.

In such sentences the plural reference is the only natural or acceptable one.

9b *Person*

A pronoun agrees with its antecedent in person—first, second, or third. The following sentences illustrate this practice:

FIRST PERSON I did the work *myself* and no one helped *me*. (*I* is the antecedent.)

SECOND PERSON Have you finished studying *your* French? (*You* is the antecedent.)

THIRD PERSON Why does she always put *her* nose in my business? (*She* is the antecedent.)

The only problems occur with the relative pronoun, which agrees with its antecedent:

I, who am treasurer, will collect the dues. (*I who am* is a chain of agreements: *I* is in the first person, the person of the speaker. *Who* is also in the first person, in agreement with its antecedent, *I*. *Am* is likewise in the first person, in agreement with *who*.)

You, who are treasurer, will collect the dues.

George, who is treasurer, will collect the dues.

344

For agreement with pronouns like *each, anyone,* etc., which all take pronouns in the third person singular (*he, her, its,* etc.), see above, 9a(4).

9c *Gender*

A pronoun agrees with its antecedent in gender—masculine, feminine, or neuter.

> Jane left her book where we found it. (*Her* agrees with the feminine *Jane, it* with the neuter *book.*)

Exercise

From the parentheses choose the appropriate form. Be prepared to justify your choice.

1. The herd is slowly making (its, their) way to the spring feeding grounds.
2. Everybody came in and picked up (his, their) examination book.
3. We found that neither the boys nor Jane knew (her, their) way to town.
4. Each of the boys now (has his, have their) own car.
5. He says that you, who (is, are) in a position to help, should write a letter.
6. A person like you should help (his, their) friends.
7. As we came in, we noticed that neither (the books nor the radio, the radio nor the books) could be seen in their usual place.
8. At the trial, each of the experts gave (his, their) opinion.
9. Anybody may say something that (he regrets, they regret) later.
10. The crowd was determined to make (its, their) demands heard.

10 Reference of Pronouns

Make sure that the meaning of every pronoun is clear. If the pronoun has an antecedent—as nearly all pronouns have

—the antecedent should be unmistakable. The reader should never be in doubt about what word or idea the pronoun refers to, for if there is uncertainty the whole sentence may be confusing. Although "Jim and me went to the dance" is not a sentence that will be admired in all circles, its intention cannot be mistaken. But "He spoke to Jim; he didn't want to go" is not clear at all. Yet it is the kind of sentence many people might write in a first draft. In revision, pay close attention to the reference of every pronoun.

10a *Prefer a stated to an unstated antecedent.*

If—as sometimes happens—a pronoun refers to an unstated idea, the writer is responsible for making sure that the reader knows at once what the idea is.

(1) The relative pronoun *which* should usually have a stated antecedent. See, however, (3) below.

> LOOSE REFERENCE   He confessed that he had lied, which was just what we wanted.
>
> REVISED   His confession that he had lied was just what we wanted.
>
> CLEAR REFERENCE   Frank asked for five dollars, which was the amount he needed.

(2) The words *this* and *that* referring to a whole statement should be given a stated noun to modify if without it there is any possibility of confusion. (But see also (3) below for acceptable "broad reference.")

> VAGUE   He has always tried to do his best in spite of his handicap. This accounts for his success.
>
> REVISED   . . . This persistence accounts for his success.

Without the word *persistence*, the reference of the pronoun would seem to be *handicap:* "This handicap accounts for his success." The fact that the reader can stop, read the sentence again, and then modify his first impression does not exempt the writer from the responsibility of making his meaning immediately clear. It is for the writer—not the reader—to do such work.

On the other hand, *this* and *that* cannot modify a noun unless the noun has already been stated or implied. In the sentence above, the idea of persistence has been stated and the word itself has been implied. "This persistence," accordingly, is correct. Suppose, however, that we had these two sentences:

> He believed he could do good work in spite of his handicap. This persistence accounted for his success.

Here the reference is poor because the idea of persistence has not been implied. "Belief" has been implied, or "thought," "hope," or "faith," but hardly "persistence."

(3) **Broad reference of *this*, *that*, and *which* (reference to a clearly implied idea) is acceptable if the meaning is unmistakable.**

> I don't want to live with them in their cottages; *that* would be a sort of prison.—D. H. LAWRENCE

Caution: If you have any doubt about whether the antecedent is *clearly* implied or not, be sure to state the antecedent.

(4) ***It, they,* and *you*** should usually have clearly stated or understood antecedents, except for the expletive *it* in expressions like *it was a cold winter* and *it's time to go*, and except for *you* as explained in the *Note* below. The popular use of *it*, *they*, and *you* is often careless and vague.

> VAGUE   As soon as there are more dollars in circulation to buy an already scarce product, *it* raises the price of that product to consumers.
>
> REVISED   As soon as there are more dollars in circulation to buy an already scarce product, the increase in purchasing power raises the price of that product to consumers.
>
> SLOVENLY AND WORDY   *It* tells here in this chapter about Columbus's fourth voyage.
>
> REVISED   This chapter tells about Columbus's fourth voyage.
>
> COLLOQUIAL (AND SOMEWHAT VAGUE)   In college *they* try to teach the student to think for himself.

REVISED (AND MORE PRECISE) College instructors try to teach the student to think for himself.

ALSO PRECISE AND ACCEPTABLE A college tries to teach a student to think for himself.

AWKWARD I don't want to take any course in which you have to do lab work.

REVISED I don't want to take any course in which I have (*or* one has) to do lab work.

Note on you *in the sense of* one: Such use seems to be gaining among very respectable writers, as the examples below show. The impersonal *you* has dangers, for it may be awkward and it may be misinterpreted as being addressed directly to the reader (*If you are caught stealing, the penalty may be severe*). But if used carefully, it often seems easier and more natural than *one*.

But if at last you drove her to break with you, the breach was permanent: you did not get back again.—G. B. SHAW

I presume you are not allowed to drop a pin in a radio studio.
—IRWIN EDMAN

10b *Make a pronoun refer clearly to one antecedent.*

Momentary ambiguity or unintentional humor will result if the pronoun has two or more possible antecedents.

AMBIGUOUS The G. I. Bill of Rights tended to equalize the opportunities of the son of the rich man and the son of the poor man because he could go to the best college in the country without help from his family.

REVISED The G. I. Bill of Rights tended to equalize the opportunities of the son of the poor man and the son of the rich man because even the poor boy could go to the best college in the country without help from his family.

AMBIGUOUS Peggy held a piece of bread and jam in one hand and the telephone receiver in the other. She kept eating it while she talked.

REVISED Peggy held in one hand the telephone receiver and in the other a piece of bread and jam, which she kept eating while she talked.

10c *Place a pronoun as close to its antecedent as possible.*

Do not separate the pronoun-antecedent pair by anything that might be mistaken for the antecedent.

CLUMSILY SEPARATED   He sat in the kitchen doing his homework, which was heated by a big old stove.

REVISED   He sat doing his homework in the kitchen, which was heated by a big old stove.

AMBIGUOUS   While cleaning it out, John bumped his head on a beam in the cellar.

REVISED   While cleaning out the cellar, John bumped his head on a beam.

10d *Make sure that a pronoun refers to an antecedent that is reasonably prominent.*

Avoid reference to subordinate or inconspicuous words— the "invisible" antecedents.

WEAK REFERENCE   She is going to wear a long blue dress to the Junior Prom next week. It is her favorite color. (One would expect a noun or pronoun to be the antecedent of *it;* an adjective like *blue* makes a weak antecedent.)

REVISED   The long dress she will wear to the Junior Prom next week will be blue—her favorite color.

WEAK REFERENCE   The headpiece was made of hawks' feathers, which he himself had killed. (A possessive, such as *hawks',* often makes a weak antecedent.)

REVISED   The headpiece was made from the feathers of hawks which he himself had killed.

10e *Do not use a pronoun in more than one sense in a sentence or in closely related sentences.* Especially common is the misuse of *it.*

CONFUSED   I wished I had brought my overcoat, for *it* had become colder and I needed *it.* (The first *it* is impersonal; the second *it* refers to *overcoat.*)

REVISED   When the weather became colder, I wished I had brought my overcoat, for I needed it. (Or: When the weather became colder, I needed my overcoat and wished I had brought it.)

10f   *Use* who, which, *and* that *correctly.*

Who refers to human beings, *which* to all nonhuman antecedents, and *that* to either human or nonhuman antecedents.

> Where is the woman *who* (or *that*) sings in the choir?
> Where is the kettle *which* (or *that*) sings on the stove?

That is useful in referring to mixed antecedents—part human and part not:

> These are the places and the people *that* we saw on our trip.

Which is often a rather heavy pronoun; *that* is lighter, less conspicuous:

> Those racks hold the suits *that* are on sale.

See also **33e(1)** Note.

10g   *Avoid needless use of the* he-or-she, his-or-her *construction.*

Unless there is some reason to distinguish between men and women, use the general *he, his, him.*

> CLUMSY   Every student should bring his or her laboratory manual.
> REVISED   Every student should bring his laboratory manual.

Exercise

In the following sentences, correct pronouns that show faulty reference. You will need to rewrite some of the sentences. Leave correct sentences unchanged and mark them C.

1. Such potent wines were drunk by the ancient Greeks that they had to be diluted with water.
2. Civilizations have been born, have developed, and have died. This might seem parallel to the life of biological organisms.
3. Each patient must wait his or her turn.
4. The people expected Orwell to shoot the elephant. Although he felt it was wrong, he shot it anyway.
5. The Romans ultimately extended citizenship to the people they conquered. This action was an example of their political intelligence.

6. Owners of early factories employed children because they could hire them at low wages and they were easy to control.

7. President Franklin Roosevelt gathered professors from all over the country, which were known as the Brain Trust.

8. In the average Broadway play they present an odd picture of American life.

9. Patricia ran down the stairs and knocked at the landlady's office, whom she had never seen before.

10. His hair was the color of dry sand, which was naturally wavy.

11. It was not monotonous even though I taught flying every day, because it seemed that every student was a different problem.

12. Tariff rates were drastically reduced, which intensified the depression.

13. My father is a lawyer. It is a profession he hopes I will enter.

14. Houses are not a good investment that bring a constant burden of repairs.

15. This girl is now attending a very good college, which was made possible by a scholarship.

16. The ballots came in sealed envelopes to the secretary. She said that since there was no opposition to any of the candidates she had opened them herself.

17. In the third chapter of the book it gives a detailed account of the development of steam power.

18. Tom gave the teacher, Mr. Drummond, an apple. He thought it might contain poison.

19. Tom is in Mr. Blunt's Spanish class, who is a demanding instructor.

20. Witches do not bother educated people, because they don't exist.

21. Although it is rather dry in Texas, it is a great cotton state.

22. The opening up of new routes to the Orient in the sixteenth century shifted commerce from the Mediterranean to the Atlantic. This now became the chief thoroughfare to the treasures of the East.

23. The opening up of new routes to the Orient in the sixteenth century shifted commerce from the Mediterranean to the Atlantic. This made England's geographical position almost central instead of peripheral.

24. The house is located in a small town which I am intending to buy.

25. When a student hands in an examination to the instructor, he is not always satisfied with it.

11 Case

Case is the form of a noun or pronoun that indicates its use in a sentence. See **7b** and **8e**.

11a *Put the subject of a verb in the subjective case.*

The *stick* broke when *he* pressed on it.

Be especially careful with compound subjects (*she and I, he and my brother*) and with *who* and *whoever*.

> WRONG CASE   Susan and *him* are going.
> REVISED   Susan and *he* are going. (The compound subject is *Susan and he.*)

> WRONG CASE   He is a man *whom* should be respected.
> REVISED   He is a man *who* should be respected. (*Who* is the subject of *should be respected.*)

> WRONG CASE   He will give advice to *whomever* asks for it.
> REVISED   He will give advice to *whoever* asks for it. (*Whoever* is not the object of *to;* it is the subject of *asks.* Although the word may seem to be both subject and object, it cannot be both. *Whoever* is the subject of the verb, and *to* has for its object the whole clause *whoever asks for it.*)

11b *Do not let a parenthetical expression like* he says, we think, he believes, *or* I feel sure *affect the case of the subject.*

> WRONG CASE   This party is presenting a candidate *whom* we know is unfit to serve.
> REVISED   This party is presenting a candidate *who* we know is unfit to serve. (*Who* is not the object of *know;* it is the subject of *is: who is unfit to serve.*)

11c *Put a pronoun complement of the verb* be *in the subjective case.*

This means that a pronoun which is equivalent to the subject and appears after words like *am, was, has been,* or *had been* is in the same case as the subject. In "This is she," *she* is equivalent to *this;* indeed we might substitute = for *is:* "This = she." (A pronoun used as *she* is used here is called the subjective complement or predicate nominative.)

WRONG CASE   It is us who must make the decision.
REVISED   It is we who must make the decision.

WRONG CASE   Tell me whom he is.
REVISED   Tell me who he is. (he = who)

FORMAL   It is I. That is I. It is he. It is she.
INFORMAL   It's me. That's me. ("It's him" and "It's her" are less common—less fully accepted—in educated speech than "It's me.")

The formal expressions are probably better for most student writing. The informal ones, though generally limited to conversation, are not therefore inferior; they are simply more familiar in tone. Personal taste and judgment of situations must tell you whether to say "It is I" or "It is me." You will find that both usages are very old. The stately language of the Bible is appropriate in the words of Jesus: "Behold my hands and feet, that it is I myself" (Luke 24:39). Shakespeare illustrates both formal and informal uses: "This is I, Hamlet the Dane" (*Hamlet* V, i, 280–81); "That's me" (*Twelfth Night* II, v, 87).

Exception: For a pronoun after the infinitive *to be,* see **11e.**

11d   Put the object of a verb or preposition in the objective form.

WRONG CASE   He asked my sister and *I.*
REVISED   He asked my sister and *me.* (*Me* is the object of the verb *asked:* "He asked . . . *me.*")

WRONG CASE   The package was addressed to my brother and *I.*
REVISED   The package was addressed to my brother and *me.* (*Me* is the object of the preposition *to:* "The package was addressed to . . . me.")

WRONG CASE   I know our candidate will lose, no matter *who* we support.

REVISED   I know our candidate will lose, no matter *whom* we support. (*Whom* is the object of the verb *support*.)

WRONG CASE   He will read his poetry to *whoever* he can find.
REVISED   He will read his poetry to *whomever* he can find. (*Whomever* is the object of the verb *can find*.)

Note on whom: In conversation, *who* often seems more natural than *whom*, especially at the beginning of sentences. But in most writing, including that done in college, you will be expected to follow the somewhat more formal practice.

CONVERSATIONAL   *Who* shall I send it to?
WRITTEN   *Whom* shall I send it to? (*Whom* is the object of the preposition *to*.)

Sometimes an unnatural or very formal *whom* can be easily avoided:

UNNATURAL ATTEMPT AT FORMALITY   The girl *whom* he asked to the dance has accepted.
NATURAL   The girl he asked to the dance has accepted.

11e   *Use the objective form for a pronoun complement after an infinitive.*

He didn't want to meet *her*.
I wanted Ann to be *her*.

Note: In the last example above, *Ann* is said to be the subject of *to be*. If no subject precedes the infinitive *to be*, formal English requires the subjective case:

Ann hopes to be *she*.

But both sentences about Ann are clumsy and should be avoided.

11f   *Ordinarily in writing use the possessive case of a noun or pronoun before a gerund (an -ing word used as a noun).*

Mary was annoyed both at *Tom's* asking to be invited and at *my* forgetting to reply to the invitation. (*Asking* and *forgetting* are gerunds.)

354

Note 1: Do not use the possessive case and gerund when to do so would result in clumsy and unnatural language.

> GOOD USAGE   Besides everyone in my family thinking I was a strange child. . . . (Not *everyone's* or *family's*. But observe that you would say: Besides everyone's thinking I was a strange child. . . .)

Note 2: Distinguish between a gerund and a participle (an –*ing* word used as an adjective).

> GERUND   I think Tom's *swimming* has improved.
> PARTICIPLE   I saw Tom *swimming* in the pool.

Note 3: In colloquial language the possessive is often not used with the gerund, as in this sentence from conversation:

> I won't stand for him doing anything really wrong.

11g *Use the possessive correctly with indefinite pronouns, with compounds, and with a series in which there is joint possession.*

(1) Such **indefinite pronouns** as *somebody* and *anyone* add *'s* to form their possessives: *somebody's, anyone's*. The plural *others* and *ones* add the apostrophe: *others', ones'*. If *else* follows an indefinite pronoun, *else*, not the pronoun, shows the possessive: *anyone else's, somebody else's*.

(2) In **compounds,** the last word is given the possessive form: *the attorney general's office, my sister-in-law's camera*.

(3) In **joint possession,** the last element is given the possessive form: *Beaumont and Fletcher's play*. But when individual possession is intended, the possessive case is used with each member of the series: *the attorney's and the doctor's fees*.

Note: Nouns referring to inanimate objects sometimes seem awkward if a possessive *'s* is used. Use *the rung of the ladder* rather than *the ladder's rung*. But there are many accepted phrases using *'s: a week's vacation, the law's delay;* and there are many other nouns which may equally well use an *'s* or an *of* phrase: *the train's speed* or *the speed of the train; the book's preface* or *the preface of the book.*

11h   Use the correct case after **than** and **as.**

After *than* and *as*, whether a pronoun should be subjective or objective depends on what is meant. "She likes him better than me" is correct if you mean "She likes him better than she likes me," but it is incorrect if you mean "She likes him better than I like him."

> Molly is younger than *I.* (Implied is the idea ". . . than I am young.")
> Give it to him rather than *her.* (Give it to him rather than *to* her.)
> I hope to be as good a student as *he.* (. . . as good a student as he *is.*)

11i   Put an appositive pronoun in the same case as the word with which it is in apposition.

> WRONG CASE   Three girls—Peggy, Joan, and *me*—were chosen for the committee.
> REVISED   Three girls—Peggy, Joan, and *I*—were chosen for the committee. (*I* is in apposition with *girls,* which is the subject of *were chosen.*)

> WRONG CASE   They chose three of us—Peggy, Joan, and *I.*
> REVISED   They chose three of us—Peggy, Joan, and *me.* (*Me* is in apposition with *three,* which is the object of *chose.*)

11j   When a pronoun is followed by an appositive, keep the pronoun in the right case.

> WRONG CASE   *Us* students have done our best.
> REVISED   *We* students have done our best. (*We* is the subject of *have done; students* is an appositive.)

> WRONG CASE   The captain threw the ball to *we* players.
> REVISED   The captain threw the ball to *us* players. (*Us* is the object of the preposition *to.*)

Exercise

In the following exercise underline the preferable form of the noun or pronoun.

1. I shall speak to (whoever, whomever) will listen to me.
2. It is (they, them) who have intensified the problem by pretending it did not exist.
3. Give it to anyone (who, whom) asks for it.
4. There were three men—the assistant coach, the trainer, and (I, me)—who scouted the Riverside game.
5. First they asked me to tell them (who, whom) I was.
6. Then they asked (who, whom) I was voting for.
7. My brother is not so independent as (I, me).
8. (Who, whom) do you think is here?
9. (We, us) girls are going to the movie.
10. My father had to wait because of (me, my) taking his car.
11. Then I told them I would vote for (whoever, whomever) I thought was the best candidate.
12. Do you have any evidence of this (man and woman, man's and woman's) having served in community activities?
13. Shall we settle this just between you and (I, me)?
14. I am sure I do not want to see (she, her) again.
15. Two of the group—Barney and (I, me)—were called on to speak.
16. Is this (someone's else, someone else's) job?
17. He called to Barney and (I, me).
18. (Kennedy and Nixon's, Kennedy's and Nixon's) campaigns made great use of airplanes.
19. Barbara Allen was attracted to a young man (who, whom) she at first believed didn't love her.
20. This new game is very popular among (we, us) girls.

12 Verbs

A verb is a word that asserts action, condition, or being.

The radio *begins* the day with this song.
The boy *has eaten* the eggs.
Ideas *are* weapons.
The book *feels* heavy.

357

By its various forms a verb indicates time (tense), mood, person, number, and voice. These are discussed below, beginning with **12c.**

12a Kinds of verbs: transitive, intransitive, and linking

(1) Transitive and intransitive verbs

When a verb is used with a direct object, the verb is said to be transitive:

> He *broke* the knife. (*Knife* is the direct object.)

When no object is present, the verb is said to be intransitive:

> He *laughed* and then he *sighed.*

Most verbs can be either transitive or intransitive, depending on whether they are followed by a direct object or not:

> He *muttered* a few indistinct words. (Transitive, with
> *words* as the direct object)
> He *muttered* indistinctly. (Intransitive)

Some verbs are transitive only—for example, *raise* and *set.* Often verbs are intransitive only—*rise* and *sit,* for example. See **12b.**

(2) Linking verbs

A linking verb is a kind of intransitive verb that connects a subject and a predicate noun, pronoun, or adjective. The most common of these verbs are *be, become, grow, seem,* and a number of verbs expressing sense impressions—*feel, look, smell, sound, taste,* and so on.

> This *is* Tommy. (The subject is *this; Tommy* is a predi-
> cate noun.)
> It *is* she who must decide. (*It* is the subject; *she* is a
> predicate pronoun.)
> He *looked* stronger than before, but he said that he *felt*
> weak. (*Stronger* and *weak* are predicate adjectives.)

12b *Use the proper forms for* lie *and* lay, rise *and* raise, *and* sit *and* set.

The principal parts are *lie, lay, lain; lay, laid, laid; rise, rose, risen; raise, raised, raised; sit, sat, sat; set, set, set.* These verbs are especially troublesome.

Lie is an intransitive verb—that is, it takes no object—and means "to recline."

> The rug *lies* on the floor today; yesterday it *lay* there; in fact it *has lain* there a long time.

In contrast, *lay* is a transitive verb—that is, it takes an object—and means "to put down."

> I now *lay* the rug on the floor; yesterday I also *laid* it there; and I *have laid* it there many times.

Rise, being intransitive, takes no object.

> He *rises* early during the gardening season.
> The flag *rose* on the pole.
> The temperature *has risen.*

Raise, a transitive verb, takes an object.

> He *raises* carrots.
> He *raised* the flag.

Sit means "to be seated" or "to be situated." *Set* means "to put something in a sitting position."

> The builder *set* the house on the hill, and it *sits* there overlooking the valley.

Whether the subject is living or not has nothing at all to do with which verb is used.

> The rug *lies* on the floor, and the baby *lies* on the floor.

The choice between *lie* and *lay, rise* and *raise,* or *sit* and *set* is made purely on use: when the subject does the action itself, it *lies, rises,* or *sits;* when it does the action to something else, it *lays* or *raises* or *sets* something.

Exercise 1

In the following exercise, underline the correct form of the verb.

1. Since his illness he has (lain, laid) down for a nap every afternoon.
2. Please (sit, set) it down there.
3. Please (sit, set) down.
4. The cost of living (rose, raised) again last month.
5. I (laid, lay) it down yesterday but I can't remember where.
6. She told the child he must (lie, lay) on the blanket.
7. The new school building has (risen, raised) in a few months.
8. I wonder why she (laid, lay) the bracelet there.
9. The sparrow hawk is (sitting, setting) on the branch.
10. The dog (rose, raised) up to greet us.
11. You will find the lamp (sitting, setting) on the table.
12. Now I (lie, lay) me down to sleep.
13. I remember how Uncle Fred would pick me up and (sit, set) me on his shoulder.
14. The dogs have been (lying, laying) in the sun.
15. The boy (rose, raised) himself to his full height.
16. After the telegram came yesterday, she just (sat, set) there as if stunned.
17. Bring the book that is (lying, laying) on the radio.
18. Many generations of students have (sat, set) in this room.
19. This is where the road (lay, laid) before the turnpike came through.
20. The smoke is (rising, raising) to the ceiling.

12c *Principal parts of verbs*

The principal parts of a verb are the present infinitive (*to play, to throw, to choose*), the past tense (*played, threw, chose*), and the past participle (*played, thrown, chosen*). For a full table of the forms of a verb, see the conjugation of *to choose,* pp. 379–380.

Most verbs are *regular*—that is, they form the past tense and the past participle by adding *ed, d,* or *t* to the infinitive:

to rain	rained	rained
to pledge	pledged	pledged
to burn	burnt (or burned)	burnt (or burned)

Some verbs are *irregular*. They usually—but not always—change a vowel in the past tense and sometimes again in the past participle.

to swim	swam	swum
to give	gave	given
to hit	hit	hit

12d Use the proper form of regular verbs.

Do not write the past tense or past participle of regular verbs without the normal *ed*, *d*, or *t*. Whether the omission of the standard ending comes from carelessness or ignorance, the mistake is generally regarded as illiterate.

NONSTANDARD PAST TENSE   He is not as busy as he *use* to be.
STANDARD   He is not as busy as he *used* to be.

NONSTANDARD PAST PARTICIPLE   The police later found that he had *reverse* the direction of the car.
STANDARD   The police later found that he had *reversed* the direction of the car.

12e Use the proper form of irregular verbs.

The following list gives the principal parts of the most common of these verbs. (Included are a few verbs that have both regular and irregular forms.)

bear	bore	born, borne [1]
beat	beat	beaten
become	became	become
begin	began	begun
bet	bet	bet
bid (command)	bade	bidden
bind	bound	bound
bite	bit	bitten
blow	blew	blown

[1] The form is *borne* when *bear* means "to carry" (The equipment was *borne* across the river); the form is *born* when *bear* means "to give birth to" (I was *born* in Wyoming).

bring	brought	brought
broadcast	broadcast (or broadcasted)	broadcast (or broadcasted)
burst	burst	burst
buy	bought	bought
cast	cast	cast
catch	caught	caught
choose	chose	chosen
cling	clung	clung
come	came	come
creep	crept	crept
deal	dealt	dealt
dig	dug	dug
dive	dived (or dove)	dived
do	did	done
draw	drew	drawn
drink	drank	drunk
drive	drove	driven
eat	ate	eaten
fall	fell	fallen
feel	felt	felt
fight	fought	fought
find	found	found
flee	fled	fled
fly	flew	flown
freeze	froze	frozen
get	got	got (or gotten)
give	gave	given
go	went	gone
grow	grew	grown
hang	hung	hung [2]
hit	hit	hit
hold	held	held
know	knew	known
lay	laid	laid
lead	led	led

[2] If *hang* means "to suspend," the principal parts are irregular, as above. If the word means "to execute," they are regular: *hang, hanged, hanged.* (The picture was *hung;* the criminal was *hanged.*)

lie	lay	lain [3]
lose	lost	lost
pay	paid	paid
put	put	put
ride	rode	ridden
ring	rang	rung
rise	rose	risen
run	ran	run
say	said	said
see	saw	seen
set	set	set
sew	sewed	sewed, sewn
shake	shook	shaken
shine	shone	shone [4]
show	showed	showed, shown
shrink	shrank	shrunk
sing	sang	sung
sink	sank	sunk
slink	slunk	slunk
sit	sat	sat
slide	slid	slid
sling	slung	slung
sow	sowed	sowed, sown
speak	spoke	spoken
spring	sprang	sprung
steal	stole	stolen
sting	stung	stung
strike	struck	struck, stricken
swear	swore	sworn
sweep	swept	swept
swim	swam	swum
swing	swung	swung
take	took	taken
teach	taught	taught
tear	tore	torn
think	thought	thought
throw	threw	thrown

[3] When *lie* means "to tell a falsehood," the principal parts are *lie, lied, lied*. (Herbert *lay* on the couch and *lied* about the fish he had caught.)

[4] If *shine* means "to glow" the principal parts are irregular, as above. In the colloquial sense of "to polish" they are regular: *shine, shined, shined*. (The sun *shone* yesterday, so I *shined* my shoes to celebrate.)

wake	waked, woke	waked, woke, woken
wear	wore	worn
weave	wove	woven
win	won	won
wind	wound	wound
wring	wrung	wrung
write	wrote	written

In addition to these irregular verbs, there is the verb *to be,* the first principal part of which is *be, am, are,* or *is;* the second part is *was* or *were;* the third part is *been.*

Exercise 2

In the following exercise, underline the accepted form of the verb.

1. We have often (rode, ridden) out to the farm for a picnic.
2. He has (drank, drunk) more cold water than he should on such a hot day.
3. The miner (led, lead) the rescuers forward cautiously.
4. The gale (blew, blowed) hard from the northwest.
5. The old road (ran, run) along here.
6. I would have (wrote, written) the letter differently.
7. After the accident he seemed badly (shook, shaken).
8. The boy had caught his coat on the barn ladder, had lost his footing, and had (hung, hanged) there yelling until we ran to pull him loose.
9. We stood in front of the school half (froze, frozen).
10. Tom asked me if I was (wore, worn) out.
11. This was the career he had (chose, chosen).
12. The first time he looked, he (saw, seen) her.
13. Have you ever (drove, driven) over that road?
14. He knew that the nail (tore, teared) his jacket.
15. When he caught the tadpole, he (slang, slung) it away.
16. Amy had (fallen, fell) out of the swing.
17. Who has ever (become, became) so popular?
18. She sat down and (wrang, wrung) her hands.
19. She wondered who had (rang, rung) the bell.
20. We (put, putted) her worry down to nervousness.
21. I never heard anyone who (sang, sung) so easily.

22. When Marvin saw me come in, he (burst, bursted, busted) out laughing.
23. How many times has he (flew, flown) the Atlantic?
24. I saw him when he (came, come) in.
25. The lamplight (shined, shone) on the water.

12f   *Auxiliary verbs*

An auxiliary is used with other verbs to make a verb phrase, which itself acts as a verb form: *have written, am writing, has been writing, did write.*

Common auxiliaries are *have, be, do, can, must, may, might, shall, should, will, would.*

12g   *Mood*

Mood (or mode) is the form of a verb that shows the attitude of a speaker or writer toward what he is saying. The indicative mood makes a statement or asks a question; the imperative makes a command or a request; the subjunctive shows doubt, possibility, a wish, or a condition contrary to fact.

INDICATIVE   You *do* excellent work. *Is* this the work?
IMPERATIVE   *Work* hard. *Do* your best.
SUBJUNCTIVE   I wish I *were* a hard worker.

Most writing is in the indicative mood. On the subjunctive, see **12m.**

12h   *Person*

The person of a verb indicates that the subject is speaking (first person), is spoken to (second person), or is spoken of (third person). The verb *to be* makes a number of changes to show person: I *am,* you *are,* he *is,* we (they) *are,* and so on; but other verbs change only the form for the third person present indicative, where an *s* is added: I, you, we, and they *think;* he, she, and it *thinks.*

12i Number

Number may be singular or plural. The form of nouns changes (*book, books; man, men*) to show number, but among verbs only *to be* changes for number—*am, is, are, was,* and *were.* (The *s* at the end of the third person singular of most verbs is an ending to indicate person, not number.)

12j Voice

There are two voices of a transitive verb, the active and the passive. In the active voice the subject does the action:

> Tom *wrote* the best theme.
> That boy *started* the fire.

In the passive voice the subject is passive—is acted upon:

> The best theme *was written* by Tom.
> The fire *was started* by that boy.

The passive voice often does not tell who did the action:

> The key *has been lost.*
> The garden *was planted* last week. (The writer is not interested in who lost the key or planted the garden.)

For the forms of the active and passive, see pp. 379–380.

12k Standard use of tense forms

Verbs vary in form to show time related to the moment of speaking or writing. The various forms are called *tenses.* The various tenses of English verbs are as follows:

(1) **Present tense** The present tense is used in a number of ways:

(a) To indicate action that is habitual at the time of speaking or writing. The action may or may not be taking place at that moment.

> He *goes* there every day.

366

(b) To indicate action or being that holds before, through, and after the moment of speaking or writing but does not emphasize that moment.

> The national capital was once New York, but now it *is* Washington.

(c) To indicate action or being in future time.

> They *march* on Washington tomorrow.

(d) To indicate facts that we consider permanently true.

> He discovered that freedom *is* more important than security.

(e) To relate incidents that occurred in the past as if they were happening in the present. (This is called the *historical present.*)

> Now Grant *decides* that there *is* no other course—he *must* use his reserves against the Confederate left wing. (In an account of a Civil War battle written today.)

(f) To indicate action going on at the moment of speaking or writing.

> The quarterback *gets* the ball and *moves* to his right.

Note: This use of the present tense is restricted almost completely to eye-witness accounts, as on radio and television. The moment of speaking or writing ordinarily is indicated by the present progressive form. See **(7)** below.

(2) Past tense The past tense shows action or being in time before the present. The time of the action must be made clear, either by a definite indication (*yesterday, when I was in high school*) or by implication.

> I *worked* yesterday.
> When I was a boy, I *worked* hard.
> During World War II, women *worked* at many jobs formerly held by men.

Note that in each of the sentences above a time in the past has been pointed out. Of course, the time need not always be stated specifically but may be made clear by other sentences, as in the following passage:

> In the 1912 election, there were three major parties: Democratic, Republican, and Progressive. The Progressives, followers of Theodore Roosevelt, were mainly former Republicans. With the Republican party thus split into two camps, the Democrats won easily.

In this paragraph only one specific time is stated—1912. Although no time is mentioned in the next two sentences, the past tense is proper and perfectly clear, because the reader understands that the year mentioned in the first sentence is to be applied to the rest of the passage.

(3) **Future tense**   The future tense shows action or being that will take place in time to come. On *shall* and *will*, see **12n.**

> I *will* (or *shall*) *work* tomorrow.
> He *will do* his best.

There are other ways of showing the future, as by the present tense—see (**1c**) above—and by the progressive form—see (**7**) below.

(4) **Present perfect tense**   The present perfect tense shows action or being that took place in the past, often with the implication that it is continuing into the present.

> I *have* often *thought* of you.
> George *has worked* at the factory for twelve years. (The tense informs us that he is still working there.)

(5) **Past perfect tense**   The past perfect tense shows action or being that took place before an indicated time in the past.

> I *had worked* there for a year before I came back to school.
> By last spring he *had worked* in the bank long enough to be pensioned.
> When the time was totaled on Saturday, we found that we *had worked* forty-three hours.

Notice that in each of these sentences the work had been completed *before* some stated time.

Warning: Do not confuse past, present perfect, and past perfect tenses. Note the difference in these statements:

PAST   I wrote a letter home last Friday.
PRESENT PERFECT   I have written a letter to my mother.
PAST PERFECT   I had written two letters before I got an answer.

(6) **Future perfect tense**   The future perfect tense shows action or being that will be completed before a definite future time.

By next month I *shall have worked* there a year.

(7) **Progressive forms**   To show the action of a verb in progress at any time, there are special forms of the verb in the various tenses. The progressive forms are made by combining the appropriate tenses of the verb *be* with the *–ing* form of the verb.

PRESENT   He is working.
PAST   He was working.
FUTURE   He will be working.
PRESENT PERFECT   He has been working.
PAST PERFECT   He had been working.
FUTURE PERFECT   He will have been working.

The progressive forms are very common, especially in the following uses:

(a) To indicate continuing action

She *was cooking* the dinner.
He *will be sitting* there after you have left.

(b) To indicate action at the present moment

Susan *is writing* a letter.
Tommy *is bothering* me.

(c) To indicate future time

We *are leaving* for Mexico in a few days.

(8) **Emphatic forms**   The emphatic forms appear in the present and past tenses.

PRESENT He *does work.*
PAST He *did work.*

These forms are used in the following principal ways:

(a) For an emphatic statement, especially a reply

Why don't you pay your bills? I *do pay* them.

(b) In negative statements and questions

He *didn't review* for the test.
Why *don't* you *help* him?

(c) In asking questions

Did you *see* him?

Exercise 3

Illustrate the eight forms discussed above by writing a sentence using each one. In parentheses after each sentence, name the form.

12l *Sequence of tenses*

The time of the verb in a dependent clause should agree logically with the time of the verb in the independent clause. Usually this means that both verbs will keep the same tense or understandably related ones. The following sentences illustrate this practice:

Bill *sleeps* while others *work.* (The time of *work* in the dependent clause *while others work* agrees with the time of *sleeps.* Both are in the present tense.)
Bill *slept* while others *worked.* (Past tense)
He *has stopped* his work because he *has inherited* a little money. (Present perfect tense)
He *will find* that his money *will* not *go* far. (Future tense)
He *says* that he *will find* a job. (Present and future logically related)
He *will find* that he *has wasted* his time. (Future and present perfect logically related)

(1) **The past and past perfect tenses need particular care.** If the verb in the independent clause is in the past or

the past perfect, the verb in the dependent clause should usually be in the past or past perfect.

> OBSCURE   When I *reached* the pier I *saw* that the boat *was* four feet lower than it *was* at high tide. (The first three verbs, *reached, saw, was,* refer to a time in the past; the fourth verb, *was,* refers to an earlier time. The past perfect is therefore more exact for the fourth verb.)
>
> REVISED   When I *reached* the pier I *saw* that the boat *was* four feet lower than it *had been* at high tide.
>
> CONFUSED   Yesterday Tom *told* us that he *has passed* the course.
>
> REVISED   Yesterday Tom *told* us that he *had passed* the course.
>
> CONFUSED   Whenever I *have reported* to the registration desk, the man there *became* angry.
>
> REVISED   Whenever I *reported* to the registration desk, the man there *became* angry.

(2) The sequence of tenses is generally not observed when the dependent clause contains a statement of what is customary or is regarded as universally true.

> He *had discovered,* at long last, that honesty *pays.*
> We already *knew* that Hawaii *has* one of the most pleasant climates on earth.
> She *learned* that a ship *sails* to the island every Tuesday.

Exercise 4

In the following sentences revise any verb forms that need to be changed. Do not make any unnecessary changes.

1. Last Wednesday Mary told her teacher that she has completed her library work.
2. I crept through the heavy snow. Suddenly, not twenty-five yards away, the largest buck I had ever seen runs into the clearing.
3. He wondered if the mail has been collected yet.
4. For several months now I took violin lessons.
5. For several months last year I took piano lessons.
6. He wanted to know whether November 5 is Guy Fawkes Day.

7. This is the first time I have been completely on my own. If I do not succeed, at least I had my opportunity.
8. I became embarrassed because I lost the money.
9. After taking my first train ride, I felt I had the most thrilling experience of my life.
10. Because he had taken the trip many times before, my brother was very casual about it.

12m   *The subjunctive*

(1) Forms

The subjunctive was once used more widely in English than it is today. Now it remains in only a few situations and appears in only a few forms. It still exists in the third person singular, present tense, where it differs from the indicative by dropping the *s* ending:

> We insist that he *go* to the hospital at once.
> I move that each delegate *appoint* an alternate.

In the indicative mood, the verbs would be *goes* and *appoints*.

The subjunctive also exists in two forms of the verb *to be:*

> PRESENT SUBJUNCTIVE   if I (you, he, we, etc.) *be*
> PAST SUBJUNCTIVE   if I (you, he, we, etc.) *were*

(2) Uses

The subjunctive is now limited to a few uses:

    (a) To express a supposition or improbable, impossible, or contrary-to-fact condition (using the past subjunctive).

> If I *were* rich, I would buy that house.
> If Jefferson *were* alive now, what would he think?
> Just suppose I *were* to propose to you right now!
> The dean wishes that I *were* doing better work.

    (b) To state formal demands, wishes, requirements, recommendations, rulings, parliamentary motions, and the like. These uses are generally preceded by *that.*

I demand that his statement *be* proved.
You must insist that he *carry* out his promises.
The law requires that he *come* to court in person.
I move that the treasurer *pay* whatever sum is necessary.
It is our desire that he *be* freed.

(3) Misuses

Do not use the subjunctive when the indicative is called for. Contrast these sentences:

SUBJUNCTIVE   If I *were* a genius, I would know the answer. (An imagined situation)

INDICATIVE   If Napoleon *was* a genius, he was one the world could have done without. (Not an imagined situation; simply a statement of fact. Note how absurd *were* would be.)

SUBJUNCTIVE   If he *were* our friend, he would stand by us now. (But he is not our friend.)

INDICATIVE   If he *is* our friend, he will stand by us now. (We do not know whether he is our friend or not.)

Do not look on the subjunctive as a form of superior elegance. "If I be elected president of the club, I'll accept" would sound affected in writing or speech at any level of formality.

Exercise 5

Choose the form—subjunctive or indicative—that is appropriate.

1. If everyone (was, were) on time, we could finish our practice early.
2. I suggest that he (leaves, leave) the cast.
3. Abe moves that Tom (is, be) allowed to take no further part in this play.
4. I would not do that if I (was, were) you.
5. I wondered if I (was, were) to be as lucky now as I was a week ago.
6. You would not be here if it (was, were) not for the opportunity Mr. Kravitz gave you.
7. If he (is, were) absent from the examination, he will have trouble passing the course.

8. If he (was, were) sitting next to you, he may be the person who picked your pockets.
9. The regulation provides that every petition (bears, bear) ten signatures.
10. You treat me as though I (was, were) an interloper.
11. If Thoreau (was, were) living today, he would still feel the same.
12. If I (was, were) present, I don't remember it.
13. If evidence (is, be) available, it must be presented to the jury.
14. I can eat a whole pie if it (is, be) in front of me.
15. The court insists that restitution (is, be) made.

Exercise 6

Write five sentences containing a verb in the subjunctive mood. Use each of the following subjunctive forms at least once: *be, were, permit, make, deny.*

12n   Shall *and* will

(1) **The distinctions between** *shall* **and** *will* **have largely disappeared,** *will* having become the common form for the simple future. The current general use is as follows:

> FIRST PERSON   I (we) will write
> SECOND PERSON   you will write
> THIRD PERSON   he (she, it, they) will write

(2) Once established in formal use and still sometimes observed is the following practice:

> FIRST PERSON   I (we) shall write
> SECOND PERSON   you will write
> THIRD PERSON   he (she, it, they) will write

In formal written English, these uses of *shall* and *will* were reversed for emphasis:

> FIRST PERSON   (emphatic) I (we) will write
> SECOND PERSON   (emphatic) you shall write
> THIRD PERSON   (emphatic) he (she, it, they) shall write

These uses still often serve to indicate determination or compulsion:

> They shall not pass.

(3) *Shall* is commonly used when there is a question about the right thing to do:

> *Shall* I bring my sister?
> *Shall* she invite her friends?
> What *shall* I say to them?

(4) In general, you are not likely to have any problems unless you use *shall* excessively. Do not get the idea that *shall* is somehow a more refined word than *will*. Write the word that seems natural to you, modifying your choice as your instructor suggests.

> UNNATURAL The price of eggs *shall* not prevent us from eating them.
> REVISED The price of eggs *will* not prevent us from eating them.

(5) The past tense of *shall* and *will* in certain sentences is expressed by *should* and *would*.

> PRESENT TENSE *Shall* I bring my sister?
> PAST TENSE He asked if he *should* bring his sister.
>
> PRESENT TENSE He *will* write the letter.
> PAST TENSE He said that he *would* write the letter.

Exercise 7

In each blank space, use *shall* or *will*.

1. My library paper _____ deal with the earliest operas.
2. When I refer to books, _____ I underline titles?
3. Professor Maslow, how _____ I arrange my note cards?
4. The professor says that we _____ write a short story next.
5. I hope the story _____ be easier for me to do than my library paper was.

13 Verbals

13a *Kinds and uses*

A verbal is a word derived from a verb and used as a noun, adjective, or adverb. A verbal, like a verb, can take an object, have voice, and have an adverb as its modifier, but it cannot act as the verb in a predicate. Verbals are of three kinds: infinitives, participles, and gerunds.

(1) Infinitives

An infinitive consists of the present or perfect form of the verb preceded by *to: to be, to run, to think, to have thought.* It is used as noun, adjective, or adverb.

> *To err* is human. (Noun, subject of *is*)
> The best route *to take* at night is Highway 38. (Adjective modifying the noun *route*)
> Your parents are eager *to see* you. (Adverb modifying the adjective *eager*)

After some verbs the *to* of the infinitive is regularly omitted:

> They made him [*to*] *toe* the mark. (Compare this with "They required him *to toe* the mark," in which *to* cannot be omitted.)

The *to* is often omitted in a series:

> He decided *to eat,* [*to*] *pack* his bags, and [*to*] *leave.*

The infinitive may be present (*to go, to write*) or perfect (*to have gone, to have written*). The present infinitive (which is the common form) expresses time concurrent with or future to the time of the main verb: *I am to go, I was to go,* etc. The perfect infinitive expresses action that happened before the time of the main verb: I was lucky *to have gone* before they got here.

(2) Participles

A participle is used as an adjective (the *fading* colors, the *faded* colors) or as part of a verb phrase (*is fading, has faded*).

The present participle ends in *ing;* it expresses time concurrent with that of the main verb.

> *Running* water is usually pure. (*Running,* acting as an adjective, modifies the noun *water.*)
>
> He started off, not *thinking* of his promise. (*Thinking* modifies the pronoun *he.*)

The past participle is the third principal part of the verb. Its use as an adjective is illustrated in these sentences:

> The *fallen* leaves must be raked up.
> I looked at my *worried* mother.

The perfect participle consists of *having* (or *having been*) and the past participle. It expresses time before that of the main verb.

> *Having escaped*, the lion ran into the woods.
> *Having written* the letter, I felt relieved.
> *Having been exposed* to his playing before, we declined the invitation.

(3) Gerunds

A gerund is used as a noun. It always ends in *ing* and so is identical in form with the present participle: *running, thinking.*

> *Running* is good exercise for some people. (*Running* is the subject of the verb *is.*)
>
> Many persons dislike *thinking*. (*Thinking* is the object of the verb *dislike.*)
>
> I've had my fill of his *whining*. (*Whining* is the object of the preposition *of.*)

13b *Time relationships of infinitives and participles*

Infinitives and participles should have a clear and logical time relationship with the main verb. Do not confuse the simple infinitive with the perfect infinitive or the present participle with the perfect participle.

> INFINITIVE   It became clear that *to spread* such ideas was dangerous. (Not *to have spread*. What was dangerous was to spread the ideas, not to have spread them at some time in the past.)
>
> INFINITIVE   He wanted *to be* there. (Not *to have been*.)
>
> PERFECT INFINITIVE   He is pleased *to have been informed* ahead of time. (The perfect infinitive is correctly used here, for what he was pleased about is that he had been informed beforehand.)
>
> PRESENT PARTICIPLE   *Looking* at his watch, he wondered how late she would be. (His wondering was done at the time he did the looking.)
>
> PERFECT PARTICIPLE   *Having looked* at his watch several times, he began to wonder how late she would be. (He wondered after he had looked.)

Exercise 1

Underline each verbal and be prepared to explain whether it is a present participle, perfect participle, past participle, gerund, infinitive noun, infinitive adjective, or infinitive adverb. If your instructor wishes, write out your explanation and hand it in.

1. The boy kicking the ball is my brother.
2. To be successful as a writer is not easy.
3. Because of the patient's condition, the surgeon is afraid to make the operation.
4. The law prohibits speeding on this road.
5. This is an experience to remember always.
6. Worrying more than necessary, she waited for the letter.
7. Worried for many days now, she watched anxiously for the letter.
8. His eccentric driving upsets me.
9. I heard that laughing even after they left.
10. The desolation was a forbidding sight.
11. It was as if we had entered a forbidden country.
12. Nancy likes walking under the elms at night.
13. She likes to hear the wind blow through the leaves.
14. Her sister was ready to go further.
15. The child asked us to wait.

16. This is the road to take.
17. To take the wrong road now would be fatal.
18. Having called the captain, we sat down and waited.
19. His brow puckered by dismay, he looked quite helpless.
20. Puckering his brow, the clerk admitted he did not know.

Exercise 2

Write ten sentences containing verbals. Use each of the following at least once: an infinitive noun, an infinitive adjective, an infinitive adverb, a perfect infinitive, a perfect participle, a gerund as subject, a gerund as object, a present participle used as adjective, and a past participle as adjective. In parentheses after each sentence, name the forms you have used.

Conjugation of the irregular verb *to choose*

Choose (principal parts: choose, chose, chosen)

INDICATIVE MOOD

Active Voice		*Passive Voice*	
Singular	*Plural*	*Singular*	*Plural*

PRESENT TENSE

1. I choose	we choose	I am chosen	we are chosen
2. you choose	you choose	you are chosen	you are chosen
3. he chooses	they choose	he is chosen	they are chosen

PAST TENSE

1. I chose	we chose	I was chosen, etc.
2. you chose	you chose	
3. he chose	they chose	

PRESENT PERFECT TENSE

1. I have chosen	we have chosen	I have been chosen, etc.
2. you have chosen	you have chosen	
3. he has chosen	they have chosen	

PAST PERFECT TENSE

1. I had chosen	we had chosen	I had been chosen, etc.
2. you had chosen	you had chosen	
3. he had chosen	they had chosen	

379

1. I will (shall) choose   we will (shall) choose   I will (shall) be
2. you will choose   you will choose   chosen, etc.
3. he will choose   they will choose

1. I will (shall)   we will (shall)   I will (shall) have been cho-
      have chosen   have chosen   sen, etc.
2. you will have   you will have
      chosen   chosen
3. he will have   they will have
      chosen   chosen

Other indicative forms are common, especially the following:

The progressive forms: I am choosing, was choosing, will be choosing, etc. See **12k(7)**.

The forms with *do:* I do choose, did choose, etc. See **12k(8)**.

Future forms with *going, about to:* I am going to choose, I am about to choose, etc.

Imperative Mood (only in the present tense): choose (passive voice: be chosen)

Subjunctive Mood: if I, you, he, we, they choose. See **12m**.

Infinitives
  Present: to choose (*passive:* to be chosen)
  Perfect: to have chosen (*passive:* to have been chosen)
Participles
  Present: choosing (*passive:* being chosen)
  Past: chosen
  Perfect: having chosen (*passive:* having been chosen)
Gerunds
  Present: choosing (*passive:* being chosen)
  Perfect: having chosen (*passive:* having been chosen)

14   Agreement of Subject and Verb

Make a verb agree with its subject in number and person. If a subject is singular, its verb must also be singular; if a subject is plural, its verb must be plural. If a subject is third person, the verb should be third person.

SINGULAR SUBJECT   A *sophomore*
SINGULAR VERBS   A sophomore *is* here. He *thinks* we can still get
tickets for the game.

PLURAL SUBJECT   *Sophomores*
PLURAL VERBS   The sophomores *are* here. They *think* we can still
get tickets for the game.

In practice, only a few difficulties arise, and practically all
of those are associated with number. Although none of us
would say, "He love his work," we may not be sure whether
to put *is* or *are* in the blank in this sentence: "The price of
all our various kinds of glasses _____ going up." Although we
would never say, "The dishes is ready," we may occasionally
wonder whether some subjects are singular or plural. Should
we say, for instance, "The orchestra is about to play" or "The
orchestra are about to play"?

Whenever we are in doubt we should make sure (1) exactly what the subject is and (2) whether it is singular or
plural. In the sentence in the preceding paragraph, "The
price of all our various kinds of glasses _____ going up," the
verb should be *is* because the subject is *price*. (What is—or
are—going up? *Price? All? Kinds? Glasses?* Obviously the
going-up idea applies to the price. Therefore the *price is*
going up.) In the sentence about the orchestra, we are thinking of a musical unit and so we should say, "The orchestra
is about to play."

The following subsections discuss the most common difficulties in subject-verb agreement.

14a   *Intervening elements*

**(1) A subject and verb agree even if other words
come between them.**

The supply of microscopes and slides *seems* unlimited.
(*Seems* agrees with *supply*.)
The repetition at the end of each stanza *helps* give unity.
(*Helps* agrees with *repetition*.)

**(2) Singular subjects are not made plural when
phrases beginning with such expressions as *with, besides,
together with,* and *as well as* are added to them.**

Dr. Jones, as well as his son, *is* going to New York. (But: Dr. Jones and his son *are* going to New York.)

The mayor, together with the council, *has* agreed to be present. (If such a sentence sounds awkward or if you feel that the subject is really plural, use *and:* The mayor and the council *have* agreed to be present.)

14b   Compound subjects

(1) A compound subject in which the parts are joined by *and* normally takes a plural verb.

The bookcase and the table were stained the same color.
Lanier and Whitman are my favorite American poets.

But when the parts joined by *and* refer to the same person or thing, the verb should be singular.

The vice-president and general manager *is* George Simpson.

Our family's lawyer and constant adviser *was* not present.

(2) A verb after a compound subject joined by *or* or *nor* (or *either . . . or, neither . . . nor*) usually agrees with the part of the subject that is nearest the verb.

French or German *is* the next language to study.
Neither architecture nor painting *appeals* to him.
Neither the teacher nor the students *were* expecting the fire drill.
Neither the students nor the teacher *was* expecting the fire drill.

If awkwardness occurs, rephrase the sentence.

(3) A compound subject joined by *and* takes the singular if it is modified by *each* or *every*.

Every man and woman in the club *is* eligible to vote.

14c   Subject following the verb

A verb usually agrees with its subject even though the subject follows the verb. Remember that *there* and *here* are not subjects in *there is* and *here is* expressions.

In her dark brown hair *were*, we saw, a few streaks of gray. (Subject: *streaks*)

Under way again *is* a bitter struggle over forest conservation. (Subject: *struggle*)

Here *come* John and his sister. (Subject: *John and his sister*)

There *are* many reasons to drop this project right now. (Subject: *reasons*)

But if the first member of a compound subject after *there* or *here* is singular, the verb is often singular:

There was the river, the widening fields, the cottonwood groves—springs, ditches, hay stacks—spelling bees, quiltings, Sabbath schools.—BERNARD DE VOTO

Note: It always takes a singular verb, even when it is used as an expletive to anticipate the real subject.

It *is* my friends I fear.

Did you know it *was* his easy ways that got him into trouble?

14d *Subjective complement*

A verb agrees with its subject, not with a subjective complement.

FAILURE IN AGREEMENT   His funny gestures *was* the only amusing thing about him. (The subject is *gestures;* the subjective complement is *thing.*)

REVISED   His funny gestures *were* the only amusing thing about him.

ALSO ACCEPTABLE   The only funny thing about him *was* his funny gestures. (In this revision *thing* has been made the subject; *gestures* has become the subjective complement.)

14e Each, either, neither, one, anyone, someone, everyone, anybody, everybody, somebody, nobody

These pronouns are considered singular in most writing (including the papers you write in college).

Each of the students *has* done his work.

Anyone who is late *is* going to be left behind.

Everybody *was* there.

Neither of the students *was* selected.

Spoken English is less strict. Quite natural in talk is something like "Everyone seems glad *their* work is done."

14f *Collective nouns*

Some nouns may be either singular or plural. If the noun treats a group as a unit, it is collective and the verb is singular; if the noun treats a group as a number of individuals, it is not collective and the verb is plural. Typical collective nouns are *committee, class, crowd, family, group, jury, majority, number, people, public, team*. There are, of course, many others.

> The family *is* the basic unit of society. (*Family* is obviously thought of here as a single thing.)
> The family *are* all coming home for Thanksgiving. (*Family* here is considered a group of individuals.)

If you have difficulty, it is likely to come from a failure in consistency—in treating the noun as singular at one time and as plural at another:

> INCONSISTENT The crowd has surged forward, showing their impatience. (*Has* indicates that *crowd* is being treated as a singular; *their* is therefore inconsistent.)
> CONSISTENT The crowd has surged forward, showing its impatience.

14g *Singular words that are plural in form*

Some nouns, though originally plural in meaning and still plural in form, are now singular in meaning.

> The news *is* alarming.
> Politics *is* the art of the possible.
> Mathematics *was* my favorite subject.

(Some of these words are always singular, but others vary between singular and plural. Thus we would say, "Politics *is* the art of the possible," but we would also probably say, "His politics *reflect* [not *reflects*] the moral standards of the community." Consult the dictionary when you are uncertain.)

14h   *Optional agreement*

Some words, like *all, none, some,* and *what,* take either a singular or plural verb, depending on the meaning. If one of these words involves a singular idea, the word is singular; if it involves a plural idea, it is plural. The same principle applies to fractions.

> *None* of the answer *is* here.
> *None* of the boys *are* volunteering their help; at least *none have* offered yet.
> *Some* of this talk *is* foolish. Is it because *some* of these people *are* foolish?
> A *third* of the term *is* over. *Half* of your themes *have* been late.

14i   *Foreign plurals*

Use the right verb form with nouns that have a foreign plural. Here are a few of these nouns:

SINGULAR	PLURAL
alumnus	alumni
crisis	crises
criterion	criteria
datum °	data °
phenomenon	phenomena

14j   *Relative pronouns*

A verb with a relative pronoun as its subject agrees with the antecedent of the pronoun.

> We who *are* about to die salute you. (*Are* agrees with its subject, *who,* which in turn agrees with its antecedent, *we.*)
> A prize will be given to the man who *makes* the best mousetrap. (*Makes* agrees with *who,* which in turn agrees with *man.*)
> This is the only one of the books that *has* interested me. (*Has* agrees with *that,* which agrees with *one.* Only one has interested me.)
> This is one of the books that *have* interested me. (*Have* agrees with *that,* which agrees with *books.* Certain books have inter-

° *Datum* is now not often used. *Data* is generally accepted as either singular or plural. See the Glossary.

385

ested me. This is one of them. Therefore, this is one of the books that *have* interested me.)

It is you who *are* to tell him. (*Are* agrees with its subject, *who*, which agrees in number and person with its antecedent, *you*.)

Exercise

In the following exercise select the correct form of the verb. Be prepared to explain your choice.

1. News from all over the world (is, are) discussed here.
2. The valedictorian and class president (is, are) George Brennan.
3. The salutatorian and marshal (is, are) John Peterson and Jim Rawlings.
4. Out of these experiences (comes, come) a new attitude.
5. The new phenomena (is, are) something we must consider.
6. None of the pie (is, are) left.
7. He is one of those happy people who (seems, seem) at home in any group.
8. Such frightening stories (is, are) the reason Johnny cannot sleep.
9. Did you say it (was, were) the new boys who caused the disturbance?
10. Another thing autumn brings to our city (is, are) the concerts.
11. Sometimes the trail plunges into cool damp shadows through which (gleams, gleam) in the dim light the fronds of the seedling hemlocks.
12. There (goes, go) Barbara and her cousin.
13. Every boy and girl (is, are) invited.
14. Everybody (has, have) heard of insulin.
15. Neither the president nor his advisers (was, were) satisfied.
16. The salary for these positions (starts, start) at $9,000 a year.
17. In college, mathematics (is, are) usually a required subject.
18. Each of the new houses (has, have) been inspected.
19. The class (is, are) ready for the examination.
20. Everyone in the graduating class (carries, carry) the stamp of the college upon him.

15 Modifiers: Adjectives and Adverbs

Adjectives and adverbs are words used to modify—that is, they describe, limit, or identify other words. Modifiers bring greater exactness or vividness to the words they modify. For example, the noun *tree* may be modified to become *dead tree, tall tree,* or *third tree,* and the verb *run* can be made more precise by adding words like *fast, slowly, hard,* or *heavily.*

15a *Adjectives: uses and kinds*

(1) Adjectives modify nouns or pronouns.

> He gave a *quick* answer. (*Quick* modifies the noun *answer.*)
> She is *unhappy.* (*Unhappy* modifies the pronoun *she.*)

Adjectives often are used in groups of two or more: *his two enormous yellow* teeth.

(2) Adjectives may be descriptive or limiting.

> DESCRIPTIVE   *modern* art, *red* barn, *split* second, *daring* acrobat
>
> LIMITING   *this* class, *that* book, *these* problems, *those* fashions (demonstrative)
> *his* French, *my* friend, *their* views (pronominal)
> *which* way? *what* price? *whose* pen? (interrogative)
> *some* person, *more* talent, *any* writer (indefinite)
> *ten* years, *fifteenth* century (numeral)
> *a* mouse, *an* act, *the* flowers (articles)
> the artist *whose* work is here (relative and pronominal)

(3) Adjectives are also classified as *common* or *proper* (as nouns are). Proper adjectives, derived from proper nouns, are capitalized:

> *Scotch* plaid, *Chinese* village

Sometimes nouns are used adjectivally, as modifiers:

> *tree* house, *house* party, *party* line, a *Toulouse-Lautrec* print

Phrases are used adjectivally:

> The top *of the house* was damaged.

So are dependent clauses:

> The student *who won the chemistry prize* has been of-
> fered three jobs.

15b *Adverbs: uses and kinds*

(1) **Adverbs modify verbs, adjectives, or other adverbs.**

> He walked *slowly*. (The adverb *slowly* modifies the verb
> *walked*.)
> He was an *unusually* faithful worker. (The adverb *un-
> usually* modifies the adjective *faithful*.)
> He walked *very* slowly. (The adverb *very* modifies the
> adverb *slowly*.)

(2) **Adverbs are usually concerned with one of the following:**

> TIME   *always, now, later*
> PLACE   *there, up, below*
> MANNER   *thus, cheerfully, quickly*
> DEGREE   *more, less, hardly, well*
> CAUSE   *consequently, therefore, hence*
> AFFIRMATION OR DENIAL   *yes, no, probably, indeed*

A phrase may be used as an adverb:

> He wrote *at top speed*.

So may a clause:

> He wrote *when he found time*.

Certain adverbs, like *however* and *therefore*, are also called
conjunctive adverbs. See **18c**.

15c *Forms of adjectives and adverbs*

Commonly the *ly* ending indicates an adverb (adjectives:
fierce, splendid, harmonious; adverbs: *fiercely, splendidly,
harmoniously*), but some adjectives end in *ly* (*friendly,*

manly). A number of the most frequently used adverbs have forms with *ly* and without. For example, the words in both columns are adverbs:

slow	slowly
soft	softly
loud	loudly

Which form to use will usually depend on the tone of the sentence. In general, the form without *ly* seems a little more colloquial and therefore more appropriate for informal occasions.

> Come *quick.*
> He came *quickly* to the point.
> Drive *slow.*
> They drove *slowly* through the canyon.

Some adverbs are identical in form with the corresponding adjectives.

> The *high* building sways in the wind.   (Adjective)
> He jumped *high* over the fence.   (Adverb. In some sentences *highly* is the only acceptable form: I think *highly* of him.)

> It was a *hard* examination.   (Adjective)
> He worked *hard.*   (Adverb)

> They had a *little* argument.   (Adjective)
> They *little* thought it would come to that.   (Adverb)

Other words which have the same form as adjective and adverb are *far, near, early, fast, late, loud, quick,* and *slow.*

15d   *Adjectives and linking verbs*

Pay particular attention to adjectives after linking verbs. A common use of linking verbs is to join a subject and its predicate adjective.

> He looks *wise.*

The important thing is to recognize such verbs and to realize that they will require predicate adjectives, not adverbs, because the subject (a substantive) is being modified, not the verb.

After forms of *be* none of us would be tempted to use anything but adjectives:

> I am *sleepy*.   (Not *sleepily*)
> She is *happy*.
> They are *generous*.

If other linking verbs are used, no change is required, because the words *sleepy, happy,* and *generous* are adjectives modifying *I, she,* and *they.*

> I *feel sleepy.*
> She *looks happy.*
> They *seem generous.*

An easy test for a linking verb is to see if you can substitute a form of *be* for the verb.

> I hope that I *appear* (= am) honest.
> They *became* (= were) angry.
> The boys *have grown* (= are) tall.
> The rose *smells* (= is) sweet.
> Her voice *sounded* (= was) tense.
> This pie *tastes* (= is) good.

Some verbs function as both linking verbs and verbs of action. *Feel,* for instance, is a link in the sentence "I feel sleepy," but it denotes action in "I feel the door." (Notice that although *am* can be substituted in the first of these sentences, it cannot be in the second.) When the verb denotes action, the action can be modified by an adverb: "I feel the door *gropingly*" or "I feel his disappointment *keenly.*"

15e   *Confusion of adjectives and adverbs*

Use adverbs, not adjectives, to modify verbs, adjectives, and other adverbs.

> INAPPROPRIATE, ESPECIALLY FOR WRITTEN WORK   He sure has
> a wide knowledge of Beethoven. (*Sure* is an adjective;
> here an adverb is needed to modify the verb *has.*)
> REVISED   He *certainly* has a wide knowledge of Beethoven.

> SUBSTANDARD   Milton wrote *good,* even when he was young.
> (*Good* is an adjective; an adverb is needed to modify the
> verb *wrote.*)
> REVISED   Milton wrote *well,* even when he was young.

INAPPROPRIATE, ESPECIALLY FOR WRITTEN WORK   They became *real* angry. (*Real* is an adjective; an adverb is needed to modify the adjective *angry*.)

REVISED   They became *very* (or *really*) angry.

INAPPROPRIATE, ESPECIALLY FOR WRITTEN WORK   Tom won *most* every game. (*Every* is an adjective; it should be modified by the adverb *almost*.)

REVISED   Tom won *almost* every game.

Exercise 1

In the following exercise select the appropriate adjective or adverb. Be prepared to explain your choice.

1. He looked at us (angry, angrily).
2. He looked (angry, angrily) as he listened to the oratory.
3. The dinner tasted (good, well).
4. The storm stopped as (sudden, suddenly) as it had begun.
5. The plan sounds (satisfactory, satisfactorily) to me.
6. He listened (attentive, attentively) to the lecture.
7. Carter looked (firm, firmly) as he stood on the platform.
8. Carter looked (firm, firmly) at the audience.
9. He worked (late, lately) last night.
10. A week in the country is pleasant (most, almost) any time.

15f *Comparison of adjectives and adverbs*

Adjectives and adverbs change form to show differences in degree. There are three degrees—positive, comparative, and superlative.

Adjectives

POSITIVE	COMPARATIVE	SUPERLATIVE
wise	wiser	wisest
good	better	best
much	more	most
active	more active	most active
	less active	least active
determined	more determined	most determined

Adverbs

wisely	more wisely	most wisely
	less wisely	least wisely
fast	faster	fastest
well	better	best

The comparative is used if two units are being compared; the superlative is used if more than two units are involved in the comparison. Adjectives are used in this way:

POSITIVE   Helen is *wise*. (A simple statement of the idea in *wise*)

The Yankees were *good* last year.

COMPARATIVE   Helen is *wiser* than Tom. (A comparison involving two units)

Last year the Yankees were *better* than the White Sox.

SUPERLATIVE   Helen is the *wisest* person in the family. (A comparison involving more than two units)

In fact, the Yankees were the *best* team in the American League.

The adverbial forms are as follows:

POSITIVE   Helen behaves *wisely*. (A simple statement of the idea with no comparison involved)

Charles writes *badly*.

COMPARATIVE   Helen behaves *more wisely* than Tom.

Charles writes *worse* than Harry.

SUPERLATIVE   Helen behaves *most wisely* of the three children.

Francis writes *worst* of the whole group.

15g *Avoid confused, illogical, and incomplete comparisons.*

(1) **Do not neglect to include *other*** (or an equivalent word) in sentences like these:

ILLOGICAL   Bob is stronger than any man on his team. (Bob is on the team; he cannot be stronger than himself.)

REVISED   Bob is stronger than any other man on his team. (You are now comparing Bob correctly with others, not with himself.)

ILLOGICAL   Helen is wiser than anyone in her family.
REVISED   Helen is wiser than anyone else in her family.
(*Else* gives an effect equivalent to *other*.)

(2) Do not leave comparisons vague, incomplete, or not really comparable.

FAULTY   He likes selling insurance better than a teacher.
REVISED   He likes selling insurance better than teaching.
(*Selling* and *teaching* are comparable.)

FAULTY   Our dormitory is just as beautiful as any other school.
REVISED   Our dormitory is just as beautiful as any other school's.

INCOMPLETE   Buy the bigger and better Buddy-Buddy candy bar. (Bigger and better than what? Leave such deliberate vagueness to high-pressure advertising.)

INCOMPLETE   She is so intelligent. (So intelligent that what?)

AMBIGUOUS   He taught me more than you. (More than he taught you—or more than you taught me?)

(3) Do not try to compare what cannot be compared. Certain words, like *dead, square, absolute, perfect, unique,* are ordinarily not compared in formal writing.

CRUDE   This is a squarer piece of paper than the other one.
REVISED   This piece of paper is *more nearly square* than the other one.

But the makers of the American Constitution wanted to form "a more perfect union," and in slang we speak of "the deadest party" we ever attended.

Exercise 2

Revise the following sentences, correcting all faulty comparisons.

1. I like poetry more than Bertha.
2. She is the best typist of any girl in the office.
3. She seems to me so skillful.

4. Bertha was a better actress than any girl in her school.
5. Her sister Clara wants to excel her at everything; Clara is definitely the most ambitious of the two sisters.
6. Their brother Richard prefers farming to a pharmacist.
7. He is busier than anyone in his pharmacy.
8. Richard looks more like Bertha than Clara.
9. Disagreements among them are probably similar to all other brothers and sisters.
10. You should taste Bertha's hamburgers; they're better.
11. Marvin has common sense far superior to children his age.
12. Coeducational colleges are more beneficial.
13. The swimming here is perhaps the best of any place on the island.
14. The environment gradually became as much a part of me as any other child.
15. The opening of Beethoven's *Fifth Symphony* is more famous than all the symphonies in the world.

16 Misplaced and Dangling Modifiers

Use modifiers clearly and accurately. Place them and word them so that they express your exact meaning. Carelessness with modifiers may make them dangle—that is, make them have only a loose connection with what you intended them to modify. Such carelessness may cause you to say something quite different from what you have in mind.

To revise a misleading or loosely related modifier, rearrange or rephrase your sentence to attach the modifier clearly and definitely to the word it is supposed to refer to.

16a *Place a modifying word so that it clearly relates to what you intend it to modify.*

AMBIGUOUS PLACING OF ADVERB He said he would like to begin by discussing the three plays already mentioned *separately*.
REVISED He said he would like to begin by discussing *separately* the three plays already mentioned.

Perhaps most likely to give trouble are the common adverbs *almost, even, ever, nearly, hardly, just,* and *only.* The meaning of the sentence can often be changed drastically by changing the position of these words. Look at a few examples:

> On Tuesday I *almost* walked to the park. (But, the sentence implies, the writer decided not to go for a walk. Ordinarily, this will not be what he means.)
> On Wednesday I walked *almost* to the park. (This is the meaning probably intended above—he started out but did not get all the way there.)
>
> He *nearly* lost ten dollars last night. (Did he have a narrow escape but lose nothing?)
> He lost *nearly* ten dollars last night. (He lost money, and we know approximately how much.)
>
> This book has *only* the answer to your question. (It contains nothing else worth bothering about.)
> *Only* this book has the answer to your question. (No other book contains the answer.)

Exercise 1

In the following sentences, place all words so that they clearly modify what they are intended to modify.

1. Let me tell you about a girl who joined an organization I belong to recently.
2. No true plants grow at the very bottom of the sea, with the exception of perhaps seaweed.
3. I do not see how I can get all this work possibly done.
4. He looked at the movie as it pictured life on Mars doubtfully.
5. The course I am taking now meets three times a week.

16b *Place phrases so that they clearly modify what you intend them to modify.*

Avoid dangling phrases, either at the beginning or at the end of a sentence.

> MISPLACED Later in the evening the family trims the tree *along with a few friends.* (Do the friends get trimmed?)
> REVISED Later in the evening the family, *along with a few friends,* trims the tree.

DANGLING *As a villain,* I think Richard III is unexcelled. (Am I a villain—or is Richard III?)

REVISED I think Richard III is unexcelled *as a villain.*

DANGLING PARTICIPIAL PHRASE AT BEGINNING *Sitting in a jar of alcohol,* I saw my tonsils. (*Sitting* seems to modify *I.*)

REVISED I saw my tonsils *sitting in a jar of alcohol.* (Now it is the tonsils that are in the alcohol.)

DANGLING PARTICIPIAL PHRASE AT END Andrew Johnson succeeded in 1865 to the office of President of the United States, *resulting from the assassination of Lincoln.* (What, exactly, does *resulting* modify?)

REVISED *After the assassination of Lincoln,* Andrew Johnson succeeded in 1865 to the office of President of the United States.

DANGLING PARTICIPIAL PHRASE AT END He broke his glasses, thus *preventing him from doing the assignment.*

REVISED He could not do his assignment because he broke his glasses.

DANGLING GERUND PHRASE *After soaking in cold water until pliable,* you tuck the head of the drum around a wooden hoop. (Who or what gets soaked?)

REVISED *After soaking the head of the drum in cold water until it is pliable,* you tuck it around a wooden hoop.

DANGLING INFINITIVE PHRASE *To understand why I wanted to change schools,* I will give the facts leading up to my decision.

REVISED *To understand why I wanted to change schools,* you will need to know the facts leading up to my decision.

ANOTHER REVISED VERSION So that you can understand why I wanted to change schools, I will give the facts leading up to my decision.

Exercise 2

Revise the following sentences.

1. She told the child to stop crying in a nasty way.
2. As a fraud, I think he will really qualify.
3. I got acquainted with the students and we were talking as though we had known each other for years in no time at all.
4. Jane will not have a hard time finding a new boy friend with her good looks.

5. The blaze was extinguished before any serious damage was done by the local fire department.
6. Then the final draft can be typed, knowing that you have done your best.
7. Cleopatra ordered a serpent to commit suicide.
8. Making all sorts of noises and walking oddly, the passerby is often frightened by an intoxicated person.
9. I was glad to be going to the party for several reasons.
10. What a strange picture this Santa on the street made, with his bell in one hand and a big cigar in the other for a small child.

16c *Avoid misplaced clauses.*

Place dependent clauses so that they clearly and immediately modify what you intend them to modify.

> MISPLACED   Richard Cory is the main character in a poem by Robinson, whose neighbors think he has everything to make him happy.
> REVISED   Richard Cory, whose neighbors think he has everything to make him happy, is the main character in a poem by Robinson.

> MISPLACED   My eyes began to wander around the room and almost made me forget why I had come while I sat in the cozy little parlor.
> REVISED   While I sat in the cozy little parlor, my eyes began to wander around the room and almost made me forget why I had come.

16d *Avoid dangling elliptical clauses.*

An elliptical clause—one in which the subject and verb are omitted but clearly implied—is useful but must be handled carefully to avoid confusion. If there is misunderstanding about what the subject and verb really are, the elliptical clause "dangles."

> DANGLING ELLIPTICAL CLAUSE   When ten years old, spinach was the vegetable I disliked most.
> REVISED   When I was ten years old, spinach was the vegetable I disliked most.
> REVISED   When ten years old, I disliked spinach more than any other vegetable.

As the revisions above illustrate, a dangling elliptical clause can be corrected either (1) by filling it out with its correct subject (When *I* was ten years old) or (2) by making the logical subject the subject also of the main verb (When ten years old, *I* . . .).

> DANGLING   If well packed, he had no trouble handling the boxes.
> REVISED   If the boxes were well packed, he had no trouble handling them.

> DANGLING   Do not mail the letter until well typed.
> REVISED   Do not mail the letter until it is well typed.

Exercise 3

Revise the following sentences.

1. Other students strive desperately for a position on the team that they will never obtain.
2. Mrs. Blaisdell is moving to an apartment to be near her daughter that she has rented for the winter.
3. While learning to read and write, my mother supervised my piano practice at home.
4. My average was the highest in the French class, which won a prize for me.
5. When filled out and returned in the enclosed envelope, I will be glad to open your checking account.
6. Several of the shirt buttons were replaced by safety pins which were missing.
7. Grandpa would never eat lobster if not boiled.
8. When straightening her clothes, the new mirror came in handy.
9. The lumberjack raised his arm above his head which was very muscular.
10. Unless cut to the ground very early, the home owner will be doubly sorry he has weeds.

16e *Avoid squinting modifiers—modifiers that may refer either to what has gone before or to what comes after.*

Sometimes the sentence can be clarified by punctuation, but usually rephrasing is better.

SQUINTER   With dessert, *available on request,* was a tray of cheese. (What is available, the dessert or the tray of cheese?)

REVISED   Available on request with dessert was a tray of cheese.

SQUINTER   All people who go to Jamaica *sooner or later* fall in love with it.

REVISED   Sooner or later, all people who go to Jamaica fall in love with it.

Exercise 4

Revise the following sentences.

1. They planned during the evening to leave by the side door.
2. The pills going down my throat after a minute tasted like sour cream.
3. Although I study my English thoroughly, because of my bad handwriting, I never receive a very good grade.
4. Because I finished writing the theme in half an hour I was ready to go on the picnic.
5. When I went back to the reference room with help from a librarian I found the book I wanted.

Exercise 5

Rewrite any of the following sentences that contain poorly related or misplaced modifiers. Mark satisfactory sentences C.

1. We were taught never to swim alone as a safety precaution.
2. Lichens can extract the moisture they need from the air, having no root system.
3. She discussed the test that her history professor marked unfairly with her friend.
4. I did not pass the course, caused by failing the examination.
5. The force of the batter's swing carried him across the plate almost falling on his face.
6. Being in dire need of valves, piston rings, and a general overhauling, he found that his car had no compression at all.
7. As the professor said, when young we are eager to learn.
8. When overloaded, a dangerous list appeared in the ship.
9. Sitting in the farm kitchen in the evening, we drank our coffee and talked over the day's activities.
10. The tourist looked at City Hall coming down Main Street.

11. Although as pretty a baby as my older sister, my birth was practically unnoticed.
12. My father will give me a job after completing my college education.
13. After completing my college education, my father will give me a job.
14. At first the paint did not dry properly causing me to do the job again.
15. Although in need of paint, she liked the car.
16. The ordinance of the township commissioners will go into effect next month forbidding fireworks after long delay.
17. Mrs. Jones said I had mowed the lawn too fast, thus causing me to do parts of it again.
18. Although tired from the trip, I intend to see the sights before I do anything else.
19. After telling him that the dog was just what she wanted, her father asked her what they should name it.
20. To ask for a raise, the boss should be approached tactfully, thus not offending him.

17   Connectives: Prepositions

A preposition is a word that relates its object (a noun or other substantive) to another part of the sentence. The preposition and its object combine to form a prepositional phrase.

17a   *Kinds of prepositions*

Most prepositions are single words, but some are word groups, called *phrasal* or *compound* prepositions. Here are examples of common prepositions.

> SINGLE-WORD PREPOSITIONS   *about, above, at, behind, between, by, for, from, in, into, on, over, through, to, under, with, without*
>
> PHRASAL OR COMPOUND PREPOSITIONS   *according to, as to, because of, in regard to, in spite of, instead of, on account of, out of*

17b *Objects of prepositions*

The object of a preposition can be any kind of substantive —noun, pronoun, gerund, phrase, or clause.

NOUN A basket *from home* arrived.
PRONOUN That was the last *of him.*
GERUND He is in no danger *of failing.*
PHRASE She stressed the importance *of making a good start.* (Gerund phrase *making a good start* is the object of *of.*)
CLAUSE Give the ticket *to whoever asks for it.* (*Whoever asks for it* is the object of *to.*)

17c *Case of objects of prepositions*

The object of a preposition is in the objective case.

This is a present to *her* from *me.*

17d *Recognizing prepositions*

Some words used as prepositions may also be adverbs or conjunctions.

AS PREPOSITION They stood *before* him.
AS ADVERB He had come in three hours *before.*
AS CONJUNCTION I had heard of her *before* I met her.

AS PREPOSITION The postman left a letter *for* him.
AS CONJUNCTION You'll need your sweater, *for* the nights are cold.

Note that the prepositions have objects.

17e *Prepositions in idioms*

Prepositions are often fixed to other words in unchangeable combinations called *idioms*. The meaning comes from the whole combination. So we say that we *agree in* an opinion, *agree on* a plan, *agree to* a proposal, and *agree with* a friend. The proper use of idiomatic prepositions is an essential part of good writing. Below are some of the most common idiomatic combinations involving prepositions. There are many others.

When you are in doubt about the form of an idiom, check

for it in your own dictionary under the principal word. If the idiom is not given, consult *Webster's New International Dictionary* (second or third edition), *The Oxford English Dictionary*, or *The Standard Handbook of Prepositions, Conjunctions, Relative Pronouns and Adverbs* (New York, Funk & Wagnalls, 1953).

abide by your decision
absolve him *from* blame
accede to his demands
accommodate yourself *to* the situation
accommodate me *with* a loan
accompanied by Uncle Ed
account for such a mistake
account to Aunt Mary
accused him *of* this error
acquaint me *with* the facts
acquitted of the crime
adapt this *to* your needs
adequate for our purposes
adequate to the expected demand
admits of no choice
admit to Jerry what you have done
aim to make this clear
angry at his behavior
angry with him
authority on a certain subject
comply with your wishes
concerned about bad habits
concerned for you
concerned in this unfortunate business
concerned with making a living
confer about the matter
confer with him
conform to his principles
contrasted this *with* that

contrast of this *to* that
convince him *of* his error
convince him *that* he should
corresponded to that in every particular
corresponds with him by letter
differ about our politics
differ from him
differ in many ways
differ with you
different from that
different than I expected (*than* when a clause follows)
disappointed in you
disappointed with my new job
identical with that
in accordance with your suggestions
infer from what you say
involved in so many activities
involved with him more than I like
negligent of his duties
part from those people
part with all my possessions
plan to talk (*not* plan on talking)
subject to change
superior to all others
try to forget (*not* try and forget)
wait for me
wait on tables

Exercise

Supply the correct preposition in each of the blanks. If there is an option of two prepositions, write both of them in the blank.

1. Does this vary (_____) what you expected?
2. It should be useful (_____) your purposes.
3. He wants to be relieved (_____) all responsibility.
4. We rejoice (_____) your success.
5. Have you become reconciled (_____) him?
6. I have a great prejudice (_____) such sneaks.
7. He hopes to be independent (_____) his family.
8. Advise him (_____) our action.
9. It is useless to try to reason (_____) him.
10. Are you reconciled (_____) what you have to do?

17f *Position of the preposition*

Much energy has been wasted in an effort to make people stop ending statements with prepositions. The practice is well established in the English language and has constantly been used by good writers. Occasional formal sentences may effectively be rephrased to end with something other than a preposition (for example: This is a subject about which I know absolutely nothing), but most sentences are better ended in more natural ways.

CLUMSY   At what is he so amused?
NATURAL   What is he so amused at?

CLUMSY   That is the matter for which I am hoping.
NATURAL   That is what I am hoping for.

Many words that might be mistaken for prepositions at the end of a sentence are really adverbs. (The car knocked the fence *down*. He set the box down and walked *in*.)

18   Connectives: Conjunctives and Conjunctive Adverbs

Conjunctions are words that link words, phrases, or clauses. They differ from prepositions in having no objects. They may be coordinating or subordinating.

18a   *Coordinating conjunctions*

Coordinating conjunctions connect parts that are equal grammatically, such as two nouns or a noun and a pronoun. They may be simple or correlative.

(1) **The simple coordinating conjunctions are** *and, but, for, or, nor, so, yet.* Here are some typical uses of them:

> He wore a sweater *and* a jacket (Connecting two nouns)
> Tom *or* I will go. (Connecting two substantives—a noun and a pronoun)
> I have not finished the work, *but* I intend to get to it to-morrow. (Connecting two independent clauses)

So is more used in speech than it is in writing. It is quite informal and easily overused. See the Glossary.

(2) **Correlatives are pairs of coordinating conjunctions:** *either . . . or, neither . . . nor, both . . . and, not only . . . but (also).* The elements that follow each part of the pair should usually be alike—two substantives, two phrases, and so on.

> *Either* Tom *or* I will go. (Two substantives are joined.)
> This is *neither* in our interest *nor* in yours. (Two phrases are joined.)
> We want to know *not only* when he gets there *but also* what he does. (Two dependent clauses are joined.)

The use of correlatives is likely to result in statements more consciously planned and more forceful than they would be with simple coordinating conjunctions. Contrast the tone of these sentences:

They blamed us and threatened to punish us.
They not only blamed us but threatened to punish us.

18b   *Subordinating conjunctions*

A subordinating conjunction joins a dependent (subordinate) clause to the main clause or to some part of it. Some of the most common conjunctions are *after, although, as, as if, because, before, if, since, then, that, till, unless, until, when, where, while.*

> *When* Jack fell down, he broke his crown.
> Jill came tumbling down *after* Jack broke his crown. (Or *because* he broke it, or *before* or *since* or *while*, depending on the meaning.)

The relative pronouns *who, which, what*, and *that* are used like subordinating conjunctions but have an additional function of acting as a subject or object in the dependent clause. *That*, which can be either pronoun or conjunction, illustrates the difference:

> This is the house that Jack built. (Relative pronoun—*that* is the object of *built*.)
> I do not know that Jack built this house. (Subordinating conjunction—not a subject or object.)

18c   *Conjunctive adverbs*

Conjunctive adverbs are adverbs which are also used as connecting words. They may connect parts of sentences, whole sentences, or even paragraphs. Some of the common conjunctive adverbs are *also, besides, consequently, furthermore, hence, however, indeed, moreover, nevertheless, otherwise, still, then, therefore.* When they join independent clauses, the resulting sentence is compound.

> There is not much to be said for his views except that they are unusual; so strange, *indeed*, are some of them that they must be labeled eccentric.

Note on use of conjunctive adverbs: The conjunctive adverb between independent clauses is not common in modern writing. To say "Tom likes Beethoven better than any other composer; however, I prefer Mozart" is to use an excessively heavy and formal construction for informal material. Most writers would probably think *but* more appropriate: "Tom likes Beethoven better than any other composer, but I prefer Mozart." Pick up almost any good magazine and see how rare the conjunctive adverb is in such sentences.

But the conjunctive adverb is often—and well—used to connect one sentence with another:

> When we read the poetry of a man like Pope, who was extraordinarily, almost abnormally, susceptible to the charms of verbal music, we can have no doubt that he was, in that one department of his existence, all sense. We are not justified, however, in going on, as a recent biographer of the little man has done, to attribute to him a sensitive heart.—MARK VAN DOREN

19 Interjections

An interjection is an exclamatory word or phrase. It may be a separate sentence.

> Oh!
> What!
> For goodness' sake!

It is grammatically independent if it appears within a sentence.

> Well, he always did have plenty of nerve.
> But now, alas, it is too late.

EFFECTIVE SENTENCES

Effective sentences are clear and interesting. They are unified and coherent and—according to the demands of the material—emphatic and varied. They have an appropriate style. Effectiveness of course assumes grammatical competence. Therefore in effective writing there will be, for example, no crude sentence fragments (4), no sentences run puzzlingly together without punctuation (6), and no subliterate sentences in which subject and verb fail to agree (14). (These matters of elementary competence are dealt with in sections 1–19 of this handbook.)

The sections that follow (20–28) are intended to help you avoid certain pitfalls and become familiar with the common paths to effective writing. Some ways to sound writing are routine—almost mechanical. For example, a good sentence does not waver uncertainly back and forth between a question and a positive statement ("She asked why was I going"; see 21e); a good sentence places parallel ideas in parallel grammatical forms ("He jumped over the fence, ran across the field, and disappeared into the woods"; see 25).

But many ways of gaining effectiveness are not at all mechanical and are considerably more complicated than, say, deciding that the active voice is usually better than the passive (27c). For example, there is no mechanical way of telling whether a sentence is unified or not. Only experience, careful thought, and "sentence sense" can tell that. And only a person with an accomplished feeling for style could write such a paragraph as the following, with its two sentences, one long and one short, and both making an effective unit:

> In his struggle to reach the captain and the boat, he reflected that when one gets properly wearied, drowning must really be a comfortable arrangement, a cessation of hostilities accompanied by a large degree of relief, and he was glad of it, for the main thing in his mind for some months had been horror of the temporary agony. He did not want to be hurt.—STEPHEN CRANE

In connection with effective sentences, you will not want to overlook one of the most basic matters of all: the kind of words you are going to use—words that are appropriate to your material and your reader. For a discussion of words that are fitting, see Chapter 6.

20   Clear Sentence Patterns

Construct your sentences in normal and complete grammatical patterns. Put your ideas in clear, grammatical, logically arranged statements. Do not mix sentence patterns.

20a   *Complete a pattern that you start.*

Do not forget how you have begun a sentence and carelessly shift constructions, breaking off one pattern and starting another.

MIXED   He began to wonder why was that necessary. (The sentence confuses indirect and direct quotation. The clause "why that was necessary" shifts to the pattern of a direct question: "Why was that necessary?")

REVISED AND CONSISTENT   He began to wonder why that was necessary.

MIXED   It is one of Thoreau's basic contentions that any man who is more right than his neighbors constitutes a majority of one, and therefore gives him the right to practice his belief. (The verb *gives* has no subject.)

REVISED   It is one of Thoreau's basic contentions that any man who is more right than his neighbors constitutes a majority of one and is therefore entitled to practice his belief.

CONFUSED   This is a ballad which like most ballads the author is unknown. (*Which* has no construction; it is not part of any completed grammatical pattern.)

REVISED   This ballad, like most others, is by an unknown author.

Exercise 1

Rephrase any mixed patterns to give clarity and consistency.

1. Each stone figure was between seventy-five to one hundred feet high.
2. It was due to this lack of an iron industry that led the South to defeat.
3. It was not until Penn had spent seven months in this wilderness, did he begin to make proposals for the purchase of land.
4. By acquiring all this information on human anatomy does not mean that we are going to become scientists.
5. From a beautiful sunset I can derive more pleasure in contrast with another new dress.
6. I took gas the first tooth I had pulled.
7. Because people invariably are disturbed by *Gulliver's Travels* seems to me to show the ability of the author.
8. It is not until after the duel does one feel relief from this hostility.
9. Greeted by unfriendliness made me want to leave Hoisington as soon as I could.
10. I believe my cousin is a person that everything he has on his back was bought on credit.

20b *Include all necessary words.*

Do not omit words required for clarity or grammatical completeness. The following sentences illustrate common mistakes.

> PREPOSITION NEEDED   I have always been a great sports fan, especially baseball. (*Of* is needed before *baseball*.)
>
> "THAT" NEEDED   One superstition she often mentions is a spider seen spinning his web at night denotes good luck. (*That* is needed after *is*.)
>
> COMPLETE AND LOGICAL PARALLELISM NEEDED   He was stout, a clean-shaven face, with horn-rimmed glasses resting on the end of his nose. (Revised: He was stout, had a clean-shaven face, and wore horn-rimmed glasses that rested on the end of his nose.)

Note on the omission of verb words: The omission of parts of a verb phrase in a pair or a series of verbs can often result in clumsy or confusing constructions. When a form is identical in two verb phrases, it can be omitted from the first.

STANDARD, ACCEPTABLE OMISSION   He could have and should have finished the work last night. (*Finished* is the word that completes both verb phrases: *could have finished* and *should have finished*. The sentence is entirely idiomatic and clear.)

STANDARD, ACCEPTABLE OMISSION   The question was not whether we should have but whether we could have done anything about it. (*Done* clearly completes *should have* as well as *could have*.)

If a form is not identical in two verb phrases, it cannot be omitted from the first one.

INCOMPLETE   He has not and will not receive any award. (The omission of *received* after *has not* is not acceptable in standard written English. Write "He has not received and will not receive any award" or rephrase to something less stiff: "He has not received any award and he will not." See below.)

When the full form of the verb phrase appears first, omission of an identical word is common and acceptable.

We promised to write and we will [write].
He has finished the work and [has] gone.

Even when the form changes for the second verb, the changed form is often omitted if the verb has already been expressed fully.

He hasn't finished the work and he won't [finish it].

Such an omission is not always acceptable. Most educated users of the language would hesitate to write the following:

QUESTIONABLE   We have gone every day and will again tomorrow.

ACCEPTABLE   We have gone every day and will go again tomorrow.

Often a form of the verb *do* is substituted for a preceding verb.

STANDARD   We have not given him permission to go, and we shall not do so. (*Do* is used instead of *give*.)

Exercise 2

Complete all sentence patterns to express the idea clearly. Supply any missing words.

1. This essay helped me understand what college football can and is doing.
2. The men asked themselves what they should do in the new circumstances they found themselves.
3. The school was too large, too many people, and too few friends.
4. On the bulletin boards were posted samples of the students' work, varying from cutouts, pictures, and handwriting.
5. Each character is convincing so far as the honesty of his feelings.
6. This is one show I think you will not regret paying an admission if necessary.
7. The student's idea may be attending college for a semester is all he wants.
8. As the Roman Empire expanded, rulers copied the idea of Augustus, that of coining the major denominations of coins himself and the coining of smaller denominations to the local governments.
9. For years he has read travel books, especially Tibet.
10. We knew that he did not dare and has never gone anywhere by himself.

20c   *Avoid using the double negative.*

You are not likely to write anything such as "I *can't* believe *nothing* you say," but you may make mistakes with other words that have a negative meaning. *Hardly* and *scarcely* are perhaps the most troublesome of these words; others are *but, only, rarely,* and *neither.* The following sentences illustrate the problem:

DOUBLE NEGATIVE   I can't hardly believe what you say.
STANDARD   I can hardly (*or* scarcely) believe what you say.

DOUBLE NEGATIVE   There weren't only (*or* but) two seats left.
STANDARD   There were only (*or* but) two seats left.

DOUBLE NEGATIVE   Students will not be able to do their best work, neither mentally nor physically.

STANDARD   Students will not be able to do their best work, either mentally or physically.

20d   *Avoid mixing figures of speech.*

MIXED   Each mile away from home was like a brick in a stone wall that separated me from those I love. (Is the wall made of bricks or of stones?)

Figures of speech are often weak because of triteness or inappropriateness. (See pages 99–100, 102.)

20e   *Avoid awkward separation of closely related sentence elements,* such as subject and verb, verb and object, or parts of a prepositional phrase, an infinitive, or a verb phrase.

A good rule to follow is to separate the parts of such expressions only when you must do so to preserve clarity and accuracy.

AWKWARD SEPARATION OF SUBJECT AND VERB   *She,* since the manager seemed to dislike her, simply *went* to the other company.
REVISED   Since the manager seemed to dislike her, *she* simply *went* to the other company.

AWKWARD SEPARATION OF VERB AND OBJECT   Charles IV *signed* at Barcelona on October 5, 1802, *Louisiana* over to France.
REVISED   On October 5, 1802, at Barcelona, Charles IV *signed Louisiana* over to France.

AWKWARD SEPARATION OF PARTS OF A PREPOSITIONAL PHRASE   The corruption of the English language, Orwell says, is caused *by* in large measure *politicians.*
REVISED   The corruption of the English language, Orwell says, is caused in large measure *by politicians.*

AWKWARD SEPARATION OF PARTS OF AN INFINITIVE (a "split" infinitive)   I was forced *to* carefully *examine* my beliefs.
REVISED   I was forced *to examine* my beliefs carefully.

AWKWARD SEPARATION OF PARTS OF A VERB PHRASE   We *were* at this time of the year *surprised* to see anyone carrying skis.
REVISED   We *were surprised* to see anyone carrying skis at this time of the year.

Do not think that separation of sentence elements is always an error. On the contrary, separation is sometimes the way to express oneself idiomatically, clearly, or naturally. For example:

> Mr. Eliot *has* simply *inverted* the old sugarcoated pill theory. . . .
> —ROBERT PENN WARREN
> But, no doubt, some kinds of knowledge cannot be made *to* directly *serve* the instinct in question. . . .—MATTHEW ARNOLD

Sometimes the separation of sentence elements gives a certain dramatic suspense:

> They had left from—of all places—Willistown.

Exercise 3

Revise the following sentences to remove any awkward separation of sentence elements.

1. I was taught that I was to never place my finger on the trigger.
2. The curtains hide the garages that can through the big double window be seen.
3. He, because he had got in the way of the soldiers, had been wounded severely.
4. A certain kind of wave has according to many reports been a signal of the coming of a typhoon.
5. Joe Louis collected through his fights millions of dollars.
6. George felt, after the game was over, depressed.
7. We are staying at, for the time being, the local hotel.
8. We knew that Alice was, when she accepted the invitation, getting herself into a tangle.
9. I am one of those unfortunate people who seem to at all times forget names.
10. He had left, as the relatives learned when the will was read, his property to charity.

21 Shifts in Sentence Elements

Keep sentence elements consistent. Avoid awkward, aimless, and illogical shifts.

21a *Keep the same grammatical subject unless there is good reason for changing.*

SHIFT   The *cast* first discusses the play, and then nightly *rehearsals* begin. (The shift is clumsy and needless.)

REVISED   The cast first discusses the play and then begins nightly rehearsals.

SHIFT   *John* worked hard for three years, and then a *job* was given him that let him use his special talent.

REVISED   John worked hard for three years and then was given a job that let him use his special talent.

Do not confuse such awkward statements with sentences in which the subject very properly changes:

Time has shifted our point of view on Bernard Shaw, yet *he* is still worth our contemplation.—EDMUND WILSON

The *work* was hard, but the *profits* were small. (The shift here is clear and is justified because the writer is making parallels between *work* and *profits* and between *hard* and *small*.)

21b *Keep the person of pronouns consistent.*

SHIFT   First *we* come into the big hall, dazed and bewildered, and then *you* are lectured at some more. (In both clauses the writer is talking about the same group of people; he has no reason to shift from the first person, *we,* to the second person, *you.*)

REVISED   First *we* come into the big hall, dazed and bewildered, and then *we* are lectured at some more.

21c *Keep the number of nouns and pronouns consistent.* (See also 9a, 14f.)

SHIFT   I think a *person* should choose *their* own friends. (Careless shift from singular *person* to plural *their*)

REVISED   I think a *person* should choose *his* own friends. (Now both are singular.)

SHIFT   The town library *needs* supplies. *They* are asking for your support. (Is *library* thought of as singular or plural?)

REVISED   The town library *needs* supplies. *It* is asking for your support.

21d *Keep the tense, mood, or voice that you have decided is the right one.* Avoid needless or careless shifts.

SHIFT IN TENSE   He *drove* the car into the side road and quickly *turns* off the motor. (The shift from past tense, *drove*, to present tense, *turns*, is awkward. Such a shift, often made with the hope of achieving dramatic excitement, is seldom successful.)

REVISED   He *drove* the car into the side road and quickly *turned* off the motor.

SHIFT IN MOOD   First *build* a fire and then you *should make* the coffee. (*Build* is in the imperative mood, *should make* in the indicative.)

REVISED   First *build* a fire and then *make* the coffee. (Both verbs are now in the imperative.)

SHIFT IN VOICE   He *drove* the car into the garage and the motor *was* quickly *stopped*. (The voice shifts from active to passive. Notice that the subject also shifts awkwardly from *he* to *motor*.)

REVISED   He *drove* the car into the garage and quickly *stopped* the motor. (Both verbs are now active: *drove* and *stopped*. The only subject is *he*. The sentence is now consistent and clear.)

21e *Keep to either direct or indirect quotation* (*also called direct and indirect discourse*).

Decide which form is better and stick to it. Do not shift from one form to the other.

SHIFT   She came over to me and asked whether I had talked to John and is he coming to the dance. (Shift from indirect to direct quotation)

REVISED   She came over to me and asked whether I had talked to John and whether he was coming to the dance. (Indirect quotation throughout)

OR REVISED   She came over to me and asked, "Have you talked to John? Is he coming to the dance?"

21f *Keep to the style or tone you have chosen.*

See pages 93–95.

21g   *Keep to any sentence pattern or construction you have chosen to use.* (See 20.)

Exercise

Revise the sentences that contain awkward shifts. Mark satisfactory sentences C and leave them unchanged. Be prepared to justify your answers and revisions.

1. If one works reasonably hard, you can learn to speak a foreign language in a few months.
2. My brother George wants to be a musician, but architecture is my future profession.
3. When I reached the pier, I suddenly notice that the tide is low.
4. As he looked at the front page, a gasp came from his throat.
5. The company is looking for an engineer to take charge of their new office in Vancouver.
6. As soon as you know the assignment, go to the library; you should take out at least two books on your subject.
7. Old cars are fun, but new ones give less trouble.
8. Will you please tell me how an inexperienced person can learn what is expected of them here?
9. He spoke to the stranger and asks what ails him.
10. He repaired the radio and then his homework received his attention.
11. Before inventors made the first steamboats, many technical problems had to be solved by them.
12. A freshman should have perseverance and flexibility and should learn to do one's assignments promptly.
13. The insects of early October were making their ancient patterns of sound; the moon, still bright, was low in the sky; and the distant hoot of an owl sounded nuts.
14. Looking at the calendar, she suddenly remembered that her cousin is coming.
15. Sometimes he won small sums of money, but they were quickly lost the next time he went to the track.

22   Sentence Unity and Coherence

A sentence should be unified—that is, it should be made up of related parts that combine to express one thought; and a sentence should be coherent—that is, the relationship between its parts should be clearly shown. Whether the sentence is extremely simple ("I like music") or somewhat more complicated ("Although music has been part of my life for as long as I can remember, until recently I was indifferent to most of the modern composers"), it should contain only a single thought or a unit of clearly related thoughts. (Connective devices that show relationships are discussed under "Transitions," **23.**)

22a   *Include only clearly related ideas.*

Revise sentences containing parts that are or appear to be unrelated by (1) rewriting to show the relationship you have in mind, (2) putting unrelated ideas in separate sentences, or (3) omitting irrelevant material.

> NOT CLEARLY RELATED   July is the hottest time of the year, and my birthday comes in this month.
>
> ONE POSSIBLE REVISION TO SHOW RELATIONSHIP   I was born in the hottest month of the year, July.
>
> ANOTHER POSSIBLE REVISION   I have never liked hot weather, even though I was born in July, the hottest month of the year.

> NOT CLEARLY RELATED   Indians spoke of hibernation as the Long Sleep; it is like being half-way to death.
>
> REVISED   Indians spoke of hibernation as the Long Sleep, but it is rather more than that. It is profound oblivion midway between sleep and death.—ALAN DEVOE

> NOT RELATED   Shakespeare, whose elder daughter, Susanna, married Dr. John Hall, is the only English dramatist before the late nineteenth century whose plays are still frequently performed. (The ideas here do not belong in the same sentence or even in the same paragraph. The sentence can be unified only by omitting one of the ideas.)

417

22b *Learn to find the dimensions of clearly unified sentences.*

Do not let sentences become cluttered with too much material. Drop ideas that are not clearly related to the central purpose of the sentence.

CLUTTERED   It took me a long time to learn to swim, but I finally did learn one day when a clay bank along a river in central Kansas where I grew up caved in under my feet and, as I soon discovered, the water was too deep for me to stand up, although I tried to do so.

REVISED   (by omitting some material and dividing the sentence into related parts)   It took me a long time to learn to swim, but I finally did learn one day when a clay riverbank caved in under my feet. As I soon discovered, the water was too deep for me to stand up, although I tried to do so.

CLUTTERED   Mexico City is great and cosmopolitan, with a fine university and ultramodern architecture, and I hope to go there this summer.

REVISED   Mexico City is great and cosmopolitan, with a fine university and ultramodern architecture. I hope to go there this summer.

Exercise

Point out the weaknesses in unity and coherence in the following sentences. Some of the sentences may be satisfactory as they stand. Suggest revisions of unsatisfactory sentences.

1. Baseball is my favorite game, and it is played in hot weather.
2. Mr. Schwartz is my chemistry instructor, but his wife is rather pretty.
3. Edward J. O'Brien made collections of American short stories, one which I like very much being "Evening" by Zona Gale, who lived in Portage, Wisconsin.
4. I don't know what experience in my early childhood accounts for my fear of snakes, but I shall not spend another summer in the pine woods.
5. Happiness is not always mere relaxation; an Einstein derives great satisfaction from understanding the nature of the physical universe.

6. The elective system, which President Eliot of Harvard introduced into the curriculum of the American college, has fragmented the common body of knowledge which all educated men once possessed.

7. There are many books in my father's library which I have not read, but book knowledge is not always a substitute for practical experience.

8. Germany, a country which possesses very rich coal reserves, attracts thousands of tourists.

9. Our school had four chemistry teachers; the students rated three as average, and the fourth was notorious for his high academic requirements.

10. Germany, a country of great natural beauty and many fine museums, attracts thousands of tourists.

11. The boy never knew his father was a gang leader who was wanted by the police for years, but they never had his description, only his suspected activities.

12. Some of Orwell's essays made me think over what I had read —whether I would do the same thing in his place and be just as guilty, and the essay called "Shooting an Elephant" is one of these essays.

13. Another suggestion that came to me when I was trying to improve my vocabulary in order to become a writer was to read a dictionary—either the big one so zealously guarded by the library dragons or the one I can never forget I got as a prize in the high-school poetry contest (I used to be quite a sonneteer)—but after taking several nights away from my favorite television programs I found that his advice was the greatest possible waste of time.

14. When she finally learned to drive a car, she did so without knowing how to get along in traffic, and this was a serious handicap to her.

15. All the social activities I have mentioned are to be recommended for the student's enjoyment but if indulged in too vigorously they will distract his mind and his grades will suffer, which is not good; because his purpose in being at a university is to get an education, which is an obvious truth often forgotten.

23   Transitional Devices That Aid Unity and Coherence

Transitional devices can help make your writing clear and smooth. Such devices may be any of various standard expressions (like "now" or "in the second place") inserted in a sentence, or they may be pronouns, or they may be repetition of important words or patterns. Whatever they are, good transitional elements make it easier for the reader to pass from one part (small or large) of a composition to another.

Remember that your reader does not know what connections you have in mind; you must often state them in your writing for him to follow your thoughts. Almost all aspects of your writing that make it seem connected, clear, and united are in a way transitions, but the term *transitional device* is applied in particular to the connective helps discussed in the sections below.

23a   *Use transitional expressions.*

Among the useful transitional expressions available to every writer are the following:

To show contrast

> but, however, still, yet, otherwise, nevertheless, in contrast, on the contrary

To show additions or to amplify a previous statement

> also, besides, again, moreover, in addition

To show result

> so, thus, therefore, as a consequence, as a result

To show order and time

> later, next, then, first, second, third, in the meantime

There are hundreds of others, common and uncommon.

(1) Transitional expressions may make connections within a sentence.

> We had wondered what could happen if you flew to London or Paris, hired a car, and simply took off into the countryside—without a prearranged plan, without reservations in advance, and *therefore* without a tight schedule. . . .—ERIC LARRABEE

(2) They may make connections between sentences.

> *In the meantime,* I had been following the rules and growing more powerful every day.—WILLIAM SAROYAN
> *Finally,* a large number of pairs could nest in the rushes of a favorable lake. . . .—LUDLOW GRISCOM
> It is *thus* a kind of French "ultra" movement. . . .—ALAN WESTIN
> It follows *therefore* that women who are beautiful should want for nothing.—REBECCA WEST

Transitional expressions are essential for clear writing, but they are not the principal means of showing relationships. You need only glance at a page of any good modern magazine or book to see that such set, mechanical transitions are probably less common than you may have thought. They are not the chief dependence of writers but only one part of a whole series of transitional methods that also involve such matters as repetition and the use of pronouns. For further discussion of transitional expressions within paragraphs, see pages 69–72.

Exercise 1

From a page of an article (not a short story) in a recent issue of the *Atlantic Monthly* or *Harper's Magazine,* list all the transitional expressions you find. Give the names of the author, the magazine, the article, and the date and page number.

23b *Use pronouns as transitional aids.*

In their normal function, most pronouns refer to antecedents and call them to mind. Skillful use of pronouns is therefore one of the easiest and most natural means of smooth transition from one part of a sentence to another. The following examples make this point clear.

(1) Within a sentence

> The broadcasters know this, however much *they* try to convince *themselves* as well as others that *they* perform a consistent public service.—MARYA MANNES
>
> Alumni whose sole interest in their alma mater is in *its* athletic standing lose *their* interest when *its* teams run on bad years.—ROBERT M. HUTCHINS

(2) Between sentences

> Possibly *I* am lucky. *I* have just lived through the teen-ages of a son and a daughter. There were moments when *I* thought murder was too good for *them;* there were moments when *they* thought murder was much too good for *me.* Sometimes *their* anguish was *my* anguish; sometimes *their* cussedness was *my* fury; occasionally *their* pleasure was *my* despair. But *I* saw *myself* sometimes distorted, sometimes all too clearly, in *them* as a mirror. *I* suspect *I* learned from *them* as much as *I* taught *them,* and *I* wouldn't have missed *it* for anything.—RUSSELL LYNES

Exercise 2

List the pronouns in the passage quoted below in **23c**, and in a few sentences discuss their value as transitional devices.

23c   *Repeat important words.*

In the following selection observe that democracy, the central idea of the paragraph, is mentioned in every sentence. The result is a clear, readable, highly concentrated passage. (The author avoids monotony by varying the structure of the sentences and by using the noun *democracy* twice and the adjective *democratic* twice.)

> The great paradox of *democracy* is that its moral ideas preceded its political and economic problems. *Democracy* drew its values and goals from the eighteenth century, its basic practical issues from the nineteenth century. Jefferson set forth the *democratic*

dream in terms so compelling and universal that they have held broadly good for all subsequent generations. But his specific *democratic* presuppositions were derived from an agricultural society of small freeholds.—ARTHUR M. SCHLESINGER, JR.

23d Repeat structural patterns within and between sentences when the thought lends itself to such repetition.

For a discussion of this device, known as *parallelism*, see **25**.

24 Subordination and Coordination

24a Use subordination and coordination in such a way as to increase sentence effectiveness.

In general, place your main thoughts in independent clauses, and put explanations and details in subordinate clauses or phrases. Place thoughts that are of equal importance in coordinate constructions.

Here, for example, are sentences from Rachel Carson's *The Sea Around Us* that show subordinate clauses (italicized) in skillful relation to the main clauses:

> *As long as there has been an earth,* the moving masses of air *that we call winds* have swept back and forth across its surface. And *as long as there has been an ocean,* its waters have stirred to the passage of the winds. . . . The waves *most of us know best* are wind waves.

And these sentences from the same work illustrate the coordinating of similar elements:

> If you visited this place and talked to the meteorologist in charge, he could tell you the life histories of the waves that are rolling in, minute by minute and hour after hour, bringing their messages of far-off places. He could tell you where the waves were created by the action of wind on water, the strength of the winds that produced them, how fast the storm is moving, and how soon, if at all, it will become necessary to raise storm warnings along the coast of England.

Note in these sentences the careful indication of coordination in the emphatic repetition of *he could tell you*, and the coordinating of the expressions after the second *he could tell you*:

> where the waves were created . . .
> the strength of the winds that produced them
> how fast the storm is moving
> how soon . . . it will become necessary.

For further discussion of coordination of similar elements, see Parallelism, **25.**

Intelligent use of subordination and coordination can help give smoothness, variety, emphasis, and unity to your writing, but to gain these effects you must think carefully about your material and distinguish between more important ideas and secondary ones. To improve your use of subordination and coordination, study the following sections.

24b   *Avoid choppy sentences*

A book for very young children, written in a style suited to their understanding, will contain passages like this:

> I see the duck. The duck is white. He swims in the water.

A college student does not write in this childish way, of course, but if we examine student sentences such as the following, we will see that they are basically not very different:

> We need new tennis courts in this city. The ones behind the Community House are the only public ones we have. They are in very bad condition. The backstops are practically worthless. This is because they are so badly torn. Also the nets are torn.

The content of this passage is more mature than the set of I-see-the-duck sentences. The form, on the other hand, is still what is sometimes called "primer style," with sentences short and unvaried. Such choppy writing is monotonous, fails to show which ideas are to be emphasized, and does not make clear how the ideas are related.

What can you do to improve such writing? The most obvious and the easiest change is to reduce the number of short sentences. This can be done in three ways: (1) by coordination—that is, by putting two statements in the same sentence:

> The backstops and the nets are torn and practically worthless.

(2) by putting one idea in a subordinate clause:

> Because the backstops are so badly torn, they are practically worthless.

or (3) by reducing one sentence to a word or phrase in another sentence, as when "Also the nets are torn" becomes a phrase:

> Because the backstops are so badly torn, they, *like the nets,* are practically worthless.

CHOPPY   The setting of most of Edith Wharton's stories is New York or Paris. These cities are world capitals. Their society is wealthy and aristocratic. Perhaps, however, the best novel Mrs. Wharton ever wrote is *Ethan Frome.* This novel tells the story of the tragic love of a poor farmer. He lived in the most remote section of Massachusetts.

REVISED   The setting of most of Edith Wharton's stories is in the wealthy and aristocratic society of those world capitals, New York and Paris. But *Ethan Frome,* perhaps her best novel, tells the story of the tragic love of a poor farmer in the most remote section of Massachusetts.

Exercise 1

Reduce the number of short sentences in the following passage. Use the methods mentioned above, but do not coordinate, subordinate, or reduce any structure at the cost of clarity or effectiveness.

> Cape Cod is a fine place for a vacation. I know because I was at the Cape last summer. I drove all day to get there. I arrived one Sunday night in July. Unfortunately, I had nowhere to stay when I got there. The Cape was a place I had never seen before. I drove around for an hour. Then I found a picturesque guest house. It was near the beach and the surf. The landlady said she had a room for rent. I went in and inspected it. I decided to take it. Following this, I got my luggage and unpacked it. Now I was free to go out on the terrace. The landlady had told me this terrace was near my room. The salty air was pleasant on my lips. It blew through my hair and made it feel cool.

I could see the white breakers rolling in. They seemed never to stop. Weariness and peace came over me. I returned to my room. I went to bed immediately.

Exercise 2

Follow the directions in Exercise 1 above.

> One critic attacks American ignorance. He says Americans know little of what is going on in the world. At least, they do not know the important things. This is true, he says, in spite of modern communications. In communications we surpass the whole world. Today every man gets the news. It comes fast from many parts of the country and around the globe. There is a great deal of news. The newspapers are big. Radios give news of happenings everywhere. So does television. But this critic still does not like it. He says we have much noise, but we are starved for understanding and truth.

24c *Avoid upside-down subordination. Distinguish between the main and the secondary parts of a statement.*

The main idea should normally be stated in the main clause, not in a modifying phrase or dependent clause. These minor constructions are for introduction, background, supplementary explanation, and qualification. The basic or emphatic part of your sentence should usually be in your main clause.

The following sentences illustrate the most common kinds of upside-down subordination:

(1) The main idea in a *when* or *where* clause
> POOR   I entered the room, when I saw a sight I shall never forget.
>
> REVISED   When I entered the room, I saw a sight I shall never forget.

(2) The main idea in a participial phrase
> UNEMPHATIC   He hit a single to left field, establishing a new record for consecutive hits.
>
> REVISED   With his single to left field he established a new record for consecutive hits.

(3) The main idea in a relative clause

POOR The game began at two o'clock that was to determine the city championship.

REVISED The game, which began at two o'clock, was to determine the city championship.

Note: Whether a particular thought should be subordinated or not often depends on the context. In other words, you cannot always be sure unless you know the circumstances in which subordination occurs. For example, in a narrative context, such a sentence as the following would be effective, even though the subordination at the end (beginning with *when*) contains the most dramatic part of the statement:

My sister had just started to fry the meat when the fat in the pan burst into high, fierce flames.

In most expository writing, however, you weaken the impact of a main idea by putting it in a dependent clause or phrase.

Exercise 3

Improve the following sentences by revising the subordination. If you think the context would make a difference, indicate what would be best in a particular context.

1. The hunter kicked around in the honeysuckle when out ran a big rabbit.
2. I ran out of ink, thus being unable to finish my theme.
3. We ran into the store where we found the biggest surprise of our lives.
4. College is a place in which we prepare ourselves for adult responsibilities.
5. The truck was rolling along smoothly when it suddenly exploded.
6. The prize was given yesterday that was for the best essay by a freshman.
7. When lightning struck a tree beside the tennis court, we were playing our first game.
8. They were bored with endless talk when they began to play games.
9. We drove from Cheyenne to Vancouver, seeing some very spectacular mountain ranges.

427

10. I was nearly through the test before I realized that I had overlooked the most important question.

24d Avoid careless and excessive coordination.

Do not string ideas together with *and, but,* and *so* when some of the ideas should be subordinated or placed in separate sentences.

> CARELESS, EXCESSIVE COORDINATION   I started to cook my first meal and I became frightened so I frantically turned the oven off and then I cried.
> SUBORDINATION USED   When I started to cook my first meal I became so frightened that I frantically turned the oven off and cried.

> CARELESS COORDINATION   To cover the floor, I ordered two hundred tiles, half a gallon of primer, and half a gallon of cement, and this was enough material for the whole job.
> SEPARATE SENTENCES USED   To cover the floor, I ordered two hundred tiles, half a gallon of primer, and half a gallon of cement. This was enough material for the whole job.

Exercise 4

Revise the following sentences to eliminate careless and excessive coordination.

1. The architect's plans look good and we were at first intending to build the house next spring, but now we have decided to wait.
2. Alice had the best grades in her high-school class and of course she is going to college.
3. I have never met Ralph but I have heard a great deal about him, so I feel as if I know him.
4. Socrates had a large group of followers and they would do almost anything for him.
5. I have not read the assigned book so I will not have my review ready so I may have trouble in this course.
6. I always come to school on the bus and it is crowded all the way.
7. California is like Italy and has a Mediterranean type of climate.

8. New York has a first-class harbor and has become the leading American port, so the city has grown into a great metropolis.
9. Manhattan is an island and the most densely populated island in the world.
10. The native houses were round and pointed and they made a pleasing contrast with the background of the forest.

25 Parallelism

Use parallel forms for parallel ideas. One of the signs of a mature mind is that it is able to recognize similarities and differences and, on the basis of this recognition, to group similar items and distinguish them clearly from other things. The writer who thinks straight will present his ideas in clear and unmistakable form. He will see to it that like things are put in a form which shows that they are alike. He will use parallel construction for parallel ideas.

Look at this sentence:

> I like dancing and to read good books.

Why should the author change from the noun (a gerund) *dancing* to the infinitive phrase *to read good books?* He likes two activities, dancing and reading. Why, by using a non-parallel construction in grammar, does he disguise this parallelism in idea? He should be consistent and use either nouns or infinitives for both activities:

> I like dancing and reading good books.
> I like to dance and to read good books.

Here is a sentence with a similar error:

> Being ambitious by nature and because I am an optimist, I think I can work my way through college.

The same awkward and pointless shifting is involved, this time from a participial phrase (*being ambitious*) to a subordinate clause (*because I am an optimist*). Again, the construction shifts when the thought calls for parallelism:

Being ambitious and optimistic, I believe I can work my way
through college.
Because I am ambitious and optimistic, I believe I can work my
way through college.

If you think, for example, that you have three aims in
coming to college, you should state these as parallel items.
Before you put these aims into written words, you should
have something like a diagram in your mind:

I have come to college to
$\left\{\begin{array}{l} \rule{6cm}{0.4pt} \\ \rule{6cm}{0.4pt} \\ \rule{6cm}{0.4pt} \end{array}\right.$

Your next step is to fill in the blanks in this imaginary diagram. You must take care to make all three of the aims alike
in form, because you will not want the reader to be puzzled
even for a moment or to wonder whether the three items are
really intended to be parallel at all.

Let us suppose that your coming to college means the fulfillment of a childhood dream of becoming a scientist, that
you have always enjoyed learning about all sorts of things,
and that you hope in college to meet people who share your
interests. You could fit this material into the diagram in the
following way:

I have come to college to
$\left\{\begin{array}{l} \textit{become} \text{ a scientist} \\ \textit{increase} \text{ my general knowledge} \\ \textit{meet} \text{ people who share my interests} \end{array}\right.$

Notice that the three items are parallel in form; each of
them contains an infinitive and a noun. You now need only
put this material into the following sentence form:

I have come to college to become a scientist, increase my general
knowledge, and meet people who share my interests.

Suppose, however, that the sentence had been this:

I have come to college to become a scientist, for increasing my
general knowledge, and so that I may meet people who share
my interests.

The three items have no parallel appearance and are left for
the reader to disentangle as best he can. Let us put the sentence into diagram form:

I have come to college
$$\begin{cases} \textit{to become} \text{ a scientist} \\ \textit{for increasing} \text{ my general knowledge} \\ \textit{so that I may meet} \text{ people who share my} \\ \quad \text{interests} \end{cases}$$

The items are not uniform, and the sentence, therefore, is not nearly as easy to grasp as it was when the items were presented in parallel form.

A lack of parallelism where it is called for will not only reduce the clarity of a sentence; it will also reduce its force. Julius Caesar's statement "I came, I saw, I conquered" has been quoted for two thousand years. It would never have been remembered had Caesar said the Latin equivalent of "I came, I was able to see, and the land was conquered."

In Lincoln's "government of the people, by the people, for the people," the phrases are parallel: each of them is made of a preposition followed by a noun. The effect would have been lost had Lincoln written: "government of the people, by popular majorities, and that will serve the best interests of its citizens."

25a Use parallel structure for coordinate sentence elements.

The following sentences illustrate typical mistakes in parallelism:

FAULTY   As time passed, his feeling turned to *anxiety, disbelief,* and finally *becoming deeply concerned.* (Nouns faultily paralleled with participial phrase)

REVISED   As time passed, his feeling turned to *anxiety, disbelief,* and finally deep *concern.* (All nouns)

FAULTY   On Christmas Day our relatives always visit each other to *see the tree, presents,* and *wish everyone a happy holiday.* (Infinitive phrases and noun faultily paralleled)

REVISED   On Christmas Day our relatives always visit each other to *see* the tree, *give* presents, and *wish* everyone a happy holiday. (Infinitives now clearly paralleled)

FAULTY   In a cafeteria one *chooses* his own food, *carries* it to a table, and no tip *is given.* (Two verbs in the active voice faultily paralleled with one in the passive voice)

REVISED   In a cafeteria one *chooses* his own food, *carries* it to a table, and *gives* no tip. (Verbs now paralleled—all active)

Note: Items in a series or list should be parallel in form. The following list is faulty:

1. Why are the living standards on the farms in this part of the state so low?
2. Can the land ever support the people?
3. What kind of crops can be grown in this region?
4. A loan might be needed to help people get started.

The first three items are in the form of questions; item 4 is not parallel. Either make the first three items affirmative rather than questions, or change the last item to something like this: "Will a loan be needed to help people get started?"

The principles of parallelism also apply to outlines. See pages 22–26.

25b *Use parallel sentence elements after both parts of a pair of correlative conjunctions* (either . . . or, neither . . . nor, both . . . and, not only . . . but also).

The correlatives are designed to set up a balance which can be maintained only if both elements are followed by parallel constructions.

AWKWARD   He believed neither *in himself* nor *did he believe in others.*

REVISED   He believed neither *in himself* nor *in others.* (Two prepositional phrases paralleled)

AWKWARD   Since we have only one desk, my roommate either studies or I do.

REVISED   . . . either my roommate studies or I do.

EFFECTIVE PARALLEL STRUCTURE   *Not only* did they find DDT in substantial quantities in the rats' body fat *but* they found that this DDT was just as effective a poison as it had been when it was sprayed on the alfalfa.—ROBERT RICE

25c *In general, repeat words that are necessary to make the parallelism instantly clear.*

CONFUSED   Thoreau stood up for his principles by not paying his taxes and spending a night in jail.

REVISED   Thoreau stood up for his principles by not paying his taxes and *by* spending a night in jail. (Preposition repeated)

CONFUSED   These are days which I want to hold on to forever but seem to slip out of my grasp.

REVISED   These are days which I want to hold on to forever but *which* seem to slip out of my grasp. (Relative pronoun repeated)

CONFUSED   He portrays the true-to-life detective and how he carries out his duties.

REVISED   He portrays the true-to-life detective and *shows* how he carries out his duties. (Verb function repeated)

25d *Do not belabor parallelism by using needless signs of it.* The italicized words in the following sentence add only stiffness and heaviness:

CLUMSY AND EXCESSIVE   She kept herself busy by baking a pie, *by* reading a magazine, and *by* writing a letter. (Omit the italicized words.)

Repeating the signal word (*by* in the preceding sentence) makes for greater formality. If you think your material needs the weight of full parallelism, repeat the signal. Remember, however, that little of your writing is highly formal and that repeating the signal needlessly may be out of keeping with an easy, informal style.

25e *Avoid faulty parallelism*

(1) Do not join with *and* or *but* an independent clause and an adjective clause beginning with *who* or *which*.

AWKWARD   I went to the dance with a girl from Memphis and who has a Southern accent.

REVISED   I went to the dance with a girl who is from Memphis and who has a Southern accent.

AWKWARD He brought his guitar to the party but which he was given no chance to play.

REVISED He brought his guitar to the party but was given no chance to play it.

(2) Avoid false, ambiguous, or illogical parallelism.

FALSE PARALLELISM The monkeys keep patrons laughing, riding bicycles, and balancing on huge balls. (*Laughing, riding,* and *balancing* appear to be parallel but are not.)

REVISED The patrons are kept laughing as they watch the monkeys riding bicycles and balancing on huge balls.

AMBIGUOUS PARALLELISM I hoped I would fall downstairs and break a leg or catch pneumonia. (Is *catch pneumonia* parallel with *fall downstairs* or with *break a leg?*)

REVISED I hoped I would catch pneumonia or fall downstairs and break a leg.

MISLEADING When not asleep, the opossum spends nearly all his time *prowling* along streams and *climbs* into treetops in search of food. (*Climbs* seems to be, but is not intended to be, parallel with *spends.*)

REVISED When not asleep, the opossum spends nearly all his time *prowling* along streams and *climbing* into treetops in search of food.

ILLOGICAL PARALLELISM If Frank Sinatra goes out in the evening, he is in the company of his manager and a disguise. (*Disguise* appears to be parallel with *manager.* There is an effect of unintentional anticlimax.)

REVISED . . . he is accompanied by his manager and is in disguise.

Such incongruous parallelism is occasionally used for comic effects, as when someone is described as "a dark-eyed, alarmingly intelligent-looking man of about fifty, who was wearing red suspenders and a weary air." (The *New Yorker*)

Exercise

Revise the following sentences by correcting any faulty or unclear parallelism.

1. I had hopes of becoming an engineer and help to build the new world.
2. Most people postpone things until the last possible minute and then having to cram like mad.
3. Her feet made no sound as she moved about the kitchen and the preparation of breakfast for the family.
4. Waddell was a man Russell had met in Lexington, and who had become his partner.
5. In the hole were placed articles such as old tin cans, clothing, broken furniture, and then filled with dirt.
6. At first glance he appeared to be about six feet tall, forty years of age, medium build, and about two hundred pounds.
7. I take a cold shower to wake me up and turn on the radio.
8. When he first smoked a cigar, he suddenly felt the room rising and falling and throbbing in his head.
9. The candidate attacked neither the program of his opponent nor offered one of his own.
10. My uncle might help send a worker's son to school or a farmer with his irrigation problems.
11. He thought the game was badly played and that it had been poorly managed.
12. The student should choose a topic that he is interested in and will help him in the future.
13. In many cases I would worry about a subject that I understood, but yet had given me trouble.
14. The team was more interested in defeating its oldest rival than to win the league championship.
15. Man's social thinking has not advanced as far as he has in his technology.
16. Hoover Dam serves the Southwest in many ways: the control of flood waters, it improves navigation, generates electrical power, and irrigation.
17. The ink splattered on the desk, spread over the floor, and there was even some on the wall.
18. Posing for snapshots, hot dogs, and soda pop helped to give the boys an exciting day.
19. It is common to speak of the Great Spirit, to whom the Indian prays and depends on for his existence.
20. The Jesuits attempted to teach the Hurons the care of domestic animals imported from Europe and to cultivate new fruits and vegetables.

26 Repetition

The effect of repeating words, structures, or ideas may be good or bad. Repetition that is stumbled into is nearly always clumsy and distracting. Deliberate repetition can be effective if it is used carefully and sparingly.

26a *Avoid careless repetition of words or ideas.*

(1) **Avoid awkward repetition of words,** sometimes in a slightly varied form. Reading over what you have written will help you catch such unfortunate sentences as these:

> I felt like a lost sheep that had lost its way.
> The result of questioning various groups about rush week resulted in a desire to investigate further.
> I can still remember that I was waiting for a bus on a busy corner in the west end of town. As I waited for the bus to come, I began to stare at the little newsstand on the corner.

(2) **Avoid aimless and unnecessary repetition of an idea.** These sentences, for example, require careful re-reading.

> Most of the boys were nearly all college students.
> People are now beginning to see and recognize the full value of nursery schools.
> What do you know about the recent educational program that has been set up in the last two or three years?

(3) **Avoid careless repetition of sounds.** Notice how distracting the sounds are in the following sentence:

> The lead pipes used by the thugs led to bloodshed.

26b *Use deliberate repetition to contribute to effectiveness.*

Repetition is especially useful to gain emphasis (**27d**), to aid in transition (**23c**), and to make parallelism clear (**25c**).

Exercise

Remove the ineffective repetition of words, sounds, or ideas in the following sentences.

1. I soon learned that when my uncle had gone to boarding school he had been unjustly mistreated.
2. Little cat feet are the feet on which the fog in Sandburg's poem came walking.
3. There is no other alternative to the course you have proposed.
4. In reality it was really Gina who did all the work.
5. Tom certainly has a tendency to overexaggerate.
6. I was transferred from that school to another school.
7. This course is to a large extent composed mainly of laboratory work.
8. Emotional feelings have no place in a scientific report.
9. Shylock was provoked into cruelty by undeserved provocations.
10. The subject I was made to pick made me sick.

27 Emphasis

Emphasis is the means by which you give desired force to your writing. It is the way you call attention to the relative importance of your various ideas—some of them of much significance, others rather incidental. Although emphasis is essential in the larger aspects of your writing—in putting together a whole composition or a paragraph—the use of emphasis in individual sentences is particularly important, for it can often contribute greatly to the effective expression of your thoughts. The following sections are intended especially to draw attention to some useful ways of gaining emphasis.

Note: Many common sentences are not subject to emphasis within themselves. They can be stated in only one natural way, and the sections below do not apply to them. Here are a few examples:

John has the measles.
Her desk is cluttered.
The sweater used to be bright green.

27a *Consider the order of words as a means of achieving emphasis.*

(1) **Use position for emphasis.** Put words in places that suit their relative importance and that contribute to the effectiveness of the whole sentence. Do not let ideas come straggling in as if by chance.

> UNEMPHATIC He will not have the endurance needed for the long training required to be a dentist, *I think.* (*I think,* the most incidental part of the sentence, has been put in an emphatic spot. The effect is a kind of anticlimax.)
>
> REVISED He will not, I think, have the endurance needed for the long training required to be a dentist.

If you experiment with sentences, you will find that you can shift emphasis by arranging parts in different orders. The sentence end is usually the place of strongest emphasis, and the beginning the place of second strongest emphasis. When it is possible, therefore, you will wish to put less important elements somewhere in the middle. (The placing of *therefore* in the preceding sentence shows what we mean.) In the following sentences, notice how you can use a relatively incidental expression like *it begins to appear* to throw emphasis to one part of a sentence or another—or by carelessness to lose emphasis.

> The traditional tools of diplomacy have been made almost unmanageable by having to operate in a condition that is neither war nor peace, or so *it begins to appear.* (The expression trails along unemphatically.)
>
> *It begins to appear* that the traditional tools of diplomacy have been made almost unmanageable by having to operate in a condition that is neither war nor peace. (A satisfactory sentence, with some attention called to the expression by its being at the beginning.)

The traditional tools of diplomacy, *it begins to appear*, have been made almost unmanageable by having to operate in a condition that is neither war nor peace. (This throws emphasis on the opening words.)

You could also place *it begins to appear* after *unmanageable* or after *that*. Each arrangement would vary the emphasis.

Note on inverting the normal sentence order: Occasionally words that have a relatively fixed position can be transposed for emphatic effect. This device should not be overused. (See also **28d**.)

> NORMAL SENTENCE ORDER He reached *sleepily* for the book.
> INVERTED ORDER *Sleepily* he reached for the book. (Attention is called to *sleepily* by the inverted order.)

Exercise 1

Rearrange groups of words in the following sentences to give greater emphasis. Do not change any words.

1. George, a solidly built man of six feet, looked clean and neat, as usual.
2. I had missed the train by this time to add to all my troubles.
3. Love is not rational but it may make the right decisions, luckily for the human race.
4. The boy fell with a painful thump on the pavement when he was learning to skate.
5. Each state in the United States is allowed to control its own affairs to a large extent.

(2) **Ordinarily arrange a series of items in climactic order**—that is, in an order that goes from the least important to the most important (or in an order that goes from the general to the specific).

> UNEMPHATIC Most of these motels were filthy, noisy, and had ugly furniture.
> REVISED Most of these motels had ugly furniture and were noisy and filthy.

The opposite of climactic order results in anticlimax. Anticlimax is often used deliberately by humorous writers, as in the following lines from Pope, which gain their satirical point by sounding as if to the young lady the second item in each pair is more important (whereas we know, of course, that it should be infinitely less so).

> [The fates, Pope says, do not let us know whether the young lady shall]
> . . . stain her honor or her new brocade;
> Forget her prayers, or miss a masquerade;
> Or lose her heart, or necklace, at a ball.

Exercise 2

Use climactic order in arranging the items in the following sentences. Since various arrangements are often defensible, be prepared to justify the order you choose.

1. The thief stole Edgar's French horn, his new suit, and the cake his mother had sent him.
2. Tom is cruel, lazy, and careless.
3. She bit her teacher, her little sister, and her fingernails.
4. The Indians came to Fort Laramie looking bloodthirsty, ragged, and hungry.
5. The dean threatened me with failure in the course, with expulsion, and with the loss of a parking space for my car.

(3) **Use periodic sentences for occasional emphasis.** The **periodic** sentence is one in which the main thought is held suspended until the end or near the end, when it is suddenly released. The **loose** sentence is one in which the main thought is completed well before the end. Contrast the following sentences, with the completion of the main thought italicized:

> PERIODIC   When last year her mother was dying of cancer and her father seemed on the verge of a breakdown, *Jane showed her real inner strength.*
>
> LOOSE   *Jane showed her real inner strength* last year when her mother was dying of cancer and her father seemed on the verge of a breakdown.
>
> PERIODIC   In his capacity to deceive himself, to seek his own advancement ruthlessly while talking about

service, and to injure others in the name of morality, *Jones was,* of all the men I have known, *easily the worst.*

LOOSE *Jones was easily the worst* of all the men I have known in his capacity to deceive himself, to seek his own advancement ruthlessly while talking about service, and to injure others in the name of morality.

PERIODIC Although he wanted the job more than anything else in the world, *he knew he had little chance of getting it.*

ALSO PERIODIC *He knew that,* although he wanted the job more than anything else in the world, *he had little chance of getting it.*

LOOSE *He knew he had little chance of getting the job,* although he wanted it more than anything else in the world.

We do not ordinarily talk or write in periodic sentences, since we usually want to express our main thought and then, if necessary, add to it. The loose sentence is more natural and informal. The periodic sentence, however, can impart emphasis by its retention of the main thought until the end. Notice how effective periodicity is in this sentence:

If Thoreau had merely left us an account of a man's life in the woods, or if he had simply retreated to the woods and there recorded his complaints about society, or even if he had contrived to include both records in one essay, *Walden* would probably not have lived a hundred years.—E. B. WHITE

Exercise 3

Make the following sentences periodic.

1. His first customer finally bought a dress after he had shown her almost everything he had in stock.
2. I spent every summer on Aunt Martha's farm, though I do not know why my parents sent me.
3. I had a hard time getting up in the morning until the day my cousin took me fishing.
4. He intends to study history if he goes to summer school.

5. She said she didn't care how she looked when the time came to get dressed for the prom.
6. The Battle of Fallen Timbers practically ended the long war on the frontier because the Indians lost hope and were ready for peace.
7. There is in Mexico a feeling of confidence in the nation's future in spite of its backwardness and poverty, as anyone who has been there knows.
8. Artists have a responsibility to society, whether they recognize it or not.
9. I still did not know why the book should have been written, even though I had forced myself to read through it at my friend's urging.
10. The Soviet Union has no farmlands comparable to those of Illinois and Iowa in all its expanse of well over eight million square miles extending from the deep Arctic to the borders of India.

27b Use suitable changes in sentence length to give emphasis to ideas.

A short sentence after a group of longer statements will sometimes startle a reader into close attention and will dramatize an idea.

> So President John Adams saw one newspaper editor after another thrown into jail, or subjected to heavy fines, for criticizing the administration; and the country came to believe that he was, if not actually a tyrant yet, in the way of becoming one. That finished him.—GERALD W. JOHNSON

27c Use the voice that is most emphatic and appropriate.

In general, the active voice is preferable because it is more direct and precise. The following sentences show the proper uses of each voice:

ACTIVE The girl gave no reason for her refusal to answer. (The passive would be clumsy and unemphatic: No reason for her refusal to answer was given by the girl.)

ACTIVE My father used to write speeches. (The passive would be weak: Speeches used to be written by my father.)

PASSIVE   Where is the man who was bitten by the dog? (The interest is on the man; the dog enters the sentence only to explain something about the man.)

PASSIVE   John Adams was elected President in 1796. (The passive is much better here; the emphasis is on the fact of the election, not on those who elected him.)

The following sentences show the kind of weak, clumsy passives that sometimes creep into beginners' writing:

The use of the slide rule was explained by the instructor at that meeting.

Long walks were taken in the woods that fall.

A serious breakdown was suffered because the doctor's orders were not followed.

Notice how much improved these sentences would be if the doer of the action were made the subject of the sentence.

On avoiding awkward shifts between active and passive, see **21d**.

Exercise 4

Change any weak passives to the active voice. If the passive is better or if the sentence contains no passive, mark the sentence C and be prepared to defend your answer.

1. We obtained good seats where no part of the game was missed.
2. Through an extravagant wife and his own gambling, his whole fortune was lost.
3. Much more effort will have to be made by John if he is to learn calculus.
4. The right of the people to bear arms shall not be infringed.
5. My going home has been looked forward to for weeks.
6. An old Swedish warship was recently lifted from the ocean floor, where it had lain for three hundred years.
7. I learned quickly that the blender had not been made to crack ice.
8. Friends were chosen for what could be got out of them by me.
9. Now that the spring has come, I want to go fishing.
10. He was greatly offended by my thoughtless words.

27d   *Repeat words, structures, or ideas for occasional emphasis.*

In the following passage all three—words, structures, and ideas—are repeated. (Only unusual emphasis, of course, justifies so much repetition.)

> Government comes from below, not above; government comes from men, not from kings or lords or military masters; government looks to the source of all power in the consent of men.
> —HENRY STEELE COMMAGER

27e   *Do not neglect mechanical devices for emphasis.*

Mechanical devices, such as commas, dashes, and italics, can sometimes give emphasis. Such devices should not be used frequently, lest by giving emphasis too often you end by giving no emphasis at all.

> COMMAS AND DASH FOR DRAMATIC EMPHASIS   The landscape, for instance, of South Dakota is in some ways the finest I have ever seen in the world—the most amazing, and the most strange, and the most beautiful.—PEARL BUCK
>
> ITALICS FOR EMPHASIS   Athletics—that is, *winning* athletics—now become a legitimate university operation.
> —HAROLD W. STOKE

> "Pray don't waste time mourning over *me*."—E. M. FORSTER

Warning: Do not ordinarily use exclamation marks for emphasis, as in the following sentence:

> I hope you can come to our picnic next Sunday!

Save exclamation marks for actual exclamations:

> What a scene!
> Help!

27f   *Consider other means of emphasis.*

There are numerous practices in writing that contribute to emphasis and that are discussed in other parts of this book. See, for example, passages on parallelism (**25c**) and on subordination (**24**).

28 Variety

Vary the form and the length of your sentences. The kind of sentences you compose will vary, of course, with what you are writing about and the tone you are giving it, but you can keep the interest of your reader more easily if you become aware of some of the resources available for giving variety. Experiment with sentences. Try writing them in more ways than one. Many phrases and dependent clauses, for instance, can be placed in various parts of a sentence.

Much variety will come naturally if you try to make your writing clear and emphatic. Indeed, variety in general depends on the thinking behind the writing. Awareness of monotony in verbal expression functions partly as a guard against monotony of thinking, and one should not look on rhetorical devices as a bundle of tricks to give an attractive facade to mediocre thinking. Become aware of rhetorical resources so that you will have the technical skill needed to reflect accurately the variety in your thinking.

28a *Vary the openings of sentences.*

Although a sentence normally begins with the subject, avoid the monotony that comes from a series of sentences with the subjects first. Try revising your writing to put an occasional phrase or clause at the beginning.

> ORIGINAL SENTENCE WITH SUBJECT FIRST A farm could be extremely isolated seventy-five years ago.
> REVISION Seventy-five years ago a farm could be extremely isolated.
> OR One who lived on a farm seventy-five years ago was isolated in a way completely unknown today.

Exercise 1

Rearrange the words in the sentences below to vary the beginnings.

445

1. Robert Louis Stevenson lived in California at one time.
2. Phoenix boasted that it led the nation last year with 3,697 hours of sunshine.
3. There was evidence last spring of considerable anxiety in the sheriff's office.
4. Science fiction is not for every reader, in my opinion.
5. Clarke has had, in the first place, an unusually thorough scientific training.

28b Vary the kinds of sentences.

Use both loose and periodic sentences. Use occasional questions, as the following paragraph does:

> Today resources exist in such abundance that a world-wide extension of the principle of welfare is physically possible. All that is lacking is the political decision to do so. Is it possible that a society which boasts of its humanity and its Christian inspiration should ignore the challenge? Is it conceivable that such a society, having done so, should deserve to survive?
>
> —BARBARA WARD

Use simple, compound, complex, and compound-complex sentences when they are appropriate for your material. In the following paragraph note that most of the sentences are simple, but the fourth and sixth are complex, and the next to the last is compound. (The fourth sentence is also periodic.)

> Protracted storms or the migration of game would produce shortages. And hunting was a daily job. The boys ranged through the woods, hillsides, and plains, usually on snowshoes. If the snow was too soft or deep for horses, they had to carry their take on their backs. There were problems of keeping the surplus from wolves. If the meat could be hung in trees it was safe from them but not from animals that could climb. Russell tells of burying some under three feet of snow and burning gunpowder on top to add another deterrent to the man-scent, but it did not work. No device worked for very long.
>
> —BERNARD DE VOTO

28c Vary the length of sentences.

Note the variety in this paragraph:

> Dusk is here now. So I switch on the lamp beside my desk. The powerhouse burns its hoarded tons of coal a week, and gives us

this instant and most marvelous current. But that light is not new. It was hurled out of the sun two hundred million years ago, and was captured by the leaves of the Carboniferous tree-fern forests, fell with the falling plant, was buried, fossilized, dug up and resurrected. It is the same light. And, in my little fig tree as in the ancient ferns, it is the same unchanging green stuff from age to age, passed without perceptible improvement from evolving plant to plant. What it is and does, so complex upon examination, lies about us tranquil and simple, with the simplicity of a miracle.—DONALD CULROSS PEATTIE

Warning: Do not gain the mere mechanical appearance of length by a crude tying together of several short sentences, as the student did who wrote this:

It is about six o'clock when we finish supper and I get ready to go to the early show at the movies because I like to get out early so I can go dancing with the crowd.

28d *Vary word order.*

Invert normal order for occasional variety. (See also 27a.)

Long was the way home.
Never had I tasted such strawberries.

This device must be used sparingly in prose. Poetry often makes striking use of it.

Me only cruel immortality
Consumes. . . .—TENNYSON

Exercise 2

Using a theme that you have written recently, make an analysis showing the following:

1. The number of sentences
2. The number of simple sentences
3. The number of compound sentences
4. The number of complex sentences
5. The number of compound-complex sentences
6. The average number of words in each sentence
7. The number of words in the shortest and longest sentences

What conclusions about your writing do you draw from this analysis? Write a brief comment.

PUNCTUATION AND MECHANICS

29 Practices and Conventions

Follow standard conventions of punctuation. If you are in doubt about what marks of punctuation to use, study the next paragraph and refer to the appropriate sections.

Punctuation is the use of certain marks to help make writing clear. *Mechanics* refers to devices like underlining.

Marks of punctuation may be grouped according to the purpose they serve. (1) They may *end* a sentence (period, question mark, exclamation mark). (2) They may *separate* parts of a sentence (chiefly comma, semicolon, dash, parentheses, colon). (3) They may *introduce* a part of a sentence or show *relationship* between parts (chiefly comma, dash, colon). For example:

(1) Period to *end* sentence: Let no dogs bark.
(2) Semicolon to *separate* parts: Let no dogs bark; we are important people.
(3) Colon to *introduce* a part: You know my purpose: to keep dogs from barking.

Do not get the impression that punctuation will make a good sentence out of a bad one. A sentence like "The plays of Shakespeare's day were listed in the Stationers' Register and by this act were supposed to prevent anyone from stealing them" is so confused that no changes in punctuation will improve it. But a basically sound sentence can often be made clear by intelligent punctuation. Consider "While painting my father fell off the ladder." This is perfectly satisfactory except that it needs a comma after *painting*.

Sometimes punctuation can change the meaning.

(a) He asked whether he would be penalized if he turned his theme in late.
The instructor answered, "No exceptions will be allowed."
(b) He asked whether he would be penalized if he turned his theme in late.
The instructor answered, "No. Exceptions will be allowed."

A few "rules" of punctuation come close to being inviolable conventions (such as the commas in an address that is part of a sentence: He lives at 1016 Hamilton Avenue, Hagerstown, Maryland), but most of them require that judgment also be used. (In many sentences where you ordinarily expect to use a comma you may instead use a semicolon or a dash. See, for example, **33a** or **33i**.) The sections that follow outline the chief practices and conventions in modern books and magazines and in the writing you will do in college and afterward. Good sense should tell you to observe these widely understood practices and to learn and use them before you go very far into the wilderness of exceptions and individual differences.

30 The Period [.]

30a *Place a period at the end of a declarative or imperative sentence or an indirect question.*

DECLARATIVE SENTENCES   The corn is four feet high. No. You're right.

IMPERATIVE SENTENCES   Turn in the questions. Please let me have your answer soon. (A strongly imperative sentence may take an exclamation mark: "Get out of here!")

INDIRECT QUESTION   She wanted to know what she should do.

30b *Place a period after most abbreviations.*

Mr., Mrs., Dr., A.B., Ph.D., F.O.B., A.M., a.m., A.D., e.g., Inc.

Some abbreviations may use periods or not.

TVA or T.V.A., FBI or F.B.I., rpm or r.p.m.

Do not use periods after such shortened forms as *lab* and *exam*, which are now full terms in their own right, not simply abbreviations of *laboratory* and *examination*. If such words are appropriate in your context, use them as words, not abbreviations.

INCORRECT   When I walked into the *lab.*, I was surprised.
REVISED (formal)   When I walked into the *laboratory*, I was surprised.
REVISED (informal)   When I walked into the *lab*, I was surprised.

30c *Use an ellipsis mark (three spaced periods) to show that a word or words have been omitted from a quoted passage.*

> With malice toward none; with charity for all . . . let us strive on to finish the work we are in. . . .
> —Lincoln's Second Inaugural Address

The four periods at the end of the quotation above show the ellipsis and a period at the end of the sentence.

An ellipsis is sometimes used, especially in narratives, to show hesitation or an unfinished thought.

> "Really! So many young men consider him . . . a bore."
> —J. F. POWERS

> "I heard him once," Mr. Kernan continued. "I forget the subject of his discourse now. Crofton and I were in the back of the . . . pit, you know. . . ."—JAMES JOYCE

Exercise 1

Put a period where it is needed.

1. The assignment is hard but interesting
2. Mr McCormick, my history instructor, had the nerve to ask me who became President when Zachary Taylor died
3. "That prof is my nemesis," she said
4. I have to pass this course to get my A B degree
5. When we came into the dorm we could hear his F M radio
6. Is your dentist named Dr Beard?
7. The train is due at 2:51 p m
8. Our lit instructor is Mrs Becker
9. This is the last year the prom will be held in the old auditorium
10. Miss Abrams is working for her Ph D

Exercise 2

Copy a sentence from a book used in a course you are now enrolled in. Then copy it over except for an ellipsis within the sentence. Do the same for another sentence, placing the ellipsis at the end.

31 The Question Mark [?]

31a *Place a question mark after a direct question, but not after an indirect question.*

DIRECT QUESTION   Where is the money you earned last summer?
DIRECT QUESTION   Why are you going?
INDIRECT QUESTION   I asked her why she was going.

Sometimes a question is phrased like a declarative statement. The question mark is the reader's only clue.

DECLARATIVE STATEMENT   You are to be there at eight o'clock.
QUESTION   You are to be there at eight o'clock?

31b *Use a question mark after an interrupting question that is set off with dashes or parentheses.*

For the third time this month—or is it the fourth?—the bus was late.
For the third time this month (or is it the fourth?) the bus was late.

31c *Punctuate a series of questions in one of a number of ways.*

Did you attend your biology class? or French? or history?
Did you attend your biology class? Or French? Or history?
Did you attend your biology class—or French—or history?

31d *Use a question mark to indicate doubt.*

Jane Seymour (1509?–1537) was the third wife of Henry VIII.
William Caxton, who was born in 1422(?), was the first English printer.

31e *Do not use a question mark to point out your wit.*

FEEBLE IRONY   He was certainly a charming (?) companion.

31f *Do not use a period or comma immediately following a question mark.*

NOT CONVENTIONAL   "Can we go?," she asked.
REVISED   "Can we go?" she asked.

31g *You may omit the question mark after a statement that is really a request even though politeness has caused it to be phrased as a question.*

Will you please see that the answers reach us by August 1?
OR   Will you please see that the answers reach us by August 1.

On the use of question marks with quotation marks, see
39k(3).

Exercise 1

Put a question mark or period where it is needed.

1. Have you had a test in that course
2. What does Jack know about the Wilmot Proviso
3. The date of the Missouri Compromise—was it 1820 or 1821—
   was one of the things the professor wanted to know
4. He also asked us when Kansas was admitted to the Union
5. That's what he calls being friendly before a test
6. Was Arkansas admitted as a state in 1820
7. I wonder whether it was admitted before Missouri
8. This is the second (or is it the third) test we have had
9. Is there any chance of putting off the test until next week
10. The professor wants to know why we are taking this course

Exercise 2

Write four original sentences:

1. A sentence containing a direct question
2. The same sentence rephrased as an indirect question
3. A sentence using a question mark to indicate doubt
4. A sentence containing an interrupting question within dashes

32 The Exclamation Mark [!]

32a *Place an exclamation mark after expressions that are exclamatory* (that, in other words, cry out with surprise or other strong feeling) *and after strong commands and other emphatic statements.*

> What a surprise!
> Poor man!
> What a fine day it is!
> Keep away from here! (A strong command)

32b *You may use an exclamation mark within a sentence after interjections.*

Often the choice of an exclamation mark or a comma will depend on the intensity of the feeling you wish to express.

> "Oh," she said, "I don't know about that."
> "Oh!" she cried, burying her face in her hands.

32c *Do not overuse the exclamation mark.*

The emotion in the following sentences is apparent without the sign of exclamation.

> POOR The Grand Canyon was the most beautiful sight I had seen!
> POOR I was certainly pleased to get your letter! Your description of Aunt Ida was lifelike! I could almost see her!

All these sentences would be better if they were ended by periods. The exclamation marks give an air of artificial and unconvincing excitement.

32d *Do not use a period or a comma immediately following an exclamation mark.*

> NOT CONVENTIONAL The cry I could not forget was "Help!."
> REVISED The cry I could not forget was "Help!"

On the use of exclamation marks with quotation marks, see **39k(3)**.

Exercise

Put an exclamation mark where it is needed. Remove any punctuation marks improperly used. Mark correct sentences C.

1. "Save me!," she cried.
2. She was not in any danger, but she was very frightened!
3. The lifeguard swam out crying "Hold on!."
4. He seemed to take his time.
5. How shocking.

33 The Comma [,]

The comma is used to separate parts of a sentence or to set a word or construction off from the rest of the sentence. If you have trouble with commas, study this section and compare the uses of the comma with the uses of related marks, especially the semicolon, colon, and dash.

33a *Ordinarily place a comma before a coordinating conjunction* (and, but, for, nor, or, so, yet) *that joins two independent clauses.*

> John was ready to abandon the project, for his brother was beginning to lose interest.
>
> Snow had blown in under the sides of the car, so the momentum he had hoped to achieve was sluggish in coming.—JOHN UPDIKE
>
> There were lots of other places to go where we boys could have enjoyed ourselves better, but we weren't consulted of course, and we'd have been surprised if we had been.—CLARENCE DAY

Be particularly careful to use the comma when the conjunction is *for*.

> CONFUSING   They called me home for supper was ready.
>
> CLEAR   They called me home, for supper was ready.
>
> CLEAR   They called me home for supper. (Here *for* is a preposition.)

454

Exceptions to the use of the comma between independent clauses joined by a coordinating conjunction are common. If the clauses are short, the comma is often omitted, especially before *and*.

> Miss Honey's nostrils pinched together and she rocked slightly, with her arms folded.—KATHERINE ANNE PORTER

If the clauses are long and themselves contain punctuation, a semicolon may be used between them.

> There may be geniuses among the gorillas; but since gorillas have no conceptual language, the thoughts and achievements of these geniuses cannot be recorded and so are lost to simian posterity.
> —ALDOUS HUXLEY

A semicolon is used occasionally even when the clauses do not contain punctuation. The effect, of course, is a considerably stronger separation than a comma gives.

> Neither my parents nor my schoolmasters ever asked themselves such questions; and had I not had the rare luck to make money as a born playwright I might now be ending as a tramp.
> —G. B. SHAW

Exercise 1

Insert a comma before each coordinating conjunction that joins two independent clauses. Do not insert other punctuation.

1. I have heard your twenty-odd reasons but I am still not convinced.
2. Darkness had been deepening for the last half hour and we were beginning to be alarmed.
3. They had worked for several hours yet they were no nearer to solving the problem.
4. You had better listen now for my answer is this.
5. You can accept this answer for what it is worth or you can find a better answer of your own.
6. Our merchants screamed and pleaded and finally the legislature passed the bill.
7. The book is hard but interesting.
8. We ate ice cream and cake and afterwards the adults joined us for games.

9. I have no idea what his reasons are for I could not understand what he was talking about.

10. This is the last time I will work with him but I am not going to tell him so.

33b *Place a comma after introductory phrases and clauses unless they are short and easily understood without the comma.*

PHRASES   Living out the months of our required residence and waiting for the long growing days to make us a crop, we saw few people.—WALLACE STEGNER

SHORT PHRASE   In this cycle a huge and exquisite balance is preserved.—PAUL HORGAN

CLAUSE NEEDING COMMA   When we reached Fargo late that night in the dead of winter, we wondered what had possessed us to leave Houston.

CLAUSE NOT NEEDING COMMA   When we reached Fargo we were ready to turn in.

Note: Often no comma is used after a rather long introductory clause if the subjects of both introductory and main clauses are the same and there is no likelihood of misreading.

After I graduated from college and ended my first year of law I took a year and a half off and taught English and history in a preparatory school.—ROBERT MAYNARD HUTCHINS

Note: Even when the introductory element is very short, a comma may be needed to prevent confusion or secure emphasis. (See **33o.**)

At first, thought was clouded by superstition.

For our fathers, to waver meant delay; for us, it may mean disaster.

But no comma is needed if the introductory phrase is followed by the verb and then the subject:

In the front seat was a huge Saint Bernard.

Exercise 2

In the following sentences insert commas where they are needed after the introductory element. Be prepared to give reasons for using or not using a comma.

456

1. In this area there is only one FM radio station.
2. Beginning at seven in the morning and continuing until eleven at night it gives news and plays records.
3. If the records are of operas Jake finds an excuse to listen.
4. Although I too have grown to like operas as I know them better I still prefer other music.
5. In brief operas are not my favorite music.
6. On either side of the white marble stairs was a statue.
7. Until we accept the decisions of our courts we cannot think of ourselves as law-abiding people.
8. In the uncivilized parts of the world many superstitions are held that seem to us fantastic.
9. While eating the duck waddled about the yard.
10. The examination over the class felt relieved.

33c *Use a comma to separate words, phrases, or short clauses in a series.*

WORDS IN A SERIES   The team was quick, heavy, and spirited.
PHRASES IN A SERIES   Lincoln has told us that government should be of the people, by the people, and for the people.
CLAUSES IN A SERIES   In the toy department trains hummed, babies cried, and Santa laughed.

Whether a comma should be placed before *and* in a series is a matter of divided usage. Although some newspapers do not use the comma in constructions like "pencils, paper and rulers," general usage seems to prefer "pencils, paper, and rulers" because it allows for greater exactness. Sometimes a comma before *and* prevents momentary delay in understanding sentences like "The restaurant served these soups: French onion, chicken broth with noodles and vegetable." A comma after *noodles* would make the sentence clear immediately.

No commas, of course, are required if the items in a series are joined by conjunctions.

The team was quick and heavy and spirited.
Neither snow nor sleet nor prayer can keep examinations from coming at the appointed times.

Exercise 3

In the sentences below insert commas where they are needed in each series.

1. Until a few years ago, immigrants to the United States landed at Ellis Island were examined there and then were sent to the mainland.
2. Sometimes, long ago, they were cheated deceived or even robbed.
3. Immigrants came in successive huge waves from Great Britain from Ireland and from southern and eastern Europe.
4. Now immigration has been slowed down made more difficult and from some countries almost stopped.
5. Since World War II much immigration has been of so-called "displaced persons" from such lands as Hungary the Ukraine and the Baltic countries.
6. Most of these immigrants have been very ambitious and intelligent and hard-working.
7. Many came here poor lonely and friendless but most have had little trouble becoming adjusted.
8. In Hungary a language is spoken that is related to the languages of Finland Lapland and Estonia.
9. Lapland is a country where extreme cold lasts for nine or ten months of the year where there is hardly any vegetation and where the ways to make a living are limited.
10. Some of the Lapps live along rivers keep reindeer and even do a little farming.

33d *Use commas to separate coordinate adjectives modifying the same noun and not connected by a conjunction.*

Adjectives in a series are coordinate when they have the same relation to the noun. In the sentence "A tall, thin, gawky boy walked in," the adjectives *tall, thin,* and *gawky* all modify the noun *boy.* They are coordinate and should be separated by commas.

A comma is not placed between adjectives that are not coordinate: "He wore a brown leather jacket." Here *leather* modifies *jacket,* but *brown* modifies the unit *leather jacket.*

458

Adjectives may be recognized as coordinate when we can shift their order without altering the sense. So we can say "a gawky, tall, thin boy" or "a thin, gawky, tall boy," but we cannot say "a leather, brown jacket" without feeling that we have changed the meaning. Another test is to see whether *and* can be placed between the adjectives without damaging the meaning (as in "a tall and thin and gawky boy"). This test is not infallible, but it often helps.

Sometimes subtle differences can be shown, as in the following pairs of sentences:

COORDINATE   He was an old, tired man.
NOT COORDINATE   He was a tired old man.

COORDINATE   I have a new, shiny penny.
NOT COORDINATE   I have a shiny new penny.

Sometimes the differences are quite obvious.

He bought the cheapest, flimsiest shirt in the store.
He bought the cheapest white shirt in the store.

Coordinate and noncoordinate adjectives can be in the same series.

He bought the cheapest, flimsiest white shirt in the store.

Note: Some modern writers occasionally omit commas between coordinate adjectives.

For Carter Harrison belonged to a warm grandiloquent personal city. . . .—ERNEST POOLE
. . . the pained confused limited mind. . . .
—KATHERINE ANNE PORTER

Such uninterrupted leveling of the adjectives can be effective. You should know, however, that the practice is not common, especially in expository prose, and is difficult to use well. You will do better to learn and use the standard practice.

Exercise 4

Underline the coordinate adjectives in the following sentences and insert commas where they are needed. Some sentences are correct as they stand.

1. It was a beautiful October morning.
2. He lived in a rambling old Elm Street home.
3. Jim Kendall was a crude practical joker.
4. The surly inconsiderate reply surprised him.
5. The deep menacing rumble of thunder was the next sound we heard.
6. The mayor made an open sneering attack on the committee.
7. The committee made a clearly contemptuous answer.
8. Herbert came in wearing an old tweed suit.
9. He had a weak old mother.
10. He had a weak helpless mother.

33e *Use commas to set off nonrestrictive dependent clauses and phrases but not to set off restrictive ones.*

A *restrictive modifier* (also called *essential* or *defining*) identifies the term it modifies. It cannot be removed from the sentence without a significant change in the meaning of the modified word or words. A restrictive modifier and the term it identifies form, for the time being, an inseparable unit. The restrictive modifier therefore cannot be set off by commas. Following are three typical restrictive modifiers:

> An automobile *that won't run* is not worth buying. (The adjective clause is essential to identify the kind of automobile meant.)
> An automobile *in poor condition* is not worth buying. (A prepositional phrase that also identifies the kind of automobile.)
> An automobile is not worth buying *if it won't run*. (An adverbial clause that is essential to the meaning of the sentence.)

A *nonrestrictive modifier* is not necessary for the clear identification of a noun or for the clear understanding of a main clause. It gives information which, though it enriches the sentence, is not essential to our identifying the term that is modified. It does not form a tightly knit unit with the modified term and can be removed from the sentence without significantly changing the meaning of the modified word or words. It is set off by commas. Contrast these sentences with the examples of restrictive modifiers:

> His automobile, *which won't run,* is for sale. (The identification is made by *his,* which tells us what automobile is meant.)

There is a tendency for adverb clauses at the beginning of a sentence to be treated as nonrestrictive. (See **33b**.) The last three sentences above would probably use commas if the dependent clauses came first. For example:

> Because he was afraid, he ran.
> If the economist hopes to emerge from the book with a clear system of economic thought, he will continue to have rough going.

(3) **Phrases may be nonrestrictive or restrictive.** They require commas or not just as clauses do.

> NONRESTRICTIVE   This play, *written in 1932*, reflects the problems of the great depression.
> RESTRICTIVE   A play *written in 1932* will probably reflect the problems of the great depression.

> NONRESTRICTIVE   Janet Myers, *in the yellow dress*, is on her way to the party.
> RESTRICTIVE   The girl *in the yellow dress* is on her way to the party.

Notice the difference in meaning that comes from using or not using commas around the prepositional phrase in this sentence:

> NONRESTRICTIVE   The last essay, by Thoreau, was the best.
> RESTRICTIVE   The last essay by Thoreau was the best.

Exercise 5

Insert commas where they are needed in the sentences below.

1. Jane Austen whose *Pride and Prejudice* was published in 1813 writes as if she had not heard of the war in France.
2. The Jane Austin you mention spells her name differently.
3. Farmers who as a group are among the first to feel the pinch of deflation should be interested in this proposal.
4. Farmers who grow export crops like wheat and cotton are more vulnerable than dairy farmers who produce only for the domestic market.
5. The electoral college which reflects state majorities but not necessarily a national majority chooses our President.

6. My dog Frisco which was hunting with the other hounds was the first to come on the scent.
7. She stood first among the girls earning their way through college.
8. Williams is a man who has devoted a good brain to trivial uses.
9. A number of books and articles dealing with the rebellion have been written.
10. He forced his way into the crowd although he certainly hadn't been invited.
11. The designer who is able to get closest to the real field conditions is the best civil engineer.
12. I encountered very little trouble when I took the test.
13. Speech that is natural is pleasanter than the kind that is elaborately prepared.
14. A man who has a poor memory for detail is of little value in our business.
15. John Masterson with his poor memory for detail will be of little value to us.
16. The cat with the short tail is named Felix.
17. He won't come to work until he has to.
18. His last final examination in History 151 was the hardest one.
19. The course I took in summer school kept me busy every minute.
20. My sister in spite of her hard work forgot many of her lines.

33f *Use commas to set off nonrestrictive appositives.*

Put commas around nonrestrictive appositives for the same reason you set off other nonrestrictive elements. Appositives are usually nonrestrictive.

> His oldest son, *John,* is home from college.
> The party, *a very happy affair,* was held in January.
> They made the best ice cream in town, *the best he had ever tasted.*
> The letter was addressed to James Craig, *M.D.,* Greencastle, Indiana. (When such abbreviated titles follow a name, they are treated as appositives.)

Some appositives are restrictive

> His son *John* is home from college. (This son, not another one)
> I mean James Craig the *dentist.*

When an appositive is part of a name, it is restrictive and takes no commas.

> Charles the Second, Peter the Great, Richard the Lion-Hearted.

If you wish to make a somewhat more definite separation of a nonrestrictive appositive, you may use dashes or parentheses.

> I forget the score of the game, the one we lost.
> I forget the score of the game—the one we lost.
> I forget the score of the game (the one we lost).

If the appositive contains punctuation, dashes are usually better than commas:

> The party—a bright, happy affair—was held in January.

Exercise 6

Insert punctuation where it is needed to set off appositives in the following sentences.

1. In Japan a poor country attendance at a college is a great privilege.
2. Boswell the biographer of Samuel Johnson was from Scotland.
3. You should see my farm the only property I have ever owned.
4. Washington the man was probably greater than Washington the general.
5. My favorite relative my Uncle Mark was a born storyteller.
6. My sister Mary is taller than my sister Pamela.
7. Cherry pie my favorite dessert is often poorly prepared.
8. The dog a cheerful little creature was interested only in food and playing.
9. We ate at the Warwick the best hotel in the city.
10. George the Third may profit by their example.

33g *Place commas around parenthetical words, phrases, and clauses that interrupt a sentence sufficiently to be set off.*

The extent of the interruption that you feel and wish to suggest must be your guide in deciding whether you will put commas before and after such expressions or not.

465

(1) One-word interrupters

Commas are frequently used to set off interrupting adverbs. The more formal ones, such as *consequently, however, furthermore, moreover, nevertheless,* and *therefore,* are likely to make heavier and sharper interruptions than lighter ones like *also* and *indeed,* but with either kind you will need to decide whether commas are desirable or not. Sometimes reading a sentence aloud will help you make the decision.

> The influence of environment on any one individual, *however,* is limited by his life-span.—RUTH BENEDICT
>
> *Nevertheless,* the Broadway audience at any performance of any hit is a very different public from the playgoers of twenty years ago.—MARYA MANNES
>
> He said that the point he was trying to make was that Cousin Mary's ways were not his ways, and that *consequently* there was no use whatever discussing them with him.—CLARENCE DAY

Slight differences in tone sometimes call for a comma in one sentence and not in another, depending on the degree of the interruption.

> *Now,* the proposition that the three angles of every triangle together make up two right angles is a proposition in Euclid. . . .—ROBERT H. THOULESS
>
> *Now* it is hard to see how anyone else can know better than I do what I am experiencing.—HAROLD LARRABEE

Caution: When words like *however* and *indeed* join main clauses, they are preceded by semicolons. See **34b.**

(2) Phrase interrupters

Phrase interrupters (such as *in fact, of course, no doubt, for example, in the first place*) are sometimes set off and sometimes not, depending on the degree of interruption.

> There were, *of course,* dissenting voices.—BERGEN EVANS
>
> *Of course* tall land animals have other difficulties.
> —J. B. S. HALDANE
>
> We knew *at last* where we were going.
>
> George is, *by all reports,* a great success.

(3) Clause interrupters

Clause interrupters are usually set off but sometimes not, depending again on how much of an interruption is felt.

> Wells has been a good prophet, *as prophets go,* and his crystal-gazing is not to be sniffed at.—E. B. WHITE
> Oliver Twitchell *when he received Professor Chartly's envelope* sat down with a strong favorable predisposition toward his task.—THEODORE MORRISON

After a coordinating conjunction (especially *and, but, or, for*), the first comma is often omitted before a following subordinate clause.

> In the speeches no violence was urged; *and when a drizzling rain set in,* the crowd began to melt away.
> —ERNEST POOLE

Caution: Except as indicated in (3) above, do not half set off interrupters by placing a comma only at the beginning or at the end; make up your mind whether to enclose the expression or not. Punctuation of the kind marked *confusing* is worse than none:

> CONFUSING We expect you, therefore to do your best.
> REVISED We expect you, therefore, to do your best.
>
> CONFUSING Why did my mother decide, at the last minute to get off the plane?
> REVISED Why did my mother decide at the last minute to get off the plane?
>
> CONFUSING The theme of Lardner's "Haircut" was it seems to me, the cruelty of small-town life.
> REVISED The theme of Lardner's "Haircut" was, it seems to me, the cruelty of small-town life.

33h *Use commas to set off absolute phrases.*

> Finally, *all his money having been spent,* he went on relief.
> *The law being clear on this matter,* there is no point in appealing the decision.

33i   *Use commas to set off contrasting expressions and questions.*

> He came to make peace, *not war.*
> Money, *not love,* was the reason for his proposal.
> The book on the table, *not the one on the shelf,* is what you need.
> You knew Uncle Fred, *didn't you?* (Such added expressions make the whole sentence a question.)

Contrasting expressions are sometimes set off by dashes.

> Money—not love—was the reason for his proposal.

33j   *Use commas to set off a word or group of words used in direct address.*

> I think, *Molly,* that you know less about the Treaty of Versailles than you should.
> Stand still, *boys,* and wait for the command.
> Here, *ladies and gentlemen,* is the real explanation.

33k   *Use a comma after introductory* yes *and* no *and after mild interjections* (those not strong enough to require an exclamation mark).

> Yes, he knows the answer.
> No, he won't tell you.
> Oh, I don't think so.
> Well, you had better look into the matter.

But

> Well! That is a strange way to behave.

33l   *Use commas with quotation marks as explained under Quotation Marks, 39k.*

33m   *Use a comma after the salutation and the complimentary close in an informal personal letter.*

> Dear Jane,
> Dear Aunt Eunice,
> Sincerely yours,
> Cordially,

468

33n *Use commas to set off parts of dates, addresses, and geographical names.*

(1) Dates

The party will be held on Friday, November 12.
She was born on April 6, 1962.
On June 22, 1941, Hitler invaded the Soviet Union.

When only the month and year appear, either of the following is now accepted:

The crisis came in April, 1861.
The crisis came in April 1861.

There is a growing tendency to write "4 February 1965," but the older form, "February 4, 1965," is still the one more often seen. Either may be used.

(2) Addresses and geographical names

He lives at 10 South Davenport Street, Minneapolis 12, Minnesota.
Youngstown, Ohio, is a great steel-producing center.

33o *Use commas wherever they are needed to prevent misreading.*

MISLEADING   After all the time had come for her to lead her own life.
REVISED   After all, the time had come for her to lead her own life.

MISLEADING   Before plastering Uncle Will cleaned the wall.
REVISED   Before plastering, Uncle Will cleaned the wall.

CLEAR   When it was time to clean up, Eric put the blocks away.
CLEAR   Just before, an anxious crowd had been yelling for him to win.
CLEAR   To her, nurses and doctors meant only painful examinations.

Exercise 7

Insert commas where they are needed in the following sentences. Be prepared to explain what you have done and to cite the section that applies.

1. She was born in Cheyenne Wyoming.
2. No matter who cooked the meals were always good.
3. I want to grow not stagnate.
4. Yes I am going to the party.
5. As you can see the counselors had many problems.
6. The will was dated January 6 1927.
7. Why here's Bob.
8. I hope to be a teacher who can stimulate thought not simply impart facts.
9. His homework being finished earlier than he expected he looked for his fishing tackle.
10. He had had to wait for Harriet was late in getting there.
11. And now my friends let me tell you the real story.
12. Dear Uncle Ray
    Do you think lending me $100 at 10 percent interest would appeal to you?
13. Well that is exactly what happened.
14. Even though it is raining workmen are still on the street.
15. You can write to him at 1218 West Martin Street Denver 10 Colorado.
16. Beverly where in the world have you been?
17. I know Julie well and like her am an only child.
18. This is my sweater isn't it?
19. Oh I know what he'll say.
20. As I recall the Harrisons and their guests were in the living room.

33p *Do not insert commas where they are useless or confusing.*

(1) Do not separate a subject and verb.

> INCORRECT Envying other people, was her greatest weakness.
>
> REVISED Envying other people was her greatest weakness.

(2) Do not separate a verb from its object or complement.

> INCORRECT I cannot decide, whether to take the job or not.
>
> REVISED I cannot decide whether to take the job or not.

INCORRECT   The real reason is, that he has no interest in clinical psychology.
REVISED   The real reason is that he has no interest in clinical psychology.

(3) Ordinarily, do not separate the parts of a short compound predicate.

POOR   Andy picked up the bat, and walked over to the plate.
REVISED   Andy picked up the bat and walked over to the plate.

But you will find that a comma is often used in somewhat longer sentences or where its use increases clarity.

A man may take to drink because he feels himself to be a failure, and then fail all the more completely because he drinks.—GEORGE ORWELL (The parts of the compound predicate begin with *may take* and *fail.*)
He liked to talk to the people in the blacksmith shop and the general store, and would sometimes stay an hour while they came and went.—EDMUND WILSON (He *liked . . .* and *would . . . stay*)

(4) Do not use a comma for mistaken emphasis or mistaken pauses.

INCORRECT   Perhaps, you know the best road to Seattle.
REVISED   Perhaps you know the best road to Seattle.

INCORRECT   I know the price is high—but, I am willing to pay it.
REVISED   I know the price is high—but I am willing to pay it.

(5) Do not break up a *so . . . that* clause by inserting a comma.

INCORRECT   Your argument is so illogical, that I hardly see how you yourself can believe it.
REVISED   Your argument is so illogical that I hardly see how you yourself can believe it.

(6) Do not use commas before the first or after the last item in a series.

471

INCORRECT   The Indians of Central America raise, potatoes, wheat, and tomatoes.
REVISED   The Indians of Central America raise potatoes,
wheat, and tomatoes.

(7) When an adjective comes directly before the substantive it modifies, do not place a comma between adjective and substantive.

INCORRECT   He moved in an intricate, graceful, dance.
REVISED   He moved in an intricate, graceful dance.

(8) Do not clutter your sentences with commas. Unless there is a reason for using a comma, omit it. Modern writers generally prefer the free flow of a sentence with few commas ("open" punctuation) to the frequent setting off of elements that are clear without punctuation ("close" punctuation).

OVERPUNCTUATED   Johnny was, of course, late again, as
we had expected. About six o'clock, he ran in and
threw his books, carelessly, on the floor.
BETTER   Johnny was of course late again, as we had expected. About six o'clock he ran in and threw his
books carelessly on the floor.

Exercise 8

Circle commas that should be omitted in the following sentences. Insert commas where they are needed.

1. I suddenly noticed, that I was no longer interested.
2. Portland, in my opinion deserves both praise and criticism.
3. Like most European countries, with a feudal economy, Spain was a monarchy.
4. The prices for this movie are so high, that I am surprised there is any audience at all.
5. She spoke with, what seemed to me a beautiful accent.
6. A man with his qualities, is what I term, an ideal citizen.
7. Any kind of freedom of expression, is dangerous to the regime.
8. In this society we must buy food, or a hunting license.
9. My brother turned on the light, and began to read.
10. But, there is more to the story than you have heard.

34 The Semicolon [;]

The semicolon indicates a sentence break greater than that shown by a comma and less than that made by a period. If you have trouble with the semicolon, be sure you know the difference between independent and dependent clauses. (See **2b.**)

34a *Use a semicolon between independent clauses that are not joined by a coordinating conjunction* (and, but, or, nor, for, so, yet).

> The housing shortage was acute; it had been severe, as a matter of fact, for a number of years.
> His books were beautiful to look at; the trouble was that he never read them. (Contrast this with the same sentence using *but* to join the clauses: His books were beautiful to look at, but the trouble was that he never read them.)

34b *Use a semicolon between two independent clauses when they are joined by a conjunctive adverb* (*or an expression equivalent to a conjunctive adverb*), *such as* however, then, hence, thus, also, otherwise, nevertheless, therefore, besides, indeed, in fact, for example, on the contrary.

> It is flexible, highly varied, and in touch with virtually the entire population; *furthermore,* it is characterized by a genuine spirit of service.—HAROLD W. STOKE
> The connection proved surprisingly durable; *in fact* it became Professor Hale's turn to be apprehensive.—THEODORE MORRISON

34c *Use a semicolon when the independent clauses joined by coordinating conjunctions are long and themselves contain punctuation.*

> He studied a little Latin, French, German, and Italian; and as you might guess, he came out of college knowing no foreign language well enough to make any use of it.

473

Nothing, therefore, can prove that Shakespeare's sonnets are, or are not, autobiographical except the discovery of outside evidence that they accord, or do not accord, with facts of his life; and no such evidence is forthcoming.—G. L. KITTREDGE

34d *Do not use the semicolon improperly or unnecessarily.*

(1) Do not use a semicolon before a series. (The normal mark is a colon.)

MISUSE These were the cities we visited; San Antonio, Phoenix, Santa Fe, and Albuquerque.

REVISED These were the cities we visited: San Antonio, Phoenix, Santa Fe, and Albuquerque.

(2) Do not use a semicolon between a phrase and an independent clause—where a comma or no punctuation at all would be normal.

MISUSE Thinking of nothing at all; I used a semicolon.
REVISED Thinking of nothing at all, I used a semicolon.

MISUSE He started down the street; going nowhere in particular.
REVISED He started down the street, going nowhere in particular.

MISUSE At sundown the ship resumed her voyage; with about fifty native fishermen on board as passengers.
REVISED At sundown the ship resumed her voyage with about fifty native fishermen on board as passengers.

(3) Do not use a semicolon between a dependent clause and an independent clause.

MISUSE As I listened to the rain blowing against my window; I felt glad to have all my errands done.
REVISED As I listened to the rain blowing against my window, I felt glad to have all my errands done.

(4) Do not use a semicolon after the salutation of a letter. (A comma or colon should be used.)

MISUSE Dear Bill; Dear Mr. Anderson;
REVISED Dear Bill, Dear Mr. Anderson:

(5) Do not use a semicolon before a conjunctive adverb in the middle of an independent clause. (See also 34b.)

MISUSE   There are; however, a few good comic books.
REVISED   There are, however, a few good comic books.

Exercise 1

Use semicolons where they are needed in the sentences below. Do not change a sentence if it is correct. Mark each correct sentence C.

1. I couldn't bring myself around to writing to distant Aunt Tillie, after all, what could you say to a relative?
2. Fortunately, blanking out before a test does not happen often, if it did I wouldn't be in college now.
3. All goes well as long as she gains her objective, when she is crossed, she is a ruthless spitfire.
4. The two of them, wet, tired, hungry, and badly frightened, searched for hours for a way out of the woods and as they told me later, they were often ready to give up.
5. I made a beginning at the work in April; I did not finish it until July.
6. We are more nearly self-contained than any other country, but we are dependent on other parts of the world for many imports.
7. No one knew anything about the accident for several hours it had occurred at a time when almost no cars were on this road.
8. The accident occurred late at night, and no one knew about it for several hours.
9. He placed the pack of cards face down on the table, after he had done this, he asked one of us to draw a card.
10. The walls of the classroom were bare and dull, they seemed indeed to be made to depress the spirits.

Exercise 2

Write six sentences, two to illustrate each of the uses of the semicolon described in **34a, b,** and **c.**

Exercise 3

Some of the following sentences illustrate improper uses of the semicolon; other sentences are correct. Be prepared to suggest appropriate punctuation when the semicolon is improper.

1. After I had walked along the path for an hour; I suddenly came upon the spring.
2. I especially remember four of Shakespeare's characters; Macbeth, Juliet, Hamlet, and Brutus.
3. The men who invented the parts for the wireless are not known, and they are; therefore, not given credit.
4. Everything seemed unreal; it was like a bad dream that would not go away.
5. I was finding friends; who had the same interests I had.
6. In my effort to throw the discus; I succeeded only in looking ridiculous.
7. Our car stopped beside the station; its engine idling as we waited for the train.
8. Paying not the slightest attention to traffic regulations; he drove the car down Pacific Street.
9. The book turned out to be very readable; after all, he felt he had known most of the characters.
10. Now the problems facing you are; where you will hold the party and how many guests you will invite.

35 The Colon [:]

Use a colon to introduce material that is to follow. The colon should be used in only certain rather well-defined situations; its effectiveness depends on its not being overused or used improperly. Often it is preceded by *as follows, the following will illustrate the point,* or a similar expression.

35a *Use a colon to introduce a statement presented formally, an example, a question, a quotation, and a series or list.*

FORMAL STATEMENT   I think the case may be better put this way: European institutions and practices wore themselves out against the abrasive frontier grindstone.

—WALTER PRESCOTT WEBB

EXAMPLE   Three teams were tied that year: Indiana, Michigan, and Ohio State.

QUESTION   And the question still remains the same as that propounded by the Greeks long ago: How, in a world certainly not at first acquaintance rational-appearing, is it possible to lead a rational life?—IRWIN EDMAN

QUOTATION   The subject of the poem is the endless, eternal, elusive change of things: "I change but I cannot die."

—ALFRED NORTH WHITEHEAD

SERIES OR LIST   Work was carried on in three fields: physiological, psychological, and historical.—RUTH BENEDICT

35b *Use a colon between two independent clauses when the second clause explains, restates, or illustrates the first.*

Not much else can be said: an item in the history of America had fulfilled itself.—BERNARD DE VOTO

There are other schools than poverty in which to learn the lesson: Thomas Jefferson learned it in a mansion.

It is only in this use that the colon approximates the semicolon. The semicolon indicates separation; the colon suggests that what is to follow is in some sense a fulfillment of what has gone before. Notice the effect if, in the examples above, you were to change the colons to semicolons.

On capitalizing the first word of the second clause, see 43b.

35c *Use the colon in certain situations where convention has established it.*

(1) **After the salutation of a business letter or a formal social letter**

Dear Sir: Dear Mrs. Jones: Dear Senator Johnson:

This usage contrasts with the practice in writing to people with whom we are on familiar terms.

> Dear Bob, Dear Aunt Mary,

(2) Between hour and minute written numerically

> The examination will begin at 9:30.

(3) Between chapter and verse in Biblical references

> Ecclesiastes 9:11 (Or a period may be used—9.11.)

(4) Between title and subtitle

> *The English Romantic Poets: A Review of Research*

35d *Do not misuse the colon.*

Especially, do not use a colon between a verb and complement, between a preposition and its object, or after *such as.*

> MISUSE My hardest subjects are: German, calculus, and English literature.
> REVISED My hardest subjects are German, calculus, and English literature.
> REVISED These are my hardest subjects: German, calculus, and English literature.

> MISUSE I have the greatest trouble with: German, calculus, and English literature.
> REVISED I have the greatest trouble with German, calculus, and English literature.

> MISUSE The new book includes stories by such writers as: Flannery O'Connor, Herbert Gold, and John Updike.
> REVISED The new book includes stories by such writers as Flannery O'Connor, Herbert Gold, and John Updike.

Exercise

Place a C before the sentences in which uses of the colon are acceptable. Be prepared to give your reasons.

1. Listen to others, but only for one purpose: to determine which of their thoughts will be useful to you.

2. Now study the following: the letters of Charles Lamb, the essays of Hazlitt, and the early poems of Wordsworth.
3. The contracts call for research in such widely separated places as: Spokane, Elmira, and Houston.
4. Franklin's work in France led to his greatest contribution to American independence: the diplomatic recognition of the United States.
5. The favorite comic actors in the early movies were: Buster Keaton, Charlie Chaplin, and Harold Lloyd.
6. The following assumption is a safe one to make: English scientific work has been, over the centuries, as great as any in the world.
7. The physical universe was once supposed to be composed of: fire, earth, air, and water.
8. Uncle George has at least one reason to be happy: he has money.
9. I ask you this question: When will you finish the work?
10. When the train came in at 8:36, we were there to meet it.

36 The Dash [—]

The dash is a rather dramatic mark of punctuation, likely to be stronger and more emphatic than other marks, for which it is sometimes substituted.

36a *Use a dash to show a sudden change of thought or of sentence direction or continuity.*

"I was just going to ask you to dance when—" John stopped suddenly.
Let's drive to—but what am I saying?

36b *Use dashes to set off a parenthetical expression that makes a sharp interruption, or that needs to be made emphatic, or that contains internal punctuation.*

And then—horror on horror—the flashlights found them.
—JOHN STEINBECK
She sneaked out onto the porch—just to get away from the smoke and the chatter for a minute.

479

You know the girl I mean—and you needn't act as if you don't. (Notice how much less emphatic a comma would be.)

The effect of a *Time* review is not to invite the reader to examine the book for himself; rather, it provides the *Time* reader—in a painless, flattering, and entertaining fashion—with the feeling that he has "got it cold."—WILLIAM VAN O'CONNOR (The passage already has so many commas that using them instead of dashes would be less clear and would clutter the sentence.)

36c *Use a dash before a summary of a preceding series.*

The motion picture, the automobile, the radio, television—these have broken down the sense of community.

36d *Use a dash to set off an appositive or a repeated word when a comma seems an insufficient separation.*

You know the girl I mean—the blonde with bangs.

It must safeguard, therefore, as sacred the rights of speech and press and assembly and petition and association—those rights which enable men to achieve through reason and consent what in the past they tried to achieve through violence.

—HENRY STEELE COMMAGER

36e *Do not overuse the dash.*

The dash is a helpful, flexible mark of punctuation, but it loses its effectiveness if it becomes a careless substitute for various other marks.

MISUSE OF DASHES It took the pioneers six weeks to get over the mountains to California—some of the party froze to death in the wild blizzards—others turned back—weary and disillusioned—to try to find their way to Santa Fe.

PROPERLY PUNCTUATED It took the pioneers six weeks to get over the mountains to California. Some of the party froze to death in the wild blizzards; others turned back, weary and disillusioned, to try to find their way to Santa Fe.

36f In typing, make the dash by using two hyphens; there should be no space before, between, or after these hyphens.

Exercise 1

Write five sentences about college students or courses, one to illustrate each of the following uses of the dash: to show a sudden change of thought or sentence direction, to set off a parenthetical expression that is emphatic, to set off a parenthetical expression containing commas, to summarize a preceding series, to set off an appositive.

Exercise 2

Punctuate the following passage from Robert Louis Stevenson. When you consider the dashes poorly used, substitute other marks. (For your information, there are four dashes in the original. Capitals—except for *I*—at the beginning of sentences have been made small letters.) Be prepared to defend your punctuation.

One day—I shall never forget it—I had taken a trail that was new to me—after a while the wood began to open—the sea to sound nearer at hand—I came upon a road—and—to my surprise—a stile—a step or two farther—and—without leaving the woods—I found myself among trim houses—I walked through street after street—parallel and at right angles—paved with sward and dotted with trees—but still undeniable streets—and each with its name posted at the corner—as in a real town —facing down the main thoroughfare—"Central Avenue"—as it was ticketed—I saw an open-air temple—with benches and sounding board—as though for an orchestra—the houses were all tightly shuttered—there was no smoke—no sound but the waves—no moving thing—I have never been in any place that seemed so dreamlike.

37 Parentheses [( )]

37a Use parentheses to set off material that you wish to be considered incidental or supplementary.

During migration the birds flew with great swiftness (forty to sixty miles per hour) in a front about a mile wide.

—LUDLOW GRISCOM

481

Occasionally this use of parentheses may give an ironic emphasis:

> Communication by the written word is a subtler (and more beautiful) thing than Dr. Flesch or General Motors imagines.
> —*The New Yorker*

Note: The writer sometimes has a choice in the use of parentheses, dashes, and commas. Study the following sentences:

> My uncle, who had not gone to college himself, was scornful of a college education.
> My uncle—who had not gone to college himself—was scornful of a college education.
> My uncle (who had not gone to college himself) was scornful of a college education.

Each of these sentences is correctly punctuated. The writer's intention and judgment must tell him the one to use. Which is best here it would be difficult to say, though if we had the context the sentence appeared in, one might seem slightly more appropriate than the others. Here is a general guide: commas are least conspicuous and, being the normal punctuation, should be used unless there is good reason not to use them; dashes will usually give most emphasis; parentheses are most useful in suggesting the independence (the parenthetical nature) of the word or statement—in setting it, so to speak, somewhat to one side.

37b   *Use parentheses to enclose explanatory and illustrative details.*

> William Dwight Whitney (1827–94) was one of our first great linguistic scholars.
> The story first appeared in the *Atlantic Monthly* (September, 1954, p. 56).
> Word formations like NATO (North Atlantic Treaty Organization) have become common in recent years.

37c   *Use parentheses to enclose numbers or letters which mark the items in a series.*

> There are three common thermometric scales: (1) the Fahrenheit, which sets the freezing point of water at 32° and the boiling

point at 212°, (2) the Réaumur, with the same points at 0°
and 80°, and (3) the centigrade, with the points at 0° and
100°.

37d *Observe standard practice when other marks are used with parentheses.*

(1) When a comma, period, or semicolon is needed, place it after a parenthetical passage within a sentence.

> If one were doing a book of snobs, as Thackeray once
> did, it would be necessary, I think (though difficult),
> to describe the Spiritual Snob. . . .—IRWIN EDMAN

(2) When a parenthetical passage is a separate sentence, place the end punctuation before the second parenthesis.

> He gave his account of the accident. (Or should we call
> it his first account?)

37e *Do not use parentheses to cancel a passage.*

Draw a line through canceled material in the following
manner:

> He constantly ~~exagerrated~~ exaggerated the story.
>   exaggerated
> He constantly ~~exagerrated~~ the story.
>   ^

Exercise 1

In a recent issue of any magazine recommended by your instructor, find five sentences containing material in parentheses.
Copy the sentences and state which of the sections above give
appropriate explanations for using the parentheses.

Exercise 2

Put parentheses in the proper places in the following sentences.

1. In some ways the most talented of eighteenth-century English
   statesmen was Charles James Fox 1749–1806, a friend of the
   young United States.

2. The temperature was exceedingly high never below a hundred degrees Fahrenheit.
3. Such willfulness hinders I might say "wastes" the talents of an actor.
4. They crossed the mountains five or six miles was sometimes a full day's journey.
5. *Harper's Weekly* December 27, 1862 contains a bitter account of the Battle of Fredericksburg.

38 Brackets [ ]

38a *Use brackets to enclose corrections or explanatory matter inserted in a quoted passage.*

> "It was about this time [1732] I conceiv'd the bold and arduous project of arriving at moral perfection."—BENJAMIN FRANKLIN
> "They [studies] perfect nature and are perfected by experience."
> —FRANCIS BACON

38b *The Latin word* sic (*meaning* thus *or* so) *in brackets may be used to show that an error in a quotation has been quoted just as it appeared in the original.*

> The next sentence begins: "The hurracane [*sic*] hit our ship early on Sunday morning."

39 Quotation Marks [" "]

American publications use double (" ") quotes as the basic quotation marks, single (' ') quotes for quotations within quotations.

39a *Use quotation marks to enclose conversation.*

> "Where's the mustard?" Ellen asked. "We can't eat these sandwiches without mustard."

484

"I thought," he replied loftily, "that you were arranging this picnic."

Some self-pity—or was it irony?—crept into her voice. "Yes, of course, I was arranging it, wasn't I? You, naturally, were too busy. So now we'll eat nice dry sandwiches."

Note the following:

(1) Each person's speech, regardless of length, is set off in a separate paragraph.

(2) Expressions like *Ellen asked* are not part of the dialogue and are therefore not included within the quotation marks.

(3) Comments by the author may accompany the dialogue.

(4) In an uninterrupted series of sentences by the same speaker, quotation marks are used only at the beginning and end of the series, not to set off each sentence.

(5) If the words of a speaker run to more than one paragraph, place quotation marks at the beginning of each paragraph and at the end of the last one.

Jim said, "You should have seen the kid run up and grab me and yell. He made so much noise it was hard to tell what was the matter with him. I didn't know whether he was mad or scared.

"Anyway, he hung on to my coat sleeves and tried to pull me off in the direction he came from—over there in the woods. And I kept tryin' to push him to one side so I could settle my business with Jerry, because I'd come a long way to talk to him."

Note: What is said above applies to dialogue. In a long quotation that is not conversation the same practice is sometimes followed, but it is now also common to indent the whole passage and use no quotation marks. (See also page 270.)

39b *Use quotation marks for short direct quotations (whether conversation or not).*

Do not use quotation marks for indirect quotations. A direct quotation gives the exact words of the writer or speaker.

DIRECT QUOTATION   It was Churchill who said, "Never have so many owed so much to so few."

INDIRECT QUOTATION   It was Churchill who said that so many had never owed so much to so few. (Here the speaker's exact words are not repeated.)

39c   Use quotation marks for short poetry quotations that do not form separate sentences: indicate the line division by a slant (/).

Keats says that the word *forlorn* is "like a bell / To toll me back from thee to my sole self!"

Quotations of more than three or four lines of prose or poetry are usually indented or centered on the page. The original line arrangement of poetry is always observed.

39d   Use single quotation marks (' ') to enclose a quotation within a quotation.

Schlesinger says, "No one ever called Jackson 'Andy Jackson' during his Presidency."

39e   Use quotation marks to enclose titles of written work not published as separate volumes: magazine articles, chapters of books, short stories, essays, and most poems. Use italics (underlining) for titles of volumes.

Matthew Arnold's essay "The Study of Poetry" first appeared as the introduction to *The English Poets*, edited by T. H. Ward.
"In Football Season," a short story by John Updike, was originally published in *The New Yorker*.

The practice advised here is common in formal writing and is followed in many periodicals, but some magazines and newspapers have a different rule. The New York *Times*, for instance, places all titles in quotes. Nearly all colleges expect the usage recommended in this section.

39f   Quotation marks are sometimes used for the names of works of art (paintings, musical compositions, and so on) and for ships, airplanes, and trains, but italics are generally preferred (42a).

39g Quotation marks may be used to indicate a word used as a word.

> The first step is to define "metaphor."—MONROE BEARDSLEY
> The explanation is called "selective migration."—RUTH BENEDICT

Note: In much formal writing, italics are more common than quotes in this use. Sometimes quotes are used, along with italics, in definitions.

> Shakespeare uses the word *gull* in the meaning of "dupe."

39h Use quotation marks to indicate a word used in a different sense than someone else has used it.

Note the change in meaning that would occur if the quotes were omitted from the following sentences:

> We need to remember that we can protect the right of free speech for the whole American people only by insisting upon the right of free speech for those with whom we disagree most violently, the "radicals," the "reds," the "fanatics," whose opinion we may least respect.—HENRY STEELE COMMAGER
> A "people's democracy" is likely to be a dictatorship. . . .
> —JOHN C. SHERWOOD

This use of quotes is easily overdone. You will seldom need it.

39i Use quotation marks at the beginning and end of a quotation.

Do not use only part of a pair of quotation marks.

> CONFUSING   He added, "If your car acts up, pull over to the side of the road and switch off the ignition. There's nothing much to do then except wait for help. (Omission of one set of quotation marks leaves the reader wondering whether the second sentence is included in the quotation or not.)
> REVISED   He added, "If your car acts up, pull over to the side of the road and switch off the ignition. There's nothing much to do then except wait for help."

39j *Do not overuse quotation marks.*

(1) Do not use quotation marks to enclose indirect quotations. (See 39b.)

(2) Do not use quotation marks to enclose common words and phrases.

> MISUSE   I knew I had been silly to make such a "fuss" about the trip.
> REVISED   I knew I had been silly to make such a fuss about the trip.

> MISUSE   I certainly "backed the wrong horse."
> REVISED   I certainly backed the wrong horse.

(3) Do not use quotation marks to enclose slang in a context where slang belongs. Ordinarily you should not use slang in college writing, but if your subject requires it, or if a slang term is the most effective term, use it without apology or false delicacy. (On the use of slang, see pages 89–90.)

> MISUSE   Who was that "guy"?
> REVISED (for context such as dialogue)   Who was that guy?
> STANDARD ENGLISH   Who was that man (or that student)?

> No one had the guts to raise a riot, but if a European woman went through the bazaars alone somebody would probably spit betel juice over her dress.
> —GEORGE ORWELL
> (Orwell considers *guts* appropriate and does not wish to weaken it by placing it within quotation marks.)

(4) Do not use quotation marks to indicate humor or irony.

> WEAK   He has "elegant" manners.
> WEAK   John weighs 250 pounds; isn't he getting "thin"?

(5) Do not use quotation marks to enclose names.

> MISUSE   Four players from the "Yankee" team were there.
> REVISED   Four players from the Yankee team. . . .

MISUSE   "Bud" Jones, "Red" Smith, "Lizzy" Brown
REVISED   Bud Jones, Red Smith, Lizzy Brown

39k *When other marks are used with quotation marks, observe the following practices:*

(1) **Use a comma after an expression like *he said* that introduces a quotation.**

> She answered, "I may be mistaken."

But quotations that are long or that are presented formally are introduced by colons. (See **35a**.)

(2) **When a comma or period occurs at the end of a quoted passage, place the comma or period before the quotation marks.**

> "I am mistaken," she said.
> She said, "I am mistaken."
> The first essay is "A Summing Up."
> "You, Andrew Marvell," a poem by Archibald MacLeish, was published in 1930.

(3) **Place a question mark or exclamation mark before the quotation marks if the quoted material is a question or exclamation, after if it is not.**

> Bob said, "Why didn't you answer my telegram?" (Notice that the whole sentence is not a question, but a statement of what Bob said. The quoted material is a question and therefore requires a question mark.)
> "Good gracious!"
> "Stop grinning!" the photographer cried.
> Did Washington really say, "I cut down the cherry tree with my hatchet"? (The whole statement is a question; the quoted material is not.)
> Where did you get that recording of "Who Stole My Gal?" (When both the whole statement and the quoted material are questions, the question mark before the quotations marks is the only one used.)

(4) **After an interrupting expression like *he said*, use a comma unless a semicolon or period is needed.** If you wonder which mark is proper, read the sentence with the interrupting expression omitted.

COMMA   "I expected you to like the play," she said, "but I despise it." (A comma is used after *she said* because it would be the normal punctuation if the interrupter were not there: "I expected you to like the play, but I despise it.")

SEMICOLON   "I don't doubt that you like the play," she answered; "you're in love with the author." (The semicolon would be used if *she answered* were omitted: "I don't doubt that you like the play; you're in love with the author.")

PERIOD   "I don't doubt that you like the play," she answered. "After all, you're in love with the author." (The period would be used if *she answered* were omitted: "I don't doubt that you like the play. After all, you're in love with the author.")

When no punctuation would be used normally, set off the interrupter with commas.

"This procedure," he answered, "is the only one possible under the circumstances."

Exercise 1

Place quotation marks where they belong in the following conversation:

Fred, Mary said, do you remember Robert Frost's poems that we read when we were in college?

A few of them. I remember one about birches and another about how far somebody had to travel before he could sleep.

Yes, that one was called, I think, Stopping by Woods on a Snowy Evening. I like it, too, but my favorite is West-running Brook. I never was sure I understood it, but the man and woman seemed very real.

Well, I only remember a couple of things about that one, he said. The man's name was Fred, and in those days you said he was condescending and reminded you of me.

Exercise 2

Check the sentences in which quotation marks are justified. Circle any marks that should be removed. Be prepared to defend your answers.

1. After he turned the theme in, he realized that "the die had been cast."
2. Some of the violent scenes in *Wuthering Heights* left me "numb."
3. "Why didn't they put the capital in Denver?" the British delegate asked, wiping his brow.
4. In Moscow it's called "deviationism" or "revisionism."
5. I especially like Caroline Gordon's story "The Last Day in the Field."
6. I think Allen is beginning to realize that he is "henpecked."
7. In England the hood of a car is called the "bonnet."
8. His trying to date my girl brought about the "beautiful" scar he has under his right eye.
9. The school cafeteria is a "haven" for gossipers who meet at a "gabfest" to exchange the latest dirt while sipping cokes and eating soggy pretzels.
10. The instructor wanted to know "why we hadn't read the assignment."
11. Last night I finally wrote to "Bill" Smith.
12. Do you know the essay "Old China," by Lamb?
13. The instructor said, "Tomorrow read Forster's essay 'My Wood.'"
14. The time had come, I felt, for me to prove that I was "a woman of the world."
15. Did your plans proceed without a "hitch"?

40 The Apostrophe [']

40a *Use an apostrophe to show the omission of a letter in contractions and, in recordings of conversation, to indicate omission in pronunciation of a letter normally sounded.*

CONTRACTIONS   *It's* been raining heavily all week. (*It's* = *it has*) *It's* going to rain again. (*It's* = *it is*) *They're* not coming after all. *Isn't* it too bad!

CONVERSATION   She said, "*I've* been *waitin'* for you."

491

40b *Use an apostrophe to indicate the plurals of letters, of words thought of as words, of signs, and of numbers.* When letters, words, signs, and numbers are referred to as such, they are italicized; the plural *s* is not.

> He told us to dot all our *i*'s.
> His sentences have too many *and*'s.
> In most writing, *&*'s are inappropriate.
> His *7*'s are hard to tell from his *4*'s.
> The early 1930's were for many people a time of despair.

40c *Use an apostrophe to indicate the possessive case of nouns and of such pronouns as* anybody *and* everybody.

Possession is generally shown by adding an apostrophe and *s* in the singular and by adding the apostrophe alone in the plural. If the *'s* causes difficulty in pronunciation, it is often omitted: *Socrates'* words, for *conscience'* sake.

> SINGULAR a *friend's* help, a *lady's* respect, *James's* coat (or *James'* coat), *Burns's* poems (or *Burns'* poems), *anyone's* guess, *nobody's* business, *somebody's* idea
> PLURAL *friends'* help, *ladies'* respect, the *Burnses'* children

The following exceptions and special usages should be noted:

(1) **For plural nouns which do not end in *s*, show possession by adding *'s*.**

> *men's* clothing, *deer's* antlers

(2) **For compounds and groups of words with a unit idea, use the possessive form in the last word only.**

> We started out in my *mother-in-law's* car.
> It seems to be nobody *else's* business.

(3) **Show joint possession by using the possessive form in the last word in the series, individual possession by using an apostrophe after each noun.**

> JOINT This is *John and Fred's* car.
> *Walton and Smith's* truck went past the corner.

INDIVIDUAL   These are *John's* and *Fred's* examinations. *Walton's* and *Smith's* trucks collided at the corner.

(4) Do not use the apostrophe with the pronouns *his, hers, its, ours, yours, theirs,* **and** *whose.*

This book is *hers.* The dog chased *its* tail. Where is the man *whose* car was hit?

(5) Use the apostrophe with certain phrases, especially of time and measurement, in which the possessive form has long been accepted. (See 11g Note.)

four *days'* leave, three *dollars'* worth of apples, two *weeks'* vacation

Exercise

Place appropriate apostrophes (or an apostrophe and *s*) in the following sentences.

1. Anybody elses answer would be the same as hers.
2. Is that the Joneses dog or the Browns that is chasing its tail?
3. Even people with the highest I.Q.s make mistakes.
4. Who hasnt had his doubts about others decisions as well as his own?
5. We lived on that street in the 1950s.
6. Its too late now to oppose your sisters marriage.
7. What would he do if his *howevers* and *notwithstandings* were forbidden him?
8. Alice question was surprising: "Do you like Sophocles plays?"
9. Aunt Kate said, "He cant believe youre goin to return after a weeks time."
10. The Secretary of States car stopped in front of my son-in-laws house.

41 The Hyphen [-]

41a *Use a hyphen at the end of a line when a word must be divided.*

In most themes and other handwritten and typewritten work, relatively few words need to be divided. Observe the following practices in dividing words:

(1) **Divide between syllables:** *seven-teenth, pen-sion, turpen-tine.* If in doubt, consult a dictionary.

(2) **Divide words with prefixes and suffixes at the joining point:** *ex-treme, re-vised, illustra-tion, driv-ing, champion-ship.*

(3) **Usually divide between double consonants** (*drug-gist, begin-ning, min-now*) **unless a suffix has been added** (*spell-ing, pass-able*). To be sure, consult a dictionary.

(4) **Do not divide words of one syllable:** *switch, brought, saints.* An *–ed* that is not pronounced as a separate syllable should not be hyphenated: *lived.*

(5) **Do not divide a one-letter syllable from the rest of the word:** *a-bout, e-vaporate, myster-y.*

(6) **Do not split a word that is already hyphenated except at a hyphen:** *brother-in-law* (not *broth-er-in-law*).

41b *Use a hyphen with numbers from twenty-one to ninety-nine and with fractions: thirty-two* students, *eighty-four* new telephones, *fifty-third* performance, *three-fourths* of the amount, five *thirty-seconds* of the distance.

41c *Use the hyphen with a number of compound nouns,* such as *forget-me-not, cure-all, bull's-eye, merry-go-round.*

But most such combinations are solid (*outgrowth, blackboard, watermelon, playwright, backhand, blowout*) or are

494

simply treated as two words (*short circuit, home plate, lawn mower*). Since practice varies greatly, you will probably need to consult a dictionary. (And you may discover that for some compounds the dictionaries themselves occasionally disagree.)

41d   *Use hyphens with prefixes in the following ways:*

(1) Use hyphens when words might otherwise be awkward or unclear.

> *re-echo, re-examine, re-lease* (to lease again, but *release*, to let go)

(2) Use hyphens when a proper name follows.

> pro-French, anti-Administration, un-American, non-European

(3) Use hyphens after *ex-* (when it means "former": ex-dean) and *self-* (self-defense).

For many of these words you will need to consult your dictionary.

41e   *Use hyphens between two or more words treated as a single adjective before a noun.*

> a man-to-man talk, a four-room apartment, a take-it-or-leave-it tone, a well-made house

Such hyphens are especially important when misreading might result without them: "He then went to the freezer and got ready to cook steaks." (For the correct meaning read *ready-to-cook*.)

Exception: A compound containing an *–ly* adverb is not hyphenated.

> a poorly revised theme, a cheaply made clock

Note: When compounds come after the noun, they are not hyphenated.

> The word was well chosen. (*But:* It was a well-chosen word.)
> They met face to face. (*But:* They had a face-to-face encounter.)

41f *Use a hyphen when in a series of compounds one part is carried over or suspended.*

When Faulkner writes of "objects which in the levelling sun resembled vari-sized and -colored tatters," he is avoiding the clumsy repetition of "vari-sized and vari-colored" by carrying over *vari*. Here is another example of part of a compound that is suspended:

> He carried sixty-, eighty-, and even hundred-pound bags of grain.

Exercise 1

In the sentences below, indicate which words need a hyphen and which should be written solid. You will need to use a dictionary frequently.

1. He caught a two pound fish.
2. This is our fifty fourth game.
3. Look at that jet black button on her snow white jacket.
4. Did you see the head line in the morning paper?
5. He now owes me eighty nine dollars.
6. Let's feed the gold fish an earth worm.
7. The ex president of the company has four hundred pet fish.
8. A jack in the box is one of the oldest toys.
9. The game of jack straws is also old.
10. I don't mean to be un neighborly, but do you own all those jack rabbits?
11. I wonder if I'll re cover from the sight of them after that exhausting ten hour trip.
12. We made a trans polar flight in a poorly built plane.
13. Well, it was better than a trans Siberian trip.
14. Please put that cross cut saw down while I cross examine you.
15. Did you look up the cross reference?
16. I rather like his get there somehow attitude.
17. Are you going to have the chair re upholstered?
18. He has done three problems out of sixty four.
19. In other words, he's three sixty fourths of the way through.
20. We were looking for a four room apartment but we took one with three rooms.

Exercise 2

Assume that you may have to split some of the following words at the end of a line. Check those which cannot be split at all. Indicate at what points others might be split. You may need to use a dictionary for some of the words.

1.	modern	11.	plucky
2.	twenty-fourth	12.	rhymed
3.	alert	13.	milling
4.	thwarting	14.	emulsion
5.	comedy	15.	evict
6.	straight	16.	windmill
7.	winning	17.	shrubbery
8.	heritage	18.	catalyst
9.	conquest	19.	oration
10.	anatomy	20.	transport

42 Italics (Underlining)

In typewritten and handwritten papers use underlining to indicate the italics of printing.

UNDERLINED   Have you read <u>Pride and Prejudice?</u>
ITALICIZED   Have you read *Pride and Prejudice?*

42a   Use italics for titles of books, magazines, newspapers, and other separately published complete works, as well as motion pictures, plays, longer poems, and other works of art.

The Good Earth
Harper's Magazine
the Washington *Post*
Shakespeare's *Julius Caesar*
the motion picture *Kind Hearts and Coronets*
Milton's *Paradise Lost*
El Greco's painting *Toledo*

Quotation marks are common for shorter pieces and parts of books and larger works, magazine and newspaper articles, short stories, short poems, chapters or essays in books.

"The Dead" was one of the stories in Joyce's *Dubliners*.

There is no uniformity in the use of quotes and italics. You will occasionally see other practices in good publications, but the usage given here is standard in most colleges. (On the use of quotation marks, see **39e**.)

Note: Also usually italicized are the names of ships, airplanes, and trains: the *Lusitania,* the Burlington *Zephyr.* Quotation marks are sometimes used for such names. (See **39f**.)

42b   *Use italics for words from foreign languages unless they have become absorbed into English.*

The grizzly bear (*Ursus horribilis*) is found mainly in mountainous areas.
In 1914 the French expected their *élan* to defeat the Germans.

But words that are common in standard English should not be italicized: antebellum, avant garde, coup d'état, ennui, per se, kamikaze. There are of course many words that are on the borderline; some writers would italicize *avant garde* or *coup d'état.*

42c   *Use italics to indicate a word used as a word.*

Suspect yourself of wordiness whenever you see an *of,* a *which* or a *that.*—SHERIDAN BAKER
Why is *blockhead* considered standard English and *bonehead* American slang?

Many writers use quotes for such words. (See **39g**.) Italics are somewhat more formal and are generally preferred in college writing.

42d   *Use italics—but very rarely—for emphasis.*

We knew what he said and did and even what he earned. We didn't know what he *was.*
We have considered the ponderable factors; we have not yet considered the *im*ponderables.

Exercise

Underline the appropriate words below. Do not underline any words unnecessarily.

1. Crossing New Mexico in the Santa Fe Chief, I read A Stillness at Appomattox.
2. A few weeks before, I had seen a review of the book in the New Republic and another review in the New York Times.
3. The crucial word in the sentence is consult.
4. In San Francisco we went to performances of Sheridan's School for Scandal and Mozart's The Magic Flute.
5. In Orson Welles' motion picture production of Macbeth, Welles himself takes the part of Macbeth.
6. Is the word school related to the French école?
7. He pronounces the oi in join to make the word rhyme with line.
8. The Olympic was the first ship to reach the Titanic's survivors.
9. Van Gogh did several versions of his famous painting The Bridge at Arles.
10. Professor Ward advised the ladies not to try to plant the bunchberry (Cornus canadensis) in a flower garden.

43 Capital Letters

43a *Capitalize the first word of a sentence, including a quoted sentence or a sentence in parentheses.*

> They sang, "What shall we do?"
> He said "No." (But why did he say it?)

Note: When the words do not form a sentence, they begin with a small letter.

> He said John was "the biggest numbskull on the campus," and I (a mere sophomore) believed him.

The use of capitals in dialogue is illustrated in **39k(4)**.

43b *After a colon an independent clause is not usually capitalized, but sometimes it is.*

NOT CAPITALIZED   I was interested in this because it bore out an opinion of mine that philosophy is an affair of character rather than of logic: the philosopher believes not according to evidence, but according to his own temperament; and his thinking merely serves to make reasonable what his instinct regards as true.—W. SOMERSET MAUGHAM

CAPITALIZED   The only reassurance we can give, to either men or women students, is this: Education is as education thinks and does.—T. V. SMITH

43c *Capitalize the first word in each line of a poem unless the original uses lowercase.*

A thing of beauty is a joy for ever:
Its loveliness increases; it will never
Pass into nothingness. . . .—KEATS

anyone lived in a pretty how town
(with up so floating many bells down)—E. E. CUMMINGS

43d *Capitalize names of individual persons and places and other proper nouns and words derived from them.*

PERSONS   James, Jim, Mrs. Allen, Jefferson (Jeffersonian)

PLACES   Virginia (Virginian), America (American and Americanize)

LANGUAGES   German, Dutch

DAYS AND MONTHS   Tuesday, Thanksgiving, March

HISTORICAL PERIODS AND EVENTS   the Dark Ages, the Battle of the Bulge

CHURCHES, ORGANIZATIONS, INSTITUTIONS, POLITICAL PARTIES, GOVERNMENTS, RACIAL AND NATIONAL GROUPS   Methodist, Catholic, International Shoe Company, the Rotary Club, the Atomic Energy Commission (also AEC), Reed College, Republicans, the Democratic Party, the Supreme Court, the State Department, the Kennedy Administration, the House of Commons, the Senecas, Indians

DEITY AND RELATED RELIGIOUS REFERENCES   God (but not the gods), the Lord, the Creator (Also commonly capitalized, but not always, are pronouns that refer to such words.)

Note: Do not capitalize words that are no longer felt to be proper nouns and adjectives: titian red, china (chinaware).

43e *Capitalize titles derived from rank and office.*

(1) **Capitalize titles that come before a person's name.**

> President Hoover, Captain Anderson

(2) **Do not capitalize titles that come after a name —or without a name—unless the office is a high one.**

> Has George Anderson been made a captain?
> Is that the captain?
> The president of the club will be elected at the next meeting.
> The President will speak here next week. (This means only the President of the country indicated in the context.)

43f *Capitalize words indicating family relationships when they are used as the equivalent of names or when they are used before names.*

> EQUIVALENT OF NAME   Jerry, where is Mother?
> BEFORE NAME   I think Aunt Catherine has the book.

But when a possessive precedes such a word, no capital is used:

> This is my mother; those are my aunts.

43g *Capitalize any common noun that is part of a specific name.*

Examples of such nouns are *college, university, high school, river, street, mountain, lake, dam, desert, theater, county.* They are not capitalized, of course, when they do not help to form a proper noun.

> Is there a junior college in Montgomery County?
> No, but York Junior College is in a neighboring county.
> The Mojave Desert is in California.
> The first pioneers had great trouble in crossing the desert.

43h   *Capitalize the names of specific academic courses but not general areas of study.*

I am having trouble with Biology 2, but I am getting along well in History 52.
I have always had more difficulty with biology than with history.
My success with French 21 led me to make French my major subject. (Names of languages are always capitalized; see **43d**.)

43i   *Capitalize a directional word that has become a place name.*

He was born in the East but his parents moved, first to the South and then to the Southwest.

Capitalize adjectives derived from such place names.

She has a Southern accent.

But for a simple direction do not capitalize.

He got in his car, turned east, then northeast.

43j   *Capitalize the first and last words of titles* (of books, magazine articles, poems, themes and other student papers, and so on) *and all other words except* a, an, *and* the, *the short conjunctions such as* and *and* or, *and short prepositions.* Prepositions having five or more letters are usually capitalized.

A Portrait of the Artist as a Young Man (Book)
Death of a Salesman (Play)
"New Findings on the Origins of Races" (Magazine article)
"What People Have to Work With" (Essay; last word capitalized, even though a preposition)
"The American Attitude Toward War and Peace" (*Toward*, a long preposition, capitalized)

For your own themes and other compositions use the same principles but omit underlining or quotation marks.

Over the Fence Is Out
Is Richard III a Maligned Monarch?

43k *Do not use capitals for the seasons.*

winter, spring, fall, summer

43l *Do not capitalize unnecessarily.*

Being a lowly Freshman, I am impressed by the Campus and the Professors. Even though a Pre-medic, I am studying History. (Only *I* and the words at the beginning of the sentences should be capitalized.)

Exercise

Use capital letters appropriately in the sentences below. Make no changes in correct sentences.

1. Who said that George is "A frustrated gangster"?
2. If I can manage to get through college next Spring, I'm going to become a Dentist.
3. The tabletop has been given a coat of japan.
4. Stephen Crane's story "the open boat" begins: "none of them knew the color of the sky."
5. My term paper in History should be called "the trouble I've seen." It would be pure Autobiography.
6. Is sergeant Smith a graduate of Colville high school?
7. I brought back some venetian glass for my aunt and a billfold for dad.
8. Does this river run east into Lake Superior?
9. I prefer History 3 to any english course at all.
10. She said, "we hear you came from the middle west but we're not sure what city you're from."

44 Numbers

Write out numbers or use figures consistently and in accordance with good practice.

44a *Ordinarily write out numbers that can be expressed in one or two words.*

There were at least two thousand in the audience.
A dog's sense of hearing and rhythm is so keen that he can dis-

criminate easily between a metronome beating one hundred times a minute and another beating ninety-six.

44b *Write out a number at the beginning of a sentence.* If the result is awkward, revise the sentence.

> Two hundred and eighty-seven passengers were on board the ship.
>
> OR   On board the ship were 287 passengers.

44c *In some cases use figures instead of writing out numbers.*

(1) Use figures for numbers that cannot be written in one or two words.

> This book runs to 346 pages.

(2) Use figures in any passage where numbers are frequent.

> He found 14 people in Section A, 23 in Section B, and 47 in Section C.

(3) Use figures for dates.

> December 27, 1959 (Note that in dates the simple numbers are preferred to numbers like 27th, 1st, and 2nd.)

(4) Use figures for addresses.

> 1920 Clymer Street   211 Peabody Hall   415 Widener Building

(5) Use figures for page numbers, chapter numbers, and the like.

> page 287   Chapter 10   stanza 8

(6) Use figures for time when a.m. or p.m. is used.

> 8 A.M. or 8 a.m. (*or:* eight o'clock)
> 3 P.M. or 3 p.m. (*or:* three in the afternoon)

(7) Use figures for most kinds of technical passages.

> At 25° Fahrenheit a car moving at 20 miles an hour travels 125 percent farther before it can be stopped than it does at 3° below zero.

44d *For a number with four or more digits, use a comma to separate each group of three figures.* Exceptions are made for dates and addresses.

> The cost will be $12,231.
> There are 2,231 students in the college now.
> He lives at 2231 Quincy Avenue.
> That won't happen until the year 2231.

44e *Except in legal papers and business contracts, do not repeat a written number with figures in parentheses.*

> He wrote his examination in forty-five minutes. *Not:* . . . in forty-five (45) minutes.

Exercise

In the following sentences, underline any numbers that are in figures but that should be written out. Circle numbers which are written out but for which figures should be used.

1. In 1840, Boston had ten thousand three hundred and seventy houses.
2. The new state park has an area of 12 square miles and parking space for ten cars.
3. He lives at 2416 Kendall Avenue.
4. Tom is moving into two hundred thirteen Johnson Hall.
5. 2/5 of the acreage will be used by these 30 farmers.
6. Turn to page nineteen and do exercise three.
7. At six A.M. the clock was three minutes fast.
8. I hate to remind you, but you owe me eighty-five (85) cents.
9. She graduated from high school on June sixteenth, 1964.
10. She was 18 years old on the same day.

45 Abbreviations

45a *Use only acceptable abbreviations*

(1) For a few common titles attached to names.

> Mr., Mrs., Dr., St. (for *Saint*), Messrs.
> I saw Dr. Blake. (*But:* I saw the doctor.)

(2) For titles.

> M.D., A.B., Jr., Ph.D., Esq.

(3) For certain technical and business terms in a proper context.

> C.O.D., r.p.m. or rpm, B.T.U., F.O.B.

(4) For certain things and groups where letters have come to be equivalent to a name or nickname.

> YMCA, TVA, WAC, NATO

(5) For a number of Latin abbreviations, though the English equivalents—written out in full—are usually preferred.

> etc. (*et cetera*), and so forth; i.e. (*id est*), that is

(6) For certain words in footnotes. See page 278.

45b *In general writing, avoid most abbreviations.*

The following and similar words should not ordinarily be abbreviated:

Virginia (*not* Va.)	pounds (*not* lbs.)
Kansas City (*not* K.C.)	company (*not* co.)
Samuel (*not* Saml.)	manufacturing (*not* mfg.)
street (*not* st.)	Wednesday (*not* Wed.)
governor (*not* gov.)	January (*not* Jan.)
square feet (*not* sq. ft.)	Christmas (*not* Xmas)

In the name of a business establishment, use the form used in the company's title.

> Bristol-Myers Co.; Block Drug Company, Inc.; G. & C. Merriam Co.

In general writing, do not use the ampersand (&) or a plus (+) instead of *and*.

45c *Observe standard practice in punctuation with abbreviations.*

(1) Use periods after most abbreviations.

> Esq., Mr., M.A., ibid., A.D.

(2) The period may be followed by a comma.

He has three degrees: B.A., Ph.D., and Ll.D.

(3) Do not use a period after abbreviations that have become familiar words in themselves.

NBC, exam, lab, Dave, Sue, Doc Thompson

Exercise

Underline any words that should have been abbreviated. Circle words that should not have been abbreviated.

1. I will be home for Xmas + will stay for two wks.
2. Where is Mister Benjamin's class?
3. I arrived in L. A. after visiting Miss Worthington for three mos.
4. I expect to start work for my A.B. degree at a jr. college.
5. Last summer when I was in Memphis, Tenn., I worked so hard I lost thirteen lbs.
6. Were you ever in St. Paul, Doctor Miller?
7. Our exam asked us about the origin of TVA.
8. I expect to leave Fla. next Wed.
9. The date to remember is A.D. 476.
10. The letter should be sent to Chas. Hazard, Esq.

SPELLING

46 Spelling

The ability to spell correctly is an accomplishment that confers no distinction. Like the ability to add and subtract, it is taken for granted among educated people. But if the ability confers no distinction, the inability imposes a severe handicap and invites the scorn of the familiar words "He can't even spell."

It should be possible for you, even though you may have entered college as a poor speller, to avoid the charge that you can't even spell, if you are willing to face your problem and give it some time and energy. Here are several suggestions.

(1) Look up in a dictionary every word that you have any doubt about. Suppose you had written this paragraph, which comes to about a hundred words. No matter how poor a speller you are, you probably would be sure of every word, except perhaps "dictionary." One word in a paragraph of a hundred words means five doubtful words in a 500-word theme. It should be possible to look up five words in less than five minutes—surely a small investment to avoid the charge that you "can't even spell."

(2) Make it a practice to read your writing once, preferably aloud, *thinking of nothing but the spelling*. Certainly you should revise your writing for such things as diction, punctuation, and sentence structure; but after all other revision has been completed, you should check for spelling alone. Every English teacher will testify that the most common spelling errors are those of carelessness and not ignorance—errors like "to" for "too," "their" for "there," and "it's" for "its." Presumably you do not need to go to a dictionary or handbook for help on errors like these; you need to read what you have written as carefully as other people may read it.

(3) Go over the list of words in **46f;** learn the spellings

you are not sure of, and add other words (**46g**) you have trouble with. There are several hundred thousand words in the English language, but relatively few give much trouble.

(4) Understand the main spelling rules (**46a**). Avoid the mispronunciations that lead to misspelling (**46b**). Do not confuse words that look or sound alike (**46c**).

46a   *Observe spelling rules.*

(1) **Silent *e* at the end of a word is kept if a suffix beginning with a consonant is added.**

> completely (complete + ly)
> excitement (excite + ment)
> lateness (late + ness)

(2) **Silent *e* at the end of a word is dropped if a suffix beginning with a vowel is added.**

> exciting (excite + ing)
> dated (date + ed)
> miner (mine + er)
> excitable (excite + able)
> assurance (assure + ance)

Exception: If words end in *ce* or *ge*, the *e* is kept before a suffix beginning with *a, o,* or *u:*

> notice, noticeable (What would be the pronunciation of *noticable?*)
> outrage, outrageous

(3) **In words of one syllable (*fat, wed*) or in words in which the last syllable is accented (*omit, refer*), a final single consonant preceded by a single vowel is doubled when a suffix beginning with a vowel is added.**

For instance, *remit* ends in a single consonant, *t*, preceded by a single vowel, *i*, in an accented syllable, *mit*. When we wish to add *ed*, we must double the final consonant, *t*, and spell the word *remitted*. (Note the odd result if the *t* is not doubled; we would have a word, *remited*, which would presumably rhyme with *blighted*.)

Note: Do not confuse words ending in a single consonant

509

with words ending in a single consonant followed by a silent *e*. The difference between *win* and *wine* and *top* and *tope* shows itself in the difference between *winning* and *wining* and between *topper* and *toper*.

Remember that words that do not meet all three requirements (*single vowel* followed by *single consonant* in *accented syllable*) do not come under the rule. Thus, though *wed* and *wedding* come under the rule, *weed* and *weeding* do not. Nor do *reveal* and *revealed*. Nor do *inherit* and *inheritance* or *inherited*, for the accent in *inherit* is not on the last syllable; we therefore have both *preference* and *preferred*.

(4) Final *y* preceded by a consonant is usually changed to *i* when it is followed by a suffix. This change is particularly common in noun plurals (*berry, berries*) and in verbs (I *spy*, he *spies*, he *spied*).

ally, alliance	ninety, ninetieth
deny, denial, denies	study, studies, studious
cry, cried	Tory, Tories
identify, identified, identification	friendly, friendliness

Exceptions:

(a) When the suffix begins with *i*, the *y* is not changed. Thus we have *flying, identifying, studying*, etc.

(b) When *y* is preceded by a vowel, the *y* usually is not changed: *play, played; employ, employed; buy, buyer.* A few very common words do make the change, however: *say, said; pay, paid; lay, laid.*

(5) The *ie-ei* combination is usually spelled *ie* when the pronunciation is ē, except after *c*. When it is pronounced ā, it is usually spelled *ei*.

believe
field
grief
niece ⎬ pronounced with long *e* (ē)
piece
relieve
yield

barrier
cashier } with other pronunciations
efficient
science

After *c* or when pronounced ā, the combination is likely to be *ei:*

ceiling
conceit, conceive
deceit, deceive } after *c*
perceive
receive

eight
freight
inveigh } pronounced ā
neighbor
weigh

Exceptions: *either, forfeit, height, leisure, neither, seize, their, weird, financier, species.*

(6) **A few additional helps may be given for plurals.**

(a) Most plurals are formed by adding *s* to the singular.

books, colleges, comparisons, radios, Belgians, slices

(b) If a singular ends in *s* or *ch, sh, x,* or *z,* add *es.*

losses, watches, dishes, taxes, quizzes

(c) Singulars ending in *o* add *s* or *es.*

solos, heroes, pianos, tomatoes

(d) Singulars in *f, ff,* and *fe* sometimes use *s* and sometimes *ves* for the plural.

waif, waifs; self, selves; cliff, cliffs; staff, staffs or staves; fife, fifes; knife, knives

(e) Some plurals are irregular.

men, women, children, sheep, dice, geese, crises, criteria, media (or mediums), formulae (or formulas)

511

There are other rules, each with exceptions, but if you learn to apply the few rules stated here, you will be helped with hundreds of common words.

46b *Take special care to avoid mispronunciations that lead to misspelling.*

Here is a list of a few words that often cause trouble because they are mispronounced. Practice pronouncing them correctly; do not hesitate to exaggerate a little as you say the syllables of words like *gov-ern-ment.*

arctic	mischievous
arthritis	perspiration
athlete	presumptuous
disastrous	remembrance
drowned	sophomore
environment	surprise
February	tragedy
irrelevant	undoubtedly

46c *Distinguish between words that look or sound alike or somewhat alike.*

Here are a few such often-confused words:

*accept, except	costumes, customs
*adapt, adopt	formally, formerly
advice, advise	*loose, lose
*affect, effect	passed, past
*allusion, illusion	persecute, prosecute
anecdote, antidote	*principal, principle
breath, breathe	respectfully, respectively
censor, censure	sight, site, cite
choose, chose	*than, then
close, clothes	*their, there, they're
*complement, compliment	*to, too, two
conscience, conscious	weather, wether, whether
consul, council, counsel	weight, wait

* Words starred are discussed in the Glossary, **47.**

46d Become familiar with common prefixes and suffixes.

If you learn the meaning of common prefixes and suffixes, you will be helped with the spelling of many words. Here are a few common prefixes and suffixes. Your dictionary will have many more.

ante– (before), antedate
anti– (against), anticlimax
–cide (kill), homicide, suicide
circum– (around), circumference
dis– (not), disappoint, disappear
–ful (full), careful, handful
hyper– (in excess), hypersensitive, hyperthyroid
hypo– (under, diminished), hypothyroid
in– (in), income, induce
in– (not), involuntary, indecent
inter– (between, among), international, interpose
intra–, intro– (within), intramural, introduce
mis– (wrong), misrule, misspelling
pre– (before), prepare, preschool
un– (not), unfair, unnatural

46e Try tricks of association to improve your spelling.

For some people, tricks of association are often more helpful than the rules. The absurdity of the association does not matter; indeed, the more absurd the association, sometimes, the more help it gives. If you have trouble remembering that the verb *lose* does not have a double o, you might think "lose an o," then say the phrase over a few times, and be sure of *lose* for the rest of your life. If you have trouble with *similar*, you might think of a phrase like "be particu*lar* about simi*lar*." Such tricks of association are often employed for other purposes by people who have trained their memories, and there is no reason why they should not be used in learning how to spell.

513

46f *Pay particular attention to troublesome words.*

Study the following list of words frequently misspelled. Check the words that have given you trouble; write each one correctly five times. Or try this method: have someone read the whole list to you as you write it; after comparing your spellings with those here, write five times each word that you misspell; during the next week write these same words every day.

From themes you have written you may be able to make a list of your own; such a list is for you better than the following or any other. (See **46g.**)

accept	clothes	equipped
accidentally	coherence	equivalent
accommodate	committee	exaggerate
accompanying	competition	exhaust
achievement	concede	existence
acquaintance	condemn	extravagant
across	conquer	familiar
advice (noun)	conqueror	fascinate
advise (verb)	conscience	February
aggressive	continuous	foreign
allege	controversial	forty-four
all right	coordinate	friend
amateur	(*Or:* co-ordinate)	fulfill
analyze	criticism	fundamental
apparent	decision	genius
arctic	definitely	grammar
argument	dependent	granary
athletic	desperate	guarantee
attendant	develop	handicap
beginning	dictionary	handicapped
believe	difference	handkerchief
benefit	disappoint	hindrance
boundary	disastrous	imitate
bouquet	discussed	immediately
breathe	eighth	imminent
category	eligible	independent
choose	embarrass	initiate
chosen	equipment	inoculate

interrupt
irrelevant
laboratory
later
latter
led
maintenance
marriage
minimum
miscellaneous
mischief
mischievous
misleading
misspell
monetary
necessary
noticeable
obstacle
occasion
occurred
omit, omitting
opportunity
parallel
pastime
perform

playwright
politics
possession
precede
prejudice
prevalent
privilege
procedure
proceed
profession
professor
psychology
pursuit
quiet
quite
receive
recommend
referred
remembrance
repetition
resistance
sanitary
schedule
secretary
seize

sensitive
separate
serviceable
siege
significant
similar
sophomore
specimen
stretch
studying
supersede
surprise
temperament
therefore
tragedy
truly
unconscious
undoubtedly
until
villain
weather
whether
woman, women
writing

46g *Keep a list of words that have been troublesome to you.*

Exercise 1

Which of the rules in **46a** or the notes accompanying them applies to each of the following words? Be prepared to explain your answers.

1. reciting	11. recital
2. insurance	12. swapped
3. indemnities	13. advantageous
4. exhibited	14. worries
5. pried	15. reference
6. valleys	16. thirtieth
7. incitement	17. neigh
8. grabbed	18. ditches
9. receipt	20. wield
10. burying	19. mannish

Exercise 2

Which rule or accompanying note in **46a** is violated by each of the following words? Spell the words correctly. Be prepared to explain your answers. (The words in parentheses are the root words.)

1. omited (omit)	11. batchs
2. shys (shy)	12. thirtyeth (thirty)
3. comming (come)	13. writter (write)
4. purly (pure)	14. feindish
5. chargable (charge)	15. occurence (occur)
6. hurring (hurry)	16. bodys (body)
7. decieve	17. wieght
8. hiting (hit)	18. poolling (pool)
9. greive	19. polling (pole)
10. redish (red)	20. allies (alley)

Exercise 3

Underline all misspellings in the following passage. On a separate piece of paper, spell each of the underlined words correctly.

The house I use to live in out in the country stands on a quite, shadey little lane in between two mapel trees. Shrubery and grass are abundant around it. The shrubbery (high mock orange and golden forsythia) greets the visiter who starts up the stone walk. Hugh trelases of red roses are at the doorway. Around the bronze male box climb mourning glories that my mother planted.

GLOSSARY

47 Glossary

This glossary includes two kinds of items. First, capitalized, are definitions, mostly of common grammatical terms. Second, not capitalized, are words and phrases often confused and misused. Neither set of items, of course, is complete: if you cannot find a grammatical term here, look in the index; for other words that you cannot find and that give you difficulty, consult a dictionary.

Absolute phrase. A group of words not part of the grammatical construction of the sentence but connected logically with the main thought. The word *absolute* is somewhat misleading; such phrases are not punctuated as separate sentences, as independent clauses can be. What is usually referred to by the term "absolute phrase" is a group of words containing a noun or pronoun followed by a participle. (The alarm having rung, we got up sleepily. We got up sleepily, the alarm still ringing in our ears.) At the beginning of a sentence, an absolute phrase such as *the alarm having rung* is characteristic of a somewhat formal style; a clause like *after the alarm rang* is less formal.

Abstract words. Words that refer to ideas, qualities, concepts (*grandeur, isolation, vigor, happiness, honesty*). They are necessarily rather general and unspecific. Their opposite is concrete words, which by naming specific things give sense impressions (*tallow candle, ashtray, copper nail, cheese sandwich, tears, rain*). Very little writing could be done without abstract words, but concrete words give pictures and refer to more definite things. In general, use language that is as concrete as possible.

accept, except. *Accept* means "to receive"; *except* means "to exclude." (He accepted the explanation. He excepted the third chapter from the examination.)

accidently. The right spelling is *accidentally*.

Active voice. See *Voice*.

adapt, adopt. *Adapt* means "to change to suit one's needs"; *adopt* means "to accept" or "to agree to." (We adapted the architect's plans to fit our requirements. The club adopted the committee's recommendations.)

Adjective. A word that describes or identifies a noun or pronoun (*blue* candles, a *hundred* freshmen, *running* water, *poor* me, *Japanese* food). See **15a.**

Adverb. A word that modifies a verb (swam *swiftly*), an adjective (*genuinely* new), or an adverb (*very* easily). See **15b.** Conjunctive adverbs (*however, indeed, therefore*) connect independent clauses or sentences. See **18c.**

affect, effect. *Affect* means "to influence" or "to assume"; *effect*, as a verb, means "to bring about." (His poor spelling affected his chances of getting the job. He wants to effect an improvement in the accounting system.) *Effect* as a noun means "result." (What was the effect of his being there?)

aggravate. In the meaning of "irritate" or "annoy," this is colloquial but long established. In formal writing, limit its meaning to "make worse." (His constant blowing on the horn annoyed me and aggravated my headache.)

Agreement. The correspondence between subject and verb (I am; he is; we are, etc.) or between pronoun and antecedent (Charles has done *his* work well).

ain't. Although a contraction of *am not* is needed, *ain't* has been condemned as illiterate and should not be used in writing or seriously in speech.

alibi. Formally, a legal term used of an accused person who says he was not at the place where the crime was committed. Do not use the word in the meaning of "excuse." (What excuse [*not* alibi] did he have for not coming to class?)

all ready, already. *All ready* means "entirely ready"; *already* means "by this (or that) time." (They were all ready to leave an hour ago; in fact, they are already on their way.)

all the farther. As a substitute for *as far as,* this is dialectal and should not be used in serious writing. (That is as far as [*not* all the farther] he went.)

all together, altogether. *All together* means "in a group"; *altogether* means "completely." (We cousins, who were all together in the living room, decided we were not altogether satisfied with the family reunion.)

allusion, delusion, illusion. *Allusion* means "an indirect reference." *Illusion* means a "misconception or false idea." *Delusion* also means "a misconception," but it intensifies the meaning and often suggests a neurotic cause for the error. (The professor made an allusion to the Greeks; he said it is an illusion to think that the ancient Athenians admired their philosophers more than their athletes. He further said that few people would have suffered from the delusion that they were Socrates or Plato.)

alot. This should be two words: *a lot.* However spelled, the expression is often vague. (The blizzard delayed me for two days [*not* a lot].)

alright. The standard spelling is *all right*—as two words.

alumnus, etc. *Alumnus* refers to a masculine graduate, *alumna* to a feminine graduate. *Alumni* is the masculine plural, *alumnae* the feminine plural. *Alumni* is used for both men and women.

among, between. *Among* applies to three or more persons or things; *between* usually refers to only two. (Her property was divided among her four children. The jewels were divided between the twins.) Sometimes *between* applies to more than two. (The elm tree marks the dividing point between the four lots.)

amount, number. *Amount* refers to quantity or bulk, *number* to things that can be counted. (The number of patients in the hospital is great; the amount of sickness is appalling.)

and. A foolish belief exists that sentences should never begin with *and* or *but.* A glance at any good book or magazine will disprove this false notion.

and etc. Redundant, because the first two letters of *etc.* are the Latin *et,* meaning "and."

Antecedent. The word or idea to which a pronoun refers. (In his haste Ed said that he could not wait for the girls, who had not yet arrived. [*Ed* is the antecedent of *his* and *he; girls* is the antecedent of *who.*])

anxious, eager. To be anxious means "to be worried or fearful"; to be eager means "to have strong, impatient longing." (Aunt Martha is anxious about her weight, but she is always eager to dine out where the servings are large.)

Appositive. An expression that follows and renames another word. In the sentence "The local radio station, WRTI, will put on our program," *WRTI* is a renaming of *the local radio station.* In meaning, the two are approximately equivalent.

Archaic. Words that are archaic have long been out of use, although they may be preserved in older literature or in the Bible (Judge not, that *ye* be not judged). Inexperienced writers sometimes think archaic expressions like *prithee* (I prithee, Bud, how art thou?) are amusing. Such humor belongs to adolescence.

Article. There are three articles in English grammar—*a, an,* and *the. A* and *an* are called indefinite articles, *the* the definite article.

as. In the causal sense, *as* is less specific than *because, for,* and *since.* (I went to the circus because [*not* as] I liked animals.) Sometimes *as* is ambiguous (As I was going to the circus, I borrowed five dollars. [Does *as* here mean "while" or "because"?])

at. Redundant after *where* in such sentences as "I don't know where I'm at" and "Where did he put it at?" In writing—and in careful speech—omit *at* in such situations.

Auxiliary verb. A verb that assists another verb to form a verb phrase: in *has eaten,* the auxiliary is *has.* The chief auxiliary verbs are the various forms of *have, do, be, can, may, shall, will, must, ought.* (We *had been* notified. He *will* know the price. She *may have* gone.) See **12f.**

awful, terrible, terrific, etc. Colloquial, overused intensives (That hairdo is awful; the apple pie is terrific). In writing, use these words with exactness (Lincoln knew his awful responsibility. The man's suffering was a terrible thing to watch. The tornado struck the town with terrific violence).

being as. Not standard English in the sense of "because." (Because [*not* being as] I was late, I missed the train.)

beside, besides. *Beside* means "at the side of"; *besides* means "in addition" or "in addition to." (He sat down beside her. Besides, they never pay their debts. Besides writing three letters he did his French assignment.)

between. See *among*.

broke. A colloquialism often essential in college speech but not appropriate in serious writing.

but. See *and* for comment on *but* at the beginning of a sentence.

but what. Use *that* instead of *but what* in sentences like "I never doubted in those days that (*not* but what) Santa Claus would come."

can, may. *Can* means "having the power to do something" (He can speak Spanish easily); *may* suggests "being possible or having permission" (He may buy a car if he can pay for it). The use of *can* in the sense of *may* is colloquial (My father says I can buy a car).

cannot help but. A mixed construction now very common colloquially but not fully accepted in formal writing. Omit *but*. (He can't help being lonely. *Not* He can't help but be lonely.)

can't hardly, can't scarcely. Since *hardly* carries a negative meaning, *can't hardly* is a double negative—as is *can't scarcely* for the same reason. Say "He can hardly spell; she can scarcely think."

case. Overused and a contributor to wordiness and vagueness. (I am opposed to Mulvaney for mayor. [*Not* In any case, I am opposed. . . .] Some of the screens are torn and must be replaced.

[*Not* Some of the screens are torn; in such cases they must be replaced.])

Case. The form a noun or pronoun takes to indicate its grammatical use—that is, its relation to other words in the sentence. Case endings are numerous in German and Latin, but few in modern English. Today we nearly always show that a word is subject or object by its position in the sentence and by using prepositions. (The basic order is subject-verb-object.) In nouns, two cases survive—the common (*boy*) and the possessive (*boy's*). For a few pronouns, there are three cases—the subjective, the case of the subject (*I, he, they*); the possessive (*my, his, their*); and the objective, the case of the direct or indirect object (*me, him, them*). See **11.**

character. Often vaguely and inaccurately used. Try to get rid of it in sentences like "His thinking was of a confused character." Better: "His thinking was confused."

Clause. A group of words containing a subject and predicate. A clause may be independent (also called *main* or *principal* clause) or dependent (also called *subordinate*). Dependent clauses may be used as nouns, adjectives, or adverbs. In the following sentence the words before the comma are a dependent clause, the words after the comma an independent clause: When she saw him, she tried to look pleased. See **2b.**

Cliché. An expression, perhaps once apt and vivid, that has been appropriated again and again by inept writers and speakers. The cliché is likely to make writing seem both empty and insincere. Clichés are also called trite or hackneyed expressions, or stereotypes. *Pure as the driven snow* and *last but not least* are examples of clichés. See page 100.

Collective noun. See *Noun.*

Colloquial language. The language used in conversation and informal writing. There is nothing wrong with it, though it may not be appropriate to certain levels of writing, especially formal levels. *Isn't* is colloquial; *is not* is the form more common in standard written English. Your subject and your audience must tell you whether colloquial language is appropriate or not. Certainly much good writing makes use of the familiar, easy tone of colloquialisms.

Common noun.   See *Noun.*

complected.   Colloquial or dialectal. Say "She has a light complexion," *not* "She is light complected."

Complement.   The word or group of words that completes the meaning of a predicate. The complement may be an object, a predicate noun, a predicate adjective, or an objective complement.
> *Object:* He broke the *glass.*
> *Predicate noun:* This is the *truth.*
> *Predicate adjective:* This is *true.*
> *Objective complement:* They named her the best *dancer.* He painted his house *white.*

Predicate nouns and predicate adjectives are called subjective complements. An objective complement renames or modifies the direct object.

Complex sentence.   See *Sentence.*

Compound sentence.   See *Sentence.*

Compound-complex sentence.   See *Sentence.*

Compound subject.   See *Subject.*

Concrete word.   See *Abstract word.*

Conjunction.   Words linking parts of sentences (words, phrases, or clauses) or whole sentences together. Conjunctions may be coordinating (simple: *and, but, for, or, nor, so, yet;* correlative: *either . . . or, both . . . and,* etc.) or subordinating (*after, although, because, if, that, unless, until, when, where,* etc.)

Conjunctive adverb.   See *Adverb.*

contact.   As a verb, overused business jargon. Instead of *contact me* say "write to me," "meet me," "get in touch with me." As a noun referring to a touching or junction of bodies, *contact* is standard usage (The wire is in contact with the ground).

continual, continuous.   In formal usage, *continual* means "often repeated"; *continuous* means "going on without a break." (The ringing of the doorbell that day was continual. The whir of the machinery in the factory was continuous.)

continue on. *On* is sometimes redundant. (He will continue with his experiments.)

Contractions. Words formed by omitting a letter or a sound— for example, *aren't, can't, isn't, I've, we'll.* Used in colloquial and most informal writing, though not in formal style.

Coordinate elements. Parts of a sentence that are the same grammatically (two nouns, two clauses, etc.): *quickly* but *ineffectively* (two adverbs), *in sickness* and *in health* (two prepositional phrases), *after we had met* but *before we had voted on anything* (two dependent clauses).

Coordinating conjunction. See *Conjunction.*

Copula. Means the same as *linking verb.* See *Verb.*

Correlative conjunction. See *Conjunction.*

could of. Illiterate for *could have.*

credible, creditable, credulous. *Credible* means "believable" (His account of the crime is so credible that no one will dispute it); *creditable* means "worthy of praise" (His generosity to the library is most creditable); a person is *credulous* if he is ready to believe, especially if he is so ready to believe that he seems gullible (The alleged proof impressed only the credulous).

data. Originally the plural of the Latin *datum, data* is now used as singular or plural. (*Singular:* Not much data has become available. *Plural:* The data he has submitted are not widely known.) Formal usage still generally treats it as plural. but there is a growing tendency to think of it as singular—as, in other words, a collective noun referring to a set of factual material.

definitely. An overused word that can usually be omitted when it is an intensive. (He likes this soup very much. [*Not* He definitely likes this soup.])

Degree. A form used in the comparison of adjectives and adverbs. The degrees are positive, comparative, and superlative (*positive:* fast, popular; *comparative:* faster, more popular, less popular; *superlative:* fastest, most popular, least popular).

delusion. See *allusion.*

Demonstrative. The demonstratives (*this, that, these, those*) point out. They may be adjectives (*this* hat, *those* shoes) or pronouns (*This* is the hat; *those* are the shoes).

Dependent clause. See *Clause.*

different from, different than. American usage prefers *different from* when a noun or pronoun follows it (College is different from high school) but *different than* when a clause follows (College is different than I expected it to be).

Direct address. The name of a person or thing spoken to directly. (Come here, *Alice.* That, *gentlemen,* finishes our business. Twinkle, twinkle, *little star.*) A name used in direct address is also called the *vocative.*

Direct object. See *Object.*

Direct question. The exact words of a question: Bob asked, "What should we do now?" The indirect form would be: Bob asked what they should do now. See **31a.**

disinterested, uninterested. *Disinterested* means "impartial, having no selfish interest"; *uninterested* means "having no interest." (A judge should be disinterested; he should not be uninterested.)

don't. Acceptable, like other contractions, in speech and informal writing as a contraction of *do not.* The contraction of *does not* is *doesn't.* (He doesn't; I don't; they don't.)

due to. As an equivalent of *because of,* this phrase is still sometimes objected to, though it seems to be on its way to general acceptance. (*Doubtful in formal writing:* Due to the janitor's confusion, the library closed an hour early. *Acceptable:* Because of the janitor's confusion, the library closed an hour early.) Since *due* is an adjective, *due to* may safely be used after forms of the verb *to be*. (The closing of the library an hour early was due to the janitor's confusion. My illness is not due to hard work.)

Ellipsis. (1) A mark (three periods) used to indicate an omission from a sentence. See **30c.** (2) A construction omitting words that are readily supplied or "understood." (He is younger than she [is young].)

enthuse. Colloquial. In writing, prefer expressions like *is enthusiastic, grew enthusiastic*, and *made me enthusiastic*.

etc. Abbreviation for *et cetera*, equivalent to *and so forth*. In ordinary writing it should almost never be used. Instead of saying that "the Yankees have good pitching, good hitting, etc.," say that "the Yankees have good pitching and good hitting." If you know of other details that should be given, give them; don't use *etc.* to avoid the bother: "The Yankees have good pitching; they can hit, especially when a hit means a run; and their reserves are almost as good as their regulars." Note, however, that *etc.* is appropriate when one is mentioning items of a list which the reader himself can continue. The abbreviation is so used at various points in this Glossary. See, for instance, under *Pronoun*.

Do not use *etc.* at the end of a list beginning with *such as*. (The class studied many prefixes, such as *geo, neo, pre,* and *post*. [*Not pre, post*, etc.])

See also *and etc.*

except. See *accept*.

Expletive. *It* and *there* are expletives when they act simply as introductory fillers. *There* is not a subject, though it stands in the position usually occupied by the subject.

There is little reason for his outburst. (Subject: reason)
It is my intention to do my best. (Here *it* is an expletive.)
Where is my hat? It is here. (*It* is not an expletive in the second sentence.)

fabulous. Leave this overused intensive to second-rate advertising.

528

fact that. The *fact that* is usually a wordy substitute for *that*. (I discovered that [*not* the fact that] Shelley and Keats were not friends.)

fellow. Colloquial for *boy, man*.

fewer, less. *Fewer* refers to number, *less* to amount. (Less corn is being raised. There will be fewer bushels to the acre. Fewer trees are being grown.)

Figure of speech. An expression used in other than its plain, literal sense or ordinary way. Figures often suggest comparisons and create pictures. It is a plain, nonfigurative statement to say that the world before World War I was completely different from the world afterwards. It is figurative to say, as Rebecca West does, that World War I was the crack that split time from side to side.

Figures may be of a number of kinds. The most common are similes and metaphors. In a simile, *like* or *as* makes a comparison explicit: something is like something else. In a metaphor the comparison is implied; no *like* or *as* is used.

Simile: The dandelions lay like spots of yellow light on the grass.
Metaphor: The dandelions were spots of yellow light on the grass.

Finite verb. See *Verb*.

fix. Colloquial in the sense of "repair" or "predicament."

Gender. The characteristic of a word that shows the sex or lack of it of the person, animal, or thing referred to. Gender in modern English presents few difficulties. A pronoun has the same gender as its antecedent.

Genitive case. This is the same case as the possessive. See *Case*.

Gerund. See *Verbal*.

good, well. *Good* is an adjective (a good man, the play was good). Do not use as an adverb (*Substandard:* He works good). *Well* is an adjective or adverb. As an adjective it means "in health" (He looks well); as an adverb it means "in a good manner" (He works well).

graduated from. The idiomatic form includes *from.* (She graduated from Westlake High School. *Not* She graduated high school.)

hanged, hung. Strict usage calls for *hanged* to refer to executions and for *hung* in other uses. (The murderer was hanged on Monday. She hung the picture on the east wall.) There is a strong and understandable tendency to use *hung* in all senses.

human. An adjective (the human race). Not fully established as a noun. Many readers will find a sentence like "A human should not live there" slightly comical. Substitute *man* or *human being.*

Idiom. A word combination peculiar to a language and sometimes difficult to explain logically or even grammatically. *To take after* (to resemble), *to take to* (to become fond of), *to take on* (to undertake) are idioms. See **17e.**

Idiomatic language. A style that follows the standard, natural patterns of a language is idiomatic. English sentences, for example, are put together differently than sentences in French or German.

> *French:* Il a dix ans. (*Literally:* He has ten years. That is, in the English idiomatic pattern: He is ten years old.)
> *German:* Ich werde ihn bald sehen. (*Literally:* I shall him soon see. The English pattern is different: I shall see him soon.)

illusion. See *allusion.*

Imperative. See *Mood.*

imply, infer. To *imply* is to hint at something or suggest it without actually stating it (In what he said the instructor implied that the test would be difficult); to *infer* is to draw a conclusion (The students inferred from what he said that they should study).

Independent clause. See *Clause.*

Indicative mood. See *Mood.*

Indirect object. See *Object.*

Indirect question. See *Direct question.*

Infinitive. See *Verbal.*

in regard to. Never say "in regards to." Often the expression is better avoided altogether. (He did not know what to do about [*not* in regard to] the letter.)

Intensive pronoun. See *Pronoun.*

Interjection. An exclamatory word or phrase, such as *oh, tut-tut, alas.*

Interrogative pronoun. See *Pronoun.*

Intransitive verb. See *Verb.*

irregardless. A substandard confusion of *regardless* and words like *irregular.* Say *regardless.*

Irregular verb. See *Verb.*

is when, is where. Wordy and often inaccurate in definitions. Revise, omitting *when* and *where.* (In baseball there are nine men on a side. [*Not* Baseball is where there are nine men on a side.] A monarchy is a country ruled by a king. [*Not* A monarchy is when a country is ruled by a king.]) *Is when* and *is where* are natural in constructions involving time (*when*) or place (*where*). (April is when you should be there. That corner is where the accident happened. This is where you get off.)

its, it's. *Its* is a possessive (The bird built its nest). *It's* is a contracted form of *it is* (It's raining) or *it has* (It's been raining).

kind, sort. Singular words. Colloquial when used in the sense of "rather," "somewhat," and so on. (She looks rather [*Not* kind of] pale.) But standard English in expressions like "What kind of tree is that?" Do not say "What kind of *a* tree. . . ."

lead, led. *Led,* the past tense and past participle of the verb, is pronounced the same as the name of the metal, *lead.* (The path led us down to the old lead mine.)

leave, let. *Leave* means "to depart" or "to abandon" (He left the book on the table. I am going to leave home); *let* means "to allow" (Let me have ten dollars. I hope she will let me go).

like, as, as if. Traditionally, *like* is used as a preposition with a noun or pronoun as its object (He wept like a child. They would never consider anyone like me for the job), and *as* and *as if* as conjunctions introducing clauses (It rains as if it would never stop. It rains here as it does in Texas). *Like* instead of *as* or *as if* is common in speech (He holds his bat like you do. It rains here like it does in Texas), but it almost never occurs in good writing.

Linking verb. See *Verb.*

literally. Overused and misused. *Literally* means that words are to be taken exactly as they are stated, not in a figurative sense. When someone says he was literally burned up or was literally boiled by the heat or has literally worked his head off, we know he is using *literally* in a careless way that weakens it. (*Exact:* He literally showed his teeth. [His teeth were visible.])

loose, lose. *Loose* is commonly used as an adjective; *lose* is always a verb. (A loose bolt caused him to lose the race.)

Main clause. Also called *independent clause.* See *Clause.*

majority. More than half of a number of voters, ballots, and the like. (The majority of the jury voted against Socrates.) The word should not be used loosely for *most.* (Most [*Not* The majority] of the radio programs were very dull.)

Metaphor. See *Figure of speech.*

might of. Illiterate for *might have.*

Mode. See *Mood.*

Modifier. A world that qualifies or describes another word or makes its meaning more precise. Modifiers are adjectives or adverbs (or words, phrases, or clauses used like them). See *Adjective* and *Adverb.*

Mood (or Mode). The mood of a verb may be indicative to make a statement or ask a question, imperative to make a command, or subjunctive to show doubt, possibility, a wish, or a condition contrary to fact.

> *Indicative:* He *finished* the painting. *Is* that the price?
> *Imperative: Keep* him here. *Leave* the rest to me.
> *Subjunctive:* I wish I *were* there.

Most writing is in the indicative mood.

morale. A noun denoting attitude as reflecting or not reflecting courage and confidence. Not to be confused with the adjective *moral* or the noun *morals*. (His moral intentions were high, but his morale was low.)

most, almost. *Most* is the superlative form of *much* and *many* (He has done most of the work. Most of the voters preferred Feldman); *almost* means "nearly" (Almost [*not* Most] everyone is here. He has done almost all [*not* most all] of the work).

nature. Contributes to vagueness and wordiness in sentences like "The talk was of a helpful nature" or "The talk was helpful in nature." Say "The talk was helpful."

Nominative case. The same as *subjective case*. See *Case.*

none. This word is singular or plural, depending on the meaning. (None of the house was damaged. None of the children were hurt.)

Nonrestrictive modifier. A clause or phrase not used to identify the word it modifies. (My report, *which is due next Wednesday*, deals with the last days of Maximilian.)

Noun. The name of a person, place, thing, idea, or condition. A noun may be *abstract* or *concrete* (see *Abstract words*). It may be *proper* (the name of a particular person or thing: *Alice, Byron, Italy*) or *common* (the name of a class of persons or things: *woman, poet, country*). Some nouns are *collective*—that is, they have a singular form but may be thought of as either singular or plural: *team, band, jury, flock.*

Number. Number is singular or plural. The form of nouns, pronouns, and verbs is affected by number.
Noun: boy, house, mouse; boys, houses, mice
Pronoun: I, he; we, they
Verb: am, is, (he) takes; are, take

Object. A substantive may be the object of a preposition or of a verb. The object of a preposition is a substantive that follows a preposition (in the *air*, for *me*, to *whoever speaks first*). The object of a verb may be direct or indirect. The direct object is the substantive that completes a transitive verb and is affected di-

533

rectly by the action of the verb. It normally follows a verb. (He gave his *answer*. Tom put the *letter* in his pocket.) The indirect object is affected indirectly by the action of the verb; it names the person to whom or for whom (or the thing to which or for which) the action is performed. The idea of the indirect object can usually be expressed in a prepositional phrase with *to* or *for*. (He handed *me* the oars. He handed the oars *to me*. He gave *his school* a great amount of money. We bought *Joan* a camera.)

Objective complement. See *Complement*.

off of. Colloquial for *off*. In writing, drop the *of*. (I think you are off [*not* off of] the subject.)

Parallel construction. Sentence elements of similar grammatical form placed so as to show similarity in purpose or meaning. For example, in the following sentence the prepositional phrases are parallel: The snow fell *in the streets, in the fields,* and *on the housetops*.

Participle. See *Verbal*.

Parts of speech. The grammatical classes that words are divided into according to their form, meaning, and use. The traditional terms (often questioned by some grammarians in recent years) are noun, pronoun, verb, adjective, adverb, conjunction, preposition, and interjection.

Passive voice. See *Voice*.

per. Except in commercial expressions (*per yard, per ounce*), *a* is better. (There will be two issues a month. They ate four times a day.)

Person. Indicates in verbs and substantives the person who is speaking (first person), the person spoken to (second person), and the person spoken of (third person). Nouns are considered of course as third person.

> *First person:* I (we) walk.
> *Second person:* You walk.
> *Third person:* He (she, it) walks, they walk, the bird sings.

phone. A colloquialism established in informal writing but not accepted yet in formal usage. (*Informal:* I phoned the office. *Formal:* I telephoned the office.)

Phrase. A group of related words acting as a grammatical unit and lacking a subject and verb. Distinguish from a clause. The phrases in the following sentence are italicized: *To cover her embarrassment* she ran *across the room.* See **2a.**

plus. Do not use loosely for *and.* "Say the parents and [*not* plus] their children."

Possessive case. The form of a noun or pronoun showing ownership (the *man's* car, *her* coat) or an analogous relationship (a *week's* delay, *his* honesty). See *Case.*

Predicate. The part of a clause that consists of the verb and any objects, complements, and modifiers associated with it. In the following sentences the predicate is italicized: I *ran.* The wind *was icy.* Leaning forward, the rider in the grey jacket *wheeled his horse sharply to the left.* See **3b.**

Predicate adjective. An adjective following a linking verb and modifying the subject that precedes the verb. See *Complement.* (The weather is *cool.* [= cool weather] His hair grew *long.* [= long hair])

Predicate nominative. See *Predicate noun.*

Predicate noun. A noun following a linking verb and renaming or identifying the subject that precedes the verb. See *Complement.* (Betty is my *cousin.* George became a *doctor.*)

Preposition. A word that relates its object (a noun or other substantive) to another part of the sentence. The preposition and its object combine to form a prepositional phrase. Some of the common prepositions are *at, to, in, into, on, of, from, for, between, about, above, with, without, behind, under, over, through, by.*

Prepositional phrase. A phrase made up of a preposition, its object, and any modifiers of the object. If the object is a pronoun, it is in the objective case. See **11d.**

A friend *of Dick's* who lives *in Montana* has asked a favor *of me.*
Send an invitation *to whoever is near.* (Clause as object)
He has had little practice *in independent thinking.* (Gerund as object)

principal, principle. *Principal* as an adjective means "chief" or "most important" (That is the principal source of trouble); as a noun it means "a leading person or thing" or "accumulated wealth" (The principal of the school found that he would have to use some of the principal of his wife's inheritance). *Principle* means "a rule of conduct" (His principal trouble is his lack of principles).

Principal parts. See *Verb.*

Progressive verb. A verb phrase that combines a form of *to be* and the present participle (ending in *ing*). (I *am swimming,* I *was reading,* I *have been listening.*)

Pronoun. A word that takes the place of a noun and that has the uses (as subject, object, etc.) of a noun. Most pronouns have an antecedent—that is, a noun or pronoun, expressed or understood—which they refer to. (The house belongs to a man *who* built *it* in *his* spare time.) Pronouns are classified as follows:

Personal: I, we, you, he, she, it, they (and the possessive and objective forms: my, our, us, etc.)

Interrogative: who, whom, whose, which, what (when they introduce a question)

Relative: who, whose, whom, which, that, whoever, etc.

Demonstrative: this, that, these, those

Indefinite: any, anyone, anything, both, each, either, everybody, everyone, neither, none, one, some, someone

Reflexive: myself, ourselves, etc. (He pinched *himself.*)

Intensive: myself, ourselves, etc. (the same form as the reflexive, but used for emphasis: He ate it *himself.*)

Reciprocal: each other, one another

Proper noun. See *Noun.*

536

real. Colloquial as an adverb meaning "really" or "very." (That dress is very [*not* real] pretty.)

reason is because. Common informally but still not accepted in formal writing. Prefer *the reason is that* (The reason he eats carrots is that [*not* because] he thinks they improve his eyesight) or a more concise restatement of the sentence (He eats carrots because he thinks they improve his eyesight).

Redundancy. Needless repetition: I knew all my fellow co-workers. (Say *my fellow workers* or *my co-workers*.)

Reflexive pronoun. See *Pronoun*.

Regular verb. See *Verb*.

Relative pronoun. See *Pronoun*.

Restrictive modifier. A phrase or clause that identifies—or helps identify—the word it modifies. (The book *that I found* belongs to Bill.)

reverend. Usage varies as follows: *Formal:* the Reverend Joseph S. Stevenson or the Reverend Mr. [or Dr.] Stevenson; *informal:* Reverend Joseph S. Stevenson or Reverend Mr. Stevenson; *substandard:* Rev. Stevenson.

said. As an adjective, this is familiar in legal jargon. In nonlegal writing it is crude. (I took said book to the library.) As humor, it is flat and juvenile.

same. As a pronoun, this is chiefly legal jargon. In ordinary writing it should usually be replaced by words like *it, that,* and *this.* (You will need to prove this [*not* the same] to me. Mary had a little lamb and brought it [*not* same] to school.)

seldom ever. Not idiomatic. Say *hardly ever, seldom, seldom if ever.*

Sentence. A word or group of related words making an independent statement and ending with a period, a question mark, or an exclamation mark. A sentence usually has a grammatical subject and predicate. Sentences are classed as simple, compound, complex, and compound-complex. See **3g**.

Simple (one independent clause): *Hamlet* is my favorite play.

Compound (two or more independent clauses): I am a freshman; he is a sophomore.

Complex (one independent clause and one or more dependent clauses): I am not going to the movies until I finish writing my history report.

Compound-complex (two or more independent clauses and one or more dependent clauses): I would like to take a vacation but I cannot get away until this work is done.

should of. Illiterate for *should have.*

Simple sentence. See *Sentence.*

so. As a connective, appropriate in casual, informal writing (I studied hard, so I got through all right) but seldom as precise as a carefully chosen connective would be. (Because the Student Council does not represent student opinion, we are urging a new voting system. [*Not* The Student Council does not represent student opinion, so we are urging a new voting system.]) As an intensive (so nice, so new) it should not be overworked.

some. Colloquial in the adverbial sense of "somewhat" (I feel some better than I did); slang as an intensive (That's some answer).

somewheres. Dialect for *somewhere.*

sort, sort of. See *kind, kind of.*

Standard English. A term indicating the language—formal and informal—that is used in magazines and books, that is expected in the carrying on of business and professional work, and that is the basis of all letters and speech except the most informal. It includes most of the words in any ordinary dictionary and also includes accepted grammatical forms, constructions, and idioms. It excludes expressions commonly considered "ungrammatical" and inappropriate for educated persons (I seen him. It wasn't no use arguing with him); it excludes dialect (This is all the farther I can go); it excludes slang (Do you really dig *Hamlet?*). Standard

English is the language every college student needs to learn to use.

Authors of course regularly use nonstandard English in records of conversation and occasionally as the chief medium of communication. *Huckleberry Finn,* for example, is told entirely in dialect.

Strong verb. A name sometimes given to what is more commonly called the *irregular verb.* See *Verb.*

Subject of a sentence. The term about which something is asserted. The subject is a substantive. The subject may be simple (Tom) or compound (Tom and Mary). See **3a.**

Subjunctive mood. See *Mood.*

Subordinate clause. "Subordinate clause" and "dependent clause" are two names for the same thing. See *Clause.*

Substantive. A noun or noun equivalent. Though the most common substantives are nouns and pronouns, clauses are often used as substantives. In "Whoever comes now will have to stand," "whoever comes now" is a substantive clause—or a noun clause (as it is more commonly called)—since it is used as a noun, as subject of the sentence. Verbals that perform the function of nouns are also substantives: "*Swimming* is fun"; "*To swim* is fun."

Superlative degree. See *Degree.*

sure. Standard as an adjective (He painted with a sure hand) but colloquial as an adverb meaning "surely" or "certainly." (That was sure an interesting story. Substitute *certainly* for *sure.*)

swell. Overused slang praising something (That performance of *King Lear* was swell). Find a more exact substitute.

Syntax. The relating of words to one another in sentence structures—putting them together into phrases, clauses, and sentences.

Tense. The characteristic of a verb that shows time. See **12k.**

terrible, terrific. See *awful.*

539

than, then. *Than* is used in comparisons (a better man than I am); *then* refers to time or sequence (I did my best work then. He sang first; then I sang).

their, there, they're. *Their* is the possessive of *they* (They lost their mittens); *there* is an adverb (I left my coat there); *they're* is the contraction of *they are* (They're in the kitchen).

to. Redundant in sentences like "Where are you going to?"

to, too, two. The confusion of these words is inexcusably careless. *To* is a preposition (Give the ticket to Jane); *too* is an adverb (He stayed too long); *two* is the number (Two hearts that beat as one).

Transitive verb. See *Verb*.

used to. Do not write *use to* for *used to*. (He used to eat here.)

Verb. A word or word group that indicates action or condition. The principal parts of a verb are the basis of the various tenses. The three principal parts are the ones found in (1) the present, (2) the past tense, and (3) the past participle: *play, played, played; know, knew, known.* Following are common classifications of verbs.

> *Finite verb.* A verb that shows time (I *do,* I *did*) and that agrees with the subject in person and number (he *does,* they *do*). A finite verb is essential in all standard sentences. Finite verbs contrast with nonfinite forms—infinitives, participles, and gerunds—which are collectively called verbals.

> *Intransitive verb.* A verb that does not take a direct object. (The sun *rose.* The boy *worked* quietly.)

> *Irregular verb.* A verb that does not form the past tense and the past participle by adding *ed, d,* or *t* to the infinitive (*tear, tore, torn*).

> *Linking verb* (also called *copula*). The chief purpose of a linking verb is to link the subject with a following noun, pronoun, or adjective. (These boys *are* my friends. This *is* she. This grass *grows* tall.)

> *Nonfinite verb.* See *Verbals*.

Regular verb. A verb that forms the past tense and the past participle by adding *ed, d,* or *t* to the infinitive (*clear, cleared, cleared*).

Transitive verb. A verb that takes a direct object to complete its meaning (The bear *broke* the hinge).

Verbal. A word derived from a verb and used as a noun, adjective, or adverb. The verbals are infinitives (*To know* him is *to distrust* him), participles (The *freezing* wind blew through the *broken* window), and gerunds (*Seeing* is *believing*).

Voice. The characteristic of a verb that shows whether the subject performs the action (active voice) or is acted upon (passive voice).

Active: I see.
Passive: I am seen.

wait on. Dialect for "wait for"; standard in the sense of "attend." (I wish that girl who waits on the table would wait for me.)

Weak verb. Same as *regular verb.* See *Verb.*

well. See *good.*

where. Although it is acceptable spoken English to say "I see where you are on the dean's list," standard written English requires "I see that you are on the dean's list." For *is where,* see under *is when.*

-wise. Established in words like *otherwise* and *clockwise,* but not to be used in clumsy constructions like *stenographer-wise, date-wise, radio-wise,* and even *radio-listener-wise.* Do not say "Money-wise, the plan is objectionable." Simply say that the plan will cost too much.

without. Do not use for *unless.* (He can't find the answer unless [*not* without] you help him.)

would have. Do not use for *had* in *if* clauses. (If you had gone when I told you [*not* if you would have gone], you would not have got into trouble.)

would of. Illiterate for *would have.*

541

Index

Be

as linking verb, 358
case of pronoun after, 352–353
followed by predicate adjective, 390

Becker, Carl, quoted, 71–72
Begging the question, 57–58
Beginning of sentence
numbers written out, 504
variety in, 445
Beginning of theme
effective and ineffective, 73
independent of title, 12
Being as, misused, 523
Beside, besides, 523
Between, 521
Bible
colon with references to, 478
concrete language in, 98
footnote reference form, 274
Bibliography in research paper
abbreviations in, 278–279
cards for, 265–266
final, 254, 277–278
sources for, 258, 262
specimen, 311
working, 264–266
Biographical dictionaries, listed and described, 262
Book review, 193–194
examples of, 195, 196–198
Book Review Digest, described, 260
Books
list of reference, 259–262
titles of
capitals with, 502
italics with, 497
Brackets, 484
in a quoted passage, 484
with *sic,* 484
Breaking word at end of line, 494
Broke, 523
But, to begin sentence, 523
But what, 523
But who, but which, 433

Call numbers, library, 259
Can, may, 523
Canceling a passage in manuscript, 483, front endpaper

Cannot help but, 523
Can't hardly, can't scarcely, 411, 523
Capitals, 499–503
academic courses, 502
after colon, 500
common nouns in names, 501
days, months, 500
first word of sentence, 499
geographic sections, 502
languages, 500
lines of poetry, 500
names of people, places, etc., 500–501
proper adjectives, 500
proper nouns, 500
religious references, 500
seasons not capitalized, 503
titles of books, articles, etc., 502
titles of people, 501
unnecessary and improper, 503
words in family relationships, 501
Card catalogue in library, 259
Cards, bibliography, 265–266
Cards, for notes, 267–268
Caret, for insertion, 483, front endpaper
Carleton, William G., quoted, 206
Carson, Rachel, quoted, 67–68, 141–142, 423–424
Case, 523
Case
defined, 524
of nouns, 338
of pronouns
after *than* and *as,* 356
appositive, 356
complements of *be,* 352
forms, 340–341
object of verb or preposition, 353–354
objective, with infinitive, 354
possessive, with gerunds, 355–356
possessive, with indefinite pronouns, compounds, series, 355–356
subject of verb, 352
when followed by appositive, 356

544

555